FIRST FACTS
IN AMERICAN
JEWISH HISTORY

Other books by Tina Levitan

The Laureates: Jewish Winners of the Nobel Prize

Islands of Compassion: A History of the Jewish Hospitals of New York

Baolam Hechadash (In the New World) in Hebrew

Jews in American Life: From 1492 to the Space Age

Viewpoints on Science and Judaism

FIRST FACTS
IN AMERICAN
JEWISH HISTORY

From 1492 to the Present

Tina Levitan

JASON ARONSON INC.
Northvale, New Jersey
London

This book was set in 10 pt. Palatino by AeroType, Inc.

10 9 8 7 6 5 4 3 2 1

Library of Congress Cataloging-in-Publication Data

Levitan, Tina,
First facts in American Jewish history : from 1492 to the present / Tina Levitan.
  p. cm.
Includes bibliographical references and index.
ISBN 1-56821-895-8 (alk. paper)
1. Jews—United States—History—Miscellanea. 2. Jews—United States—Biography. 3. United States—Civilization—Jewish Influences. I. Title.
E184.J5L5738   1996
973'.04924—dc20   96-1791
                                                           CIP

Manufactured in the United States of America. Jason Aronson Inc. offers books and cassettes. For information and catalog write to Jason Aronson Inc., 230 Livingston Street, Northvale, New Jersey 07647.

Dedicated to the Memory of My Mother and Father

BELLA AND JULIUS LEVITAN

Who Bequeathed To Me a Love for the

Strength and Beauty of the Jewish Tradition

Contents

III — WE PAY OUR DEBT TO AMERICA

Preface

This is a book of American Jewish historical beginnings—of first times, first places, first institutions, first people, and first things. Each chapter marks a pioneering effort, a beginning out of the far-flung and diversified assortment that history presents.

Jews have lived in America since its discovery by Columbus. The contributions of Jewish voyagers, mapmakers, and scientists were indispensable to Columbus in planning his expedition. In Columbus's crew the first man to step ashore in the New World was of Jewish origin. And down through the history of our country, Jewish people have been among the "first" to settle a newly discovered continent; to build cities; develop trade; found new industries; advance science, economic ideals, and philanthropy; or pursue a cultural life.

From the days of the founding fathers, as the years rolled on, Jews—changing and developing with their experiences on the American scene, preserving individuality and inherited characteristics, yet integrated in the surrounding life—united with their neighbors in building, upholding, and cherishing a new nation. They risked their lives for liberty on every battlefield. They gave us geniuses whose mental attitudes and intellectual viewpoints introduced new elements, new temperaments, and new tones in art, music, and literature in the superabundant energy and talent that America's openness released in them.

In a way, the role of the Jew in the modern world has been that of pioneering. From the days of the expulsion from Spain to the days of the expulsion from Germany and thereafter, Jewish pioneers have proved influential if not dominating factors in basic situations that helped build America. Their ideas, often revolutionary in thought and expression, formed the pattern of this country and made it what it is.

In the colonial period, Jewish immigration had to a great extent come from Spain or Portugal, often through Holland, England, or South America. Daring Sephardic merchants (Jews originally of the Spanish peninsula or long settled in the Mediterranean perimeter), adventurous shipowners, and ubiquitous traders, they joined whichever struggling settlement chance drew them to. They shared in their founding, their commerce, and their upbuilding and strongly supported the separation from England. They pioneered in risky new businesses like the fur trade and the making of spermaceti candles. Even greater than these endeavors has been the contribution made by Judaism in the form of the Bible in the founding of this republic.

The Puritans, who were the most important settlers of early New England and who largely established the character of the future America, based their civil and criminal laws, their constitutions and their daily life, on the Old Testament (the term applied to the Hebrew Bible by the Christians).

The Plymouth Colony Code of Laws of 1636, the Massachusetts one of 1647, and the Connecticut Code of 1650 were all based on the laws of Moses. So great was the interest in Hebrew culture that Hebrew was taught at Harvard College as early as 1655, at the very beginning of higher education in the New World.

When the time came for revolution and freedom, the Hebrew Scriptures were the great inspiration for the leading thinkers; they were quoted on every hand and won many supporters for the cause of freedom among the pious farmers and traders of the colonies.

And perhaps there is no more notable contribution to the spirit of America than the inscription on the Liberty Bell taken from the Bible: "Proclaim liberty throughout the land unto all the inhabitants thereof" (Leviticus 25:10).

At the time of the signing of the Declaration of Independence, the Jewish population scarcely numbered 2,500 individuals. Yet this small group made significant contributions toward winning American freedom. Their efforts were apparently appreciated and perhaps influenced the framers of the Constitution to ban any religious test for holding public office. Jewish settlers proved the point that a minority adhering faithfully to a religion abhorent to the majority, yet discharging to the full all obligations of good citizenship, caused no danger to the state in establishing freedom of worship – a newly enlarged policy of religious liberty for the first time in a modern state.

While the number of Jews coming to America tapered off in the post-Revolutionary period as the emigration of Spanish and Portuguese Jews lessened, emigration of Jews from other European countries gradually increased in earnest beginning in 1820. The poverty of the Germanic states after the Napoleonic wars and the suppression of all liberal thought after the failure of the Revolution of 1848 led German Jews to seek a more congenial haven than their fatherland. They turned to America, swelling the tiny trickle to which Jewish emigration had shrunk into a rising tide of another generation of enterprising immigrants. Many of the newcomers settled in the cities and towns of the North and South; others were caught in the great American rush westward, which was then creating for our country a new empire stretching to the Pacific. Living lives of loneliness in little outposts, following rugged trails through mountain passes, tracking a path across the vast prairies into new communities—they started life anew, peddling their wares on foot or with a wagon, building synagogues, establishing schools, founding periodicals and banding together in fraternal orders, hospitals, social and charitable organizations that continue to flourish to this day.

By the time the Civil War broke out, the Jewish population is estimated to have risen to 150,000. Swept by the passions of the day in their newly found homes, Jews served with distinction on both sides of the conflict. In the Union forces, at least ten Jews held the title of general in some form, and seven Jews were awarded the Congressional Medal of Honor. In the Confederate Cabinet of Jefferson Davis, Judah P. Benjamin was Secretary of State. In the post-Civil War period, these immigrants and their children were of the generation that built industrial America.

Former peddlers opened stores and transformed the retail business of haggling to the reliable and dignified shopping of the department store, which had a tremendous influence on lowering prices and bringing a great variety of the choice of merchandise available to the masses in the cities, towns, and villages across the land.

Before the American advent of the German Jew and his progress from peddler to storekeeper, to merchant, merchandise jobber, and finally to manufacturer or department store proprietor, there was such a wide difference between the dress and living standards of the rich oligarchy of aristocrats and the American proletariat that class distinction made itself apparent wherever people assembled. It has been well said that the genius of the German Jew as garment manufacturer and distributor of merchandise helped make democracy work in the United States. These Jews abolished that class distinction in dress that from colonial days had always enabled the haves and the have-nots to be told apart before they had taken hold of clothing America.

Within two generations Jews were entering the professions, assuming public service and joining in every phase of American life.

Hays, Baruch, Jacobi, and other physicians contributed to the progress of American medicine, which soon attained the world's highest standards. The Seligmans, the Schiffs, the Warburgs and the Lehmans, who produced a noted governor and United States senator—Herbert H. Lehman—reached an eminent position in banking and finance. The theater benefited enormously through the pioneering efforts, management, direction, and taste of Belasco, Frohman, the Shuberts, and a host of lesser producers.

In heavy industry the Guggenheims became for a time the world's largest miners, smelters, and refiners of copper and other metals.

The German Jews, led by university-educated rabbis, began the movement that became Reform Judaism. Prussian-Posen Jews created congregations that are today Conservative.

The German Jewish immigrant dominated the spiritual and cultural life of American Jewry until rivaled by East European immigrants.

From 1881 to 1920, a general total of 25,500,000 immigrants entered the United States. Of this number, nearly two and a quarter million were Jews who came from Czarist Russia, Poland, Romania, Austro-Hungary, and the Baltic countries. These people, like those who had preceded them earlier, left their homes because of the lack of economic opportunity and the intolerable persecutions to which they were subjected.

They rushed to the Atlantic seaports, bringing new ghettos to our great eastern cities. The struggle for existence of vast numbers of these Jews—sturdy, ambitious, and intelligent—soon made itself felt in our economic life.

Those having obsolete skills took to the peddler's pack. Those who could scrape together a little capital opened "hole-in-the-wall" enterprises: candy stalls, tailor shops, and grocery stores. Those having skills demanded by the American economy, especially in the needle trades, found immediate employment.

As the cycle swung toward the last quarter of the nineteenth century, Jews from Eastern Europe—largely Russian Jews—took over the clothing and garment trades where the German Jews had left off. Soon fashions of the minute were almost instantaneously available within the means of the shopgirl as well as that of the society queen. To them is due the credit for making the United States the best-dressed nation on earth and for fashionable styles having been placed within the reach of the slenderest purse.

From their midst—as urban workers in mass-production industries—labor leaders arose to make labor unions of Jews, pacesetters in giving to the American labor movement progressive leadership in many directions—socially, economically and politically. Another astonishing Jewish performance was the creation of the motion picture industry in a little more than a decade that enlarged the horizons of millions throughout the world. Very similar patterns extended to radio as that medium reached toward a mass audience starting in 1925.

No greater contribution to science has been offered to the world in this century, perhaps since Galileo, than that of Albert Einstein, whose Theory of Relativity revolutionized the concepts of the physical universe and ushered in the atomic age, and the Jewish physicists who played a disproportionally large role in laying its foundation.

Since World War II, Jews have entered into the mainstream of American life, gaining admission into segments of the economy formerly closed to them—an economy that still held out special rewards for those daring to be commercial entrepreneurs. Jews became prominent in the nascent plastic manufacturing, air-conditioning, and electronics industries, as well as in hundreds of different kinds of consulting businesses. They have taken a central role in American cultural life, and they have been in the forefront of the postwar thrust to extend equality and opportunity to those to whom it has been denied. The Jews' sense of security in America has enabled them to make the plight of their brethren abroad and support for the State of Israel their chief concern, and to make philanthropy and political activism their first domestic priorities.

The following chapters show how from the very beginning, the Jewish influence in the upbuilding of America has been distinctive. They offer an impressive array of fascinating stories of American Jews whose individual paths of life added their impact to the forging of a great democracy and to enriching life and freedom in America.

I refer those readers interested in more specialized coverage to the bibliography that follows at the end of this book.

Only those "Jewish Firsts" of which definite records are available are included here. Even in the most prosaic cases, historians often disagree as to the time, place, and participation of events. Counterclaims exist in many fields because of the lack of authentic records and unattainable testimony of the trail blazers, the discoverers, or whatever the case may be. It is possible that further research into unpublished records may reveal additional data.

In the preparation of this book many libraries were visited, ranging from one-room rural setups and specialized collections to the immense holdings of the Library of Congress and the Jewish Division of the New York Public Library, whose staff were of particular assistance.

Information has also been obtained from organizations and societies, government departments, chambers of commerce, public records, and from the achievers themselves or their descendants, many of whom I have been fortunate enough to meet.

With unstinting generosity, scholars gave of their time and knowledge in the areas of their specialization. For their kind assistance, I am especially grateful and appreciative.

I am also deeply indebted to a host of preceding historians, biographers, research works, and especially to the American Jewish Historical Society, whose archival resources, manuscript collections, and published and unpublished papers have enriched every aspect of my work.

I should indeed be ungrateful if I did not also thank Jason Aronson Inc. and its vice president and editor, Arthur Kurzweil, for making the publication of this book possible.

It is hoped that *First Facts in American Jewish History: From 1492 to the Present* will prove valuable for general reading and for reference, and that it will further the appreciation and understanding of the impact of the Jew on American life.

TINA LEVITAN

New York, New York
September 1, 1995

I

We Settle in America

THE FIRST JEW IN AMERICA

1492

The history of the Jews in America starts in the year 1492. Up to that time in Spain for hundreds of years the Jews had lived in what is still remembered as the Golden Age. They had produced philosophers, scientists, musicians, and poets. They helped make Spain famous for learning and culture. But on March 31, 1492, Ferdinand, king of Spain culminated a long succession of persecutions by signing the Decree of Expulsion ordering more than four hundred thousand Spanish Jews to leave Spain in four months or convert to Christianity. The inhuman Inquisition—a ruthless "system of inquiry" into the religious beliefs of the people—was set up, and many Jews, to conceal their identity and escape death, accepted Christianity and became known as Marranos. Others chose to remain Jews openly and fled to Portugal, France, Holland, England, and the Ottoman Empire.

On Friday, August 3, 1492, a little before sunrise, the day after the expulsion of the Jews from Spain, Columbus with his fleet of three ships—the *Nina*, the *Pinta*, and the *Santa Maria*—started out on his great journey. His voyage was financed by a number of Marranos. Among them were Luis de Santangel, chancellor of the royal Spanish household, who gave Columbus his largest private contribution for the voyage (1,140,000 maravedis), and Gabriel Sanchez, chief treasurer of Aragon. He also received much information from Jewish voyagers and scientists, including Judah Cresques, known as "the map Jew" and "the compass Jew," who headed a school of navigation; Abraham Zacuto, astronomer and mathematician of Salamanca, whose *Almanach Perpetuum* with its tables of declination was the most important work in any sailor's library; and Levi ben Gershon, inventor of nautical instruments. He took with him on his voyage at least five Marranos: Rodrigo de Triana, who was the first to see land; Alonso de la Calle, a former resident of Jews' Lane, for which he was named; Marco, the surgeon, Maestre Bernal, the fleet's physician; and Luis de Torres, the interpreter, who was to be the first to step upon American soil.

Finally, after three months of traveling, on October 12, 1492, on the Jewish festival of *Hoshannah Rabba* (the seventh day of the Autumn holiday of Sukkoth), Columbus and his crew reached a little island in the West Indies. San Salvador was now named and proclaimed by the Admiral of the Ocean Seas for Spain. When land was sighted, Luis de Torres, a man of great learning who could speak Hebrew, Aramaic, and Arabic, was sent ahead by Columbus to head the first inland expedition of any kind taken by white men in America.

After traveling twelve leagues into the interior of the mainland now known as Cuba, in search of the capital city of the Great Khan of Tartary, much to his amazement he discovered a town containing fifty straw huts built in the form of tents. It was inhabited by a thousand copper-colored men and women who spoke a tongue not known to white men. However, de Torres, making himself understood by gestures and sign language, soon gained their friendship. The natives were so delighted with him that they brought cotton, ornaments, and live parrots to trade.

De Torres returned to Columbus with a detailed and lively description of the natives, their customs, of the vegetation he encountered, and of all the strange sights he saw. Not the least of the wonders de Torres reported to Columbus was that he saw men putting rolls of dry leaves, which they called tobacco, into their mouths, lighting them and blowing out clouds of smoke through the mouth and nose. Luis de Torres was thus one of the first Europeans to discover the use of tobacco. Later he was the first white man to introduce its use into the Old World.

De Torres was also the first person of Jewish birth to settle in the New World. He was delighted with the magnificent, heavily laden fruit trees, beautiful flowers, and balmy climate of the island and persuaded Columbus to allow him to settle there. He was awarded a grant of land from an Indian chieftain whose friendship he won, and with a pension from King Ferdinand, built a house. Here he had fine gardens and meadows and began to grow tobacco and traded with the Indians.

De Torres lost no time in inviting his coreligionists to come and join him in the New World that was free from religious persecution and where he believed himself safe from the Inquisition. In the same Hebrew letter to his old home, he gives the great American bird, the turkey, its name, calling it "tukki," from the Hebrew word for "peacock."

The first white man and the first Jew to settle in Cuba, de Torres lived a peaceful and honorable life there and was a symbol of the great need for freedom and security of the Spanish Jews who came to these shores and of the bold and pioneering spirit of those who followed him.

Thus Jews from the very beginning helped to discover America. In the year of their exile from their happiest and most beautiful medieval abode, they helped to found the land that was to be their refuge and home in modern times.

A few scholars believe that Columbus was of Jewish origin. They say that no Spanish Jew could have expected aid from the King and Queen of Spain, so the discoverer claimed to be an Italian Catholic. On the four hundredth anniversary of the discovery of America, in 1892, the Spanish government invited the historian Moritz (Meyer) Kayserling to investigate the origin of the discoverer. From him we learn that Cristobol Colon (who never called himself Christopher Columbus and who never wrote or spoke Italian; his writings and correspondence were couched either in Latin or Castilian) was the son of Susanna Fonterossa and Domingo Colon of Pontevedra, Spain, where those bearing such surnames were former Jews turned Marranos, some of whom were brought before the Spanish Inquisition and who lived in Galicia, in northern Spain. A royal Spanish commission was appointed to study the subject further, to proclaim the great discoverer of Spanish birth. Its judgment was that since Columbus's exact place and birth cannot be ascertained, very definite proof would be needed to contradict the explorer's claim of being an Italian Catholic.

There were already rumors about Columbus's Jewish ancestry during his lifetime. Letters written by him to strangers have the customary X at the top to indicate the Catholic faith of the writer, but of the thirteen letters written to his son, only one bears an X, and that letter was meant to be shown to the King of Spain. The others have, in the place of an X, a sign that looks like the Hebrew letters B and H, nothing more or less than an old Hebrew greeting used by religious Jews, an abbreviation of *B'ezras Hashem,* meaning "With the Help of God."

We find the first reference to Columbus's Jewishness in a document dated eighty-five years after the explorer's death. Writing home, the French ambassador to Spain, Burdau, refers to "Columbus, the Jew." Similar references have appeared variously in extensive Columbian literature over the centuries. In the late nineteenth century, the possible Jewish origin of Columbus became a highly controversial issue between Spanish historians and Columbian researchers.

Whether or not Christopher Columbus was a Jew was the most frequently asked question in 1992 among Jewish observers in the course of the quincentennial celebration of the discovery of America. The issue remained controversial. Historians and novelists gearing their narrative and creative talents towards publication in time for that significant year postulated theories and offered facts that cause us to consider that the mystery regarding Columbus's origins is largely impossible to exclude or confirm the hypothesis that he was descended from a Jewish or formerly Jewish family, due to his own mendacity.

Eighty-seven out of the ninety crew members who made the voyage with Columbus have been identified by name and occupation. At least five could be recognized as of Jewish origin. For how could they have survived and sailed if they were so known? All of them had been baptized; on the second day of August 1492—which happened to fall on the propitious fast day of the Ninth of Av, commemorating the destruction of the Temple in Jerusalem—the last Jewish exiles had departed from Spain, and the following day the admiral's little argosy had sailed out of the port of Palos. But is it too hard to believe that when in the course of the seven weeks voyage the fleet was lashed by wind and wave, Luis de Torres, who could chant the Psalms in Hebrew, or Mastre Bernal, the doctor, who had once suffered public penance for practicing Judaism in secret, prayed silently but fervently to the God of Abraham, Isaac, and Jacob?

THE FIRST BOOK OF IMPORTANCE PUBLISHED IN NORTH AMERICA

1640

The Pilgrim fathers who founded Plymouth, the first English colony in North America, were a Bible-loving people. Although they did not know many Jews personally, the Bible was their guide and Moses, their lawgiver. They compared their flight to America to the flight of the Jews out of Egypt and thought of the Massachusetts Bay Colony as the New Jerusalem. When they drew up laws to govern themselves, they followed the code that Moses had given to the Jews. The Plymouth Colony Code of Laws of 1636, the Connecticut Code of 1650, and the first code of laws drawn up at the request of the General Court of Massachusetts in 1647 were derived from the Hebrew Bible. Not only were their civil and criminal laws based on Jewish statutes, their political constitution was as well, with its threefold form of government—executive, legislative, and judicial—which was derived from the Hebrew Commonwealth in its Shofet, or chief executive; its Sanhedrin, or Senate; and its Congregation, or popular assembly.

The Pilgrims established feasts and fasts after the Jewish model, especially the holiday of Thanksgiving, which was copied directly from the Sukkoth holiday, except that the differences in seasons between ancient Palestine and New England made the great American Thanksgiving festival come two months after Sukkoth. Thanksgiving is, like its original, a Fall harvest festival of Thanksgiving to God, the giver of the harvest.

So great was the interest in Hebraic culture in colonial America that in Harvard College the study of Hebrew was for a time compulsory. It was taught in Harvard as early as 1655, at the very beginning of higher education in the New World.

It is not surprising, then, to find that the first triumph of the American press should be biblically inspired. The first book of importance published in North America was the *Bay Psalm Book,* originally called *The Whole Book of Psalms, Faithfully Translated Into English Meter.*

In 1636 several New England theologians, including Richard Mather, John Eliot, and Thomas Welde, undertook the work of translating the

Psalms from the original Hebrew into English, a task completed in the Summer of 1638. In 1640, an edition of one thousand seven hundred copies was printed at a cost of thirty-three pounds by the first printing establishment to be set up in English America in Cambridge, Massachusetts, in the house of John Dunster, the first president of Harvard College. The new *Bay Psalm Book*, immediately adopted by nearly every congregation in the Massachusetts Bay Colony, was a notable achievement of the time. Fittingly enough, there are to be found in it several Hebrew words, as well as the Hebrew alphabet, the letters of which all bear the earmarks of local American workmanship.

In the top rank of the world's most famous books, the *Bay Psalm Book* is considered far rarer than a Shakespeare First Folio and can be compared in rarity and value to a Gutenberg Bible.

The highest amount ever paid for a book in auction up to that time — $151,000 — was attained by the celebrated *Bay Psalm Book* on January 28, 1948, when it was sold in New York City at the Parke-Bernet Galleries (now Sotheby's).

The auctioned book, known as the Crowninshield-Stevens-Brinley-Vanderbilt-Whitney Copy, is one of eleven known to exist and one of four in private hands.

The first Hebrew edition of the *Book of Psalms* published in Cambridge, Massachusetts, in 1809, is believed to be the first Hebrew publication of this kind in America.

The first book to be published in North America by Jews appeared in 1761 in colonial New York and was an English translation of a High Holiday prayer book. This, the first published translation of the Jewish liturgy into English, came into being in response to the strongly felt needs of a community that numbered but a few hundred. It consisted of "The Form of Prayer Which Was Performed at the Jews' Synagogue in the City of New York on Thursday, October 23, 1760" and was so titled. A more complete High Holiday prayer book appeared in English in 1766; it was made necessary — as the translator, Isaac Pinto, explains in his preface — "because in the British Dominions in America our brethren could best understand our prayers . . . in the language of the country wherein it hath pleased the Divine Providence to appoint his lot."

Although the heads of the leading London congregation would not permit the use of Pinto's translation, Ezra Stiles, the president of Yale University whom Pinto befriended, referred to him in his Literary Diary in 1790 as "a learned Jew in New York" and considered him a good Hebrew scholar.

These are the first translations of the Hebrew prayer book. They antedate the German translations of the Hebrew Scriptures by Moses Mendelssohn, which were made in 1780–1783.

THE FIRST HEBREW AUTHOR IN AMERICA

1646

Prior of the coming of the Jews to North America, the record is replete with cases of Jewish migration to South America, the earliest settlers going to that section that was first settled. It was not, however, until 1642, that the first organized Jewish community on American soil came into existence. The Dutch had captured Recife, at that time capital of Brazil, and had driven out the Spanish rulers who brought the Inquisition with them to the New World. Many of the secret Jews living there and in other parts of South America took advantage of Holland's liberal policy by settling there and openly returning to Judaism. The settlement increased rapidly until, with the arrival of six hundred Jews from Holland, it comprised about five thousand people.

The Jews of Recife formed a congregation called *Kahal Kodesh Zur Yisroel* (The Holy Congregation Rock of Israel). They built fine homes, established sugar mills, and began an extensive trade with Holland and other countries. They decided to hire a *haham*, or rabbi, as their spiritual leader and teacher. Rabbi Isaac Aboab da Fonseca, who had studied under the noted *Haham* Isaac Uzziel in Amsterdam and who at the age of twenty-one became *haham* of the Amsterdam Congregation Bet Israel, was summoned. For thirteen years Aboab continued to serve as the spiritual mentor of the first Jewish community in the Americas.

Rabbi Aboab was the author of the first Hebrew book written on American soil, the original of which may be seen in the Library of the Jewish Theological Seminary in Amsterdam. It is called *Zecher Rab (The Great Remembrance)* and describes the sufferings of the Jews due to their loyalty to the Dutch rulers in the war with the Portuguese. In 1646, just as their prosperity and freedom seemed assured and their future most rosy, the Portuguese laid siege to Recife. Life for the Jews became unbearable.

At first the Jews discovered a Portuguese conspiracy against the Dutch and averted the danger. Then the siege began. Jews at once volunteered for the defense in large numbers. The Dutch later acknowledged in full their bravery and sufferings. Wealthy merchants raised all the money they could to contribute supplies to the defenders. After the repulse of the Portuguese attack on the city in 1646, Aboab composed a long thanksgiving narrative poem describing the past sufferings. He wrote: "Many of the Jewish immigrants were killed by the enemy; many died of starvation. Those who were accustomed to delicacies were glad to be able to satisfy their hunger with dry bread; soon they could not obtain even this. They were in want of everything and were preserved alive as if by a miracle . . . I made record of the mighty deeds of God."

For nine long years the siege continued. Isaac Aboab da Fonseca went about encouraging the weary soldiers and their starving families and leading prayers for victory. But at last, in 1654, hopelessly weakened and outnumbered, the Dutch surrendered to the Portuguese. Honorably mindful of their loyal Dutch–Jewish subjects, the Dutch requested that Portugal show mercy to them. But the Portuguese governor, Francisco de Barreto, provided sixteen ships on which Jews were ordered to embark and leave Brazil.

Quitting their homes, the fields they had planted, the mills and factories they had built, the Jews of Recife departed from the city where their Holy Congregation had known such joy.

Those who could returned to Amsterdam. Some went to the Dutch colonies of Surinam—or Dutch Guiana—and Curaçao in the Dutch West Indies. Twenty-three landed in New Amsterdam, as New York was first called. A few Jews, nevertheless, remained in Brazil to suffer continued hardships. Thus, the first work written by a Jew in America was a history of suffering related in verse.

Kayserling has described Aboab as "an excellent Hebrew poet who left us magnificently enduring works worthy of his talents and learning."

Aboab made his way back to Amsterdam in 1654. He was appointed to his former position as *haham* of the Amsterdam congregation as well as a teacher in the Talmud Torah, principal of a yeshiva, and member of the *Beth Din* (rabbinical court). He endeared himself to the congregation that he served for more than sixty years.

Aboab became celebrated as a preacher, and some of his sermons and eulogies have been published. It was a pulpit address of his delivered in 1671 that prompted the construction of the magnificent synagogue of the Sephardic community in Amsterdam.

He translated from Spanish into Hebrew two works dealing with mystic lore of the philosopher of religion and Kabbalist Abraham de Herrera, one called *Beit Elohim* (*The House of God*) and the other *Shaar Ha-Shamaim* (*The Gate of Heaven*). Aboab's Hebrew translations were both published in Amsterdam in 1655. The first edition of the latter in its original leather binding was acquired in 1947 by the Boston Hebrew College from the private collection of Rabbi Emanuel Eckstein of Cleveland; it is being studied and preserved for the future. Rabbi Aboab's most ambitious production, however, was the rendering of the Pentateuch into Spanish together with a commentary (*Parafrasis Commentado Sobre el Penta-teucho*, Amsterdam 1688).

Aboab died in Amsterdam on April 4, 1693 at the age of 88. Their bereavement over the loss of their spiritual guide was so keenly felt by Amsterdam Jewry that for many years the name Aboab and the date of his death was engraved on the border of all marriage certificates issued by the community.

The breadth of Aboab's interest in Hebrew literature is illustrated in the sale catalogue of his library, which appeared shortly after his death. It consisted of 18 manuscripts, 373 Hebrew books, and 53 secular works. It is one of the earliest known in Hebrew bibliography.

THE FIRST JEWISH SETTLER IN NEW AMSTERDAM

1654

The first Jew to set foot on North American soil was probably Elias Legardo, who sailed to Virginia on the *Abigail* in 1621. By 1624 Rebecca Isaake was a resident there. John Levy received a grant of land of two hundred acres in 1652. David Da Costa was a tobacco importer there around 1658. However, Virginia attracted very few Jews before the American Revolution, for it had neither large cities nor a merchant class.

The records of the Great and General Court of Massachusetts Bay show that in 1649, Solomon Franco, a Jew, proposed to settle in the nineteen-year-old town of Boston but was paid to leave the province. From that day, throughout the colonial era, although other Jews had made Boston their home, their number was small, and as they learned of better opportunities or hospitality elsewhere, they had deserted Boston.

Although there are records of possible Jewish settlers in other colonies, Jacob Barsimson, a Sephardic Jew of Holland, who came as one of a party of emigrants sent by the Dutch West India Company to help populate its colony in New Amsterdam—as the Dutch called New York—seems to have the honor of being the first permanent Jewish settler in what is now the United States. He came to New Amsterdam directly from Holland on the ship *Peartree* on August 22, 1654, a month ahead of a larger group of Jews from Brazil.

New Amsterdam had been founded twenty-eight years before by the Dutch West India Company. It had gained a reputation as a fur trading center and for its excellent harbor.

Barsimson was allotted a weatherbeaten hut in the woods outside the settlement where Indians had bartered furs for beads and Peter Minuit had, in 1628, bought Manhattan Island for sixty guilders. For his neighbors he found a mixed people who were still celebrating the granting of a city charter with gay flags and bunting. He traded with the Indians, cleared land, planted gardens and orchards, and for a period of time hired himself out as a manual laborer.

As in the case of the majority of Jews who followed him, Barsimson was poor in worldly goods at the time of his arrival; it is even doubtful whether he possessed the thirty-six guilders required to pay for his passage. That he did not immediately improve his condition can be adduced from the fact that the military tax of October 12, 1655, imposed upon him was only six guilders, while others of his coreligionists in the colony paid one hundred guilders. In the course of several years, however, records of a number of litigations involving Barsimson show him as prospering.

From the very outset after his arrival in New Amsterdam, Barsimson was a champion of equal rights for the Jews of the colony. Claiming the burgher right to perform guard duty in lieu of paying a tax or fine, Barsimson joined with Asser Levy in a petition submitted to the town council against the imposition of a fine of sixty-five stivers ($1.20) per month of forced exclusion from military service. Although this petition was denied, they persisted for two years in carrying on the fight, finally compelling Governor Peter Stuyvesant to accede to their wishes in June 1657.

The first case in the colonies in which the observance of the Jewish Sabbath was recognized by the authorities as a good reason for failure to attend court when summoned was that of Jacob Barsimson in 1658. The record reads: "Though the defendant is absent, yet no default is entered against him as he is summoned on his Sabbath." What the case related to is not noted, and no further entry appears.

This ruling in recognition of Jewish religious observance was doubtless the first of its kind made in America.

One month after Barsimson disembarked in New Amsterdam in 1654, a little ship, the *Sainte Catherine* (later mistakenly identified as the *St. Charles*)—after a narrow escape from fallen Recife, the Dutch colony in Brazil, and pirate-infested seas—was making its slow, uncertain way toward the same port. Barsimson and these new arrivals were to constitute the first Jewish community in North America, which was to have other "firsts" as well, such as the first Jewish congregation, the first Jewish cemetery, the first Jewish school, and the first Jewish citizen.

From September 1954 to May 1955, the three hundredth anniversary of the arrival of these first Jewish settlers was widely celebrated under the auspices of the American Tercentenary Committee with the active participation of Christian and nonsectarian groups.

In 1976, American Jewry observed the bicentennial of American independence and, eleven years later, the bicentennial of the framing of the United States Constitution, when it became an interesting exercise in comparative law to examine aspects of the Constitution in the light of the Hebrew Bible.

In the spirit and essence of the constitution, the influence of the Bible and the ancient Hebrew commonwealth in Palestine was paramount in that it was not only the highest authority for the principle "Rebellion to tyrants is obedience to God" (*The Book of Maccabees*) but also because it was in itself a divine precedent for a pure democracy as distinguished from monarchy, aristocracy, or any other form of government. By that means and to that extent it had a decisive influence in guiding the American people in the selection of their form of government.

In 1992, American Jews, too, shared in the quincentenary of the anniversary of Columbus's famous discovery, not only as part of American society but also as Jews. A new surge of public interest in the American Jewish past was generated, resulting in new publications, new lecture series, as well as library and museum exhibits.

THE FIRST JEWISH SETTLEMENT IN NORTH AMERICA

1654

On a warm, bright day in the first week in September 1654, thirty-four years after the *Mayflower* with its load of Pilgrim fathers landed at Plymouth Rock, a French man-of-war, the *Sainte Catherine*, sailed into the harbor of New York, then known as New Amsterdam. On board were twenty-three poor but healthy Jewish refugees from Brazil. These four men, six women, and thirteen young people were to found the first Jewish settlement in what is now the United States. Most of the newcomers were Dutch or Italian Sephardim (Jews originally from the Spanish peninsula), but a few were probably Ashkenazim—Jews of Central European ancestry.

These Jews had suffered great perils, and the sight of land was sweet to them. They had been forced to leave their home in Recife, Brazil, when the colony was recaptured by the Portuguese from the Dutch. One day early in May 1654, tying together their few belongings, they secretly made their way out of Brazil aboard a boat bound for one of the other Dutch colonies in South America. Several days out of port, their ship was captured by a band of Spanish pirates, but destiny intervened. A French armed ship, the *Sainte Catherine*, commanded by Captain Jacques de la Motte and headed north, made a timely appearance. The Jews negotiated a contract with the captain, who agreed to transport them to New Amsterdam, the Dutch West India Company's little outpost on the mainland of North America, for the exorbitant fee of twenty-five hundred guilders, nine hundred to be paid in advance. Sufficient funds were not realized by the Jews to pay the full amount of their passage money; they did, however, expect remittance from Holland on their arrival in New Amsterdam. After many weeks of sailing, this vessel brought them to the little fortress town of New Amsterdam, "capital" of New Netherlands.

Although it was a pleasant change from the ship, the view of New Amsterdam that greeted the little group was not that of another London or Paris, but it compared favorably with Jamestown or Plymouth or the recently founded village of Boston. Gay with red roofs and a stalwart windmill, the small community of some eight hundred broad-shouldered citizens boasted a church, a fort, a storehouse of the Dutch West India Company, a pier, a crane for loading and unloading ships, and a city tavern that in 1653 had been converted to the City Hall.

A considerable sum remained due the captain of the *Sainte Catherine* for the Recife immigrants' board and passage. As the principle men among them had signed an agreement whereby they had become liable for the whole amount, vigorous proceedings were taken against them. A public auction was held of their goods. The newcomers being unable to discharge their indebtedness, two of the group—David Israel and Moses Ambrosius—were ordered into confinement and jailed for the balance due. Then Asser Levy was arrested. There they remained until October, when kinsmen from Amsterdam finally dispatched the necessary funds.

It was an inauspicious beginning. They were poor. They were alien. They were not wanted. Governor Peter Stuyvesant, who ruled the colony, was angered to see these people trying to enter his town. He lost no time in making his sentiments felt. Some two weeks after their arrival, he wrote a letter of protest to his superiors in Holland, the Dutch West India Company. The Jews, threatened with expulsion, wrote at the same time and were backed by Dutch Jews.

The directors of the Dutch West India Company did not see eye to eye with the disgruntled Stuyvesant. They pointed out that it was in the latter's interest that Jews be permitted to live and trade in all parts of the Dutch empire. It would enable the Jewish merchants of Amsterdam to establish loyal and reliable business relationships in the New World with family members and coreligionists.

A reply was sent to Governor Stuyvesant on April 26, 1655. It stated that to refuse the Jews admission would be unreasonable and unfair, especially because of their considerable losses in defending Brazil from the Portuguese and also "because of the large amount of capital their nation had invested in the shares of this company. Therefore . . . these people may travel and trade in New Netherlands, and live and remain there, provided the poor among them shall be supported by their own nation." This is the charter of Jewish settlement and the beginning of Jewish liberty in North America. The condition laid down, to care for their own poor, was kept by the original settlers, and the great Jewish community that followed never forgot this promise.

The governor and his supporters were not at all satisfied. Even before this order came, they tried to drive out all the Jews from the colony because one of them had kept his shop open on Sunday. This expulsion was stopped by the same order that permitted the Jews to settle, although other petty persecutions went on from time to time.

Stuyvesant would not permit the Jews to engage in the lucrative fur trade, to practice a handicraft, own a house, hold public office, or serve in the militia. Neither were they allowed to "exercise their religion in a synagogue." When Stuyvesant ventured a protest that "giving them liberty, we cannot refuse the Lutherans and the Papists," the directors of the Dutch West India Company in Holland had an answer for that, too. It was for the Jews to conduct their religious activities in private and to refrain from building a public house of worship. Public worship was officially denied the Jews as it was to all other groups other than the established Dutch Reformed Church.

The newcomers, meanwhile, set about earning their livelihoods. They subsisted as peddlers, traders, importers, and metal workers. Renting their lodgings, securing access to their own burial grounds (which was at first denied), they also managed to provide for their indigent and orphaned. In 1655, Jewish taxpayers paid eight percent of the cost of the Palisade or "Waal," later the site of Wall Street, while they comprised only about two percent of the assessed population at that time.

Less than a year after their initial appearance in New Netherlands, Jewish traders petitioned the authorities to be allowed to trade in the Delaware River area. This, too, was refused. But since Jews already had a trading expedition in that region, undertaken without official consent, they were allowed to send two agents to the South River section to wind up their affairs.

It was more than trading privileges that Jewish settlers wanted. They battered with all their might against discrimination. They demanded the right to perform their civic duties like other settlers. Jacob Barsimson, Asser Levy, Abraham de Lucena, Jacob Cohen Hendriques, and other New Amsterdam Jews kept putting pressure on Stuyvesant for full citizenship rights. They insisted on the right to serve in the militia and do guard duty on the walls of the city to protect the settlers from the raids and attacks of the Indians and the Swedes. They continued their petitions and pressure until the governor finally granted them full citizenship on April 21, 1657. It was a milestone and a victory. It was a date to remember in the annals of Jewish history in America.

Within the ten years that Jews lived in New Amsterdam under Dutch rule, they progressed and established a firm foothold in that part of the world. They began as a small and insignificant group, but by the time the British wrested the colony from the Dutch in 1664 and renamed it New York, there were a number of wealthy tradesmen among them. The economic activities of the Jews of New Amsterdam were not far-reaching, but they are interesting as the first undertaken by them on the North American continent.

These first Jewish settlers for the most part were merchants and traders. Some were engaged in manual trades. There were tailors, shoemakers, wigmakers, saddlers, bakers, and distillers among them.

In 1695, forty-one years after the founding of this settlement, the Jewish population of New York numbered about one hundred. By the time the first Constitution of the State of New York was adopted in 1777, Jews were on an equality with all other citizens, New York having been the first state to grant full religious liberty.

These Spanish and Portuguese Jewish settlers proved the point that a minority adhering faithfully to a religion abhorrent to the majority, yet discharging to the full all obligations of good citizenship, caused no danger to the state in establishing freedom of worship—a new enlarged liberal policy of religious liberty for the first time in a modern state.

On May 20, 1955, a commemorative plaque and flagpole, marking the arrival of the first Jewish settlers in 1654, was dedicated in New York City's Battery Park under the auspices of the New York Joint Legislative Committee of the American Jewish Tercentenary.

Each year during the month of September a ceremony takes place under the aegis of the American Jewish Historical Society and the Jewish Historical Society of New York, commemorating the arrival of the first Jews in New Amsterdam in 1654.

That tiny group of New Amsterdam Jews laid the foundation of what was to become, here in the United States, the largest Jewish community under one flag, the strongest and freest in the two thousand years that this people has been dispersed all over the earth.

THE FIRST JEWISH CONGREGATION IN NORTH AMERICA

1654

In September 1654, twenty-three Jewish refugees from Recife, Brazil, disembarked in the harbor of New York, then known as New Amsterdam. These Jews had suffered great perils, and the sight of land was sweet to them. They had been forced to leave their homes in Brazil, when that colony was recaptured by the Portuguese from the Dutch, who had held it more than a decade. One day early in May 1654 tying together their few belongings, they secretly made their way out of Brazil on board a boat bound for one of the other Dutch colonies in South America. Several days out of port, with a stiff wind behind them, their ship was captured by a band of Spanish pirates. But destiny intervened. The ship was stranded off one of the West Indian Islands; a French ship—the *Sainte Catherine*, headed north—made a timely appearance and rescued them from the hands of the outlaws. After many weeks of sailing, this vessel brought them to New Amsterdam, on the western tip of Manhattan Island, administered under government charter by the West India Company of Amsterdam.

This small group arrived in New Amsterdam several days before Rosh Hashanah, the Jewish New Year. There was no synagogue and no facilities to accommodate their religious needs. As they celebrated that new year, they founded the Spanish and Portuguese Congregation Shearith Israel, the "remnant of Israel." Thus begins the story of the oldest Jewish congregation in North America and of Jewish life in the United States.

By a law of February 1, 1656, no type of religious assembly—only family prayers in private homes—was permissible outside the confines of the established church in the Dutch colony of New Amsterdam. Even the Dutch Lutherans had been unable to break through the vested privileges of New Amsterdam's Dutch Reformed Church. Therefore, from the start, it was useless for the Jews to hope for the right to conduct public worship in their own quarters. But they tried. At first they held services under the branches of friendly trees and then in private homes.

We do not know the exact date when the legal impediment to the establishment of a synagogue was removed; but evidence exists to show that before the end of the seventeenth century, in 1682, a house rented for the purpose was used by the congregation as a public place of worship. The structure—a small, rough one-story and one-room building, not very different from the homes of the settlers or the churches of their neighbors, of which there were six in New York County—was situated in what is now called Beaver Street, between Broadway and Broad streets.

In 1728, the little congregation, which had grown to twenty families out of a total population of 855 families, was ready to build a house of worship of their own. After preliminary preparations, by September 8, 1729, the foundation stone of the first permanent Jewish place of worship in North America was laid on Mill Street, where a mill then stood. Completed on April 8, 1730, the building remained in use for almost a century. Originally a little stone building with a fence around it, it stood at the present site of South William Street, where the great banks and office buildings of today contain nothing to remind us of the Dutch burghers and pioneer Jews of those early days.

Luis Gomez, a New York merchant who had achieved an enviable position in the import and export of wheat and other products, gave the synagogue a liberal contribution for its support and was elected its first president.

The first *hazzan*, or reader of service, was Saul Brown (originally Pardo), one of the merchants who had been admitted to the burgher rights in 1685. For his annual salary he received fifty British pounds plus six cords of wood and a supply of matzoth (unleavened bread eaten on Passover) for his family. The *shamash*, or helper, received a salary of sixteen pounds plus six cords of wood and a supply of matzoth. The Reverend Gershom Mendez Seixas, the "patriot-rabbi of the American Revolution," served as minister of this congregation for more than fifty years. During this time some of the most prominent Jewish merchants of colonial New York were numbered among its members.

The community revolved entirely around the synagogue, which was not only a house of prayer, but the school, the social center, the scene of weddings and other events of rejoicing.

Members attended the synagogue morning and evening. An elaborate system of fines and penalties helped not only to maintain the synagogue but to discourage laxity or indifference in religious matters.

In 1817, the influx of new immigrants and the large size of families began to strain the accommodations of the original Mill Street synagogue building. It was decided to rebuild and enlarge the aging structure on an adjacent site. The second Mill Street synagogue was built of stone and brick and provided seats for 167 men and 137 women. The women's gallery was reached by a passageway from the upper story of the adjoining brick schoolhouse on the north.

In 1834, with the Jewish population of New York City having shifted uptown, Congregation Shearith Israel moved to Crosby Street, where a new, enlarged synagogue building was erected. This synagogue served the congregation for twenty-five years. As New York City continued to grow, in 1860 Shearith Israel moved once more, farther uptown to its fourth home on Nineteenth Street, west of Fifth Avenue.

Congregation Shearith Israel, also known as the Spanish and Portuguese Synagogue, still exists today, the oldest Jewish congregation in North America and one of the oldest bodies of worship of any kind. It now flanks Central Park West at 70th Street in Manhattan and still observes the Orthodox Sephardic ritual.

Its present building, the fifth the congregation has occupied, was erected in 1897 at a cost of $250,000, a large sum of money in those days. At its dedication ceremony on May 18 of that year, the doors were ceremoniously opened by Dr. Horatio Gomez, a great-grandson of Luiz Gomez, president of the congregation when the first synagogue on Mill Street was dedicated in 1730.

The synagogue building of Renaissance Greek style was designed by Arnold Brunner, New York City's first Jewish architect. In the north entrance hall are two massive millstones, five inches thick, dating back to the mill erected in the latter part of the seventeenth century at the place where Mill Street became Mill Lane. These were brought to the synagogue in 1894 and were taken from the site of the first Mill Street synagogue.

The interior of the present synagogue is constructed in the style of traditional Jewish houses of worship since ancient days. To assure that the reader's words will carry, the reading desk used during services is set near the center of the synagogue. So that the present congregation can stand in prayer where their forefathers stood, the floorboards came from the reading desk of the Nineteenth Street Synagogue, to which they were brought from the Crosby Street Synagogue in 1834 and, it is said, originally from the Mill Street Synagogue building of 1730.

Three of the Torah Scrolls in the Ark come from the Sephardic Congregation of the Hague. The oldest pair of *riemonim* (decorative silver bells crowning the Torah scrolls) bear the Hebrew date of 5497 (1737). Another pair bears the name of Myer Myers (1721–1795), New York's first Jewish silversmith. Two of the pointers used in the reading of the Torah are inscribed with the date 1846, although they may be older. The beaten brass menorah (eight-arm candleholder kindled during Hanukkah) may well be over two hundred fifty years old. Four lamps on the eastern wall of the main synagogue are dedicated in memory of men who died during the First World War.

A charming smaller chapel that abuts the main synagogue is known as the Little Synagogue. It is used daily for morning and evening services, small weddings, baby namings, and *Bris Milahs* (circumcision ceremonies). It is a composite of the synagogues occupied by Shearith Israel for more than three centuries under the Dutch, British, and, since 1783, the United States. Included are a reader's desk with exquisite spindles holding four candlesticks that on close inspection seem to be *Havdalah* sets (used in blessing ceremony over wine, spices, and lights at the close of the Sabbath). Made of Spanish brass, the candlesticks are thought to date from the fifteenth century, when Marranos (professing Christians practicing Judaism in secret) in Spain or Portugal may have designated them as hidden ritual objects. There is an 1817 Ner Tamid (Eternal Light) and 1834 *bancas* (benches) as well as 1896 Tiffany stained-glass windows.

The Polonies Talmud Torah (Hebrew school), founded in 1802, and the Adult Education Institute are maintained by the Congregation, as well as are many congregational societies, including the Sisterhood, Men's Club, League and Youth Services. In addition, it sponsors the *Hebra Hased Va-Emet*, founded in 1802, and the Hebrew Relief Society, dating back to 1828 – the oldest burial and charitable societies in the United States.

The Reverend Dr. David de Sola Pool, a graduate of Jews' College, London and the Hildesheimer Rabbinical Seminary in Berlin, came to Shearith Israel in 1907 and served as minister there until his death in 1970.

Dr. Pool wrote several significant works and monographs in the fields of American Jewish history, religion, education, and Zionism, and edited and translated Sephardi and Ashkenazi Hebrew liturgical works.

Today Shearith Israel is under the spiritual leadership of the Rabbi Dr. Marc D. Angel, who was ordained at the Rabbi Isaac Elchanan Theological Seminary of Yeshiva University.

Rabbi Angel's commitment to things Sephardic and adherence to things Jewish emerges with crystal clarity in his most recent book, *Seeking Good, Speaking Peace* (1994), a collection of essays, articles, and addresses written by Rabbi Angel at different points in his career as rabbi, activist, author, and editor of thirteen books.

The Reverend Louis C. Gerstein, a graduate of the Jewish Theological Seminary of America, champion of Shearith Israel's *minhag* (customs) and the Sephardic tradition, is minister emeritus of Congregation Shearith Israel.

On May 8, 1994, the stately Sephardic Synagogue invited New York Jews to a tour of its building, as well as to view a week-long exhibition of documents, portraits, objects d'art, and films spanning the synagogue's 340-year history.

THE FIRST CHAIR OF HEBREW AT AN AMERICAN COLLEGE

1655

The first college founded in North America was Harvard, which opened in 1636 only a few years after the first settlers came to Massachusetts. It was named after a minister, John Harvard, who left the college his library and four hundred pounds when he died.

During the first few decades after the founding of Harvard College, no course of study figured more largely than Hebrew. It was not an elective course, but a prescribed subject. Because most of the students attending were preparing for the ministry, it was therefore required that they be able to read the Bible in the language they believed the Almighty spoke and in which the Oracles of God were written.

From the start, Hebrew was taught by the president of the college and the tutors along with the other undergraduate studies. In 1655 one of the first endowed professorships—that of Hebrew and Oriental languages—was established. Harvard students were required to spend one day each week for three years on Hebrew and allied tongues. The principle text used was the Bible. (Twelve copies with the students' inscriptions in them for the years 1651 to 1746 are extant.) Another text used was Wilhelm Schickard's *Horologium Hebraeum* (*The Hebrew Sun Dial*), which professed to teach the elements of the language in twenty-four hours. Following the Harvard pattern, other colleges such as Yale, Columbia, Dartmouth, Brown, Princeton, Johns Hopkins, and the University of Pennsylvania also taught Hebrew from their inception and are teaching it to this day.

The large number of Hebrew grammar books and lexicons published in this country over a long period of time indicate the popularity of Hebrew and biblical learning.

The first complete Hebrew grammar book published in North America was written by Judah Monis, the first Jew to receive a college degree as well as the only Jew to receive a Harvard degree before 1800.

Monis was born in Italy in 1683 into a family of Portuguese Marranos. Of his early years we know little. He studied in Leghorn and Amsterdam before serving as a rabbi on the island of Jamaica; then he moved to New York, where he was admitted as a freeman on February 28, 1715. He was listed then as a merchant. Four years later he appears in Boston. Here he seems to have met a number of crusading preachers.

Judah Monis easily impressed certain Harvard professors in nearby Cambridge with his Hebrew scholarship. He submitted his manuscript on Hebrew grammar, which could be published as a most useful book for teaching the subject to Harvard College students. It was accepted, and on June 14, 1720, he received the degree of Master of Arts. But he did not remain a Jew for long, for in 1722 — less than two years later — at the insistence of some of the Christian ministers, including Cotton Mather and his father, Increase Mather, he was baptized in the Harvard College Hall and became a Christian convert (but continued to observe Saturday as the Sabbath for the rest of his life). The following month he was appointed instructor of Hebrew at Harvard, but it is open to question whether Monis would have obtained this position if he had not joined their congregational church. He took charge of all of the Hebrew classes at Harvard, a position he held for almost forty years. He began dictating his grammar book, to be copied in longhand by his students until given a grant by the college to publish it under the title of *Dickdook Leshon Gnebreet: A Grammar of the Hebrew Tongue*. Hebrew type was imported from England but arrived in an imperfect condition and had to be supplemented by a later shipment. It was finally published in 1735.

Monis's grammar was used at a number of New England colleges including Dartmouth, but because of its inaccuracies and inconsistencies, it was eventually replaced by Israel Lyons's *The Scholar's Instructor of Hebrew Grammar*. The method of this grammar was simpler and was probably introduced because of its greater practical utility.

Yale, founded in 1701, offered Hebrew in its early years. The founders of the Collegiate School from which Yale developed stated that students would spend their first year in "practice of tongues, especially Hebrew." Yale was later to become a center of interest in Hebrew under its president Ezra Stiles, who assumed leadership of the college in 1777. Stiles study of the language deepened to include readings in rabbinic and Kabbalistic

(Jewish mysticism) literature. These endeavors led to his establishing friendships with six European and Palestinian rabbis.

After the American Revolution education generally shifted from a religious to a political basis. Yet at the time of the Revolution, there were some who advocated that the country abandon English and use Hebrew as the vehicle of speech.

At Harvard, Hebrew ceased to be an obligatory subject by 1817. At Yale it was no longer required after 1789. Upon granting his students' request that the obligation to study Hebrew be lifted, Stiles confided to his diary that he feared for their souls—for they would not understand the Psalms when they were admitted to the heavenly court.

The influence of Hebrew culture went far beyond the bounds of technical scholarship and professional training of theologians. It has permeated and colored the thought and feeling of this country ever since its beginning.

The influence of the Hebrew language has found its way into American speech. About half of the verses of the Book of Psalms have virtually become English idioms. Many of the phrases of Proverbs, the Song of Songs, Ecclesiastes, Job, and other books embodied in the wisdom literature of the Bible have been adopted by English-speaking peoples. Hebrew words such as amen, cherubim, hallelujah, seraphim, shiboleths, chutzpah, and so forth, have become part of the English vernacular. Cities with Hebrew names and derivative can be found in every part of the United States. For example, we have Sharon and Salem, Massachusetts; New Canaan, Connecticut; Bethlehem, New Hampshire; Mount Hebron, California; Joseph, Idaho; and Goshen, New York, just to mention a few.

To this day, Hebrew remains a living part of America. As a language, it is taught in nearly five hundred American universities and high schools. Its spirit is reflected in the best of contemporary literature, art, and thought.

THE FIRST JEWISH DOCTOR

1656

Spanish and Portuguese Jewish physicians of note came to the New World at an early date and practiced medicine in Recife, the first Jewish settlement in Brazil. Dr. Jacob Lumbrozo, a Portuguese physician who arrived in Maryland on January 24, 1656, two years after the arrival of the first Jews in New Amsterdam, was North America's earliest Jewish physician. He was the first known Jew to settle in the colony of Maryland and was the only Jew there at the time. Making no effort to hide his Jewishness, he was generally known as "Ye Jew doctor."

Dr. Lumbrozo not only practiced his profession but was an active trader and money lender; between December 1, 1657, and December 1, 1658, he was rendered judgments or attachments on nine persons because of debts owing him. His medical practice and business interests must have been very successful, for he acquired a good deal of property. He imported a servant, began raising tobacco, became a country squire, and for nearly a decade continued as an important figure in Maryland's economic activity.

Although the early proprietors of Maryland, the Calverts, were Roman Catholics and intended the colony as an asylum only for the persecuted members of their faith, Dr. Lumbrozo was not disturbed in the practice of his religion until 1658, when he was arrested and charged with blaspheming against the Christian religion by a group of zealots from Virginia who had temporarily assumed control of the colony. He was tried for being a nonconformist in violation of the Act Concerning Religion, which had become a law. The so-called Edict of Toleration, promulgated in 1649, guaranteed religious toleration to Christians only. Lumbrozo, a Jew, was by his very religious beliefs subject under the law to imprisonment or death. The case was the sole one of its kind brought against a Jew in all the thirteen colonies. He was saved only by the general amnesty proclaimed on March 3, 1659, when Richard Cromwell succeeded his father as Lord Protector of England.

During the eight remaining years of his life, Dr. Lumbrozo continued to reside in the colony, acquiring certain civil rights and a grant of land that was known for some time as Lumbrozie's Discovery.

Following Dr. Lumbrozo's example, practically every Jewish community after his time had its own physician. To inform the public of their presence, doctors would print announcements to the effect that they intended to practice the art of healing and agreed to cure persons free of charge if they could show a certificate from a clergyman that they were really poor. Letters addressed to them were expected to be postpaid, and those who lived at a distance and desired aid were requested to send a horse for transportation.

One of the most interesting of these early physicians, Dr. John Siccary, also a Portuguese Jew who settled in Virginia in 1745, was the first to introduce the tomato as an edible foodstuff. It had for long been considered poisonous and had been used as a garden ornament. Dr. Siccary called tomatoes "apples" and believed that a person who ate enough of them would never die. No one knows how many tomatoes Dr. Siccary ate, but he lived to a ripe old age.

Before the American Revolution at least four doctors were members of Congregation Shearith Israel, which was founded in 1654 by the first Jewish settlers in New Amsterdam, as New York was first called. They were: Dr. Woolin, who came from Bohemia in 1740; Dr. Jacob Isaac; Dr. Nunez; and Dr. Isaac Abraham.

Another American Jewish physician of early date was Dr. Isaac Hays. Born in Philadelphia, he graduated from the University of Pennsylvania in 1816 and received his M.D. degree there in 1820. Dr. Hays was the first one to present a resolution to the New York Medical Convention in 1846 proposing a National Medical Association, and in 1847 he composed its code of ethics. This code is still used by every state and country medical society in the United States.

Dr. Hays was among the earliest practitioners in this country to make diseases of the eye a specialty. He invented the first cylindrical lenses to correct astigmatism; he introduced many important opthalmic instruments; and he wrote a score of scientific books on medicine. In addition, he made an indelible mark in the field of medical literature. As early as 1841 he edited the *American Journal of Medical Sciences*, popularly called *Hays' Journal*, which continued to influence medical thought in this country for more than half a century. In 1843, in collaboration with his son, Isaac Minis Hays, he established the journal known as *Medical News*, which continued publication until 1905. In 1874, he founded another journal, *The Monthly Abstract of Medical Sciences*. In this way he paved the way for American medical journalism, attracted the best medical writers to his journal, and inspired gifted young men to attempt medico-literary work.

THE FIRST JEWISH CEMETERY IN NORTH AMERICA

1656

In July 1656, when Abraham de Lucena, Salvador Dandrada, and Joseph Jacob Cohen, three of the original settlers who had come to New Amsterdam on the *Sainte Catherine* from Recife, Brazil, in 1654, petitioned Governor Peter Stuyvesant and the directors of the colony for the right "to be permitted to purchase a burying place for their nation," they were told they could have one when the need arose. There was a need the following year, for on July 14, 1656, one of the newcomers died, and a tract of land was set aside from the colony lands situated outside the city.

In the absence of all records concerning the ground allotted in 1656 — almost three hundred and forty years ago — the site of this, the first Jewish burial ground in New York City, can no longer be traced.

The earliest extant document belonging to the Shearith Israel Congregation, the first Jewish congregation in America, is a deed of 1701, confirming the community's title to the second cemetery purchased in 1682, a quarter century after the first grant made by the Dutch city fathers.

Early in 1682, Joseph Bueno de Mesquita stands out as the representative of the Jewish community who purchased from William Merrett and his wife, Margery, a piece of land about fifty-two by fifty feet in size "for a Jew burying place." The site was outside the village, north of Wall Street, where the British had built the city wall, near the present location of Chatham Square and Oliver Street on the New Bowery.

Benjamin Bueno de Mesquita, a kinsman of the man who made the purchase on behalf of the community, was the first person known to be buried there. Benjamin's grave and tombstone, which is still preserved, is dated 1683.

During the Revolutionary War, the cemetery was fortified by the patriots as one of the defenses of the city.

A small part of the cemetery, with only a few tombstones bearing both Hebrew and Spanish inscriptions, still exists today, although the stones that mark the graves are so eroded that many of the inscriptions are no longer legible and have been almost completely lost with the growth of the city. Among those known to have been buried there are eighteen Jewish soldiers and patriots of the American Revolutionary War. Here lies Simon Nathan, a private under Captain Andrew Geyer's Third Company of the Philadelphia Militia, who at the risk of his life supplied the Continental Army with canvas and powder. A direct descendant of Simon Nathan and Abraham de Lucena is Congregation Shearith Israel's Honorary Parnas (president) today, Edgar J. Nathan III, the son and grandson of the synagogue's former presidents, Edgar J. Nathan and Edgar J. Nathan II. Here also lies the Reverend Gershom Mendes Seixas, known as the "Patriot Rabbi of the American Revolution," who closed the doors of Congregation Shearith Israel when the Redcoats entered New York City. Next to him lies his brother, Benjamin Mendes Seixas, who served as a lieutenant in the New York Militia and who, together with Ephraim Hart, helped to found the New York Stock Exchange.

At annual Memorial Day exercises at this ancient burial grounds of Shearith Israel—known variously as the Chatham Square, the New Bowery, and the Oliver Street Cemetery—the Asser Levy Garrison of the Army and Navy Union, named after the American Jewish pioneer, decorates each of the graves with an American flag. At the same time, the spiritual leader of Congregation Shearith Israel recounts the deeds of the men beneath the stones. A tablet marking the remains of this cemetery, which is the oldest Jewish landmark in the United States, was erected in 1903 under the auspices of the American Scenic and Historic Preservation Society and the American Jewish Historical Society. In 1966, this historic site associated with the American Revolution was declared a "landmark site" by the City of New York.

A second cemetery of the Spanish and Portuguese Synagogue in New York City is located on Eleventh Street, east of Sixth Avenue. It was consecrated on February 27, 1805, as *Beth Chaim Sheni* (the Second Cemetery). Shortly after the yellow fever scourge of 1822, it became the only Jewish cemetery in New York that could be used. In 1830, the city opened up Eleventh Street and condemned the entire burial grounds. The congregation successfully petitioned the city for use of that part of the cemetery that would not interfere with the street. Among the few still buried in this cemetery is Ephraim Hart, one of the founders of the New York Stock Exchange.

A third Congregation Shearith Israel cemetery is on Twenty-First Street, west of Sixth Avenue. Consecrated on August 17, 1829, the ground bore the name *Beth Chaim Shelishi*. The graveyard served Congregation Shearith Israel for almost twenty-two years. Mordecai Manuel Noah, the playwright who tried to found a Jewish colony on Grand Island in the Niagara River, was one of the last persons to be buried there.

On August 3, 1851, with the prohibition of further burials south of 86th Street, Congregation Shearith Israel consecrated a tract of nearly seven acres as the *Beth Olam Cemetery* on the heights of Cypress Hills in Brooklyn, overlooking Jamaica Bay, which is still in use today.

The Jewish cemetery in Newport, Rhode Island, which was founded in 1677, adjacent to the Newport Synagogue – Congregation Jeshuat Israel, also known as the Touro Synagogue – is the oldest Jewish cemetery still existing in its entirety to this day. In accordance with the wishes expressed in their respective wills, both Judah and Abraham Touro, the sons of Isaac Touro, the first *hazzan* and spiritual leader of the Newport Synagogue and the first of America's Jewish philanthropists, lie in this beautiful cemetery. Henry Wadsworth Longfellow, inspired by the tombstones bearing Hebrew and Spanish inscriptions, wrote a poem in 1852, "The Jewish Cemetery in Newport," at a time when no Jews at all were living in the city. Longfellow wrote using his knowledge of Jewish life and the Hebrew language:

Gone are the living, but the dead remain
    And not neglected, for a hand unseen
Scattering its bounty, like a summer rain
    Still keeps their graves and remembrance green.
How came they here? What burst of Christian hate,
    What persecution, merciless and blind,
Drove o'er the sea – the desert desolate –
    These Ishmaels and Hagars of mankind?
Pride and humiliation hand in hand
    Walked with them through the world where'er they went,
Trampled and beaten they were as sand,
    And yet unshaken as the continent.

THE FIRST JEWISH CITIZEN

1657

The defense of New Amsterdam, the little Dutch settlement clustering on the tip of Manhattan Island, was in the hands of the colonists, the burghers, or citizen soldiers who had obtained such guns, pistols, shot, and powder as they could. The lurking Indians and marauding Swedes made no distinction between young and old, Jew or Christian. Following the custom established in Holland, Jews were excluded from military duty but were required to pay a tax that amounted to a dollar and twenty cents a month.

In the New World, the early Jewish settlers had hoped to reside in a country where they could stand alongside their Christian neighbors and with them share the hazards of defense as well as the responsibilities of peace. Accordingly, on November 5, 1655, a handful of Jews under the leadership of Jacob Barsimson, the first Jewish settler who had come directly from Holland, and Asser Levy, one of the original twenty-three Jews who had arrived on the *Sainte Catherine* in 1654, demanded from the Dutch authorities the right to stand guard at the stockade of New Amsterdam. They objected to the discriminatory tax that was levied upon the Jews as a compulsory substitute for the customary military service exacted from all inhabitants. They were met with a prompt refusal and were further informed that if they thought the denial injurious, permission was granted "to depart whenever and whither it pleases them."

Not to be discouraged, Asser Levy proceeded to perform his military duties and passed many a watchful hour peering over the stockades into the wilderness of Manhattan. Apparently, his services were accepted, for he presented a second petition to the Court of Burgomasters and Schepens dated April 9, 1657, to the effect that since he now had kept watch and ward in common with other burghers, he requested to be admitted as a burgher. He stated further that he had been a burgher in New Amsterdam. Again the court denied his request. This time, however, the opportunity was left open for him to appeal to the director general and council of the colony. On April 27, 1657, they allowed his appeal, and he was admitted to the burgher right, thus becoming the first American Jewish citizen. He paved the way for citizenship rights for his people and other minority groups. These rights were continued when the British wrested the colony from the Dutch in August 1664 and renamed it New York. These rights gave tolerance rather than complete freedom; but they were far in advance of the rights given to the Jews by other nations, and they were one step towards the liberty embodied later in the Constitution of the United States.

Thanks are also due to Levy and his associates for establishing the right of free trade throughout the colony. Levy had set himself up as a trader. In those days, trading with the Indians for furs was the "big business" of the community. He soon extended his activities into regions as far distant as Albany (Fort Orange), much to the dislike of the local traders. They tried to stop him, and when he still persisted, they appealed to the authorities in Holland to cut off his competition. The Amsterdam authorities seemed to be sympathetic to the objectors. (Asser, however, forestalled any adverse action from them by bringing in the local authorities to keep the trade open to all alike.)

Levy was also the first Jewish landowner in North America who ventured into taking mortgages on property in such Dutch–American villages as Breucklyn (Brooklyn) and Vlackbos (Flatbush). In 1661 he purchased property in Albany and acquired a piece of land on South William Street in New York. When in 1660 he was licensed as a butcher at a time when licenses were restricted to only six in the colony, he was excused from slaughtering hogs. The same year he built the first Jewish slaughterhouse in North America so that "all persons should have the liberty to kill and hang therein meat." Later he also owned a celebrated tavern near his slaughterhouse.

By the time of the British occupation in 1664, Asser Levy was a man of wealth and the only Jew deemed prominent enough to be called upon to swear allegiance to the new governor. Although frequently engaged in litigation in which he was the plaintiff, insisting on his rights, he impressed Jews and non-Jews alike with his integrity.

No other Jew of his time seems to have had so many dealings with Christians. He was frequently named executor in the wills of many Christian merchants. In 1671 he lent money to build the first Lutheran Church in New York.

In that same year, he served on a jury, a rare privilege for a Jew in colonial times. Again in 1671, he helped a poor Jew of New England to have a fine abated, the court doing so "as a token of their respect to the said Asser Levy."

At the time of his death in 1681, Levy was considered among the wealthiest inhabitants of the colony. His grounds and buildings were appraised at two hundred and eighteen pounds and the slaughterhouse, which was located outside the city gates, at eighteen hundred pounds. In the inventory of his estate we find listed: two brass candlesticks, one Sabbath lamb (sic), three silver goblets, one ditto cup with two ears, one ditto spice box, a parcel of old books, and nine pictures. The candlesticks were evidently for Sabbath and holiday rituals, the spice box was for *Havdalah* (a ceremony for the conclusion of the Sabbath), and the cup with the two ears may have been used for the ritual of washing of the hands of the Priests and Levites (of whom Asser Levy was one) in the synagogue.

The name of Asser Levy stands out as that of a determined and admirable character whose life work made its considerable contribution to the building of a new continent. His efforts helped to lay the foundation for the abolition of the limitations imposed on Jews by the civic authorities of a less tolerant age and forced the recognition of Jews in New York as individuals entitled to share, on the same basis as all others, in the common benefits and burdens of citizenship.

One of his descendants, also named Asser Levy, was an officer in the American Revolutionary Army, a hundred years later. An ensign in the First New Jersey Regiment, he was probably the only Jew to serve with the New Jersey troops.

On February 22, 1955, during the celebration of the three hundreth anniversary of the first Jewish settlement in North America, Asser Levy Place, running from Twenty-third to Twenty-fifth streets, between First Avenue and Franklin D. Roosevelt Drive on New York City's East Side, was dedicated.

The Jews' search for rights and privileges was the central theme of Congregation Shearith Israel's week-long exhibit that opened on May 8, 1994, and was called "The 340 Year Saga for Freedom and Human Dignity." The oldest object in the exhibit was the inventory of the estate of Asser Levy, the first such document for an American Jew.

THE FIRST JEWISH SCHOOL

1728

Long before the days of the free public school system throughout the nation, the most significant means of education among Jews were the congregational schools. True to the teachings of the Hebrew prophets—"and thou shalt teach them to thy children"—each congregation conducted some kind of Jewish education and general school training.

The first of these schools, known as *Yeshivat Minhat Areb,* was established in 1728 by Congregation Shearith Israel in New York City, the same year they erected their first regular synagogue building. Children came on foot or horseback from all over the island to sit on backless benches in a building adjacent to the synagogue that was used as a schoolhouse. In charge of education was the *hazzan,* or reader of services and a special teacher, presumably for the secular subjects. In this early period, in keeping with the traditional outlook and practice of the Jews in Europe, the Bible, Hebrew, and allied studies were the main ones taught.

In 1755, Shearith Israel opened one of the earliest schools combining secular and Hebrew education, a practice unheard of at that time in many countries. The school continued to exist until the American Revolution, when most of the Jews left New York. The children were taught Spanish, English writing, and arithmetic, along with Hebrew. The hours of study were from nine to twelve in the morning and two to five in the afternoon, all through the year. Most of the day was devoted to Hebrew; English and arithmetic could not have taken more than a hour and Spanish at the most another hour. In 1762 the synagogue secured the services of Abraham Israel Abrahams, a professional teacher, at the salary of four hundred dollars a year. The trustees visited the school regularly in rotation.

In 1802 the Shearith Israel Congregational School was reorganized as the Polonies Talmud Torah, bearing the name of its chief benefactor, Mayer Polonies. It is the oldest religious school still in existence in North America today. The regular day-school pattern was continued until 1840, when it finally became limited to religious and Hebrew instruction only. As the public school system developed, the congregational schools became supplementary, meeting on afternoons or on Sundays or both.

Rebecca Gratz, a pioneer in the modern religious instruction of American Jewish youth and the model for the heroine of Sir Walter Scott's well-known novel, *Ivanhoe*, founded in 1838 the Hebrew Sunday School of Philadelphia, the first of its kind in the United States. She was concerned with religious training not only for the children of Mikveh Israel, her synagogue, but for all the Jewish children of the city. Rosa Mordecai reports in her "Recollections of the First Hebrew Sunday School" that Rebecca Gratz composed a prayer for its service and remained its supervisor, president, and active, energetic head until her eighty-third year. This school still exists in Philadelphia, where the Protestant Sunday School movement began. The idea took root, especially in Reform Judaism, and spread to every American city that has a Jewish community.

The Reverend Isaac Leeser, a self-educated rabbi, editor, and educator, founded the Hebrew Education Association in Philadelphia in 1848. The association organized a small school with twenty-two pupils that expanded bit by bit. It was the first Jewish religious school to meet in America on afternoons and Sundays. The Hebrew language, the Bible, and Jewish history were the subjects taught, and the school became known as the Talmud Torah. Eventually, Leeser himself produced a series of Jewish textbooks, which he dedicated to Rebecca Gratz, with simplified Bible and history lessons, some of them accompanied by two-tone sepia illustrations.

Today the Talmud Torahs are still a category of Jewish schools in this country by which Jewish children can learn of their religious heritage and of the great deeds of their people, although the yeshiva or

Hebrew All Day parochial school, which combines both Hebrew and Judaic and secular subjects, has shown a tremendous rise in enrollment in the last several decades.

There are now 532 elementary and secondary Hebrew Day Schools throughout the United States. Torah Umesorah, a national society for Hebrew Day Schools, helped found and services many of these schools by sending emissaries to communities across the country. These schools now have a total enrollment of 181,988.

A major conclusion of a study conducted by Brandeis University and the Jewish Educational Service of North America (JESNA) in the spring of 1994 indicates that virtually all Jewish children in Orthodox homes receive a Jewish education. The figure falls to seventy nine percent among those in Conservative households and seventy seven percent in Reform.

The study also estimates that the aggregate enrollment in all types of Jewish schools in the United States—including Sunday, weekday after-noon Talmud Torah, the Hebrew All Day School, Yiddish, congregational, and noncongregational—numbers 470,000.

THE FIRST JEWISH ARTIST/SILVERSMITH

1746

Myer Myers, a silversmith who was born in New York City in 1721 where his parents had migrated from Holland, is probably the first native-born artist of English America—certainly the first Jew who made a contribution to American art.

Young Myers who learned his trade at an early age, was apprenticed to a master artisan who worked in gold and silver. After completing the legally required seven years of training, Myer Myers opened his workshop on Lower Wall Street, where he not only engaged successfully in his craft but also sold coffee, spices, and tobacco. By 1755 he had expanded his trade to Philadelphia.

Myers was a highly skilled and versatile master craftsman who created the first American examples of Jewish ceremonial objects and was also distinguished for his general ornamental and functional pieces. Several of his exquisite Hanukkah lamps, spice boxes, and other ceremonial objects, as well as a silver tankard showing the coat of arms of the Livingston family, still exist. Examples of his work, representing fifty years of activity, may still be seen in museums, synagogues, churches, and important private collections. For the synagogues of New York, Newport, and Philadelphia he made *rimonim* (pomegranates with a crown and silver tinkling bells that decorate the Torah scrolls) that are still in use. All the objects carry his trademark *MM* embossed in a rectangle or his name engraved in script.

Myers's craftsmanship and intricate workmanship produced highly valued pieces. They cover three periods of eighteenth century design—the midcentury, the classical, and the federal. Ironically, one of his pieces even found its way into the collection of the czar of Russia.

During the American Revolution, Myers was a patriot stalwart and, together with the Reverend Gershom Mendez Seixas and most members of Congregation Shearith Israel, fled with his family from New York during the British occupation, first to Norwalk, Connecticut, and later to Philadelphia. There he used his skill to melt down household goods and turn them into bullets. Myers returned to New York in 1783 and was a signatory, with two other members of Shearith Israel, to a letter conveying the loyal sentiments of New York's returned Israelites to Governor De Witt Clinton upon his return.

The name of Myer Myers occurs repeatedly in the synagogue records of Congregation Shearith Israel during a half century from earlier than 1749, when he contributed the generous sum of eight pounds to a "public and free subscription to buy wood," to the time of his death in 1795 at the age of seventy-three. His services to the community were varied and constant, if the records refer, as they seem to, to the same man. They range from minor offices to that of president from 1759 to 1770. In 1786 he was elected president of the Silversmith's Society of New York, thus becoming North America's first Jewish president and member of a trade guild. Like his fellow silversmith, Paul Revere, Myers was attracted to Masonry and became Senior Warden of King David's Lodge in New York.

A devoted follower of Judaism, the artist-silversmith seems to have been free from the fanaticism that discourages one from making ritual objects of another creed. The Museum of the City of New York displays a baptismal bowl Myers cast for the Brick Presbyterian Church, and the Metropolitan Museum of Art cherishes the broken alms basin he made for the First Presbyterian Church at the request of Peter H. Livingston. But for the synagogues of New York, Newport, and Philadelphia, he reserved the emotion he felt for his ancestral faith.

Myer Myers married twice and had a large family. Many of his descendants had distinguished careers in law and politics, in letters, business, and banking and especially in the army, fighting on both sides of the Civil War.

He is buried in the Shearith Israel cemetery that still exists off Chatham Square in Lower Manhattan and which in 1966 was declared a landmark site by the City of New York.

There is still another early American Jewish artist who deserves mention: Joshua Cantir of Charleston, South Carolina. Another, perhaps

America's third Jewish craftsman, whose name has been preserved for us is David Lopez, also of Charleston, the builder and architect of the present synagogue Kahal Kodesh Beth Elohim. The third oldest congregation in the United States, it was organized the day following Rosh Hashanah in 1750.

Solomon Nunes Carvalho, who in 1853 joined Colonel John C. Fremont's expedition to explore the Far West, is still another early American artist. Carvalho made the maps that first wagon trails, then railways, and finally modern highways followed over the Rockies into California. Born in 1815 in Charleston, South Carolina, he became a portrait painter in his twentieth year and received a silver medal from the South Carolina Institute for his painting of "Moses Receiving the Tablets of the Law on Sinai," which was destroyed in 1838 when the Beth Elohim Synagogue burned down. Fortunately, Carvalho had drawn a sketch of the synagogue's interior so that today we can still see the "spacious and elegant synagogue" described by Lafayette and dedicated in 1794. His best-known portraits include those of Abraham Lincoln, Judah Touro, and Isaac Leeser and can be found not only in Baltimore but also at Brandeis University in Waltham, Massachusetts, and in the Touro Infirmary in New Orleans.

When in 1853 Colonel John Fremont sought to map out the most desirable route for a transcontinental railway, Carvalho was the official photographer and sketcher. Besides being a painter, he was an expert in handling the recently invented daguerreotype photography, never before utilized in exploration. Carvalho eagerly accepted the invitation to accompany Fremont's party to make daguerreotype photographs, thus becoming the first official photographer in the United States to accompany a scientific expedition. Some historians believe that Carvalho was also the first Jew to cross the Rockies. Others deny him this distinction; they claim that Emanuel Lazarus, who was one of an exploring party of seventeen white men to enter California from the East in 1826, deserves this honor. But there is no definite proof that Lazarus was a Jew.

In any event, Carvalho made the most of his opportunities. He kept a careful record of the hardships suffered by the twenty-two men of the expedition party as in the winter cold they crossed the Rockies on foot. Later he described his experiences in his book, *Incidents of Travel and Adventures in the Far West with Colonel Fremont's Last Expedition Across the Rocky Mountains.* This work, which was published in New York in 1857, is the only account of this expedition that survived and is of the greatest value to historians of the early West.

Throughout his life Carvalho took a strong interest in fostering Jewish education. He is credited with founding the first Jewish communal organization in California after his arrival there in 1854. The first Sephardic synagogue in Baltimore credits him as being one of its founders. His wife,

Sarah Solis, established the first Jewish Sunday School in Baltimore in 1856. She had served as a teacher in the Sunday School of Rebecca Gratz in Philadelphia.

Carvalho could paint, and he could write, and he had a thousand anecdotes to relate. He was also an inventor. In the late nineteenth century he patented a number of heating devices that were quite lucrative. While not a great artist, his paintings are, nevertheless, sought by collectors. They would consider it a fortunate stroke to find anything from the brush of the dashing artist who achieved fame as a pathfinder in a great American adventure.

THE FIRST JEWISH OFFICERS

1747

Although lovers of peace from the days of Solomon and Jeremiah, Jews have fought in all wars of this country with honor and distinction.

The story of the participation of Jews in the armed forces of North American lands goes back to the days when the Marrano smith Hernando Alonso fought with Cortés in Mexico (New Spain) against the Aztec Indians—when he was suddenly denounced as a heretic for practicing Jewish customs in secret, condemned to the stake, and burned to death by order of the chief inquisitor of Mexico City in 1528. More than 130 years later, as we have seen above, Asser Levy was the first to precede his brethren in standing guard at the stockade of New Amsterdam in 1656 to guard the city from possible attack by Indians and Swedes.

One of the first Jews to bear arms as a soldier in British North America was Joseph Isaks, who enlisted in the New York Militia some time before 1690.

The first instance of a Jew participating as an officer in the armed forces of the colonies was at the opening of the French and Indian War in 1747, the conflict that finally decided the destiny of the North American continent. It started when the expanding empires of France and Great Britain clashed in the land beyond the Appalachian Mountains.

The French were then entrenched along a line of scattered points from the Great Lakes south of the Ohio River, with outposts in the Allegheny Mountains. As a result, the entire northern frontier of the British colonies was exposed to attack from the Indian allies of the French. Jacob Judah volunteered in the campaign of 1747. Michael Isaacs fought gallantly in 1755. Isaac Moses marched in the company of Captain J. Whiting in 1755.

In 1754 Isaac Meyers called a town meeting at the Rising Sun Inn and set up a company of soldiers of which he was chosen captain of an expedition across the Allegheny Mountains.

Other Jews were alert to the growing dangers in French and Indian campaigns, and the names of Jewish soldiers appear in a record of skirmishes and battles of the period. Jacob Wolf and Jacob Wexler served in the ranks. Lieutenant Joseph Levy participated in the Cherokee uprising in South Carolina in 1761. Captain Elias Meyer was a member of the Royal American Regiment and whose recommendations for promotion stated that he was an engineer—probably America's first Jewish engineer of whom we have a record—and had previously served as a lieutenant.

On the seventeenth of April in 1775, when Paul Revere rode through "every Middlesex village and farm" alerting the embattled citizens and farmers that the redcoats were about to land and attack, there were about twenty-five hundred Jews in all the thirteen colonies. That meant there were only about a few hundred of military age.

The Continental Army had its share of Jewish soldiers and officers. Although the records are incomplete, we know there were more than twenty-seven officers, including three lieutenant colonels, three majors, and six captains.

We know of over forty Jews who fought directly under George Washington, as well as a number of others who served in other ways.

In South Carolina there was a "Jews' Company," commanded by Captain Richard Lushington. It derived its name from the fact that it had been recruited from a section of Charleston in which Jews predominated and the majority of its members were Jews. The company, comprising some two dozen men, saw service in the Battle of Beaufort.

Three Jews—David Salisbury Franks, Isaac Franks, and Solomon Bush—won the rank of lieutenant colonel. Of the three, David S. Frank's career was the most exciting. A Canadian at the time he was arrested for his outspoken sympathies for the rebels, he enlisted in the Massachusetts Regiment immediately on his release from custody and soon became an aide-de-camp of Benedict Arnold. When Arnold's treason was discovered, suspicion fell on David Franks, but he was acquitted of all charges leveled against him. However, the terms of the verdict displeased him, and he insisted on a review of the trial by a special court of inquiry. In 1789 not only was he completely exonerated of complicity in Arnold's treason, he was promoted to the rank of lieutenant colonel. In 1781 he was sent to bring government dispatches to John Jay in Madrid and to Benjamin Franklin in Paris. Following his honorable discharge after the Revolutionary War, he was awarded a large grant of land for his exceptionally zealous service to his country.

Isaac Franks, a cousin of David S. Franks, fought under George Washington in the Battle of Long Island on August 27, 1776—a battle that nearly wrecked the Continental Army and the colonial cause. He was taken prisoner but soon escaped. He received high rank—lieutenant colonel—as an officer in the Pennsylvania Militia after the war. History also identifies him as host to George Washington when Washington sought refuge in Germantown to escape the yellow fever epidemic rampant in Philadelphia, which was then the capital of the country.

Solomon Bush, who hailed from the City of Brotherly Love, had joined the Revolutionary Army because he wanted, as he stated, to "revenge the wrongs of my injured country." Appointed a deputy adjutant general in the state militia, he was ultimately commissioned a lieutenant colonel. Bush appears to have been the Jewish officer who held the highest rank in any combat unit of the Continental Army. He was severely wounded and taken prisoner in the fall of 1777, when General Washington's army was badly defeated in the Battle of Philadelphia. He was later freed in an exchange of prisoners between the British and the Americans.

Upon his release in 1779, he applied for rations and back pay. The Supreme Executive of the Continental Army reviewed his request and records. The review disclosed the brilliant and distinguished military service that Bush had rendered in the winter of 1776 in and out of battle, especially "when the service was critical and hazardous."

After the war, Colonel Bush went to England seeking better medical care for his war wound. While he was there, he again found himself in a position to serve his country.

When he returned to America, Colonel Bush applied for the position of postmaster general, which had recently been vacated. He was the first Jew known to have been considered for a cabinet rank in the government. He failed to get this appointment but seems to have found consolation in being elevated to the office of grand master of the Masonic lodge of his state. Freemasonry appears to have had a strong appeal to the Jews in colonial America.

His unhealed war injury hastened his death in 1796.

The first Jewish graduate of West Point was Simon M. Levy, class of 1801. He partook in the Indian War in the Northeast and became known as the "hero of the Maumee Rapids." Upon his graduation from West Point, he was appointed an instructor there. He resigned his commission in 1805, two years before his death.

THE FIRST JEWISH CANDLE MANUFACTURER

1754

As early as 1754, the Jews of Newport, Rhode Island, who had learned the art of the manufacture of spermaceti candles in Lisbon, began to manufacture sperm oil and spermaceti candles. The romantic and touching beginnings of this Jewish community were followed by a period of real importance in the fifty years before the American Revolution. Some of the Jews who had come to Newport during the middle of the eighteenth century, directly following the Lisbon earthquake, were of Sephardic origin. Many of them were Marranos (Jews who had become Christian converts to escape persecution) who had held high offices in their native lands. During their long estrangement from Judaism, they secretly nourished their faith with a love made strong and sacred through oppression. But here, in Newport, they practiced their faith openly and with great fervor, as though to make up for the lost years.

At that time Newport was more important a port than New York, following only Boston and Philadelphia. Much of its commerce was traceable to the Jews from Spain and Portugal and the West Indies. These were wealthy and influential men with business connections in their former homes as well as in other American colonies. At least fifty-eight Jewish families were living in Newport before the American Revolution with a *hazzan* — literally "cantor" — who served as officiating rabbi, along with visiting rabbis and scholars.

These Newport Jews were among the leading businessmen of their day in pioneering projects. They were largely responsible for the high standing that Newport had as a seaport, which it lost after the Revolution.

One of these men, Jacob Rodriguez Rivera, introduced the sperm oil industry to America. Rivera is thought to have discovered a method for manufacturing the best candles on the market by using ingredients obtained from sperm whales. This proved a much better mode of lighting than the old tallow candles, and, indirectly, Rivera advanced the whaling industry, as well. For a century thereafter, whaling was among the leading industries in New England.

Rivera had left New York — where he had gone with his father, Abraham Rodriguez Rivera, a Marrano from Spain, in the early part of the eighteenth century — to try his luck in Curaçao. There he lived for a time, marrying a widow originally of the Pimental family. He then returned to New York, where his child, Sarah, later the wife of Aaron Lopez, was born. Rivera was naturalized in New York in 1746; two years later he moved to Newport, where among the city's entrepreneurs he soon ranked second only to his son-in-law, Aaron Lopez, known as the "Merchant Prince of New England."

Rivera was so successful in the manufacture of spermaceti candles that Newport became the center of the whale oil, candle, and soap industry in America. By 1760, Newport had seventeen factories engaged in such activity.

Rivera's honesty in business dealings was a byword in the community. The story is told how recouping his losses after being forced to take advantage of the bankruptcy law in his first attempt to set himself up in business, he held a banquet for his creditors, each of whom found underneath his napkin a check for the exact amount, plus interest, due him.

In 1761 nine spermaceti candle manufacturers, all located in New England and of whom three were the Jewish firms of Newport, came together and formulated what is perhaps the earliest attempt at monopoly in American commerce. They formed an association under the name of the United Company of Spermaceti Candlers with the avowed aim of checking competition among its members by fixing the maximum price at which they could sell their product and adjusting their output "to the needs of the time."

As an example of a trade monopoly, the working out of this scheme holds its own in contrast with attempts to control industry by later "captains of industry."

Rivera espoused the colonial cause during the American Revolution and was among the first who fled to Leicester, Massachusetts, with Aaron Lopez and his family when the British came to Newport. When peace was declared, Rivera returned to Newport and resumed the manufacture and shipping of spermaceti candles. At the time of his death he left an estate of over $100,000, a considerable amount of money in those days.

Rivera was a leading individual in the establishment of—and the first president of—the Newport Synagogue, Congregation Jeshuat Israel, also known as the Touro Synagogue, the oldest synagogue building still in existence in North America and now a federal shrine.

Rivera was also one of the original founders of America's first Jewish club, organized by the great Jewish merchants of Newport.

At his death in 1789, Rivera was mourned by the entire community as a devout Jew and honorable citizen. He was survived by his wife, Hannah, who died at nearly one hundred years of age in New York City. His son, Abraham, left an only son, Aaron, the last of the Riveras, who settled in Wilmington, Delaware.

THE FIRST INDIGO PLANT

1756

Moses Lindo, a Portuguese Jew who came to Charleston, South Carolina, in 1756, after having spent several years in England, introduced the indigo industry into the thirteen colonies. On his large plantation in Charleston, he established the first indigo plant in North America and invested some two hundred pounds in the business. He is said to have learned about indigo production in London, where he attended the Merchant Taylor's School and there obtained practical experience in the trade. He continued a correspondence with the dyers of the London Royal Society and was continually making improvements in keeping with their findings. He even is said to have offered prizes to induce new methods of production.

The Philosophical Transactions, a publication of the British Royal Society of London, contains a letter that describes his discovery of a new dye made from pouck, a native weed of South Carolina, cooked in Bristol water. He was convinced of the superiority of the Carolinian over French indigo.

Due to his pioneering efforts, a fabulous Carolina indigo trade developed that was responsible for the wealth of the colony, and he became its leading exporter and importer. It was his mark of inspection that qualified the Carolina-grown product for acceptance in British markets. In recognition of his work in the field, in 1762, he was appointed Surveyor and Inspector-General of Indigo Dyes and Drugs for the Carolina provinces and had the right to use the royal coat of arms of George III over his door.

The petition to appoint him inspector, issued by the Board of Trade, was signed by the lieutenant-governor, council members, members of the assembly, merchants, and planters of Charleston. It stated that "because of the services rendered to this province by Moses Lindo, and as testimonial of his abilities he be made public inspector; he is the only person known to us capable of rendering this province public service in this article."

Until 1756, the annual export of indigo seldom reached 350,000 pounds. After that year, Charleston exported more than one million pounds, and the amount increased until it ranked second to rice.

After serving as Inspector-General of Indigo for the Carolinas for ten years, Lindo resigned in 1772 because, as he wrote, he could not bring himself to accept and certify inferior indigo.

Lindo was familiar with the practice of English universities in excluding Jews and was greatly impressed by Brown University in Providence, Rhode Island, with its atmosphere of tolerance and enlightenment. He was the magnanimous donor of twenty pounds, one of the largest amounts ever given to the institution to that time. Brown already had a provision excluding attendance on the Sabbath, but following acceptance of his gift we find a resolution passed by the university that reads: " . . . voted that the children of the Jews may be admitted to this institution and entirely enjoy the freedom of their religion, without any restraint or imposition whatsoever."

Though more is known about Lindo's years in South Carolina than his early life, there have been several errors prevalent in historical writings about his true position in the colony. Barnett Elzas definitely proved in *The Jews of South Carolina* (1903) that Lindo never was a soldier, a planter, or a slaveholder, as stated in earlier histories.

THE FIRST JEWISH INTERCOLONIAL FURRIER

1760

Alive to the rich potentials of North America, Jews in the early colonial days contributed their best efforts in laying the economic foundations of the country. By the 1750s, Jews accounted for possibly fifteen percent of the colonies' import-export firms, dealing largely in cocoa, rum, wine, fur, and textiles. They grew indigo in the Carolinas and furthered the whale and candle industry in New England. From the very beginning of the conflict between the colonies and the mother country, when the Non-Importation Resolutions of 1765 with England went into effect, true to the teachings of their faith—which is predominantly the faith of liberty—they signed the agreement and firmly abided by it. Jewish shippers then turned to the fur trade, sending their trappers, hunters, and agents as far west as the Mississippi. These traders were among the first pioneers and colonizers, holding the country until land-hungry settlers could follow the trails they had blazed.

It is difficult to overestimate the part played by the firms of Joseph Simon, the Franks, and the Gratz brothers in opening up the lands that were someday to become the states of Ohio, West Virginia, Kentucky, Indiana, Illinois, and Missouri. The first breath of civilization frequently came with these fur traders and hunters who settled in the regions they had explored.

During the last half of the seventeenth century, one of the leading Jewish merchants was Hayman Levy, who traded with the Indians. Recent arrivals in colonial New York might have watched the Indians with fear and wonder as they crowded Beaver Street in front of Hayman Levy's warehouse.

Born in Hanover, Germany, in 1721, young Hayman followed his Bavarian King George to England, then found his way to the colonies shortly before 1748. He was naturalized and made a freeman of New York in 1750. Trading in the northern wilds of New York province, he formed early friendships with the Indians.

By 1760, Hayman Levy became one of the greatest Jewish merchants of the period, head of the New York firm of Levy, Lyons, and Company, and the largest fur trader in the colonies. His firm was one of the principal mercantile firms in the city and had a branch in Europe known as Levy, Solomon, and Company. For many years, Levy carried on an extensive trade with the Indians, who brought the finest furs to his headquarters. They brought skins, wampums, belts, maize, antler horns, and medicinal bark to trade for calico, hatchets, blankets, beads, and rings. They appeared satisfied that the white trader gave them the best deal obtainable in the big city of wood and stone wigwams. The Indians who came to the city dealt largely with Levy and at certain times of the year seemed to be lining the streets in the vicinity of his warehouse.

There are entries in Levy's account books that show that he was the first employer of John Jacob Astor, ancestor of the millionaire Astors of today, who received one dollar a day from him for beating furs and peltries. Nicholas Low, ancestor of Seth Low, former president of Columbia University, served as Levy's clerk for seven years and later laid the foundation for his great fortune through a hogshead of rum purchased from his former employer, who rendered him substantial assistance besides.

During the French and Indian War, Hayman Levy fitted out ships to prey on the enemy's commerce. Privateering was a hazardous business but approved and encouraged by governments before submarines sank belligerent shipping on the high seas. The new restrictions that the British imposed on colonial businesses added to his troubles. Perhaps resentment against measures designed to ruin American merchants induced Levy to sign the historic Non-Importation Act of 1765, agreeing not to import or use English merchandise.

The restrictive acts of Parliament and the general colonial policy pursued by the government produced a disastrous effect upon business, and Hayman Levy failed in 1768. But Levy's creditors received full payment of principal and interest after helping him make a fresh start.

Soon Levy owned a string of buildings on Beaver Street. With the American Revolution now in full blast, the great fire of 1776 destroyed all his property. A patriotic reputation enabled him to continue to do business with the armed forces—two resolutions adopted by the Continental Congress of 1776 authorized payments to Hyman Levy for supplies—but the fortunes of war turned against him. George Washington retreated from Long Island, and the Americans prepared to abandon the heights on Manhattan overlooking the Hudson, later named after their general. Together with other patriots, Levy fled New York and took refuge in Philadelphia, the only functioning capital of the young nation and the only Jewish community left functioning in the free republic. He took the oath of allegiance to Pennsylvania and, although in his late fifties, joined the state militia as a private. He was one of the founders of Congregation Mikveh Israel in Philadelphia and served on the first board of trustees of the congregation.

After the war, Levy returned to New York with his family and in-laws. Together with his brother-in-law—the native-born noted artist-silversmith Myer Myers—he addressed a letter of welcome to Governor De Witt Clinton upon his return. They reminded their governor that though "the ancient congregation of Israelites lately returned from exile . . . is but small when compared with other religious societies . . . yet none has manifested a more zealous attachment to the sacred cause of America in the late war with Great Britain."

Levy continued to carry on the fur trade on his own account until his death in 1790.

At one time Levy was elected president of Congregation Shearith Israel in New York. But at the same meeting he was fined twenty shillings for "indecent and abusive language" uttered in the synagogue yard to the then-presiding officer. He refused to serve as president and was again fined for declining the office. On another occasion, in 1765, he was further fined for insulting the *hazzan,* a Mr. Pinto. Two years later he was on the receiving side of an insult, and a different Mr. Pinto had to pay forty shillings for insulting the acting president, Mr. Levy himself.

When Hayman Levy died, he was described in the press as a gentleman much respected by all denominations who had the pleasure of his acquaintance. *The Journal of Philadelphia* wrote of him:

> His character as a merchant was without blemish, he was a true patriot, a friend of the United States, an affectionate husband, a tender father, and a sincere friend. The widow, the orphan, and the poor will lament his loss; he was benevolent, and charitable to a great degree; his house was open to all strangers of good character to partake of his liberality.

Levy had eleven children who became important members of the New York community.

THE FIRST JEWISH CLUB

1761

As early as 1761, the great Jewish merchants of colonial Newport, Rhode Island, organized and maintained America's first Jewish social club. It was of much the same character as those of English and Bostonian merchants.

On November 25, 1761, nine men—including Moses Lopez, Isaac Polock, Jacob Isaacs, Abraham Sarzedas, Naphtali Hart, Moses Levy, Issachar Polock, Naphtali Hart, Jr., and Jacob Rodriguez Rivera—adopted a set of rules for the club that illustrated both their traveled experience and urbanity.

The roll naming these nine club members comprises the social and commercial leadership of the small Jewish community of Newport. They represented families that had emigrated from at least four different countries—Spain, Portugal, Poland, and England. Jews had come to this little New England seaport at its very beginning, attracted by the declaration of tolerance and liberty promulgated by Roger Williams, its founder.

Inasmuch as it has been recorded that the Newport community in 1760 numbered fifty-eight Jewish families, the club must have included a fair portion of its adult Jewish males. Strangely enough, the name of Aaron Lopez—not yet recognized as Newport's greatest merchant but already holding an important position as merchant and shipowner—does not appear on the list of members. Accordingly, it has been speculated that when signatures were obtained, he was away on one of his frequent business trips.

The club first developed through more or less formal meetings, with a fine social feature at the end centering around an elaborate meal with formal toasts and liberal allowance for drinks.

Patterned after the clubs of England, meetings were held in taverns or at the homes of club members. During the winter months it met every Wednesday evening. After one month, or four club nights, a new chairman was elected. Each meeting followed a specific pattern. From five until eight, each member was at liberty to divert himself with cards. At eight an elaborate meal was brought in with formidable portions of wine gathered on the members' ships' voyages from the vineyards of distant lands. When the afterdinner speaker was unknown, and when the meal was an impressive succession of elaborate courses, a "loyal toast" was a postprandial ceremony of solemnity, proposed by the chairman and drunk in glasses filled to the brim by the standing assembly. After ten o'clock, at the conclusion of the meal, no more glasses were allowed, and club business was attended to.

The energy and boldness of this little group of Jews had greatly contributed toward making Newport an important center of trade, until more ships were sailing from this port than from old New York. They were active merchants, ship owners, importers of products from Europe and of the neighboring colonies as well as of those of the West Indies. They were manufacturers and shopkeepers all at the same time. Rivera, whose fleet sailed to all the Atlantic ports where trade flourished, established the first spermaceti candle factory in America. Jacob Isaacs, successively active as shopkeeper and shipbuilder, invented a method for converting salt water into fresh water that through Thomas Jefferson he sought to sell to the government. At the time of George Washington's visit to Newport in 1790, Isaacs presented him with a bottle of this water, extracted from ocean water, so free from saline matter as to answer for all common and culinary purposes.

The members of this club for the most part belonged to St. John's Lodge of Masons. They had been founders and supporters of Newport's famous Redwood Library and were all active in various aspects of the city's communal and social life. Their chief interest, however, centered around their synagogue. These nine men not only took turns in succeeding each other in the high offices of that institution, most of them were numbered among its founders who had brought the most notable architect in mid-eighteenth-century America—Peter Harrison—to build the synagogue that is still one of Newport's prized ornaments. With consummate skill he applied his great talents to the assignment and succeeded in erecting a synagogue building of outstanding beauty, dignity, and impressiveness.

Congregation Jeshuat Israel at 85 Touro Street, Newport, is known also as the Touro Synagogue. It memorializes the Touro family—the father, Isaac—its first spiritual leader—who officiated at the synagogue's dedication—and his sons Abraham and Judah, whose generosity had preserved the structure.

Nurtured in commercial life by their uncle Moses Hays of Boston, Abraham and Judah had made fortunes. Both were outstanding philanthropists. Abraham, upon his death in 1822, left a $10,000 fund for the care and preservation of the synagogue. Abraham's bequest was certainly among the earliest in America for the purpose of preserving an unoccupied historic building. Judah Touro, who died in 1854, left another trust fund of $10,000 for the salary of a reader or minister to officiate in the synagogue. It is the oldest synagogue building in the United States still standing. On March 5, 1946, it was dedicated a national shrine by the National Park Service of the United States Department of the Interior.

THE FIRST JEWISH MERCHANT PRINCE

1767

In the Spring of 1658, fifteen Spanish and Portuguese Jewish families arrived in Newport, Rhode Island, to constitute the second Jewish settlement in North America and the first in an English colony. As time went on, other Jews from Holland, England, Poland, and the West Indies came to this haven of tolerance set up by Roger Williams. These Jews, some of whom were Marranos, wanted to start a new life in a land where they could live as free men and practice the religion of their fathers without hindrance or fear. They believed this to be possible in the colony of Rhode Island because of the assurance of freedom of religion and liberty of conscience by Governor Williams to all who came within its borders.

The Lopez family came from Portugal, the Rivera family came from Spain. Both of them had fled, a few fugitives at a time, to escape the Inquisition. After two and a half centuries as Marranos, living with the daily fear of the Inquisition, they had finally escaped to a land where they might openly live as Jews.

The Jewish community contributed not only to Newport's trade but to its manufacturing. James Lucena introduced the making of soap, a skill he had acquired in the King of Portugal's workshops. Jacob Rodriguez Rivera produced candles made out of sperm oil. Moses Lopez obtained a license from the General Assembly for the manufacture of potash, a rare commodity even in eighteenth-century England.

Into this beehive of activity came Aaron Lopez, who was born in Portugal in 1731. At the age of twenty-one, he renounced his Marrano past and openly resumed his ancestral faith. With his father-in-law, Jacob Rodriguez Rivera, he saw the commercial possibilities of Newport harbor. As a man for whom business was "real happiness," Lopez started in the spermaceti candle trade, and from his shop on Thames Street he eventually supplied customers with everything from Bibles and bottled beer to looking-glasses and violins. He soon became known as the "Merchant Prince of New England" and is credited in a larger degree more than anyone else with the rapid commercial development that made Newport for a quarter of a century the formidable business rival of New York. A record of his seafaring and commercial activities could serve as a cross section of American colonial economic activity. Through his letters, papers, inventories, and deeds, which are in the possession of the American Jewish Historical Society, we may trace his career from its modest beginnings up to the time when the entire city felt the impact of his phenomenal rise. By 1775, he owned in whole or in part with the Rivera family thirty transoceanic vessels and over one hundred coastal schooners. They carried clothing, fish, lumber, horses, whale oil, spermaceti candles, molasses, and rum to and from Newfoundland, Surinam, the West Indies, Lisbon, Gibraltar, Cape Nicholas, Amsterdam, Bristol, and Curaçao, besides the ports of call of the American colonies. Lopez had agents in these ports of call and traded in tobacco, meats, turpentine, tar, and pitch. Following the custom of the times, his ships brought slaves from Africa and carried ivory, gold dust, palm oil, and camwood to European ports. Newport became the American export-import clearinghouse, with Aaron Lopez as director.

Tradition has it that Lopez's whalers were the first to seek whales as far off as the Falkland Islands. An outgrowth of Lopez's involvement in the whaling industry resulted in his organizing with Jacob Rodriguez Rivera and a group of Newport Jewish merchants, the first American trust in 1761–the United Company of Spermaceti Candlers, which was formed with the avowed aim of checking competition among its members by fixing the maximum price they would pay for the "brown oyl," the minimum price they would sell their product for, and adjusting their output "to the needs of the time."

Lopez followed rigidly the tenets of Orthodox Judaism. The lay leader of the Jewish community, he contributed liberally to Newport's synagogue, also known as Touro Synagogue, now designated a federal shrine. He personally laid the cornerstone of this famous building.

No ship ever left his dock (still called Lopez Dock) on Saturday, and out of deference to Christian sentiment, his large business establishment was also closed on Sundays. Yet with all the vastness of his enterprises, Lopez was a man of charm and genuine humility. Ezra Stiles, Christian pastor and later to become seventh president of Yale, wrote of him in his diary: "He was a Merchant of the first Eminence, for Honor and Extent of Commerce probably surpassed by no merchant in America." Of his personal characteristics, Stiles wrote that Lopez was noted for a "Sweetness of Manners . . . the most universally beloved of an extensive Acquaintance of any man I ever knew."

On the eve of the American Revolution, Lopez was Newport's largest taxpayer. Probably no man in the colonies suffered a greater financial loss in the Revolution than he did. From the very start he espoused the patriot cause and donated much wealth to it, but his fleet fell into the hands of the British, who blockaded the coast, put a stop to fishing in British waters, and confiscated American ships wherever they were found. When the British occupied Newport, Lopez saw most of his wealth disappear. Part of the Jewish community followed him to Leicester in central Massachusetts, where they constituted the first Jewish settlement in that state. These Jews remained in Leicester during the Revolution, conducting there certain types of business. When peace came, some of them returned to Newport, but its standing as a seaport had been destroyed.

Strangely enough, when Aaron Lopez, Newport's distinguished resident, petitioned the General Assembly of Rhode Island for citizenship in 1762, he received this reply: "The free and quiet enjoyment of the Christian religion were the principal views with which this colony was settled."

The court unanimously dismissed this ruling as wholly inconsistent with the principles upon which the colony was founded. Lopez, however, did not appeal the decision; he made application in nearby Taunton, where it was quickly approved. Thus, he became the first Jew naturalized in Massachusetts.

As a public-spirited citizen, he helped generously in the founding of the Redwood Library in 1747, perhaps the finest in all the colonies. His portrait was painted by Gilbert Stuart, of whom he was an early patron.

The Revolutionary War brought ruin to the opulence of Newport. Lopez was able to rescue only a pittance out of the wreckage of his vast holdings. After Washington's victory at Yorktown had secured peace, Lopez set out with his vast family to rebuild his commercial empire and restore the prestige of Newport. On the road his horse suddenly bolted and threw him into treacherous quicksand. He struggled helplessly until submerged and was drowned. With his death, Newport lost the opportunity to regain its commercial prestige.

Aaron Lopez was buried in the Jewish Cemetery in Newport. In his will he founded the Leicester Academy—this at a time when large philanthropic gifts were rare. The Newporters to whose prosperity Lopez had contributed so significantly before the American Revolution mourned him, wrote Ezra Stiles in his diary, "With a demonstration of universal sorrow."

With his death Newport lost the opportunity to regain its commercial prestige. Today, while highly regarded as a summer resort for fashionable society, it thrives year-round on its natural beauty and historic architecture.

THE FIRST AMERICAN-BORN JEWISH CLERGYMAN

1768

The Reverend Gershom Mendes Seixas, who became the minister of the first Jewish congregation in North America, Congregation Shearith Israel in New York City in 1768, and who continued in this post for almost fifty years, was the first American-born Jewish clergyman.

Born in New York City on January 15, 1746, Seixas was related to the elite Sephardim of the congregation. His father, Isaac Seixas, a Marrano in Portugal, had reentered the convenant of Judaism and married the daughter of Moses Levy, leader of the New York Jewish community of the early eighteenth century. As a young boy, Gershom received his education at the congregational school established at Shearith Israel. History does not inform us how he received his later training. There was no rabbinical seminary, nor even a rabbi in the United States. It must have been his own spirit, his constant attendance at synagogue services, the Jewish life in his home, and what he learned from Shearith Israel's *hazzan* Joseph Jessurun Pinto that qualified him in the summer of 1768, when he was 23, to present himself as a candidate for the position. There were no other applicants, and the trustees elected the youthful "rabbi" enthusiastically.

Gershom Mendes Seixas did not organize a new officiant for the synagogue; but in him the *hazzan*-preacher found complete expression as religious leader. In the course of his ministry, the few times he was called upon to cite Jewish law, he was able to refer to the *Shulhan Arukh* (authoritative code of Jewish law). His ability to write Hebrew is evidenced by a manuscript copy of a Hebrew oration he wrote for Sampson Simson when the latter was graduated from Columbia College in 1800 (the first Jew to receive a degree from that institution). Seixas served the community, attending to ritual matters concerning birth, marriage, and death and other considerations of synagogue services. He was instrumental in saving Shearith Israel's cemetery at Chatham Square, New York, from obliteration. He helped to establish the *Hebra Hased Va-Emet* in 1802 and the Hebrew Relief Society in 1828, the oldest burial and charitable societies in the United States. He was also a self-taught *mohel* (one who performs circumcisions) and a *shochet* (slaughterer of cattle or fowl in accordance with Jewish law).

The revolutionary spirit swept Seixas along in its current. Although most Christian ministers in New York were Tories and stood by the Crown at the outbreak of the American Revolution, Gershom Mendes Seixas at once espoused the patriot cause. Possibly active with the minutemen, he had reason for apprehension after Washington's retreat from Long Island. Seixas refused to remain in New York. The English did not interfere with religious freedom, yet he took no chances. At the approach of the British in August 1776, he preached a patriotic sermon and closed the synagogue doors. He departed with the sacred Torah scrolls, the ceremonial objects and prayerbooks. The greater part of the congregation, being patriots, followed him, first to Stratford, Connecticut, and later to Philadelphia, where they remained until the end of the conflict.

In Philadelphia, the members of Shearith Israel, together with other refugees, swelled the existing congregation into the largest Jewish community in North America. In 1782, the Philadelphian congregants carried out an old ambition to build a new synagogue. For their first minister they engaged the Reverend Gershom Mendes Seixas, who assisted them in organizing Mikveh Israel (the Hope of Israel), the congregation that ranked second in the days of the early republic.

After the Treaty of Peace, many war refugees returned to their homes. The Reverend Gershom Mendes Seixas might have remained with Mikveh Israel but for the insistent demand that he return to New York. Before leaving, Seixas, as spiritual leader of Philadelphia's synagogue, with Bernard Gratz and Haym Salomon and others, petitioned the Pennsylvania authorities to amend the state constitution by removing the New Testament oath required by anyone taking public office. This was but a variant of the British oath—"on the true faith of a Christian"—devised against would-be Jewish members of Parliament. No action was taken, but the petition was not drawn up in vain. Four years later, the framers of the federal Constitution assembled in Philadelphia adopted a provision that no religious test ever be required to hold public office in the United States.

The Reverend Seixas returned to New York in 1784 and resumed his former pulpit. For two generations he was repeatedly honored by Jews and Christians as prime religious authority, patriot, and civic leader. He was one of the fourteen ministers of all sects who participated in the New

York inauguration of George Washington as first president of the United States on April 30, 1789.

Gershom Mendes Seixas was the first spiritual leader to abandon Spanish in his sermons for English and the first of his denomination to speak in the churches of America in an attempt to create goodwill. Seixas preached the first Thanksgiving sermon of any faith—Catholic, Protestant, or Jewish. Thousands of copies of this sermon were printed and sold, but he did not keep the royalties for himself. He gave them to a fund for widows and orphans of men who had died in the War of Independence. He was also the first cleric to institute a prayer for the government in English. He was a trustee of the Humane Society and in 1784 was elected by the New York State Legislature to the first Board of Regents of the University of the State of New York.

One of the incorporators of Columbia College, he served as trustee for thirty years and rendered services on various committees of this institution. As a tribute to his memory, his portrait was struck on a bronze medal issued by Columbia University, and a painting of him was unveiled at the institution on its 175th anniversary.

In his time and place, Seixas was a very important man. He won the respect of his contemporaries and was looked up to by his peers, winning fame throughout the entire American Jewish population. He served his congregation with devotion and unswerving fidelity—though it was not uncommon for him to know want. He preached and taught, wishing to give the people a pride in their faith and a religious consciousness that centered around a hope for a messianic future.

Gershom Mendes Seixas died on July 2, 1816, at the age of seventy. He was buried in the Chatham Square Cemetery of Congregation Shearith Israel in Lower Manhattan. Every year during Memorial Day Services at the cemetery, an American flag is placed on his grave.

Today upon entering Congregation Shearith Israel, one sees a bronze tablet on which is inscribed in a few words the story of the Reverend Gershom Mendes Seixas, the "patriot rabbi of the American Revolution."

Not until 1845 did a rabbi ordained in Europe officiate on any pulpit in the United States. The *hazzan-shochet-mohel* continued to function as religious head of many a Jewish community, until displaced in a later day by the yeshiva- or seminary-trained American rabbi.

THE FIRST PROPOSED UNITED STATES SEAL

1776

In 1776 Benjamin Franklin, Thomas Jefferson, and John Adams recommended for the first official seal of the newly proclaimed United States a design whose theme was the escape of the Israelites from Egypt. It had pictured on it the Israelites crossing the Red Sea with Pharaoh and his legions pursuing and perishing in the background. Rays from a pillar of fire beaming on Moses—who is represented as standing on the shores extending his hand over the sea, causing it to split and overwhelm Pharaoh—also appeared on the design. Around the edges of the proposed seal ran the motto: "Rebellion to tyrants is obedience to God" (The Book of Maccabees). This motto pleased Jefferson so much that he took it as his own and had it engraved on his private seal.

It is not surprising that the committee—appointed the day after the Declaration of Independence was adopted—should propose such a design. The Founding Fathers of the United States drew heavily on the Bible and Hebraic traditions in laying the foundations of the new republic.

In colonial America, the Bible was the one familiar book that was read morning, noon, and night, and everywhere its words kindled a sparking enthusiasm. The early colonists found in it a strong analogy between themselves and the ancient Israelites seeking freedom in the Promised Land. They identified George III with Pharaoh. America was called "the Promised Land." The Pilgrims were referred to as "Our happy Israel in America" and William Bradford, the second governor of Plymouth, as Moses. Cotton Mather called the early magistrates of the Massachusetts Bay Colony *hasidim harishonim* (the first pious men), while John Winthrop, who was governor of the Massachusetts Bay Colony, was called "Nehemias Americanus" after Nehemiah, governor of Judaea, who administered in Palestine when the Israelites returned from exile in Babylonia.

The earliest settlers of New England retained an unbounded admiration for the ancient Chosen People and testified to their affection by choosing Hebraic names for themselves and their children.

The American Revolution was cradled in the Hebraic love of freedom and liberty. Biblical influence had helped not a little in favoring and strengthening opposition to the parliamentary claim. Several decades before the Declaration of Independence was proclaimed, the biblical injunction "Proclaim liberty throughout the land unto all the inhabitants thereof" (Leviticus 25:10) was inscribed on the Liberty Bell that hangs in Independence Hall in Philadelphia and made the great watchword of the American people.

To discredit the monarchy, preachers like the bold and brilliant Jonathan Mayhew of Boston held up the warning of the prophet Samuel against royalty. Wherever the Bible was read, it fired men with dreams and hopes of freedom. The Founding Fathers were eminently capable in the expositing of all its justification for rebellion. To them the exodus from Egypt was an inspired precedent. They knew the arguments from Holy Writ that would most powerfully influence the people. It required no stretch of the imagination to demonstrate that the children of Israel, making bricks without straw in Egypt, had their modern counterpart in the colonists enduring the imposition of taxation without representation. In the darkest hours of the struggle during the long winter at Valley Forge, George Washington and his troops took courage by recalling the suffering of the Jews in Egypt in biblical days.

When the American people were ready to form their own government, they were inspired by the Hebrew commonwealth in ancient Palestine, which was composed of a threefold form of government—its *Shofet*, or chief executive; its *Sanhedrin*, or Senate; and its Congregation, or popular assembly. Following the pattern of this threefold division, they patterned their own government.

The piety of the Americans of the past is further reflected in the words of our coinage, "In God We Trust." The Hebraic influences manifest in colonial America were so considerable that the seal of Yale University is a depiction of the ancient Hebrew breastplate of the *Urim v'Thumim* worn by the priests in the temple in Jerusalem, and the Dartmouth College seal carries two Hebrew words: *El Shadai*, meaning "God Almighty"—two among numerous college seals that bear Hebrew inscriptions to this day.

It was in truth that the eminent nineteenth-century British historian William Lecky, in his classic work *History of the Rise and Influence of the Spirit of Rationalism in Europe*, declared that "Hebraic Mortar cemented the foundations of American democracy."

The twenty-five hundred or fewer Jews living in the thirteen colonies did their part on the battlefield and off; the great ideas given by Judaism to the world played an even greater role in the founding of the American Republic.

The spirit of the Bible, as well as Jewish history and custom, were all expressed in the first Thanksgiving celebrated by the Pilgrims in the autumn of 1621, who borrowed their idea of Thanksgiving from the ancient Hebrew festival of Succoth. It is this Thanksgiving that was proclaimed a national holiday by Abraham Lincoln in 1863 and that is observed by all Americans today.

The biblical phrase continues to color American speech. Hebrew ethics and philosophy motivates America in its strivings for political and social justice and ideal democracy.

THE FIRST JEW IN AMERICA TO GIVE HIS LIFE FOR HIS COUNTRY

1776

From 1776 to the present time, men and women of the Jewish faith have been fighting and dying to preserve American independence.

On August 1, 1776, in one of the earliest encounters following the Declaration of Independence on July 4, less than one month after the earnest band of patriots in Philadelphia pledged to liberty "our lives, our fortunes, and our sacred honor," Francis Salvador, colorful plantation owner of South Carolina, who won the sobriquet "the Southern Paul Revere," was killed in battle. The site was near his plantation along the Keowee River in South Carolina. With a small army of 330 men, Salvador was defending the frontier settlers against a British-incited attack by Cherokee Indians.

Salvador, a brilliant, young English Jew of Portuguese ancestry who was born in London in 1747, had arrived in Charleston in 1773 to develop and farm extensive family holdings there. He became famous as a legislator, patriot, and soldier. Together with Charles Pinckney and Edward Rutledge, he was among the first revolutionary characters of the state.

In 1774, although a resident of America for only a year, Salvador was elected to the General Assembly of South Carolina, the first Jew to represent the people in a legislative body in America and probably the first Jew in the modern world to serve as an elective officer. Because of his active part in the patriotic cause, his district made him its representative to the First and Second South Carolina Provincial Congress, which took active steps to revolt against the British. There he was named to various committees concerned with the conduct of the war and was conspicuous in debates. He was elected to the first General Assembly of the new state.

The assembly set up the Republic of South Carolina, and Salvador was appointed a commissioner to sign and stamp South Carolina's new currency. He served as financial adviser to the assembly, participated in reorganizing the courts and the selecting of magistrates, and advised the assembly as to the proper selection procedures. He also participated in drafting South Carolina's constitution.

At the very beginning of the Revolution, on August 1, 1776, the Cherokee Indians, incited by the English, struck near Salvador's plantation. Major Andrew Williamson took command, with Salvador as his chief adviser. The frontier was now on fire. Salvador urged President John Rutledge to send reinforcements of men and arms.

Together with Major Williamson, Salvador set out on an expedition to round up volunteer troops to save the colonists from attack. The little army proceeded in the silence of the moonless night. Suddenly a fusillade of shots poured out from behind bushes, trees, and fences. The Americans were ambushed. Major Anderson had sent a detachment to ford the Keowee River and remained with Salvador at the head of the company. With the first volley, Salvador was shot and swayed heavily in his saddle. The Indians closed in on all sides, but the militia soon repulsed them. Williamson found Salvador lying in a bush, scalped but still alive. He asked whether the enemy was beaten. "Yes," was the answer. He shook Williamson's hand, said farewell, and died in his twenty-ninth year, unaware of the promulgation of the Declaration of Independence.

"The whole army regretted his loss," wrote a Continental journal, *The Remembrance*, "as he was universally loved and esteemed by them."

In the brief period of three years, Salvador, a Jew and a stranger, sat in the representative assembly of the Provincial Congresses, was listened to with unusual respect for one his age, and died a patriot of the American Revolution, the first Jew to give his life for his country.

A memorial plaque was dedicated in Francis Salvador's memory in 1950 in the City Hall of Charleston, South Carolina, at the time of the bicentennial celebration of the Jewish community. It reads: "Born an aristocrat, he became a democrat; an Englishman, he cast his lot with America; true to his ancient faith, he gave his life for new hopes of human liberty and understanding."

The first Jew in the modern world to hold an elective office and die on the battlefield, a willing martyr for freedom, Francis Salvador opens the chapter of Jewish participation and integration in Western society.

THE FIRST AMERICAN JEWISH GOVERNMENT BROKER

1776

During the American Revolutionary War, Jews contributed their full share of patriotism off the battlefield as well as on it. When funds were needed in 1776 to support George Washington's army in the field, the names of Jews were conspicuous among the contributors. When bills of credit were issued from which the element of credit was greatly lacking, Jews were prominent among the subscribers. But the one who did more for the cause of the American Revolution than any other civilian or soldier was Haym Salomon.

Born in Lissa, Poland, about 1740, he had traveled in Europe, acquiring a knowledge of a number of languages and an unusual understanding of finance before arriving in New York in 1772. Like many Jewish immigrants, he probably began his career by peddling and must have traveled to Albany and farther north, for in June 1776, an Albany merchant recommended him to General Phillip Schuyler as a supplier and patriot among the troops at Lake George.

For the next two years, Salomon was in New York, where he opened a commission merchant's office and brokerage on Broad Street. Although New York was the seat of British power in the colonies, he cast his fortune with the Sons of Liberty, underground colonial patriots.

At the outbreak of the Revolutionary War, Salomon's clandestine activities resulted in his arrest as a spy and being condemned to death by the British. He was at first confined to the Citadel, known as the Old Sugar House, and then transferred to the Provost Prison. When his knowledge of different languages was discovered, he was appointed jail interpreter. In this capacity he was instrumental in persuading Hessian mercenary troops to join the American cause, and he assisted in the escape of French and American prisoners of war. With the help of patriotic friends, he himself managed to flee to Philadelphia in 1778.

Soon after his arrival there, Salomon opened an office as a broker in a plain little house on Front Street, between Market and Arch, and set about negotiating the sale of Continental Bills of Exchange. From this base of operations he was to render his magnificent services to the colonies. From the outset, Haym Salomon succeeded in Philadelphia. Most of the business of the port was with foreign markets whose trade conditions he knew intimately. His straightforward, honest methods of transacting business won him an enviable reputation.

Haym Salomon's first official recognition as an able businessman came from France. Soon after his arrival in Philadelphia, French minister Chevalier de la Luzerne appointed Salomon agent for the French government and paymaster-general for the French army in America.

In 1781, Salomon attracted the attention of Robert Morris just when the latter assumed the newly created post of superintendent of finances of the young republic, authorized to manage and improve its financial affairs. This was the crucial year of the decisive Yorktown campaign. The French supplied not only much of the military and naval forces for the purpose, but also a substantial subsidy to Congress as well. It became Morris's responsibility to convert this grant into American funds at the best possible rates, and Salomon served him ably and loyally in accomplishing this.

It is apparent from early entries in Robert Morris's financial diary that when money was needed to carry on the Revolutionary War, he negotiated with other brokers before he began writing that almost-daily phrase about seventy-five times, from August 1781 to April 1784: "I sent for Haym Salomon." He was not long in learning that he needed Salomon's vision, integrity, and unselfish devotion to the cause of liberty. Salomon was regularly consulted and his sound judgment and clear thinking saved the colonists immense sums of money.

Salomon's official title was Broker to the Office of Finance of the United States. That is, he was the broker through whom Robert Morris sold the securities of the weak, infant government. Morris received hides, tobacco, and agricultural products in lieu of money from the colonies. Salomon sold them for the account of the federal treasury. He was also called upon to act as government agent to sell captured merchandise. He asked only one quarter of one percent commission for himself on the transactions.

Handling hundreds of bills of exchange for the superintendent of finances was only part of Haym Salomon's contribution to the cause of freedom. He floated loans, endorsed notes, contributed generously to needy soldiers, equipped military units with his own money, and transcribed heavily to all government loans.

The multilingual and knowledgeable financier also advanced money to several delegates of the Continental Congress, for many of them were poor and their states did not always send them their expense money on time. In fact, James Madison, afterward president of the United States, wrote back to Virginia: "I have been a pensioner for some time on the favor of Haym Salomon."

Other needy delegates of the Continental Congress to whom Salomon lent money without interest were Thomas Jefferson, James Monroe, Edmund Randolph, and James Wilson. All had long been dependent on his generosity for their own livelihoods or for the maintenance of the particular government function for which they were responsible.

In 1783, Salomon was one of the prominent Philadelphian Jews who, on behalf of the community, petitioned the Council of Censors of Pennsylvania for the removal of the Religious Test Oath of the state, which demanded that each member elected to the assembly affirm that both "the Scriptures of the Old and New Testament were given by divine inspiration." This protest failed, but it doubtless was a contributing factor in the ultimate abolition of the Test Clause in 1790 in the Pennsylvania State Constitution and in the federal Constitution.

At Salomon's sudden and untimely death in January 1785 at the age of forty-five, it is said that he held over a third of a million dollars in paper money in Continental stocks and bonds. This would seem like a comfortable legacy for his family, but the sum, badly depreciated, went with other assets to repay what he had contracted in the interests of the new republic.

Haym Salomon died bankrupt during the terrible confusion at the end of the war and before the adoption of the Constitution, leaving his young wife, Rachel Franks, of the famous Franks family, destitute with four young children. His entire estate was in the form of various securities of the Continental Congress, which at the time were practically worthless. His poverty-stricken family received nothing but the furniture of their home. After the government was established and government obligations were again available, bills were repeatedly brought up in Congress to repay his family. These bills were investigated and recommended in committees of both the House and the Senate, but they always failed to pass Congress. No compensation or adjustment was ever made.

The depth of gratitude the nation owes Salomon, a loyal and unselfish patriot of his adopted country, was in part paid by the erection of a statue in a Chicago park, sponsored by Chicagoans, showing George Washington with his arms around Robert Morris and Haym Salomon.

Some years ago, Warner Brothers made a short motion picture called *My Country First*, written by the celebrated actor George Jessel, that portrayed some of the highlights of the life of Haym Salomon.

During the incumbency of Mayor Fiorello La Guardia of New York, a proclamation was issued, setting aside a "Haym Salomon Day." It was the mayor's intent to make all Americans conscious of the great contributions made during the Revolutionary War by a young Jew who believed in liberty "with all his heart, with all his soul, and with all his might."

On March 25, 1975, the United States Postal Service issued a commemorative stamp in tribute to Haym Salomon. This Haym Salomon issue was one of four Contributors-to-the-Cause set featuring unheralded persons who had played important roles in the American Revolution.

THE FIRST COOPERATIVE CHARITY VENTURE

1776

Mordecai Sheftall, who was the first white child and the first Jew to be born in Savannah, Georgia (in 1735), and in all the South, was the original founding member of the Union Society. This society, the first cooperative charity venture in America, sought to unite in its work Protestants, Catholics, and Jews, in the belief that men of different faiths could work together for a common social cause. It exerted a profound influence for social betterment, particularly in aiding widows and orphans during the early history of Georgia.

Sheftall was the older son of Benjamin Sheftall, who came to Savannah in 1733 with a group of Portuguese Jewish immigrants shortly after the arrival of James Oglethorpe himself, the founder of the colony. At the outbreak of the American Revolution he owned a farm and cattle ranch; he operated a sawmill and tannery; he kept stores and shipped out produce. When the War for Independence was on, Sheftall threw himself heart and soul into the struggle. Georgia, like the other colonies, was divided into Whig and Tory camps, and its Parochial Committee soon became the *de facto* government. As chairman of the Parochial Committee, which opposed Britain's tyranny and was organized in Savannah to safeguard the city's freedom, Mordecai Sheftall incurred the wrath of the royal regime, which denounced and persecuted him with utmost severity.

As the war progressed, Mordecai Sheftall was appointed Commissary General of Purchases and Issues of the state's militia. In the following year, General Robert Howe appointed him Deputy Commissary General of Issues to the Continental Troops in South Carolina and Georgia, an office that carried with it the rank of colonel. His son Sheftall Sheftall, then only sixteen years of age, was already an Assistant Commissary of Issues, serving as his father's deputy.

In 1778, the British determined to capture Savannah and sweep through the Carolinas, hoping to wipe away the shame incurred the preceding year by Burgoyne's surrender at Saratoga. Late in December, Lieutenant Colonel Archibald Campbell landed near Savannah, found a way through the swamps, and routed the smaller force of defending American militiamen under General Howe. Both Mordecai Sheftall and his son were among those captured when the city fell on December 29, 1778.

Sheftall and his son tried to escape the enemy with 185 Revolutionary officers and men by crossing the Musgrove Creek, but his son could not swim. The British encircled them, and, after a brief skirmish, Mordecai and his son and the others surrendered. Mordecai had the satisfaction of hearing the British commander refer to him as "a very great rebel." Refusing to talk, the Americans were thrown into the British garrison in Savannah. Ill-treated by the drunken soldiers and denied food for two days, their end seemed near. But German-Yiddish saved them. A Hessian officer, delighted to hear someone speak his native tongue in a foreign country, took good care of the Jewish prisoners.

Mordecai and his son spent several months on a prison ship. Paroled with others, they were confined to Sunbury, a town in Georgia. Ultimately, in June 1780, they were released and permitted to go to Philadelphia after promising not to continue active participation in the war and being exchanged for prisoners of equal rank.

While prisoners of war, Sheftall and two others continued to hold meetings of the Union Society to keep it alive. In 1825 when Lafayette laid the cornerstone of the Pulaski Monument in Savannah, a relic was deposited within it with the words: "A piece of oaktree from Sunbury County, Georgia, under which in 1779 the charter of the Union Society was preserved, and Mr. Mordecai Sheftall, then a prisoner of war, was elected president."

After the war, Mordecai Sheftall continued his mercantile career in his native city of Savannah, where he received a grant of land from the government in recognition of his wartime services.

Mordecai Sheftall was an observant Jew and took part in Jewish communal work. He helped reorganize Congregation Mikveh Israel in Philadelphia, and though at the time he was financially disabled, he donated three pounds for building the synagogue. He made a tiresome journey to Charleston to be present at the dedication of the Beth Elohim Synagogue. In his own community, besides donating ground for a cemetery, he furnished a room in his home for group prayer and assisted in the establishment of Mikveh Israel Congregation in Savannah. He was also prominent as a freemason and conducted a correspondence with the leading men of his time.

He was widely respected in the larger Gentile community, holding minor civic appointments until his death in 1797.

Moses Sheftall, Mordecai's second son, who was born in Savannah in 1769, was the first Jewish doctor born in America and was trained by Benjamin Rush. In 1804 he founded the first medical society in Georgia and did much to raise the standards of the medical profession. During the War of 1812 he volunteered for service in the army. Upon his return he was the first Jew in Georgia to be elected judge of the county court and was not long thereafter elected to the state legislature.

Visitors to Savannah today may view the old Jewish cemetery on Broughton Street donated by Mordecai Sheftall in 1773, a historic landmark since 1850.

THE FIRST JEWISH LAWYER

1778

In New Amsterdam, as New York was called during the Dutch regime, there was no class of professional lawyers. Cases were tried before the court, but neither the magistrates nor those who pleaded before them had any legal education. For example, the name of Jacob Barsimson, the earliest settler we have on record, appears as attorney in 1654 in the court records of New Amsterdam although he had no legal training. No name is more prominent than that of Asser Levy, whose almost uniform successes against Governor Peter Stuyvesant in defending the rights of his people accounts for the fact that he appears as attorney for others also.

The colonial colleges for the most part catered to prospective clergymen and attorneys. At that time Jews were businessmen and merchants, not ministers or lawyers. Merchants' sons who might follow in their fathers' footsteps did not receive an academic education.

Philadelphia was the seat of culture, one of the great educational centers of the world. Not a few of the institutions of the city bore the imprint of Benjamin Franklin, who was founder of the College of Philadelphia, later to be known as the University of Pennsylvania. The preparatory school associated with the college was the Academy. Five Jewish boys were enrolled there before 1770. One of these, Moses Levy—who was born in Philadelphia in 1757, the son of Samson Levy, a prominent merchant and signer of the Non-Importation Resolution—completed the college course and received an A.B. degree in the class of 1772. He was the only student of Jewish origin to graduate from the institution in pre-Revolutionary times. After continuing his course of study in the law school, he was admitted to the bar in 1778, the first Jew to qualify as a lawyer in the United States.

Levy became one of the outstanding lawyers of Philadelphia and was one of the defense council in the trial of Bache, editor of the anti-Federalist *Aurora* for "libelling the President and the Executive Government in a manner tending to excite sedition and opposition to the law."

From 1802 to 1806 he was a member of the Pennsylvania legislature and held other public offices. While Moses Levy was recorder (municipal judge) of Philadelphia, eight shoemakers were arrested and charged with (1) demanding $5.00 for making fancy boots, $4.00 for back-strap boots, and $3.00 for long-strap boots or cossaks, a wage higher than the current scale; (2) conspiring to prevent others from working at lower wages than demanded; and (3) designing to form a combination to make arbitrary by-laws for governing each other, for exacting "great sums of money" for refusing to work with a master who employed such labor or broke other rules or accepted lower pay.

This so-called Cordwainers Case attracted wide attention as one of the first in America where a court interfered to prevent a strike or form a union. The case also had its political repercussions. The monied and propertied Federalists stood by the employers, whose rights were consistently upheld by the highest courts of England.

Judge Levy, caught in the center of the politico-economic storm, could hardly escape the abuse of the losing side. The jury found the strikers guilty. This case helped to establish the precedent against trade unions and striking until reversed in 1842 by Chief Justice Shaw of Massachusetts.

The results of this famous trial pleased the powerful, and Moses Levy was appointed presiding judge for the District Court of the City and County of Pennsylvania, the nation's most important trial court.

In 1802 Levy's own college elected him a trustee, a position he held for twenty-five years until the time of his death. He appears to have been a man of property, for he sold his house on Chestnut Street for $10,000 to the Bank of North America, the first bank in the United States.

As counsel in many important cases and because of his brilliant record as a judge, Levy won the highest esteem of his associates. At one time his name was mentioned as a worthy candidate for the office of attorney general of the United States. President Thomas Jefferson wanted to appoint Levy to the post and on September 1, 1794, wrote the following to Albert Gallatin, secretary of the treasury: "I ask the favor of you to inquire into the legal knowledge, judgment, and moral and social character of Levy. We must have none but a good-humored man." Gallatin replied: "As a lawyer he is superior to Dickinson, and would, I presume do tolerably well."

When the president preferred "a good lawyer, and rather that he should be from Pennsylvania," he merely reflected the current faith in the "Philadelphia lawyer," a term that became a popular byword for a sound, ingenious, learned, and resourceful attorney.

After the outbreak of the American Revolution, Moses Levy had joined the Continental Army and was one of a group of selected soldiers who on Christmas Night in 1776 made the celebrated crossing of the Delaware with General George Washington to fight in the Battles of Princeton and Trenton. Later, and for many years, he was an active member of the Pennsylvania Militia.

His painted portrait by Rembrandt Peale shows the scholarly face and powdered white wig of an eighteenth-century gentleman.

When Levy died in 1826, the Philadelphia Bar Association requested that its members wear a black armband for thirty days.

THE FIRST JEWISH MAJOR

1780

Benjamin Nones, one of a group of Frenchmen who had come to America in 1777 at about the same time as the Marquis de Lafayette, was America's first Jewish major. Living in Bordeaux, France, at the time the American colonies were seething against the repressive British, "liberty, independence, rights of man . . . created equal" were heady words the idealistic Nones heard from across the ocean. He was deeply impressed and influenced by the example of Lafayette, who, intent upon helping the Americans, had outfitted his own ship at Bordeaux for sailing to their aid.

Believing heart and soul in freedom, Nones left a thriving wine business behind in Bordeaux and also came to the assistance of the embattled Americans.

Soon after his arrival in Philadelphia in 1777, Nones enlisted as a volunteer private first under General Pulaski, then under Baron De Kalb, and finally as a major and staff officer under Lafayette and Washington. He went through the entire war, from the early campaign in the south to the final ones that ended the struggle.

Nones was as devoted to his religion as he was to his adopted country. Soon after joining the army, he explained to his superior officer that he was a Jew and respectfully requested exemption from military duties on the Sabbath. The officer was much impressed by the young man's attachment to his faith and ordered that he be permitted to observe his holy day. The order, the first of its kind in this country, is still preserved in the annals of the Revolutionary War. It reads as follows: "Benjamin Nones, being of the Jewish religion, and having signified that it is inconsistent with his Jewish religion to perform military duties on Friday nights, it is ordered that he be exempted from military duties that night of the week."

Gallant conduct, especially during the siege of Savannah, in 1780 brought him promotion to the rank of major. Major Nones, with those under his command at the Battle of Savannah, shared the hardships of that sanguinary day. He became major of a battalion of four hundred men, fancifully called "the Hebrew Legion," either because of its leader or its large number of Jewish enlistments. They were attached to Baron De Kalb's command. At the Battle of Camden, on August 16, 1780, General De Kalb, mortally wounded, was carried off the battlefield by Major Nones and two other Jewish officers, Captain Jacob de la Motte and Captain Jacob de Leon, at the risk of their lives.

Major Nones was cited by General Pulaski for valor in action in the following letter written by Captain Verdier of his staff:

> Benjamin Nones has served as a volunteer in my company during the campaign this year at the siege of Savannah in Georgia . . . his behavior under fire in all the bloody actions we fought has been marked by bravery and courage, which a military man is expected to show for the liberties of his country, and which acts of said Nones gained in his favor the esteem of General Pulaski, as well as that of all the officers who witnessed his daring conduct.

After Yorktown, fighting virtually ceased. Major Nones settled in Philadelphia and went into a business partnership with Haym Salomon. But all chances of prosperity vanished when Salomon, the patriotic financier from Poland, died. Nones became an official interpreter of French, Spanish, and Portuguese for the Board of Health and for the United States government. Yet he barely earned enough to feed his steadily increasing family of fourteen children.

Feeling at home in the Sephardic ritual of Philadelphia's first synagogue, Nones joined Congregation Mikveh Israel and served as its president before and during the turn of the century.

Nones took an active part in politics. He was a leader of the Democrat-Republicans. His courage and bravery were again called on when he, his people, and his cause were scurrilously attacked in an anonymous letter published in the Federalist newspaper *The Gazette of the United States* on August 5, 1800. Nones sent a reply to the *Gazette*, but the paper refused to print it. The Philadelphia *Aurora*, however, a Republican newspaper, promptly published Nones's passionate self-defense as a feature article on August 13, 1800.

Nones ran for public office. We have a most interesting campaign letter in which he tells that he is accused of being a Jew, of being a Republican, and of being poor. He proudly states that he is all three of these terrible things but that in his opinion, these make him still more worthy of election.

His son, Joseph Nones (1797–1887), was wounded while serving as a midshipman in a battle against Algerian pirates in the War of 1812. Joseph was a pioneer in processing concentrated foods, and in 1829 he proposed a program to combat scurvy in the Navy.

A younger son, Captain Henry Nones (1804–1868) was stationed in Wilmington, Delaware, with the U.S. Navy and cited for bravery during the Mexican War.

THE FIRST JEWISH INSURER

1784

For many years the ships that sailed out of America with cargoes for Europe and Asia were insured, if at all, in London. The only way the owner of a ship could insure it against the risks of shipwreck, piracy, and other ocean dangers was to take out a policy from Lloyd's of London. By the eighteenth century, sea traffic was so heavy that it seemed sensible to transfer the writing of insurance to Boston. Settled ten years after the Pilgrims landed, the marsh-covered Shawmut Peninsula (later named Boston), quickly became an important port and shipbuilding center.

Moses Michael Hays was the first Jew to open a marine insurance office in Boston. Born in New York City in 1739, Hays was the son of Judah Hays, a Dutch Jewish immigrant, and worked in his father's trading and shipping business until Judah's death in 1764. In 1766, Moses Hays married Rachel Myers, sister of the New York artist-silversmith, Myer Myers.

The amazing success story of Aaron Lopez drew ambitious young men like Moses Hays to Newport. Emulating Lopez as the ideal merchant, Hays aspired to importing and exporting. During the British occupation of Newport, he sought refuge in Philadelphia. Later, he settled in Boston and prospered in the marine insurance business.

In 1784, setting himself up at 68 State Street as a maritime insurance broker, Hays would make out a policy describing the vessel, the voyage it was to make, and the rate and amount of insurance. Bostonian merchants who wished to share in the risks signed their names to the policy with the amounts they were willing to underwrite. Hays prospered in the business and at a later date added to this "an assurance office for houses and household goods from loss and damage by fire in any part of the Province." In 1798 his name appears in a petition for a charter of the Massachusetts Mutual Fire Insurance Company, a pioneer venture in Boston.

Hays was equally active in large-scale merchandising, exporting, and money lending. In 1784 a group of nine merchants called on him to help make plans for a bank to serve them like the Bank of England, receiving deposits and discounting loans. He played an important role in the establishment of the first permanent, successful bank in Boston, the Massachusetts Bank. Hays was among the prominent Bostonian merchants who raised the capital subscription for the bank, which opened on July 5, 1784. He was also the first depositor of record and the first to withdraw funds. Hays was among the bank's most active clients during his lifetime and contributed to the bank's twentyfold growth in its first twenty years. This bank became a direct ancestor of the First National Bank of Boston, the largest in New England and one of the ten largest in the United States.

As a man of business acumen, Hays corresponded with Robert Morris, the first superintendent of finances of the United States, about taxation, finances, and the creation of a sound monetary system.

Like most of his contemporaries, Hays exhibited strong attachment to his own religion. With patriarchal authority, he instilled in his family circle devotion to Judaism and respect for the faith of others. Philanthropy was taught by precept and example. His household included his sister Reyna, the widow of the Reverend Isaac Touro of Newport, the first *hazzan* and spiritual leader of the Touro Synagogue, and her two sons, Judah and Abraham, and daughter, Rebecca.

Hays conducted regular worship services in his home, educated his children and nephews and niece in the Hebrew language and traditional devotions, and supported synagogues in Newport and New York City.

To Hays's home came many notables of the day. He enjoyed the esteem of United States Senator Harrison J. Otis, son of James Otis, patriot of the American Revolution; Thomas H. Perkins, pioneer of American railroads; Robert Treat Paine, son of a signer of the Declaration of Independence; and others in the upper class of society. Louisa May Alcott's grandfather Samuel May remembered growing up with the Hays and Touro children.

Hays, a Federalist, sought public office but was swamped by the rising tide of Jeffersonian Republicanism. Political disappointments were, however, repaid with high honors in Freemasonry. He became a leading figure in Masonic circles and was responsible for the introduction into North America of the "Ancient Accepted Scottish Rite of Masonry," which comprised thirty-three degrees. In recognition of his contribution, he was elected grand master of the Grand Lodge at annual elections from 1788 to 1792. In 1793 he became a member of a subordinate lodge and was again elected grand master. Paul Revere served as a deputy grand master under him. The eleven deputies he appointed exercised high powers in the lodges of different states. Hays's son and grandsons were the only Jewish Masons in Massachusetts before 1810.

Hays was the first Jewish benefactor of Harvard College, and his name appears on the donors lists as early as 1780.

A portrait of Moses Michael Hays hangs today in the Masonic Temple of Boston. A copy of the Gilbert Stuart original, which was lost in a fire, it shows a handsome face, firm mouth, strong chin, and dark, appraising eyes.

Hays died in Boston on May 9, 1805, at the age of sixty-six and was buried in the famous Jewish cemetery in Newport, Rhode Island, adjoining the Touro Synagogue. In his obituary the *Boston Centinel* wrote: "He walked abroad fearing no man but loving all. . . . He was without guile, detesting hypocrisy as he despised meanness! Take him for all in all, he was indeed a man."

He left what was for that day a large estate, appraised at $82,000. Among his assets—as diverse as lands in Georgia and Rhode Island, bonds, and a house in Boston—there were twenty-two Hebrew books.

Hays family members followed his example of public service, with his son Judah being an original stockholder of the Boston Athenaeum.

In June 1990 the American Jewish Historical Society and the Bank of Boston presented an exhibition entitled *A Most Valuable Citizen: Moses Michael Hays and the Establishment of Post-Revolutionary Boston*. The exhibit recounted the contributions of Moses Michael Hays and the members of his family to the economic and cultural life of the community.

THE FIRST JEW TO FOUND A SETTLEMENT IN AMERICA

1786

The first town in America planned by and named for a Jew is Aaronsburg, Pennsylvania, which soon after its founding acquired a population of 250. The town still exists in the heart of Pennsylvania Dutch country. A marker placed by the State of Pennsylvania on State Road #45, which passes along there, reads: "Aaronsburg, named for Aaron Levy, founded 1786."

Aaron Levy, who was well-known in the community, was born in Amsterdam, Holland, in 1742 and came to this country while in his late teens, hoping to find his fortune in the American colonies. For about a decade Aaron trafficked about between Philadelphia, Northumberland, and Lancaster, where the example and advice of Joseph Simon induced him to trade with the Indians. He furnished supplies to his colony. He was a patriot. His name appeared in 1778 as a signer of a document wherein the colony was asked to protect the petitioners against the inroads of the British and the Indians. During the Revolutionary War he advanced large sums of money to the Continental Congress through Superintendent of Finance Robert Morris, with whom Levy had substantial business transactions.

Most of his life Levy lived on the frontier himself, in Northumberland County, where the tract of land was located. As he grew older, he apparently sought out Jewish communal life and ultimately moved back to more-settled areas, first to Lancaster and then to Philadelphia, where he was one of the founders of Congregation Mikveh Israel.

But merchandising and Indian trade were incidental. Aaron Levy's fame rests on real estate. As a real estate operator, he ranks with the foremost among the numerous land speculators in all the colonies. The number and extent of his transactions are astonishing. He appears to have owned land in every county of Pennsylvania. In his study on Aaron Levy, Dr. Sidney M. Fish tabulates seventy-four transactions in Northumberland and eighty-eight in Centre County. The deals range from single lots to 26,000-acre tracts as revealed in recorded documents.

One of these tracts lying in Penn Valley and situated in Centre County was particularly beautiful. Thirty miles from Northumberland, surrounded by fertile soil, the spot promised to be ideal for farmers to sell their produce. This tract, it was presumed, would become the seat of county government. A new projected highway to Fort Pitt (Pittsburgh) would surely cross at this strategic point. The imagination of Aaron Levy envisioned a thriving community that would become a prosperous city of commerce and civilized living.

On May 23, 1786, he issued a public notice declaring that he "hath laid out a town called Aaronsburg, very pleasantly situated in the beautiful, healthy, and fertile settlement called Penn Valley." The town comprised 612 lots in all, each measuring 60 by 220 feet. Houses were to be laid out with taste and skill. He named the intersecting one hundred-foot boulevard Rachel's Way, in honor of his wife. The lots were auctioned off at six dollars each, with a dollar annual ground rent, the purchaser to receive full title on paying twenty "Spanish silver-milled dollars."

On November 16, 1789, Aaron Levy gave the trustees of the Salem Lutheran Church two lots for the construction of a house of worship, a school, and a cemetery. The opening of the church as the first house of worship of the Lutheran community marked one of the brightest chapters in brotherhood and interfaith relations in the United States.

On October 23, 1949, in observance of the sesquicentennial of the opening of the church, one of the highlights of the ceremony was the presentation by the Salem Lutheran Church of a kiddush cup (a cup used for blessing over wine during Sabbaths and Jewish festivals), to Congregation Shearith Israel of New York, the oldest Jewish congregation in the United States. The cup symbolized the "Return of the Gift."

Aaron Levy anticipated a large emigration to the free Republic of the West following the peace treaty at the conclusion of the Revolutionary War. But the government, without stability and heavily in debt, had to sustain a severe economic depression that settled over the new country. Levy was among the heavy losers. Instead of becoming a tycoon, he was left land-poor. He turned land agent to obtain cash and placed his abilities at the disposal of other land speculators. As a land agent he looms large, buying hundreds of thousands of acres for Robert Morris and Supreme Court Justice James Wilson.

In 1936, on the 150th anniversary of the founding of Aaronsburg, the town was the scene of a great demonstration as thirty thousand Americans from far and near and of all faiths came to spend a Sunday there to celebrate its founding. The event received national publicity. Prominent figures, including Supreme Court Judge Felix Frankfurter; Dr. Ralph Bunche, United Nations mediator and Nobel Peace Prize winner; and the Reverend Daniel Poling, distinguished clergyman, spoke on interfaith goodwill as the American way of life.

Today, in spite of American prosperity and with all the industrial development of Pennsylvania, Aaronsburg has not more than four hundred inhabitants. It has become a symbol and gathering place for those seeking a formula for national serenity and world peace through brotherhood and understanding. In the summer of 1953, a three-day conference of the Aaronsburg Assembly, which is dedicated to this aim, again brought together a group of men and women of outstanding prominence in the political and religious life of the country. Aaron Levy again played a handsome, posthumous role.

Today there is a series of villages and towns from Aaronsburg, Pennsylvania, that extend across the country along the old trails to Roseville, California; Heppner, Oregon; and Montezuma, Kansas, named after hardy Jewish souls, who, like Aaron Levy, brought with them the first breath of civilization to hitherto untrampled territory.

After World War II William Levitt, a second-generation American Jew, built not just houses but entire communities, first on Long Island and then all over the United States. He thereby practically invented the modern suburb while fulfilling the dreams of home ownership for thousands of middle-income families.

He and his family had been successful builders, mostly on Long Island, before World War II. They purchased the old Vanderbilt estate on which they built some three hundred large homes designed by Alfred Levitt. They also began a shopping center in the same area. During the war, the firm built 750 units of housing in Virginia for naval officers and sixteen hundred more for shipyard workers.

During the severe housing shortage of the immediate post-World War II period, Levitt borrowed funds to purchase four thousand areas of potato-farming land near the town of Hempstead on Long Island, outside New York City. There during the late 1940s and early 1950s, Levitt used cut-rate production techniques to build seventeen thousand eight-hundred-square-foot Tudor-style single-family homes, which he sold at prices young families could afford. On this same tract, Levitt simultaneously laid out six "village greens," twenty-four playing fields, and nine community swimming pools, as well as ample sights for schools and a house of worship. Ultimately, "Levittown" became a pleasant and clean community of 57,000 people.

In later years, Levitt developed similar projects in other parts of the United States, and afterward in Europe.

II

We Grow with the Nation

THE FIRST JEWISH BOOKDEALER

1791

As the years went by and schools grew in numbers, people became more interested in books and learning. In 1791, the first American Jewish bookdealer opened his shop. Benjamin Gomez, the owner, was a man of intelligence and high character. It was his own taste for reading that led him to become the earliest Jewish bookdealer in the United States.

Benjamin Gomez, son of Mattias and Rachel Gomez, born in New York on September 17, 1769, stemmed from one of the most distinguished early American Jewish families. He traced his ancestry to Isaac Gomez, a Spanish nobleman, who in about 1600 was forced to flee from Spain because of the Inquisition. When Isaac Gomez found refuge in France, in gratitude to King Louis XIV for the kindly reception he received there, he caused his son Moses, to assume the name of Lewis Moses Gomez. This Lewis Moses later left France for England to escape the persecutions that followed the revocation of the Edict of Nantes in 1685. Toward the close of the seventeenth century he emigrated with his family to New York. In New York the family comprised important merchants and shipowners and assumed a position of leadership in the Jewish community.

Benjamin Gomez's father was a son of the fifth son of Lewis Moses Gomez. The Gomez House built by Lewis Moses in 1710 in Newburgh, Orange County, New York, near a stream called Jews' Creek, still stands as the oldest Jewish residence in all of North America. Its interior looks very much the way it did when the Gomez family sold it in 1772.

Benjamin Gomez first appeared in the New York directory of 1791 as a bookseller, when he was located at 32 Maiden Lane, "near the Fly Market," where also his brother, Isaac Gomez, carried on business as a broker. It is surprising how wide a choice of books Benjamin Gomez offered. A few months after he opened his shop, he ran a full-page notice in the local paper to say that he had many volumes for sale including some "just imported from Dublin," in addition to his former assortment. His advertised stock consisted of histories, essays, medical-scientific works, volumes on law, Bibles, Shakespeare, novels, travel books, poetry, sermons, and lectures "too numerous for advertisement in the newspaper."

The following year Gomez extended his bookselling activities to include publishing. Twenty-one of the books he published are still known to us. They include Hugh Gaines's edition of *Pilgrim's Progress*, an abridged edition of *Robinson Crusoe, Captain Cook's Third and Last Voyage*, as well as Goethe's *Sorrows of Werther*.

In 1794 he published a volume of 131 pages combining Dr. Joseph Priestly's *Letters to the Jews Inviting Them to Amicable Discussion of the Evidences of Christianity*. The famous scientist, not content with his great contributions to chemistry, was religious minded and concerned with converting the Jews. In the same volume, Gomez printed the rejoinder entitled *Letters to Dr. Priestly in Answer to Those Addressed to the Jews Inviting Them to Amicable Discussion of the Evidences of Christianity* by David Levi, author of *Lingua Sacra, The Ceremonies of the Jews*. Levi, the foremost Hebrew scholar in eighteenth-century England, an author and translator, was the first Jew to write a vindication of Judaism in English. The original Priestly letter had been published in London in 1786–7. The Gomez edition bears the imprint "Reprinted by J. Harrison for B. Gomez, Bookseller and Stationer, No.97, Maiden Lane, 1794."

The fact that Gomez, as a loyal Jew and prominent member of New York's Congregation Shearith Israel, should have chosen to publish this particular work raises an interesting speculation as pointed out by the eminent historian, Lee Friedman. Was Gomez, as a shrewd businessman, publishing this merely because he hoped it would prove to be a bestseller of the day? Or did he think David Levi had the better argument and thus might do the Jews a service by educating their Christian neighbors to the validity and reasonableness of the Jewish viewpoint?

At any rate, Levi's polemic against Priestly attracted wide attention. Its publication by Gomez was more than justified when it drew the notice of Thomas Jefferson who wrote to John Adams:

> I have lately been amusing myself with Levi's book in answer to Dr. Priestly. It is a curious and tough work. Some of his doctrines were new to me. He avails himself of his advantage over his adversaries by his superior knowledge of Hebrew, speaking in the very language of the divine communication, while they can only fumble on with conflicting and disputed translations. Such is the war of giants. And how can such pigmies as you and I decide between them?

Gomez took in a full stock of general stationery so customary among booksellers of the time to stimulate business. At about this point Gomez advertised "a great allowance will be made to those who buy and sell again. Binding of all kinds done with neatness, accuracy, and dispatch," and that his stock in trade included "quills, slates, and slate pencils, sealing wax, primers, chap books and spelling books, demi folio, quarto, post and foolscap writing paper, writing do, journals, day books & ledgers, invoice books, etc."

Evidently Gomez's success as a publisher was sufficient to cause Naphtali Judah of New York, in 1795, to enter the trade as America's second Jewish bookseller, who shared some of Gomez's later imprints.

Like so many members of his family, Benjamin Gomez served Congregation Shearith Israel in various offices including that of *Parnas* (president) and treasurer.

Gomez was also an early Jewish juror in New York City.

Although the name Gomez disappeared in later generations, the family line has been carried through marriages of its daughters into the Hart, Lopez, Rivera, Solis, Seixas, and Cardozo families.

THE FIRST JEWISH COFOUNDER OF THE NEW YORK STOCK EXCHANGE

1792

The first Congress of the United States under the Constitution, which met during 1789–1790 in Federal Hall at the corner of Broad and Wall streets in New York City, issued $80 million of six percent government bonds to pay Revolutionary War debts. This action created the need for a marketplace for the public sale of these securities. Orders came into New York in such volume that some merchants and auctioneers began to devote most of their time to the business. By the Spring of 1792, attempts were made by these stockbrokers to organize, and their efforts culminated in the signing of the agreement of May 17, 1792, which marked the founding of the Stockbrokers Guild, later the New York Stock Exchange. It is known as the "Buttonwood Agreement" from the fact that it was signed under a large buttonwood (sycamore) tree that stood in front of the present 68 Wall Street. The twenty-four stockbrokers and merchants who gathered together and set down the terms on which they would buy and sell stock were the first members of the New York Stock Exchange.

This was the beginning of a formal stockbrokers association in New York. The idea of drawing buyers and sellers to an organized central market to share in the risks and rewards of investing generated new opportunities for investors to help develop the nation.

By 1817 it had been formally incorporated with a set of rules that by today's standards are delightfully lax, but which did require a listing of companies whose shares were being offered for trading. By the early nineteenth century, people were investing in government securities, in stocks that had been issued to finance the Erie Canal, in banks, insurance companies, and then in the railroads that opened the whole continent to trade.

By 1911 investors were buying automobile stock, one of a host of industries that helped create the kind of economy the world had never seen before. Today more than two thousand companies from around the world list their shares on the New York Stock Exchange. About fifty-one million Americans directly own stock or shares in stock mutual funds. Each day at the Stock Exchange millions of shares of some of the world's most important corporations are bought and sold.

There have always been Jews on the exchange, and by 1824 they were exercising authority as officers. One of the twenty-four original brokers who helped organize the loose confederation of New York security traders in 1792 was Ephraim Hart (1747–1825). Hart was willing to accept the membership requirements of the New York Stock Exchange and pledged:

> not to buy or sell from this day to any person whatsoever, any kind of public stock at a rate less than one quarter percent commission on the specie value.

Thus was born the antecedent of the New York Stock Exchange.

We know from the Hart account books and correspondence that for many years he continued to do a large and important trade.

The son of Samuel Hart, Ephraim was born in Furth, Bavaria, in 1747 and came to this country in the early 1770s. A number of his fellow countrymen had already settled in New York, and one of them may have encouraged him to emigrate. He set up residence there prior to the British occupancy of September 15, 1776. The confusion and uncertainty of war made it impossible for him to establish himself immediately. When the British took the port of New York, he refused to remain under British redcoat rule. As an American patriot, he felt he could not live and work in a community that had lost its liberty. With his friend Jonas Phillips and other New York Jews, he left for Philadelphia. Later Phillips was to have the distinction of being the only outside person to address the convention assembled in Philadelphia to formulate the Constitution of the United States.

Ephraim Hart remained in Philadelphia for several years. Gradually family after family moved to Philadelphia to join the growing Jewish community in that city. Early in 1782 he was present at the dedication of Philadelphia's Mikveh Israel Synagogue.

About this time we find him a merchant, residing at 398 Third Street. He married Frances Noah, sister of Manuel Noah, long a resident of Philadelphia and aunt of the noted Mordecai Manuel Noah of New York. Several years later, when the Revolutionary War was over, Ephraim Hart disposed of his possessions in Philadelphia, among them certain parcels of ground, and returned to New York.

He started in the business of stockbroker at 52 Broad Street and later at 74 Wall Street. He became a successful businessman, made many friends, and was foremost in many important enterprises. When in 1798 the Bank of Manhattan was organized by Jeffersonians as a people's bank, Ephraim Hart, with three other Jews, was among its original stockholders. He was at this time a wealthy man and owned much valuable real estate on Wall Street. In 1810, Hart sat on the New York State Senate.

Ephraim Hart identified himself closely with the Jewish community of New York. He was a charitable man and greatly interested in the religious affairs of New York Jewry. When the time came to enlarge the original Mill Street building of Shearith Israel, he contributed funds and participated actively in the plan.

Ephraim Hart lived to be a very old man, beloved and honored not only by his fellow Jews but by his Christian neighbors, as well. He died on July 16, 1825, and was buried in the cemetery of Congregation Shearith Israel near the present location of Chatham Square and Oliver Street on the New Bowery.

In 1804 his daughter, Harriet Judith, met and married Benjamin Hart, son of Aaron Hart of Canada, who in 1800 was styled the wealthiest colonist in the British Empire.

Dr. Joel Hart, the only son of Ephraim Hart, was educated in England and was a graduate of the Royal College of Surgeons in London. In 1806 he became one of the charter members of the Medical Society of the County of New York.

Ephraim Hart's distant kinsman, Bernard Hart, was secretary of the New York Stock Exchange from 1831 to 1853.

THE FIRST PRESIDENTIAL RESIDENCE OWNED BY A JEW

1793

American Jews can point with pride to the part played by their people in colonial and revolutionary times. In private life George Washington had met many Jews at an early date. Hezekiah Levy was a member of the Fredericksburg Lodge in Virginia in 1771, Washington's own Masonic Lodge. In the ensuing struggle for American independence, he came to know several Jewish soldiers. He had on his personal staff Manuel Mordecai Noah of South Carolina (father of Mordecai Manuel Noah), David Salisbury Franks, of Philadelphia and Major Benjamin Nones, a French volunteer. He was also familiar with Philip Moses Russell, a surgeon's mate, who shared the hardships of Valley Forge, and he knew Private Asher Pollack of the Second Rhode Island Battalion.

As commander in chief during the war, Washington had occasion to watch and work with Isaac Franks, who had a varied career in the field of battle and who received high rank as an officer in the Pennsylvania Militia after the war.

A member of the famous Franks family of colonial merchants dating back to pre-Revolutionary times, Isaac Franks was born in New York in 1759. He was still in his teens shortly before the Battle of Lexington, when the Revolutionary War broke out into open warfare. At the beginning of the war, he began his military career by joining Colonel Lasher's regiment in New York and took part in the Battle of Long Island. This regiment was annexed to the Continental Army under the immediate command of General Washington. After the Battle of Long Island, Franks retreated with the army to New York and was on guard on the East River when the British took possession of the city on September 15, 1776. Franks was taken prisoner. After being held for almost three months in Cunningham's notorious Provost Prison, he escaped in a small, leaky rowboat with one single paddle to the New Jersey shore. During the next four years he was in the Quartermaster's Division. In 1781, he was commissioned ensign in the Seventh Massachusetts Regiment. At the end of the year, "being severely afflicted with the gravel," he was compelled to resign.

With the war over, Franks returned to public life. He became one of Washington's closest friends. It was in speaking of Franks that the President said: "He was a soldier that served his country well and was concerned more with the welfare of his country than the glory of his person."

The years immediately following the war found Franks in reduced circumstances, but later his fortunes improved. He acquired a home in Germantown, Pennsylvania, that was known to be comfortable. Built in 1774, it had been occupied by Sir William Howe, after the Battle of Germantown. Here the British commander entertained the future King William IV, then a midshipman in the Royal Navy. In 1782 the building was purchased by Colonel Franks. During the winter of 1793, when a yellow fever epidemic was raging in Philadelphia, George Washington leased this house as his presidential residence. The seat of the federal government was temporarily moved from Philadelphia to Germantown.

For two months the presidential family lived in the two-story house. The bill of occupancy presented to the president is amusing. In addition to the rent, which was sixty-six dollars for the two months, Washington paid for a missing flatiron, four platters, and one fork. He was also charged for "the damages done to a large [japanned] waiter made use of in the services of the President." The sum of two dollars and fifty cents was expended by Franks "for cleaning my house and in putting it in the same condition the President rec'd it in." The fact remains that the Franks' home was once the nation's capital.

For many years Isaac Franks continued to be a prosperous citizen. With the celebrated Dr. Benjamin Rush of Philadelphia, he bought vast tracts of land in Westmoreland County in what was to become the state of Indiana. Finally, in his old age, he became poor. During the last four years of his life, he was the recipient of a Revolutionary War pension and held several civil posts. He was the first Jew to sit for Gilbert Stuart, who is famous for his portraits of George Washington and other colonial leaders.

Isaac Franks often recalled his military record with pride, not failing to add that he was "a native born citizen and a uniform Republican."

Franks's sister Rachel is said to have been the wife of Haym Salomon, who rendered far greater, if less spectacular, services to the revolutionary cause.

THE FIRST COPPER-ROLLING MILL

1812

The Soho Copper-Rolling Mill, the first copper-rolling mill in America, was built by Harmon Hendricks in Belleville, New Jersey, in 1812. Hendricks was also the owner of a copper store on Mill Street (now South William Street) in New York City. The Hendricks firm was a pioneer in the production of copper sheeting and exercised an influence in the development of the copper industry in the United States. Within a few years of the opening of the Soho Copper-Rolling Mill, most of the rum produced in America was coming from stills made of Hendricks copper. This company was owned and operated by descendants of Harmon Hendricks until 1939, when the Hendricks Company went out of business and sold its plant to the Andrew Jergens Company as the site of a new factory. A stone wall and brick building near the Jergens plant are the last vestiges of this pioneer industrial enterprise, which existed for many years as the oldest Jewish-founded business concern in America.

Following a seventeenth-century trend, Haim Hendricks, grandfather of Harmon Hendricks, left his native Amsterdam for London. His son Uriah migrated to New York in 1755 and did well enough in seven years to marry the daughter of the socially prominent Mordecai Gomez. Their eight children became ancestors of a family that spread over many states. Besides operating a general store that offered numerous articles of merchandise, Uriah became an "ironmonger" and opened a metal business that remained with his descendants for 175 years.

Uriah Hendricks supplied the colonies in the French and Indian Wars with copper and other metals and laid the groundwork for a great fortune. As tensions began to mount with England and lead to war, the sympathies of Uriah Hendricks continued with the mother country. Born in England, he considered separation from the mother country unnecessary. Besides, he might have felt a loyal attachment to Cromwell's land, which treated his coreligionists better than they were treated anywhere in Europe, excepting Holland. He was one of the Tories who signed the Loyalist address to the British admiral Howe in 1776, when the British took New York. His Tory affiliations came in handy during the British occupation. He, Barak Hays, and Alexander Zuntz, the Hessian commissary, prevailed upon the British authorities to spare Congregation Shearith Israel from military seizure, something many churches were unable to do. With the advent of peace, we hear of no ill feeling against him. He remained in the city and died in 1798 of yellow fever.

His son Harmon, born in New York in 1771, suffered no such conflicting loyalties. He continued the family's metal business traditions, establishing the first copper-rolling mill in America in 1812 in Belleville, New Jersey, and in turn handed it down to his four sons. We know from the Hendricks account books and correspondence that from modest beginnings the firm reached out to all corners of the earth for their copper supply—England, Russia, the Mediterranean, and South America.

There was a close relationship between the Bostonian firm of Paul Revere and Son and that of the Hendricks. For years the Hendricks firm acted as Paul Revere's New York agent and supplied the Reveres with material needed in their factory, some of which went into the famous warship *Constitution* (nicknamed "Old Ironsides") and the *Clermont,* the first steamship launched successfully by Robert Fulton. In 1812 Hendricks's brother-in-law and business associate, Solomon I. Isaacs, acted as sales and financial agent for the Reveres. He carefully allocated his goods to shut off competition and tried to consolidate his customers soundly in behalf of the Reveres. As an example of a trade monopoly, this scheme holds its own in contrast with attempts to control industry by our later captains of industry.

During the War of 1812, Harmon Hendricks gave $40,000 as a loan to help the government finance its war with the British when the United States treasury was having difficulty with the sale of war bonds. This was one of the largest individual subscriptions for bonds ever made in the annals of American history up to that date.

Harmon Hendricks's name appears often in the records of Congregation Shearith Israel, which he served as *Parnas.* While serving as *Parnas* of Shearith Israel, a group of congregants seceded to form another congregation. Such a step usually promotes acrimony—yet Harmon Hendricks was the speaker who dedicated the newly formed Congregation B'nai Jeshurun, the first Jewish house of worship in New York City to adopt the Ashkenazic (Central European) ritual. To this competitive synagogue, he even advanced $5,000 on a mortgage for five years and charged one percent interest per annum. When payment time came around, Henricks accepted $4,850 and canceled the debt.

Harmon Hendricks died in 1838. According to one report he was "immensely rich, leaving over three million dollars and a great deal of real estate." His daughter Judith was married to Benjamin Nathan, a stockbroker in Wall Street, who sold Hendricks copper shares, which were considered among the blue chips of the era.

In his book *The Old Merchants of New York City*, published in 1863, Walter Barrett eulogized the "great copper merchant of former years" and says: "No man stood higher in his community while he lived, and no man has left a memory more revered than Harmon Hendricks. When he died, the synagogue which he attended lost one of its best friends, and the rising generation of that numerous family could not have a better example."

Henry S. Hendricks (1892–1959), for many years honorary president of Congregation Shearith Israel, was a direct descendant of Harmon Hendricks. Henry Hendricks presented family heirlooms of historic interest to the Metropolitan Museum of Art, the Museum of the City of New York, and to the Jewish Museum. These, dating from a letter book of Uriah Hendricks of the years 1758 and 1759, include many records, letters, ledgers, and books of the Hendricks Copper Mill of Belleville, New Jersey, which are of value and interest in the history of the American copper industry of the eighteenth and nineteenth centuries.

THE FIRST AMERICAN JEWISH HEROINE OF FICTION

1819

Rebecca Gratz, the beautiful, cultured, and idealistic belle of Philadelphian society, the daughter of the prominent merchant and land developer, Michael Gratz, is the first American Jewess upon whom literary immortality has been conferred. She is the original of the character of Rebecca in Sir Walter Scott's novel *Ivanhoe*, published in England in 1819 and which first appeared in American editions simultaneously in New York and Philadelphia in 1823.

Born in Philadelphia in 1781, the year Washington's cannon were booming in Yorktown, Rebecca Gratz lived long enough to see the Union restored after the surrender of Lee at Appomattox. Her purity of heart, beauty of face, her charm and loyalty to her race, inspired the imagination of her friend Washington Irving, author of "Rip Van Winkle" and other popular tales, who frequently enjoyed the hospitality of the spacious Gratz home on Chestnut Street.

In 1807, Irving wrote to Rebecca about the proposed visit to Philadelphia of Thomas Sully, the artist, saying: "I think I can render him no favor of which he ought to be more grateful than in introducing him to notice of yourself and your connections."

In the Spring of 1809, Washington Irving's fiancée, Matilda Hoffman, died of consumption (as tuberculosis was then called), having been nursed tenderly for the last six months of her life by Rebecca Gratz who had been her childhood friend. Going abroad to overcome his grief, Irving visited the great author Sir Walter Scott, then at the height of his fame and all but the acknowledged author of the *Waverly Novels*. For each of them it was a great encounter. It laid the foundation of a great friendship. "To this friendship," says Gratz Van Rensselaer, "we owe the character of Rebecca in *Ivanhoe*." For Scott was then planning to write a novel of chivalry in the time of Richard the Lionhearted. One of the characters, Scott told the American visitor, was to be a Jewish moneylender, Isaac of York.

With the skill of an experienced storyteller, Washington Irving spoke of Rebecca Gratz's beauty, her devotion to her religion, her nobility of character, self-sacrificing generosity, and refusal to marry a Christian.

Scott was interested. He immediately determined to introduce a Jewish female character in his novel, and on the strength of Irving's vivid description, he named his heroine Rebecca. When Scott finished his novel in 1819, he sent a copy to Irving with a note expressing the hope that the Rebecca in *Ivanhoe* typified all that was noble in the real Rebecca. The qualities in *Ivanhoe*'s Rebecca precisely fit the original and are the ones for which Scott's Rebecca became such a popular heroine.

Rebecca Gratz read *Ivanhoe* in 1820. She wrote on the fourth of April to her sister-in-law: "Have you received *Ivanhoe*? When you read it, tell me what you think of my namesake Rebecca."

Scott's pen portrait of Rebecca might well have been written about Miss Gratz of whom there are two excellent portraits, one by the artist Sully, the other by Malbone. Sully said:

> He had never seen a more striking Hebraic face. The easy pose, suggestive of perfect health, the delicately turned neck and shoulders with the firmly posed head and its profusion of dark, curling hair, large clear black eyes, the contour of the face, the fine white skin, the expressive mouth and firmly chiseled nose, with its strength of character, left no doubt as to the race from which she had sprung. Possessed of an elegant bearing, a melodiously sympathetic voice, a simple and frank and gracious womanliness, there was about Rebecca Gratz all that a princess of the blood Royal might have coveted.

Rebecca Gratz had always welcomed social and philanthropic service and filled her life with the performance of numerous duties and obligations. She made a home for her unmarried brothers. She mothered and reared the nine orphaned children of her sister, Rachel Moses.

In her twenty-first year, she organized the Female Association for the Relief of Women and Children in Reduced Circumstances in Philadelphia. She served as its first secretary and was a motivating force in its administration and in raising much-needed funds. She was also one of the founders of the nonsectarian Philadelphia Orphan Asylum, chartered in 1815, and served as its secretary for over forty years.

Sensing there was a need to serve the needy and unfortunate in the Jewish community, she founded and organized the Female Hebrew Benevolent Society in 1819 to care for the large number of Jewish immigrants then entering the United States. This organization was the first Jewish philanthropic agency apart from a synagogue and was the inspiration for all Jewish welfare agencies to later appear. She founded the Jewish Foster Home and Orphan Asylum in 1855 and helped found other organizations, among them the Fuel Society and Sewing Circle.

Rebecca Gratz was concerned about the religious education of Jewish children. After having observed how the Christians taught their children one day a week in the Christian Sunday Schools, she drew up plans in 1838 for the first Jewish Sunday School. She was its first president and supervisor for twenty-six years. There were no textbooks for the religious education of Jewish children, so Miss Gratz not only planned the lessons to be studied but wrote the lesson outlines she handed her inexperienced teachers. The idea of the Jewish Sunday School took root in the 1840s and 1850s, especially in Reform Judaism, and spread to every American city that had a Jewish community, becoming truly communal institutions where Jewish children could obtain a religious education, modest though it might be.

Too beautiful to escape romance, she was too genuine and loyal to her religion to benefit from the love she inspired. Rebecca Gratz refused to marry outside her faith and remained a lifelong spinster even though the man she loved, Samuel Ewing, was the literary and handsome son of Dr. John Ewing, noted clergyman, educator, and provost of the University of Pennsylvania.

When she was laid to rest in Mikveh Israel Cemetery in 1869 at the age of eighty-eight, she was mourned as the foremost Jewess in the United States and one of the noblest women in the world.

Rebecca Gratz wrote many letters during her lifetime in which she left full evidence of the wide range of her interests. Her letters mention many names of Jewish and Christian friends. Quite apart from their Jewish significance, these letters are an important contribution to social history, for the running commentary on men, on books, on the arts, on important events, of a keen and observant mind during those significant years from 1811 to 1866 cannot but be a marked addition to American history.

THE FIRST JEWISH NEWSPAPERS

1823

The first Jewish newspaper published in the United States devoted exclusively to Jewish affairs was known as *The Jew*. It was published monthly in New York beginning in March 1823 by Solomon Henry Jackson, the first Jewish printer in the city who had a virtual monopoly on all synagogue printing and who wrote English with style. It was sold for one dollar and fifty cents a year and was delivered to New York subscribers at their dwellings and to distant subscribers through the New York post office. It ran for two years and was published primarily as a defense of Judaism against all attacks of *Israel's Advocate*, which was the house organ of the American Society for Meliorating the Condition of Jews, a missionary society that had set about spreading false ideas about the Jew.

The valiant fight of Solomon Jackson reads somewhat like the public religious disputations in the Middle Ages. His polemics contradicted the editorials, the pamphlets, and the preachments of the missionaries. He reiterated the Jewish arguments against Christianity and cited in support the words of the Hebrew prophets by chapter, line, and verse. His editorials criticized the methods used by the American Society for Meliorating the Condition of Jews. In short, he used every weapon in his arsenal to confute, demolish, and defeat his opponents.

In 1825, when Jackson's paper was discontinued, the Jews of New York had to rely on the local press for news of Jewish interest until 1843, when the Reverend Isaac Leeser, outstanding spokesman of American Jewry, educator, and editor, founded *The Occident and American Jewish Advocate* in Philadelphia. This was a monthly devoted mainly to religious articles from a traditionalist point of view, but it contained news items as well and promoted the educational and philanthropic projects of which Leeser was chief architect. By 1849, however, New York Jews began to venture into the field of Jewish periodical publication, and thereafter the community never lacked organs for the dissemination of news. In that year there appeared in German *Israel's Herald*, launched by Isidor Bush, a recently arrived refugee from the Austrian counterrevolution of 1848. The purpose of *Israel's Herald* was to bring about unity among the Jews regardless of religious, social, and political differences.

In the 1850s, a New York newspaper, *The Asmonian*, described as a "Family Journal of Commerce, Politics, Religion, and Literature Devoted to the Interests of the American Israelites," was published by Robert Lyon, an English Jew. Its pages reflected the life, manners, folkways, opinions, and anecdotes of the day. In 1852 it listed trades in which Jews were engaged in as including "cigar-makers, tailors, bakers, bookbinders, paperhangers, pocketbook makers, gold and silversmiths, mechanical dentists, printers, and compositors." With the rise of other periodicals, it began to decline.

In 1854 Rabbi Isaac Mayer Wise, the founder of Reform Judaism in America, began publishing a weekly in Cincinnati, *The American Israelite*. Probably the most popular of the weeklies, it had a large national circulation for it was geared to the man on the street. Readers relied on it for international and domestic Jewish news, for theological essays, and on doctrinal and liturgical concerns in an era when the course of Reform Judaism was being chartered. *The American Israelite* is still being published in Cincinnati, making it the oldest Jewish periodical in the United States.

The earliest Jewish newspaper to be established in the South was *The Corner Stone*, founded by Solomon Jacobs in New York in 1858 but later moved by him to New Orleans, where it had a brief existence in 1860.

The beginning of Jewish journalistic activity in California can be traced to San Francisco's *Weekly Gleaner*, which began publishing in 1857 and appeared until 1865. It is a frequently consulted chronicle of the post-Gold Rush communities of the time. The first Jewish newspaper to appear in Chicago was the postconfligration latercomer on the American scene, *The Occident* (1873–1896?), which was followed by *The Chicago Israelite* (1886). St. Louis was the sight of the first Jewish newspaper west of the Mississippi with its *Jewish Sentinel* (1868–1869). In Baltimore, Dr. David Einhorn, who attacked slavery most bitterly in his paper, edited *Sinai*, which ran for six years (1856–1862).

Another early example of these types of publications was the New York *Jewish Messenger*, founded in 1857 by the Orthodox rabbi Samuel M. Isaacs. It fought with vigor the new forces of Reform Judaism, which were becoming vocal. It attacked slavery. It thundered against injustice in whatever guise it reared its head. In 1902 it united with *The American Hebrew*, established by a group of five young men in 1879. Traditional in its religious views, it continued publication until 1956, when it combined with *The Jewish Examiner*. It represented, perhaps, the best level to which this class of journals attained.

One of the most long-lived Anglo–Jewish weeklies established in the early years of the twentieth century is *The Jewish Advocate*, founded in Boston in 1903 by Jacob de Haas, a journalist who had been secretary to Theodor Herzl and served as his collaborator in Zionist affairs in Britain. It reflects the affluence and culture of Greater Boston Jewish life, and—the voice of the Jewish establishment—"Americanism, Judaism, Social Justice" continues as its motto today.

The cultural impact of Jewish newspapers was strong. Many of them borrowed material or ideas from Jewish newspapers published in Germany. They were filled with articles on Jewish history, theology, interpretations of the Bible, sermons, and necrologies; the editorial page was often a delight to read. There were serials, novels, and stories to satisfy any taste.

As the earlier periodicals left the field, they called for successors. Various weekly magazines and newspapers were projected from time to time, from humorous illustrated journals to the internationally acclaimed monthly periodical *Commentary*, founded by the American Jewish Committee in 1954 and read by decision makers and the intelligensia. These periodicals added color, picturesqueness, and cultural content to Jewish newspaperdom.

Today there is no shortage of Jewish periodicals in the form of newspapers and magazines serving a broad spectrum of Jews in varying Zionist ideologies, cultural interests, and religious beliefs within the broad spectrum of the organized American Jewish community represented by Orthodox, Conservative, Reform, and Reconstructionist Judaism. The periodicals with the largest circulation are those published by Jewish organizations for their membership as exemplified by *Hadassah Magazine*, reaching over 385,000 readers, almost equalled by the Los Angeles-based Simon Wiesenthal Center's house organ *Response*, with a circulation of 375,500 copies as of 1990.

Some attempts were made to publish Yiddish newspapers in the New World even before the stream of Jewish immigrants began to arrive from Eastern Europe in the 1880s. In 1870, J. K. Buchner founded *The Yiddisher Zeitung* (*The Jewish Times*) in New York, and two years later, Kasriel Sarasohn established *The New Yorker Yiddish Zeitung* (*The New York Jewish Times*). They were both weeklies and suspended publication after a struggle of several months. Sarasohn, however, was to become the pioneer in the field and began publishing the *Yiddishe Gazette* (the *Yiddish Gazette*) in 1874. This had a better reception than his previous undertakings, for by this time the Jewish population had been augmented by a considerable influx of new arrivals. By 1885 Sarasohn felt sufficiently encouraged to launch a Yiddish daily. Thus, the *Yiddish Tageblatt* (*The Yiddish Daily*) was born. It continued for many years to be the outstanding exponent of Orthodox Judaism and the foremost supporter of the Zionist ideal. In 1928 it merged with the *Yiddishe Morgan Zhurnal* (*The Jewish Morning Journal*) and until 1952 was published under that name.

The second Yiddish daily was *Der Taegliche Herald* (*The Daily Herald*, founded in 1891); the third was the *Abenblatt*, the organ of the Jewish labor elements and socialist groups, established in 1894. Out of a division in the ranks of the radicals came a new newspaper, the *Forverts* (Yiddish *Forward*), established in New York City in 1897 as a mouthpiece of the laboring masses. It soon became the largest and most influential newspaper in the Jewish world. The first editor was the Lithuanian-born dynamic Abraham Cahan, who remained at the helm for half a century, guiding the daily's policies, among which Americanism ranked high. He was responsible for one of the most successful human-interest features, "A Bintel Brief" (Bundle of Letters), a column that printed especially interesting letters from Lower East Side readers that described the problems of East European Jewish immigrants and answered them with thoughtful advice.

The *Forverts* today, with its positive position on all Jewish issues and infused with the spice of human interest, remains the voice of Yiddish culture and literature. It also publishes a weekly newspaper in English, launched in 1990, *The Forward*, which retains a prominent writing staff and list of contributors. Its appearance coincided with a surge of Jewish news. Within weeks of the newspaper's launch, Saddam Hussein invaded Kuwait and the politics of the Middle East were changed. Today its circulation is about twenty thousand nationwide, but sixty percent of it is in New York City.

Jacob Saphirstein, Louis E. Miller, Jacob Fishman, and Zvi Hirsch Masliansky were among the noted personalities associated with the launching of other memorable Yiddish dailies, the chain having been extended from Boston, Chicago, Philadelphia, Cleveland, and many other cities.

Yiddish newspapers had performed a vital civic function by interpreting the lofty American ideals and traditions to postwar immigrants and creating a firm bridge of understanding between newcomers and the land of their dreams. Numerous articles had appeared describing various sections and cities, featuring significant periods in American Jewish history, and embodying biographical sketches of refugees who achieved unusual success.

In 1927 the Yiddish dailies attained a peak circulation of 598,347, of which over two hundred thousand represented readers from the *Forvets*. These newspapers served as a powerful media of opinion and literary expression, and they attained a special position as primary sources of Jewish news, derived from all over the world.

A periodical press—weeklies, monthlies, and annuals—also flourished. Practically all of these included literary and cultural material, but some were also politically oriented, pressing upon the public precepts and programs of their ideological factions.

Die Frie Arbeiter Shtimme, founded in 1899, respected the "socialist anarchist" elements, and *Der Yiddisher Kempfer*, established in 1905, was the organ of Labor Zionists. The oldest monthly and one of the best Yiddish periodicals, the *Zukunft* (*Future*), was established in 1892 as the vehicle for serious literary and cultural expression. The character of this journal was molded by the poet Abraham Liessin, who served as editor from 1913 to 1938. Some of the best Yiddish poetry appeared in this magazine, and it still attracts the foremost in current Yiddish literature.

The years after World War I marked the beginning of the decline of the Yiddish press in the United States. The restrictive immigration act of 1924 cut off the flow of Yiddish-speaking immigrants to the United States. Throughout the 1920s and 1930s, falling circulation forced Yiddish dailies to cut back on the size of their staffs and editions.

At the height of the Jewish immigration to the United States, the Yiddish newspapers deemed it of major importance to instruct their readers, to educate them, and to elevate them; hence translations from the best of world literature were printed in serial or abridged form, as were articles on a variety of subjects, among them civic duties. The Yiddish press was enlivened by readers' forums, controversies of a political, social, cultural, and literary nature. The most abstruse philosophical arguments were elucidated, and they sparked an unusual intellectual exuberance among the readers. Indeed, the Yiddish press has been a unique kind of lively journalism.

As early as 1871, *Hatzofeh be-Eretz ha-Chadash* (*The New World Scout*), the first all-Hebrew newspaper in the United States, made its appearance and managed to survive for six years. An eight-page paper, it was edited by Hirsch Bernstein and sold for ten cents a copy. Its first section was made up of editorials and information on Jewish life throughout the world; the second part was devoted to scholarly and literary expression. The latter section demonstrated the editor's determination to help the immigrants in adjusting to their new surroundings.

In the succeeding decades, other Hebrew papers—including Gershon Rosenzweig's *Ha-Ivri* (*The Hebrew*) in New York, W. Schur's *HaPisgah* (*The Summit*) in Chicago, and the short-lived *Ner Harabi* (*Evening Light*), came and went. In 1921 *Hadoar* (*The Post*), edited by M. Lipson, first appeared as a Hebrew daily. Three years later it became a weekly, and the position of its editor was occupied by Menachem Ribalow, an indefatigable worker. Ribalow nurtured *Hadoar* until it became the central organ of American Hebrew writers and soon launched additional literary projects. He made the supplements *Hadoar Lanoar* and *Musaf Lakore Hatzair,* containing suitable reading material for children and youth, regular features of the magazine. Today, *Hadoar,* edited by Shlomo Shamir and Dr. Yael Feldman, published by Histadrut Ivrith of America, an organization that aims to disseminate a knowledge of spoken and written Hebrew in the Diaspora, is the only Hebrew bi-weekly in the world outside of Israel.

Histadrut Ivrith also publishes *Lamishpaha* (*For the Family*), a monthly Hebrew magazine that carries illustrated articles on Zionist and Israeli news, personalities, customs, and holidays, and crossword puzzles, too.

The American Jewish press today has developed an extraordinary influence on its readers in all matters of interest to Jews. These include Jewish affairs, religious developments, Israel's international relations, the

Middle East, world and national affairs as they impact on the Jewish community, communal and organizational matters, and Jewish life in the United States and Canada. It now comprises some 525 newspapers, magazines, journals, and newsletters, written in English, Yiddish, and Hebrew, which serve the informational and educational needs of Jews in the United States and Canada. The combined circulation of these in 1994 has grown to about 4,500,000, an extraordinary rise of over 3,500,000 since 1950. In the past decade, Jewish federations have expanded their presence across the United States, giving rise to many new newspapers. Jewish activists and religious segments have come out with new publications that are eagerly read. Jewish studies programs, which have proliferated on college campuses since the 1960s, when there were only two endowed Jewish chairs in the country—Harry Wolfson's at Harvard and Salo Baron's at Columbia— have also generated fascinating new publications.

THE FIRST AMERICAN ZIONIST

1824

Since the destruction of the Second Temple in Jerusalem in the year 70 C.E., throughout the ages, Jews have always looked in constant hope and prayer for their return to the land of their birth. Modern Zionism was actually begun, and practical work for the reestablishment of the State of Israel as the Jewish national homeland started, when the first Zionist Congress was called by Theodor Herzl in 1897. Though modern Zionism made its appearance on the American scene almost at the beginning of the world movement, the first Zionist endeavor in America dates back many years before. Major Mordecai Manuel Noah—who in 1824 declared, "We will return to Zion as we went forth, bringing back the faith we carried away with us"—is considered the first articulate American Zionist. With that statement he had anticipated by over a century and a half the Zionism of today.

Noah, an ardent and devoted Jew, was a man whose life was dominated by two passions: loyalty to Judaism and patriotism to the young republic. He was born in Philadelphia on July 19, 1785, the son of a Sephardic mother and Manuel Noah, an Ashkenazi Jew who was a soldier in the American Revolutionary War. There is a legend that George Washington attended the wedding of his parents.

When Mordecai was ten, his mother died, and he went to live with his maternal grandfather, Jonas Phillips, a Revolutionary patriot. After working as an apprentice builder and carver, a clerk in the United States Treasury, and a reporter, he moved to Charleston, South Carolina, where he became editor of *The City Gazette* and studied law. This was to be the beginning of a career remarkable for its versatility. Later he edited among other newspapers *The New York Enquirer, The Evening Star,* and *The Union.* He helped James Gordon Bennett establish *The New York World.* Journalism and politics went hand in hand. He entered with zest the rough-and-tumble of local and national politics. He served as high sheriff of New York, Surveyor of the Port, and judge of the Court of Sessions. His speechmaking and journalism must have been valued in Washington.

In 1813 President James Madison appointed Noah the American consul to Tunis in North Africa, thus making him the first Jew in America to hold a high diplomatic post in the foreign service of his country. President Madison instructed Noah to ransom a group of American sailors held captive by Barbary pirates. It was a difficult task requiring considerable adroitness; but he spent more than his allotment for the purpose, and his commission was revoked, the letter of recall affirming that his religion was deemed to disqualify from the post. Apparently, some of his enemies had been at work in Washington. The bey knew nothing of Noah's religion; besides, in those days the African Moslem states were accustomed to have Jewish agents represent them at home and in Europe. In time, however, Noah got a clean bill of health in the conduct of his mission, and the sums he advanced in performing it were reimbursed.

One of Noah's reasons for going to Tunis, in fact, was to inform himself of the situation of the Jews in Barbary. He felt sorrow over the plight of the homeless Jews in the Orient and Europe, and it was while he was in Tunis that he began to dream of a land for them. He wanted to see Palestine returned to them, but knowing how difficult it would be to establish such a concession from the Turkish rulers, his thoughts turned to the great open spaces of America. It was after his return from Algiers that he sought to found an island of asylum for the oppressed Jews of the world.

In 1824 the New York State Legislature decided to sell a tract of land on Grand Island in the Niagara River, northwest of Buffalo. Stirred to action, Noah organized a syndicate and persuaded a land agent, Samuel Leggett, to put up $17,000 on his behalf. With this sum, Noah was able to buy 2,555 acres of the land as a site for Jewish settlement. It was to represent a temporary haven for all Jews before their eventual return to the Holy Land.

Giving himself the title of "Governor and Judge of Israel," Noah issued a proclamation to Jews all over the world to come and settle in the new colony. He commanded that a census be taken of Jews throughout the world; he forbade polygamy and levied taxes on all Jews to finance his project. This fantastic document concluded with a plan for organizing the mass migration of Jews to Grand Island. Because his name was Noah, he called the new settlement Ararat, where the ark of the biblical Noah found a resting place after the great deluge. The settlement was to be under the protection of the United States.

In September 1825 (just one month before the opening of the Erie Canal) Noah set out for upstate New York to arrange dedication ceremonies. Grand Island itself was an inaccessible wasteland. Accordingly, Noah planned the event in nearby Buffalo, where he rented the city's largest public facility, St. Paul's Episcopal Church. A cornerstone had been ordered, which bore the impressive inscription in Hebrew:

> Shema Yisroel Adonai Elohenu Adonai Echod
> ARARAT
> A City of Refuge for the Jews
> Founded by Mordecai Manuel Noah
> In the month of Tishri (September) 1825
> & in the Fiftieth Year of American Independence

Noah's Ararat was not intended to supplant the Zion of Holy Writ; it would be a temporary haven for the persecuted Jews until the fulfillment of biblical prophecy. In some mysterious way the fifty square miles of Grand Island would sustain millions until the sounding of the great Shofar of Redemption.

On September 15, 1825, imposing dedication ceremonies of Ararat took place in Buffalo. At the celebration, a cannon boomed and there was a magnificent procession of city officials, army officers, Masonic dignitaries, clergymen, Knights Templar, and Indians (Noah was one of those who believed that the American aborigines were descended from the Ten Lost Tribes of Israel). Noah, the central figure in this procession, clothed in austere black draped with a mantle of crimson silk and white ermine, repeated his fantastic proclamation. As "Governor and Judge of Israel," Major Noah thus marched into Jewish history.

The dedication in Buffalo was the beginning and end of the enterprise. Grand Island did not serve as the abode of even one Jew for a single day. Not a single building was erected. Eventually the cornerstone commemorating the venture found its way into the Buffalo Historical Society as a tourist attraction.

Noah did not despair when the island of his dreams remained a wilderness. Twenty years later we find him writing a pamphlet in which he advocated the restoration of Zion by Jewish self-effort, demanded support of the Christian world for Jewish resettlement in Palestine, and suggested that the land be acquired through purchase. Little did he realize that three quarters of a century thereafter, another dreamer and man of action, Theodor Herzl, would call upon the Jews of the world to follow him and that his dream would become the State of Israel.

In a long letter to the editor of *The Occident and Jewish Advocate,* Noah addressed himself to Isaac Leeser's criticism of his plan, saying: "We in this generation may be compelled to commence the good work which succeeding generations will accomplish."

Noah continued to serve many Jewish and communal causes. In 1840 he delivered the principal address at a meeting at Congregation B'nai Jeshurun in New York, protesting the Damascus Affair. He supported the idea of a Jewish hospital, and a year after his death such an institution was founded by Sampson Simson, which ultimately became Mount Sinai Medical Center. He was a founder of New York University.

His theatrical work was popular. The American scene and American history remained among his favorite subjects. He wrote *Fortress of Sorrento* (1808), *She Would Be a Soldier* (1819), and *The Siege of Tripoli* (1820), which was produced many times under many different names. Students at Columbia University staged his play *Marion, or The Hero of Lake George* in 1932, one hundred fifty years after it was written.

When Mordecai Manuel Noah died in 1851, crowds lined the route of his funeral cortege, which is said to have been one of the most elaborate in the history of the city. One of the last Jews to be buried within the limits of the Old City of New York, his last resting place is in Congregation Shearith Israel's Second Cemetery, *Beth Chaim Sheni* on West 21st Street.

Soon after his death conflicting opinions about his character, especially in regard to his colonization project, appeared in the press. While Noah's scheme earned him ridicule and condemnation, the historian Max Raisin wrote: "He was the first real Zionist whose only fault had been that he was far ahead of his times."

THE FIRST REFORM CONGREGATION IN AMERICA

1824

Strictly Orthodox in their religion, the Spanish and Portuguese Jews established six congregations upon their arrival in America and planted the seeds of Judaism in this country. The early German immigration brought new blood into the Jewish communities and also the seeds of the Reform movement, which had begun in Germany in the early years of the nineteenth century.

At that time, the old Sephardic congregation of Charleston, South Carolina—Kahal Kodesh Beth Elohim—was the largest and richest in the United States. Although it had been founded by Sephardim in 1750 and followed their ritual as well as the custom of complete religious domination over the members of the congregation, it included a large portion of German Jews.

In 1824 a group of forty-seven members petitioned the trustees for reforms in the services and ritual to effect "a more wholesome and more respectable state of discipline." First they asked:

> With regard to such parts of the service as it is desired should undergo this change, your memorialists would strenuously recommend that the most solemn portions be retained and everything superfluous excluded; and that the principle parts, and if it is possible all that is read in HEBREW should also be read in ENGLISH, so as to enable every member of the congregation fully to understand every part of the service.

Second, they asked that Sabbath services be abridged; Third, that the custom of offerings at the altar, then still recited in the Spanish language, be abolished, that there be an English sermon weekly; and finally that the synagogue rely wholly on membership subscriptions.

When the trustees rejected the petition and changes in the services were refused, a new group organized under the name of the Reform Society of Israelites, led by Isaac Harby, a Charleston-born schoolmaster and well-known journalist of his day. The society lasted eight years. The congregation had no rabbi, and its services were conducted and the sermons preached by laymen. Abraham Moise, David Nunes Carvalho, and Isaac Harby prepared and printed a prayerbook in which there appeared many Christian hymns. They voiced their own Articles of Faith without presuming "to restrict the faith or conscience of any man."

By its first anniversary the congregation had fifty members. At a meeting in 1833, the society decided to abandon its fight for reform and passed out of existence.

By 1840 twenty-two of the original seceders rejoined Beth Elohim, where the Reverend Gustav Poznanski was the preacher and *hazzan*. He was a Polish Jew who had lived some years in Hamburg and had known the Hamburg Temple, the cradle of Reform Judaism in Germany. In 1840 the cornerstone of a new synagogue was laid to replace the old, which had been destroyed in the fire of 1838. Before the new building was completed, thirty-eight members petitioned the trustees "that an organ be erected in the synagogue to assist in the vocal parts of the service."

In his dedication sermon not only did the Reverend Poznanski approve of the use of an organ but declared the observance of the second day of the festivals to be unnecessary and recommended its abandonment. Thus Reform Judaism took root in the United States.

Under the leadership of Rabbi Isaac Mayer Wise, who had come to America from Bohemia in 1846, the practice and philosophy of Reform Judaism were subject to further modernization. He introduced confirmation to replace Bar Mitzvah, choral singing, and the seating of men and women together in the pews during the services. These and other changes in Jewish ceremony and the introduction of English in religious services were accompanied by strife and dissensions between its Orthodox and Reform members.

The Union of American Hebrew Congregations (1872); the Hebrew Union College (1875), the first successful rabbinical school in America; and the Central Conference of American Rabbis (1898) were all offspring of the work of Rabbi Wise.

As time went on Rabbi Wise inclined toward more radical changes in Judaism. The policies of the institutions founded by him were set forth in a meeting of Reform rabbis that took place in Pittsburgh in 1885, and the principles there adopted became known as the Pittsburgh Platform. It emphasized the prophetic ideals of the Bible as against the regulations of the Talmud. It declared some of the Mosaic legislation no longer applicable, among these the dietary laws. It rejected a return to Palestine. It denied the expectations of a Messiah and substituted the hope for a messianic era—that is, an era of peace and perfection that would come to the world through cultural and scientific progress. It argued that Jews were a group with a mission of spreading godliness among the peoples of the world.

A revision of these principles took place in 1937 at the meeting of the Central Conference of American Rabbis in Columbus, Ohio. The conference defined Judaism as the "historical religious experience of the Jewish people," thereby including not only the Jewish belief and ethic but also granting a place to tradition and ceremonialism. It expressed a fervent hope for the establishment of a Jewish homeland as the center of spiritual life.

Were he alive today, Rabbi Isaac Mayer Wise would hardly recognize the Reform movement he led over a century ago. Practices once considered anathema to his movement—wearing a *tallit* (prayer shawl) and *kipah* (skullcap), celebrating the second day of Rosh Hashanah, and chanting the reader's *Kaddish* (memorial prayer for the dead) and the *Avot* prayers during worship service—are now regularly used in a majority of Reform congregations.

Not long ago, a typical Reform service included a paid choir singing the few Hebrew parts of the service and the congregants reading mostly English-language liturgy. Today, there are fewer professional choirs and more Hebrew in the services and more congregational singing and chanting.

Other elements in the services that were once standard in Reform temples, such as the use of accompanying organs, have become less common.

To the Orthodox Jew, Reform Judaism was not only distasteful but shocking. Convinced that it would spell the downfall of Judaism, the Orthodox leaders, all East European Jews, carried on a bitter and relentless fight against Reform.

As the conflict sharpened, it was inevitable that a third group should develop along the middle of the road. These were Jews who believed that Reform was right in some respects and Orthodoxy in others. The Conservatives believed that some changes ought to be made, but that beyond these Judaism required no further modification.

If the Pittsburgh Platform served as a rallying point for Reformers, it also solidified the opposition to Reform and thus destroyed whatever hope there had been of unifying American Judaism. Dr. Sabato Morais, an Italian Jew who arrived in Philadelphia in 1851 as successor to Isaac Leeser as minister of Congregation Mikveh Israel in Philadelphia, had given his support to the Hebrew Union College. But when it became clear that radicalism rather than moderation would be in control, Morais began to plan a new institution for the training of rabbis. His plans resulted in the establishment of the Jewish Theological Seminary of America. The New School opened in New York in 1886, with Sabato Morais as president.

Conservative Judaism received a new and powerful stimulus when the famous Dr. Solomon Schechter arrived from England in 1902. He held the position of Reader in Rabbinics at Cambridge University and had become internationally famous when he discovered the original Hebrew text of the Book of Ecclesiasticus, known to the world until then only through a Greek translation. Triumphantly, he brought his discovery to the world. This striking personality, revered by all, became president of the Seminary in 1902.

Though a staunch traditionalist, Schechter admitted the possibility of change. However, he felt that changes should not be introduced arbitrarily. In the era of Solomon Schechter, Conservative Judaism was an ideological reaction to Reform. It was a reaffirmation of the authority of *halakah* (Jewish law), as a living, albeit changing, system of law, custom, and tradition. It emphasized the total historical religious experience of the Jewish people. His teaching was a middle-of-the-road doctrine, holding to the old but trying to reinterpret it for the present day.

To carry out his plans, Dr. Schechter brought to the Seminary a faculty unsurpassed by other institutions of higher Jewish learning. Chief among them was Louis Ginzberg, a Talmudic scholar; joined by Alexander Marx, historian and bibliographer, who made the Seminary Library the greatest repository of Jewish books and manuscripts ever assembled; and Israel Friedlander, professor of Bible.

In 1913, Dr. Schechter founded the United Synagogue, the movement's federation of congregations, which he characterized as "my proudest achievement." During the next two decades, Conservative Judaism grew as an increasing number of Jews and their children spoke English instead of Yiddish, built synagogues instead of praying in homes or rented facilities, or otherwise acculturated. Seminary-trained rabbis and educators helped immigrant Jews bridge the American and Jewish worlds. They taught traditional values in an accessible way to men and women living in a new world in which Jewish affiliation and observance were freely chosen.

Dr. Schechter died in 1915 just as the influence of his vibrant personality began to bear fruit. The Jewish Theological Seminary, however, continued to grow in influence under his successor, Dr. Cyrus Adler, particularly during the next period, when the American-born children of the East European Jews attained maturity.

The creedal differences between the Conservative and the Reform became more explicit. This found expression in the Constitution of the United Synagogue of America. Among the aims adopted by the new group were:

> To assert and establish loyalty to the Torah and its historical exposition.
> To further the observance of the Sabbath and dietary laws;
> To preserve in the service the reference to Israel's past and hopes for Israel's restoration.
> To maintain the traditional character of the liturgy with Hebrew as the language of prayer.

The group to which the influx from Eastern Europe added most strength was, of course, the Orthodox. Indeed, the leaders of the Seminary looked to the dramatically emerging East European Jewish community in America as a source of students and congregations for its graduates.

Three major types of religious thought emerged from the debates at the end of the previous century: Orthodox, Conservative, and Reform. Each type developed institutions for the furtherance of its point of view. The Hebrew Union College, which merged with the Jewish Institute of Religion founded by Rabbi Stephen S. Wise in 1922 to provide training in all branches of Judaism, continued through its highly gifted alumni to exert unusual influence on American Jewish life. Conservative Judaism began to make progress through alumni of the Jewish Theological Seminary of America. Orthodox Judaism established many schools of higher Jewish learning and synagogues.

In 1915, the Rabbi Isaac Elchanan Theological Seminary, founded in 1896, as a school for the training of Orthodox rabbis, was reorganized under the imaginative leadership of Dr. Bernard Revel. In 1928 he added a College of Arts and Sciences to the institution, which, in 1945, under the leadership of his successor, Dr. Samuel Belkin, was raised to the status of a university and became the key institution of Orthodoxy in America. Shortly after the middle of the century, it embarked on the establishment of the Albert Einstein College of Medicine and Medical Center. Thus had the Orthodox wing achieved a degree of organization comparable to that of the other two trends, embracing a union of congregations, a rabbinical body, and schools for the training of teachers, and, in addition, a medical school.

Other theological schools of Orthodox orientation were established during the same period. The Hebrew Theological College was founded in Chicago in 1922 by Rabbis Saul Silber, Ephraim Epstein, Abraham Cardon, and Chaim Z. Rubinstein. It was an outgrowth of the Hebrew high school, Yeshiva Eitz Chaim, organized in 1899 and was the first Orthodox rabbinical institution in America to require courses in Bible, Jewish philosophy, and history in addition to Talmud and Codes.

Many leaders of American Orthodox Jewry are also provided by the Ner Israel Rabbinical College of Baltimore (founded in 1933), which in 1953 was given the authority to grant degrees of Master and Doctor of Talmudic Law by the Maryland State Board of Education. This was the first time in Jewish history, and indeed in the history of education, that a doctorate has been authorized purely for the study of Talmud.

A fourth group—and newest among American Jewry—is that of the Reconstructionists who are dedicated to the advancement of Judaism as a religious civilization. Its leader and founder was Dr. Mordecai Kaplan, who for many years headed the Teachers' Institute of the Jewish Theological Seminary of America. In 1922, Dr. Kaplan and his supporters established the Society for the Advancement of Judaism at whose building in New York City Reconstructionist services are held. To further the dissemination of Reconstructionism, *The Reconstructionist* journal was founded in 1934 and the Reconstructionist Foundation formed in 1940. American Jewry has witnessed a prolific production of religious literature by Dr. Kaplan and his associates, Ira Eisenstein, Eugene Kohn, Milton Steinberg, and Jack J. Cohen, among others. Today there are seventy-eight Reconstructionist synagogues throughout the United States affiliated with the movement, more than triple the number of member congregations it had in 1980.

Within the last decade, Reform congregations have increased from 757 to 858, Conservative to 800, and the number of Orthodox congregations has reached 3,000. Many of these congregations themselves have enjoyed an explosive growth in membership.

THE FIRST JEWISH POETESS

1830

During the greater part of Rebecca Gratz's life there was a younger woman living in Charleston, South Carolina, who is the earliest-known Jewish poetess. She was Penina Moise, the daughter of Sarah and Abraham Moise, French Jews who had emigrated from Alsace-Lorraine to the West Indies and then, in 1791, to Charleston, the cultured center of the South in the latter years of the eighteenth and early years of the nineteenth centuries.

Penina Moise was born in Charleston in 1797. When she was twelve years old her father died and left to her the care and support of a paralyzed mother and large family. She had to work hard to battle against poverty but still managed to study, read, and write. The extent of her self-education was phenomenal. A legend has it that Penina would even study by moonlight.

While still in her teens, Penina began to write verses. In 1830 her poems and prose started appearing in print. She was a contributor to *The Charleston Courier, The Boston Daily Times, The New Orleans Commercial Times, The Washington Union, Godey's Lady's Book,* and *The Charleston Book,* as well as other widely read publications of the day.

In 1853 some of Penina's verses were collected and published in a volume entitled *Fancy's Sketch Book.* She became known the country over, and people looked forward to her poems that now appeared as often as three times a week. Some of the most cultured leaders of Charleston offered her their friendship and invited her to their literary teas. Later her own home became the center of Charleston writers and scholars.

Although her work was sometimes light and humerous, her best efforts were those when, as an aroused Jewess, she championed the cause of her people. Her poetry on these themes appeared in such publications as *The Occident and American Jewish Advocate,* a periodical founded by Isaac Leeser. "The Rejection of the Jew Bill in the House of Lords," "The Jews of Damascus," and "To Sir Moses Montefiore" were among her most popular works.

Her most important literary contribution consisted of a volume of 190 Hebrew hymns composed in the declining half of her lengthy life with its full measure of physical and mental pain. To this task, Penina Moise brought spiritual strivings and pious resignation, a pure heart and contrite spirit together with a passionate love for Judaism. She wrote the hymns for the use of Congregation Beth Elohim of Charleston when the Reform service was introduced. The collection was reprinted a number of times, and now there are more of her hymns in the hymnal of the Union of American Hebrew Congregations (the Reform group) than that of any other writer. They are still recited in Charleston, in other American cities, and even abroad, wherever English is spoken.

We can find space here for a few random selections. She paraphrases Psalm XXXVIII in the following verses:

Rebuke me not nor chasten me,
    In thy displeasure, Lord!
But let a frail transgressor be
    To virtue's path restored.
My heart like grass is withered up,
    Sorrow my strength destroys;
Sin's bitter drop within my cup,
    Life's sparkling draught alloys.

And she concludes:

For with unbroken trust will I
    In Thee, my God! confide,
Who deigns the meek to dignify,
    The arrogant to chide.

She piously meditates on the Jewish New Year:

Into the tomb of ages past
    Another year has now been cast;
Shall time, unheeded, take its flight,
Nor leave one ray of mortal light,
That on man's pilgrimage may shine,
And lead his soul to spheres divine?

Of "Man's Dignity" she echoes the following:

O God! within Thy temple walls,
    Light my spirit seems, and free,
Regardless of whose worldly calls,
    That withdraw it oft from Thee,
Faith to the proudest whispers: Here
    Riches Are but righteous deeds,
And he who dries a human tear,
    Ne'er to mercy vainly pleads.

Penina Moise was also a teacher. She taught at Kahal Kodesh Beth Elohim's Sunday School, which was organized only a few months after Rebecca Gratz founded the first Jewish Sunday School in Philadelphia. With her widowed sister she also conducted an exceptionally fine girl's school for many years, although she became totally blind during the last twenty-five years of her life.

She died on September 18, 1880, at the age of eight-three. Her last words to her family were: "Lay no flowers on my grave. They are for those who have lived in the sun, and I have always lived in the shadow."

In 1911 the Charleston Section of the Council of Jewish Women published a selection of Penina Moise's poetry and some of her prose.

THE FIRST JEWISH DENTIST

1832

In colonial America, dentistry received considerable impetus in the arrival from England and France of practitioners familiar with European techniques. Two such immigrants from France were Le Mayeur and Gardette, who began practicing in Philadelphia in 1783 and became dentists to George Washington.

Dentistry as an organized profession is one of the youngest in this country. Beginning with Dr. Benjamin Adolph Rodriguez, of Charleston, South Carolina, we find representatives of the Jewish faith among the leaders throughout its history. A highly intellectual man and a devoted student of the arts and sciences, Dr. Rodriguez lived and worked during the period of the birth and growth of the dental profession.

After having graduated from Charleston High School, Rodriguez became apprenticed to Dr. V. Starr Brewster, a prominent dentist who attended the most cultured residents of the city. In 1832, upon finishing his apprenticeship, young Rodriguez received a diploma from his preceptor that qualified him to perform any operation pertaining to dentistry. Fame and fortune awaited him when Dr. Brewster departed the United States for Paris and left his extensive and prosperous practice to the young dentist.

Rodriguez's desire for dental knowledge was so great that after succeeding to Dr. Brewster's practice, he completed the dental course in the Medical College of South Carolina, being graduated on March 3, 1834.

Throughout his career, Dr. Rodriguez was often called on as a lecturer before important dental societies. His work was quoted in standard textbooks on dental surgery, and he was an early contributor to the *American Journal of Dental Science,* very probably the world's first periodical in the discipline of dentistry.

As a dental practitioner, he directed his attention largely to the surgical phase of dental practice and to the correction of irregularities of the teeth and jaw. In 1850 he invented one of the first cleft palate obturators (a prosthetic device that closes an opening). He also devised many outstanding orthodontic appliances both for natural dentures and abnormalities resulting from surgical interference. For his sincere interest and effort in advancing dental science, the Baltimore College of Dental Surgery conferred on him the honorary degree of Doctor of Dental Surgery in 1850.

Thus from the start Jews have contributed to the dental profession and to the public dental health of America. They may be credited with a preponderant share of dental progress not only as specialists, educators, and dental scientists but also in their organization for the advancement of the dental profession, in their development and perfection of dental appliances, in their contributions to dental literature, and in obtaining recognition for the dental profession as an ally of the medical profession. Old and young alike have benefited from the pioneering labors of the Jewish practitioner in the dental field.

THE FIRST JEWISH WOMAN REFORMER

1837

At the time when women in America were rebelling at their lack of independence in a changing world, Ernestine Rose, the daughter of an Orthodox rabbi, circulated the first petition for the property rights of women. As early as 1837 she appeared before the New York State legislature to fight for the passage of the liberalizing statute, a fight she continued for over nine years.

A practical idealist, constructive and keen minded, her development and career were extraordinary. She was born in 1810 as Sismondi Potowski in Piotrkow, a Polish ghetto, and died in London in 1892. As a child she studied the Bible under her father's tutelage and was observant in her practice of Judaism. But at fourteen she shocked the Orthodox community of her native village by accumulating a great many doubts. Moreover, she boldly advocated equal rights for women in all spheres of communal activity.

When Sismondi Potowski was seventeen, upon her mother's death, she left home to become an apostle of humanitarianism. She traveled far and wide at her own expense and held forth on a broad range of reform topics. Alone she visited Poland, Russia, Germany, Holland, Belgium, France, and England.

The young girl appears to have had little difficulty in associating with leaders, thinkers, and celebrities. In Berlin, Sismondi conferred with the Prussian king and castigated him for restrictions against Jews. Frederick III was impressed, and she was permitted to stay as long as she liked. In Paris, she witnessed the Revolution of 1830. In the Hague, the case of a sailor's wife unjustly accused moved her girlish compassion.

Hitherto a rebel merely against social inequalities or religious tyranny, she acquired a more positive philosophy of government and society in 1832 upon coming under the influence of Robert Owen, the founder of Utopian Socialism in England. About this time Sismondi Potowski met William H. Rose, an abolitionist and silversmith, who was a non-Jewish Owenite. She warmly espoused his social philosophy. They married and left England for the United States. Soon the country was to hear of Ernestine Rose as a militant reformer.

Traveling throughout the eastern states, Ernestine Rose became involved with the struggle for human rights. Speaking with a slight and attractive foreign accent, using animated, fluent, direct, and impressive language, she advocated free public schools and called attention to the evils of the social system, the wickedness of black slavery in the South, injustices to women in the North, and the shortcomings of human character. Wherever she went she lifted the hearts of her listeners and bound them together in the magical bond of understanding. At conventions she took a leading part as organizer, orator, parliamentarian, and politician. She campaigned especially for the passage of a married woman's property rights bill in New York State, which finally passed the legislature in 1848.

In 1850 she was elected delegate to the first National Woman's Rights Convention in Worcester, Massachusetts. Here she met and won the respect and admiration of such liberal leaders as Lucretia Mott, William Lloyd Garrison, Julia Ward Howe, and Wendell Phillips, all advocates of women's rights, abolitionism, and religious liberty. She continued as a delegate to all the Women's Rights Conventions for thirty years until her health failed.

During the Civil War she joined with Elizabeth Stanton and Susan B. Anthony, Mrs. Chalkstone—a Jewess—and other anti-slavery crusaders to form the Women's National Loyal League and was active in collecting signatures to petition President Lincoln to issue the Emancipation Proclamation.

When Susan B. Anthony felt the time had come to storm the Capitol, "she gathered up Ernestine Rose and went to Washington."

Her coworkers thought Ernestine beautiful. Her portrait shows her to be rather plain looking with large eyes, a wide mouth, and rows of little sausage curls framing her face. But the impression the photograph conveys is a person of tremendous discipline and vitality.

She was the first to begin woman's suffrage agitation in the West and was largely responsible for the adoption of woman's suffrage by the state of Wyoming in 1869. However, she did not live long enough to see the fruits of her labors that was finally enacted into the Nineteenth Amendment in 1920, granting full equality for woman for the first time in American history.

Ernestine Rose seemed to attach no particular significance to her Jewish background until 1863, when she engaged in a published debate with Horace Seaver, the abolitionist editor of *The Boston Investigator,* whom she accused of being an anti-Semite.

It is not known to what extent Ernestine succeeded in freeing the editor from his false and erroneous notations about Jews, but in the course of her attempt to do so, the readers of *The Boston Investigator* certainly got an education about Jews and Jewish history from one who knew her subject well.

She died in 1892 after returning to England, having devoted practically her whole lifetime fighting injustice on many fronts. One paper wrote about her: "Ernestine Rose has accomplished for the elevation of her sex and bettering of social conditions a work which can be ascribed to few women of our times. Battling black slavery in the South and feminine subjugation in the North, she struggled against overwhelming odds to make her adopted land move towards fulfilling its promise of liberty and justice for all."

The Judah L. Magnes Museum in Berkeley, California named Ernestine Rose as its 1994 Jewish-American Hall of Fame honoree and issued a number of medals bearing her likeness.

THE FIRST PROTEST MEETING HELD BY AMERICAN JEWRY

1840

From the beginning, America has offered a chance for survival and a haven of refuge for the many sections of Jewry who have faced extinction. Throughout its development, this great democracy has stood for Jews, protecting their rights at home and abroad and taking issue with other governments when they turned to discrimination and persecution.

In 1840 word came to America that in far off Damascus thirteen Jews had been imprisoned and tortured on the charge of ritual murder, the myth that has often plagued innocent Jews. The disappearance on February 5 of that year of the Capuchin monk Tomasco and his Damascus servant was picked up by the enemies of the Jews as a means of pressing the ritual murder lie against them. The French were then the protectors of the Roman Catholics in the East, and French officials aimed in every way possible to strengthen their government's position in the Orient. Evidence to prove that a Turkish mule driver had threatened the monk's life was suppressed. A young Jew who ventured information that would lead to the discovery of the guilty party was beaten to death. The aged Joseph

Laniado died as a result of tortures by the inquisitors. Moses Abulafia embraced Islam to escape pain and indignities.

The civilized world was aroused. Protest meetings of Christians as well as Jews were held during July and August of 1840 in London and Manchester, England. For the first time American Jews made an appeal to the United States Government to help their unfortunate compatriots abroad. This set a historic precedent. A meeting was held in New York, and a letter was sent to President Martin Van Buren. The secretary of state soon informed the Jewish community that five days before the arrival of their letter, the government had already interposed on behalf of the Jews of Damascus. The expressions of sympathy on the part of the English-speaking countries led to the honorable release of the innocent victims, following a mission to Syria by leading European Jews headed by Sir Moses Montefiore, the British philanthropist who devoted most of his life and millions to assisting his fellow Jews everywhere.

A second series of incidents arose when in 1850 a treaty was drawn up between the United States and the Swiss Republic with a clause guaranteeing only to Christians certain rights and privileges. The Senate refused to ratify the treaty. The clauses were amended and the treaty ratified, although some of the discriminatory sting still remained. Later, an American Jew was ordered expelled from Switzerland. Protest meetings were held and letters sent to Washington. Diplomatic conferences followed. Finally the Swiss Constitution was amended in 1874, but the crowning event came in Lincoln's administration, when he appointed a Jew, Mr. Bernays, consul to Zurich.

In the decade of the Russian pogroms in the early years of this century, a petition was submitted to the czar by President Theodore Roosevelt against the persecutions in Kishinev and elsewhere in Russia's Pale of Settlement. A similar protest submitted by the American government to Romania in 1802, together with the efforts of Jews in America and Europe, eventually led to the action of the Congress of Berlin, which in 1878 granted Romania the status of a sovereign state upon the express condition that the Jews be given full religious and political rights.

It was not until 1906 that an organization—the American Jewish Committee, planned from the beginning as a national body—was formed to concern itself with safeguarding the civil and religious rights of Jews in this country and abroad. Using their prestige and wealth to influence government officials—the president, secretary of state, and others—they sought to bring the growing power of American policy to persuade the czar's government to desist in its persecution of Jews. The committee did succeed in getting President Taft to abrogate a treaty with Russia. Originally an elitist organization of fifty members from around the country, the committee often alerted the American public to an awareness of Jewish rights.

During World War I, the American Jewish Congress emerged, at first for the purpose of securing rights for Jews in the peace treaty that would end the war but later as a voice for the Jewish masses. As the committee and congress evolved, each began developing its own viewpoint, symptomatic of its leadership. The American Jewish Committee, long led by Louis Marshall, preferred to work somewhat quietly behind the scenes, educating people in power, applying funds for public education. The American Jewish Congress, eventually led by Rabbi Stephen S. Wise, one of the key leaders of American Jewry for a period of fifty years, preferred the open challenge of court cases to rectify wrongs.

In 1914 the American Jewish Committee, in cooperation with other Jewish organizations, helped to organize the American Jewish Joint Distribution Committee for Jewish overseas relief. After the First World War it assisted in securing the insertion of clauses guaranteeing the rights of minorities in the treaties establishing the new states of Eastern and Central Europe.

Before and during the Hitler regime, the American Jewish Committee had made studies of the growth and nature of anti-Semitism, and through its publications and representations to the United States Government alerted the public to the German outrages against the Jews.

After World War II, the American Jewish Committee became heavily involved in intergroup-relations work. Active in the movement for civil rights, the agency also developed programming in Jewish-Christian relations and interethnic understanding.

THE FIRST SPOKESMAN OF AMERICAN JEWRY

1841

"Practically every form of Jewish activity which supports American Jewish life today," wrote historian and Reform Rabbi Bertram Wallace Korn, "was established or envisaged by one man—Isaac Leeser" and "almost every kind of publication which is essential to Jewish survival was written, translated, or fostered by him."

It is no exaggeration to call the antebellum Civil War period in American Jewish history "the Age of Isaac Leeser." Included among his "firsts" were the first volumes of sermons delivered and published by an American Jewish religious leader (1837–1868); the first complete American translation of the Sephardic prayerbook (1837); the first Hebrew primer for children (1838); the first successful American Jewish newspaper—the *Occident and American Jewish Advocate* (1834–1869); the first American Jewish publication society (1845); the first complete English translation of the

Ashkenazic prayerbook (1848); the first Hebrew high school (1849); the first English translation of the entire Bible by an American Jew (1853); and the founding of the first American Jewish theological seminary—the short-lived Maimonides College (1867).

Spokesman, editor, rabbi, orator, teacher, and educator, Isaac Leeser was the first to attain large-scale leadership in American Jewry.

Isaac Leeser was born in Westphalia, Germany (then Prussia), in 1806. After graduating from a German gymnasium and completing several tractates of the Talmud with Rabbi Benjamin Cohen and then with Rabbi Abrahm Sutro, eighteen-year-old Isaac crossed the ocean to accept a job in his uncle's store in Richmond, Virginia. Modest and humble, he found ample recreation in voracious reading during the spare time that he could snatch from serving as an assistant to the reverend of a small Richmond synagogue. The calm of his studious life was broken by one of those slanderous attacks that come periodically upon Jews and Judaism. In 1828 a New York newspaper reprinted a series of articles that appeared in the *London Quarterly Review,* defaming the character and faith of Israel. The obscure young store clerk came to the defense in the *Richmond Whig,* with an answer of six essays that attracted wide attention. The trustees of Philadelphia's Mikveh Israel Congregation, in need of a *hazzan,* immediately offered the post to the twenty-two-year-old newcomer, hardly yet at home in the English language.

Isaac Leeser was never ordained for the rabbinate, yet he exercised rabbinic functions with high distinction. His fame spread far beyond the Philadelphia congregation. His advice was sought and recommendations accepted by old communities on the Atlantic seaboard and new congregations springing up as far as the Pacific coast. He traveled far and wide, enthralling audiences with his learning and eloquence. Until the Reform movement led by Wise, Einhorn, and Lilienthal got under way, Isaac Leeser remained the unofficial spokesman of all American Jewry.

One of the most important of his many accomplishments was the founding of the *Occident and American Jewish Advocate.* The leading Jewish writers contributed to this paper, which, until Rabbi Isaac Mayer Wise established the *American Israelite,* was the only widely read Jewish newspaper published in the United States. Scanning through this journal today is like reviewing the record of American Jews through twenty-five of the most formative years of our history.

Isaac Leeser was a tireless writer. Although he was the greatest Jewish scholar in America at this period, he did not feel it beneath his dignity to prepare a very simple textbook for young children, which he dedicated to Rebecca Gratz, the founder and first superintendant of the first Jewish Sunday school in Philadelphia. He prepared a Sephardic prayerbook and made many translations from the Hebrew. Perhaps his greatest service to our people was his translation of the Bible from Hebrew into English.

Up to that time Jews without sufficient Hebrew knowledge to read the original Hebrew scriptures were forced to depend on the King James version. This translation by a group of English biblical scholars had always been considered a literary masterpiece. But few Jews found pleasure in reading it as the Christian translators scattered frequent references to the New Testament through their version of the Old Testament. Isaac Leeser's translation was not only acceptable to Jewish scholars, it was so readable that it became the standard translation among Jewish readers for more than fifty years. Finally it was replaced by a translation that was the work of a commission of Orthodox, Conservative, and Reform Jewish scholars.

The Jewish community of Leeser's day hardly numbered one hundred thousand souls. Yet, he anticipated the needs of a century later, when the population would exceed five million. Imaginative intuition prompted him to pioneer in every field of Jewish endeavor. He called attention to flagrant abuses in dispensing charity. His ideas as to overall communal responsibility in collecting and disbursing funds by a central agency gave rise to the United Hebrew Charities of Philadelphia. Here we have the earliest stages of federations that would later raise gigantic sums for local, national, and overseas relief. He urged agricultural settlements that would place Jewish farmers on American soil.

Instinctively Leeser sensed the need of unity for American Jews. Disturbing news from abroad pointed to the necessity for organized effort. The recurrence in 1840 of the medieval blood libel in Damascus, for the first time in a Moslem land, was followed by discrimination against American citizens traveling to Switzerland. In 1841 he made an unsuccessful attempt to organize the Jewish community. The Board of Delegates of American Israelites, largely due to the labors of Isaac Leeser, functioned from 1859 to 1878 as a union of Jewish congregations. By 1861 the number of its affiliated congregations was twenty-four. By 1868 it would reach sixty-eight. Forerunner of both the American Jewish Committee and the American Jewish Congress of the following century, it remained the only authentic voice for Jews in the United States until absorbed by the Commission on Social Action of the Union of American Hebrew Congregations.

Although today Isaac Leeser is regarded as the champion and preserver of Orthodox Judaism and the enemy of the Reformers, he himself objected to labels and desired to serve a united Jewry. Once he said, "For our part, strange as it may seem, we belong to no party. We commenced life with certain convictions and have not swerved from them. If you wish to call this Orthodoxy, you may do so."

Such Herculean tasks were too onerous for the frail and lonely scholar, the pockmarked bachelor whose only offspring were the institutions he created. He broke down and died in his sixty-second year, in 1868, and left no successor behind. In the year after his death, the *Occident and American Jewish Advocate* ceased publication. The Maimonides College closed after graduating four students. The Board of Delegates of American Israelites was taken over and transformed by Rabbi Isaac Mayer Wise to become the social action agency of Reform Judaism.

THE FIRST PUBLICATIONS ON AMERICAN-JEWISH HISTORY

1842

The first attempt in North America to write Jewish history was made by Cotton Mather, the personification of Puritanism and its most learned minister. Unpublished in six large volumes in the Archives of the Massachusetts Historical Society in Boston, his *Biblia Americana* may still be seen today.

Mather had always shown a keen interest in Jews and in Hebrew. In 1693, at the age of thirty-one, he began writing a history of the Jews from biblical times to his own day. However, his labor was not finished, and although he worked on what he called "one of the greatest works that I ever undertook in my life" for seven years, it never got into print.

A long interval ensued before Robert Thomas's curious medly was published in 1791 in Boston, under the title of "A Brief Account of the Persecution of the Jews," in the first *Old Farmers' Almanac*. Although the first narration of post-biblical Jewish history to get into print, it was merely journalistic.

The second serious attempt by an American of a post-biblical history of the Jews was not made until 1812. In that year, Boston bluestocking Hannah Adams, of the noted presidential family, published *The History of the Jews from the Destruction of Jerusalem to the Nineteenth Century*. Hannah Adams had shown an active interest in the conversion of the Jews and was associated with America's first missionary society—The American Society for Meliorating the Condition of the Jews. Although the book went through several editions, only a single chapter of eighteen pages is devoted to "The Jews in America."

It was not until thirty years later, in 1842, that Jewish history written by a Jewish author came to be published. In that year Joseph Jonas, Jewish pioneer of the Ohio Valley, who had settled there as early as 1817, submitted a series of articles on "The Jews of the Ohio Valley" to the *Occident and American Jewish Advocate*, the first permanent American Jewish periodical, founded and edited by Isaac Leeser, spokesman, leader, and educator of American Jewry. The problems of the isolated Jew, the struggle to build up a religious community, the tendency to modify ritual and custom, the debate as to the forms of Jewish education, and the relation to non-Jews are all reflected here. Subsequently, this proved to be a valuable source of information concerning the history of the early Jewish pioneers.

The first guidebook to the American Jewish community appeared in 1854, when Jacques J. Lyons and Abraham de Sola published a Jewish calendar for fifty years and appended a list of synagogues, philanthropies, and societies. There were then, all told, one hundred organizations, serving fewer than one hundred thousand Jews in the land.

The same year, Rabbi Isaac Mayer Wise in Albany printed the first volume of *A History of the Israelitish Nation from Abraham to the Present Time*, but he apparently abandoned his plan and left the work unfinished before he reached post-biblical times.

The first complete history of the Jews in America did not appear until 1888, when Isaac Markens published *The Hebrews in America*. This was followed in 1893 by the more popularly known *Settlement of the Jews in North America*, by Charles P. Daly. The year before, in 1892, in answer to a call issued by Dr. Cyrus Adler of the Jewish Theological Seminary of America, the American Jewish Historical Society was founded and dedicated to the collection, preservation, and dissemination of information on the history of Jews on the American continent. It began collecting early records, minute books of congregations, as well as fraternal lodge letters, manuscripts, and documents pertaining to early American Jewish history.

The American Jewish Historical Society, the oldest ethnic historical society continuously in existence in the United States, is located on the campus of Brandeis University in Waltham, Massachusetts. The society is one of the chief repositories of documents and other primary source material related to Jewish life in North America. Its headquarters houses over ninety thousand volumes in its library, as well as over twelve million manuscripts; the most complete collection of American Jewish newspapers in English, Hebrew, and Yiddish; 250 paintings and handcrafts; and over five hundred American Yiddish theater and film posters (administrated by the National Center for Jewish Film).

The results of its research into the past and the interpretation of its meaning have been primarily disseminated through a scholarly journal initially called *Publications of the American Jewish Historical Society*, later the *American Jewish Historical Quarterly*, and today, *American Jewish History*, of which eighty-three volumes have been published to date.

In 1992, on the five hundredth anniversary of Columbus's landing and in conjunction with its centennial celebration, the American Jewish Historical Society sponsored the publication of a five-volume history *The Jewish People in America* under the general editorship of Professor Henry L. Feingold of Baruch College of the City University of New York.

In 1947, one of the phases of the expanded programs of the Hebrew Union College-Jewish Institute of Religion was the establishment of the American Jewish Archives under the director of Dr. Jacob Rader Marcus, pioneer historian and prolific author in the field, who has contributed substantially in his multifaceted learned endeavors toward the professionalism of American Jewish historiography and its recognition as a legitimate field of scholarship to be cultivated academically.

Dedicated to the preservation of American Jewish historical records and their study, the American Jewish Archives does not compete with but rather supplements the American Jewish Historical Society.

One of the collections of the American Jewish Archives in its headquarters in Cincinnati, the oldest Jewish settlement west of the Alleghenies, is the personal and business papers of the Gratz family, which spans approximately two-thirds of the 340 years of Jewish settlement in North America. It was made available by Mrs. Henry Joseph, a niece of Rebecca Gratz.

THE FIRST DEPARTMENT STORE

1842

Though Jews of German origin had settled in this country in the early eighteenth century, the bulk of German-Jewish immigrants emigrated to the United States in the period from 1840 to 1860. These Jews were merchants, buyers, sellers, and traders. They loved commerce and the clash of wits. Their hard work, enterprising spirit, and ability to organize won for them a place of prominence in the growing nation.

As in Europe, a characteristic early Jewish offshoot of shop retailing was peddlery, especially in the agricultural frontier where general stores were few and far between. The immigrant German Jew was by no means the original in country peddling. Throughout the eighteenth century it was the itinerant Yankee who dominated the field. By the 1800s, however, the Yankee had settled in as a small-town shopkeeper and the German Jew was freer to cater specifically to his fellow German Jews, whose language, tastes, and needs he understood from the Old Country. Thus the immigrant peddler made his way from New York, Philadelpia, Baltimore, or New Orleans to the hinterland. His routes were determined by the new canals and roads to upstate villages and Western farms and particularly by the Ohio River system, the region encompassing the largest German immigration. By 1850, some ten thousand country peddlers—overwhelmingly German Jews—were at work in the United States, and by 1860 there were perhaps fifteen or sixteen thousand.

One of the earliest of this group of German-Jewish immigrants was a humble peddler from the province of Bavaria by the name of Adam Gimbel, with whom the story of the department store in this country is bound.

When Adam Gimbel was eighteen, he left Bavaria and landed in New Orleans, alone and penniless. He found arduous and ill-paid work on the docks but soon began to look around for a better way of life. He heard that people who lived far away from the cities were clamoring for the kind of goods they could not obtain in their bleak wilderness. With the money he had saved by scraping and pinching, Gimbel bought up a variety of goods, including combs, yarn, pins, needles, thimbles, broadcloth, knives, tobacco, and clocks. Then Adam Gimbel, the young peddler, flung the pack over his shoulder and set out, rifle in hand, for the Mississippi Valley. Thus modestly began an American trade empire.

After a few years of incredible hardship, eased only by the many friends he made among the trappers, rivermen, and Indians, Gimbel decided to settle down in one place. In 1842, at the age of twenty-five, he opened a small shop in Vincennes, Indiana, and became a storekeeper— but a most unusual storekeeper. First he drew up a handbill to advertise the opening of his new establishment. Then he set up policies for the store's operation. He insisted that all customers—rich and poor, white and Indian—receive the same prompt and courteous service. More startling still, he offered to refund the purchase price to any customer not satisfied with what he bought. These novel ideas, as well as an honest description of goods, brought customers flocking to his store. Because most of them could not come in as often as they would have liked, Gimbel made their buying easy by stocking up a great many varieties of wares under the same roof, thus making his place the first modern department store.

Though Gimbel maintained the Vincennes business for more than forty years, expanding it until it included four stores in the city at the turn of the century, he finally sold out the firm to join his seven sons who had entered the merchandising field in other cities and had spread the gospel of the department store across the land.

Philadelphia was the site of a new venture, and in 1894 Gimbel Brothers bought out the business of Granville B. Hays there. At the time Adam Gimbel retired from active business, his son Isaac assumed the presidency.

By 1908, Isaac Gimbel was in New York City, spearheading the Gimbel Brothers most daring venture and crashing the tautly competitive market. With his young son, Bernard, Isaac began constructing the eleven-story, completely modern department store in Herald Square between Thirty-second and Thirty-third streets. He supervised the hiring and training of a staff of five thousand employees. The store opened to the public in 1910. Within the next five years two older firms had been absorbed into the business. A still further advance was made in New York City in 1923 when Saks and Company was purchased. Eventually, a Saks subsidiary was established as a second store on upper Fifth Avenue, which introduced new fashion in women's wear.

The growth spiral continued with the acquisition of the Pittsburgh department store of Kaufman and Baer in 1925. After three years of physical improvements, the name of the store was officially changed to Gimbel Brothers, Pittsburgh—the fourth major Gimbel store.

Main store developments were followed quickly by suburban expansion. Outstanding architects and designers were engaged to create ultramodern store designs. Construction continued at breathtaking speed and suburban Gimbel's stores opened everywhere.

From a frontier trading post, Gimbel's grew to become a merchandising colossus. All the stores in the various cities were under the supervision of the Gimbel family, descendants of Adam Gimbel or his brother, Lemuel.

In recent decades, Gimbel's has more often been thought of in terms of enormous problems than in terms of the growth and creativity that characterized its first century. So also with its stores, long the model and measure of originality and greatness, the paradigm of the American department store. In the early 1980s, it ceased to seek out a solution to its many problems and sold out to the British-American Tobacco Company and became only a small part of an international conglomerate.

In 1990, Saks Fifth Avenue, which had built its reputation as a shopping place for the fashion conscious, became a privately held company and was purchased by Investcorp, an investment group based in Bahrain and London, who bought it for $1.6 billion from Batus, the American retailing arm of B.A.T. Industries.

During the early years of the twentieth century, Jewish department store families began consolidating their impressive prewar role in mass merchandising. By the postwar period, R.H. Macy & Company (owned by the Strauses), Gimbel's, Abraham and Straus, Altman's, Lord and Taylor, Ohrbach's, Bergdorf Goodman, Franklin Simon, and Bloomingdale's dominated the New York market. By then, too, many great department stores of the nation stood as monuments of triumphant achievement, bearing the names of their German-Jewish peddler founders such as Filene's (founded by William Katz) in Boston, Rich's in Atlanta, I. Magnin and Company in San Francisco, Spiegel's in Chicago, and the Dallas-based Neiman Marcus, the largest and most prestigious department store in the Southwest.

The evolution of American retailing was further accelerated by the growth of the small midwestern mail-order firm of Sears, Roebuck &

Company, through the efforts of Julius Rosenwald under whose direction it developed into the largest retail chain in the world and whose philanthropies to his own people and African-Americans in the South were legion.

Rosenwald was responsible for opening factories that produced much of the firm's merchandise, introduced the famous "money-back-if-not-satisfied" guarantee, and expanded distribution of the firm's mail-order catalog to forty million copies annually. Its catalog brought uniformity to American styles in clothing, home furnishings, and notions—and to his family one of America's great fortunes.

Great mercantile emporiums still proudly bear their Jewish founders' names, but few remain with their founders as owners or managers, having been gobbled up by giant conglomerates.

THE FIRST NATIONAL JEWISH ORGANIZATION

1843

The first national Jewish organization to be formed in the United States— and still one of the world's most important in its influence and work— is the Independent Order of B'nai B'rith, or Sons of the Covenant. It was started in New York City in 1843 by twelve German Jews who called themselves Bundes Bruder for the purpose of ameliorating the regrettable conditions of hatred and disunity then existing among American Jewry. The founders were all humble men, shopkeepers and artisans of whom the acknowledged leader was Henry Jones, the efficient clerk of the Anshe Chesed Synagogue and who was considered there the power behind the throne.

This devoted member of Anshe Chesed (the first synagogue in New York City founded by Ashkenazim, or Jews of Central or Eastern Europe, or their descendants), told of bitter complaints that came to him from his brethren whose applications for membership were rejected by the Independent Order of Odd Fellows. He, himself, however, an Odd Fellow and a Mason, could not attribute such conduct to anti-Jewish prejudice.

The suggestion was made that an all-Jewish lodge of Masons or Odd Fellows be formed, but this was opposed by the men who founded B'nai B'rith. Instead they saw the need for an all-Jewish order of an entirely different sort, one that would bring together all the warring factions, thus healing the growing antagonism between the Orthodox and new Reformers among American Jewry.

At a time when unified action was virtually nonexistent, Henry Jones stepped in to create the first working alliance of American Jews. He laid out the philosophic foundation for the order and outlined its ideals and fundamental goals. He drafted the original constitution with the help of William Renau.

On October 11, 1843, the twelve founders met in the gaslight of Sinsheimer's Cafe on Essex Street on New York City's Lower East Side. Gazing into the future, they envisioned a movement that while based on the teachings of Judaism, cut across doctrinal lines and became a rallying point for Jews of varying origins, religious viewpoints, and economic backgrounds.

The first lodge was not formed until a few weeks later. Meanwhile, on October 21, the founders came together again and by that time had their statements and principles all worked out.

The Masonic Room at the corner of Oliver and Henry streets was rented for two dollars a night. On November 12 at 8:00 P.M. the first meeting of the first lodge of B'nai B'rith was called to order with Henry Jones as temporary chairman. It was the birth of New York Lodge Number One, which still flourishes to this day.

Although Henry Jones was the founder of B'nai B'rith, he was not its first president. Perhaps it was characteristic modesty on his part, but he accepted the post of secretary of the new group. But Julius Bien, B'nai B'rith's official historian and president for thirty-two years, remembered: "His was the strong hand that kept the wheel straight on the course that he had determined upon, and only a man endowed as he was with strength of intellect and character could succeed in his great purpose."

Unlike some of the organizations that began as local clubs and then spread by chance to national proportions, B'nai B'rith was planned from the beginning as a national body. The preamble to the B'nai B'rith constitution is still the preamble today. It reads:

B'nai B'rith has taken upon itself the mission of uniting Israelites in the work of promoting their highest interests and those of humanity; of developing and elevating the mental and moral character of the people of our faith; of inculcating the purest principles of philanthropy, honor, and patriotism; of supporting science and art; alleviating the wants of the poor and needy; visiting and attending the sick; coming to the rescue of victims of persecution; providing for, protecting, and assisting the widow and the orphan on the broadest principles of humanity.

At first the order grew slowly in different parts of the country. By 1850 it had acquired three thousand members. Although in theory any Jew as eligible for membership, in practice the first members were all German Jews, and for the first seven years all club proceedings were conducted in that language. It was only later that the order succeeded in bringing together in the same lodge the rich and the poor, the German and the Russian-born Jew, the Polish and Romanian, the Orthodox and Reform.

During the post-Civil War days, it acquired twenty thousand members and has been growing steadily ever since. Along with philanthropic work, such as the erection of orphan homes and old people's homes for the needy, B'nai B'rith began to take steps to protect and aid Jews everywhere. Out of this grew the Anti-Defamation League (ADL)—first organized in 1913—to protect the good name of the Jew, to combat anti-Semitism, and to secure justice and fair treatment for all citizens through law and through programs and services that counteract hatred, prejudice, and bigotry.

In the 1920s, ADL joined other groups in fighting the Ku Klux Klan. In the 1930s and 1940s, ADL's focus shifted to confront Fascism in America and its link to Nazi-front organizations. After World War II, ADL turned to the issue of discrimination in American life.

In the 1980s and 1990s, ADL continued to be involved in issues of concern to American Jewry, such as the plight of Jews in the Soviet Union, the American commitment to Israel, black-Jewish relations, and the ongoing fight against anti-Semitism.

ADL's work today includes active resistance and counteraction against haters and bigots. Its 28 regional offices closely monitor the emergence and activities of youth gangs such as the neo-Nazi skinheads. Its concern about religious rights, expressions of intolerance, scapegoating, and hostility toward church-state separation remains undiminished.

In 1923 the B'nai B'rith began establishing the B'nai B'rith Hillel Foundations in American universities for a vast array of religious, educational, cultural, and social programs among Jewish students. From the time of Rabbi Benjamin Frankel—first Hillel director at the University of Illinois—and Dr. Abram Sachar—who directed the University of Illinois Hillel unit from 1929 to 1933 and then served as first national director of Hillel Foundations from 1933 to 1948 and whose vision and creativity built Hillel into a national network (and who later became founding president of Brandeis University)—Hillel Foundations have extended from the University of Alberta in the Canadian North to the University of Havana in the Caribbean South, serving over 250,000 college students on more than 450 campuses. The Hillel Foundations, however, were not the first Jewish campus organizations, for as early as 1906, the Menorah Society had been founded at Harvard University, coming eight years after the first Jewish fraternity, Zeta Beta Tau.

In 1923, the B'nai B'rith Youth Organization for teenagers was created to serve—like Hillel—their religious, cultural, and social community service and counseling needs.

The growth and work of B'nai B'rith after its one hundredth anniversary almost doubled. During the first two years of American participation in World War II, it sold $162,000,000 worth of war bonds. In addition, the order took an active part in providing blood donors and shared in the National War Fund Drive. That service brought the B'nai B'rith the first citation made by both the U.S. Army and U.S. Navy to any civilian agency in the country.

The B'nai B'rith involvement in the birth of the State of Israel is an important part in the history of the Jewish state. Among its present-day Israel projects are investments in Israel's economy; land development, reclamation, and reforestation; encouragement of *aliyah* (migration to Israel); and education of its worldwide membership about Israel's history, culture, problems, and needs. The first B'nai B'rith lodge in Palestine was founded in 1888; today, many lodges and units flourish in Israel.

B'nai B'rith Women, founded in 1897, is a branch for developing programs for women and support of the youth program. A highlight of its ongoing program is the B'nai B'rith Women Children's Home in Jerusalem. In 1990, at its biennial convention, B'nai B'rith admitted women to full membership. At the same time the B'nai B'rith Women became a part of B'nai B'rith through a formal affiliation agreement, with its own agenda and with female members only.

B'nai B'rith subsidiaries—like its Hillel Foundations; B'nai B'rith Youth Organization; B'nai B'rith Women; the Anti-Defamation League; the Adult Jewish Education Committee; its Community-Volunteer Services; its magazine, the *International Jewish Monthly*; its Institutes of Judaism; and a host of other activities—have left an indelible mark on American and world Jewish affairs.

B'nai B'rith, now over one hundred fifty years old, has a membership of half a million men, women, and young adults. Its one thousand four hundred lodges (all male) and units (male and female) are found in fifty-four countries, a thousand of them in the United States.

As passionate advocates of freedom and democracy, it combats racism and bigotry and is in the forefront of the battle for human rights. It adopts its program initiative to meet new needs in the world Jewish community whenever and wherever it is most necessary. Thus, for Jews in the former Soviet Republics it has established fourteen new units to date—from the Baltics to Birobidjan—to help stem the rising tide of anti-Semitism. For Jews of Eastern and Central Europe, B'nai B'rith strives to overcome the ethnic and national hatreds that threatens to overwhelm attempts to revive the once-vibrant Jewish life destroyed in World War II.

B'nai B'rith is present at virtually every international forum. It has official recognition as a nongovernmental organization at the United Nations, where it led in the battle to nullify the odious "Zionism is Racism" resolution. It also has nongovernmental organizational status at the Organization of American States and is represented in the European Economic Community (EEC) and the European Parliament.

In September 1994, Tommy Baer, a Virginia attorney on the Board of the Richmond Jewish Federation's Community Relations Council and long-time leader of the organization, was elected president of B'nai B'rith at its biennial convention. He succeeded Kent Schiner, who concluded his second two-year term in office.

THE FIRST JEWISH HOSPITAL

1852

Overlooking the rolling greens and winding drives of upper Central Park in New York City is an institution known throughout the United States and the world. Mount Sinai Medical Center's twenty-two buildings stretch along stately Fifth and Madison avenues, from 98th to 102nd street for five crowded city blocks, and it is still expanding. Last year alone it served a patient population of almost four hundred thousand in its hospital and 160 clinics.

Mount Sinai, one of the world's leading teaching hospitals and the first Jewish-sponsored hospital in the United States, was established in 1852 as the Jews' Hospital "for benevolent, charitable, and scientific purposes" and was kosher (food prepared ritually and permissible for usage by pious Jews).

The original hospital building was completed at a cost of $35,000 and on June 8, 1855, took in its first patient. A four-story brownstone building with forty-five beds, it stood at 138 West 28th Street between Seventh and Eighth avenues in downtown Manhattan, where a tomato patch once grew and where people were accustomed to building bonfires and roasting potatoes. The hospital was founded almost single-handedly by an American Jew who bore the name Sampson Simson, Esquire.

In the mid-nineteenth century New York City, like the rest of the country, was suffering from growing pains. A railroad had just been laid between New York and Lake Erie. Thousands of immigrants were pouring in from Europe, and housing conditions were getting worse every day. The rate of illness rose alarmingly. A large portion of new Americans fell victim to tuberculosis brought on by poor housing, malnutrition, unemployment, and overcrowding. City hospitals like Bellevue existed, but for the Jewish community this was not enough. The erection of a hospital, an institution, sponsored by the Jewish community itself was a project everyone had been discussing for a long time. The Young Men's Fuel Society and the Bachelor's Loan Society offered ideas that got lost in a sea of hesitation and argument. It was then that Sampson Simson, who had lived a long and colorful life, came forward and broke through all of the difficulties.

Sampson Simson, seventy-two years old at the time, had taken a lifelong interest in communal affairs. In 1800 he had delivered his baccalaureate oration in Hebrew on "One Hundred and Fifty Years of Jewish History" when he graduated from Columbia College, the first Jew to receive a degree from that institution. Sampson can also rank as the first Jewish lawyer to pass the New York bar examination.

As a young man he had studied law in New York while working as confidential clerk to Aaron Burr, former vice-president of the United States. Sampson then had desk space in the office of the prominent Riker law firm. His practice was slight, confined chiefly to personal affairs and benevolent and religious matters. Then in 1813, after being beaten up in a night attack on the streets of New York City, he retired from the growing bustle of the city to live as a country gentleman on his estate in Yonkers. Always a pious, Orthodox Jew, he even baked his own matzoh for Passover at home.

Constantly concerned with the welfare of Jews in Palestine, he was one of the first Americans to donate sums of money for Jerusalem charities. Finally in 1852 he called upon his good friends, all prominent leaders of Congregation Shearith Israel, the oldest synagogue in the city, to hear his plan for a Jews' Hospital.

They met in the Trustees Room of Congregation Shearith Israel on a wintry day. His plan, he said, was simple. Ignoring all the existing societies, he wished to enroll members at five dollars a year; these members would elect trustees to guide the hospital. A group of young people had promised to run a ball and raise $1,000, he declared; he himself would provide the organization with two lots of land on 28th Street near Seventh Avenue.

The community accepted the plans wholeheartedly; incorporation papers were drawn up, and Sampson Simson was elected the first president.

By Thanksgiving Day 1853, the cornerstone of the first Jewish hospital in New York City was laid. On June 8, 1855, the Jews' Hospital was completed at a cost of $35,000 and took in its first patient. A generous legacy of $20,000 was willed to the hospital by Judah Touro, the wealthy philanthropist from New Orleans, which sped its opening. Proudly, the founders inscribed the name of the institution over its door—JEWS' HOSPITAL—and in Hebrew they wrote BET HOLIM.

In its first full year of operations the hospital cared for 225 patients; operating expenses were $5,493.76.

Originally a sectarian hospital, it accepted those outside the Jewish faith only in cases of accident or emergency. However, care of the wounded Federal soldiers during the Civil War, the Draft Riots, and the Orange Day Parade Riots prompted the idea of changing into a nonsectarian institution.

The hospital grew with the mushrooming of the city itself. In 1886, to make it clear that it served the community without regard to race, color, or creed, by a special act of the Legislature the institution's name was changed from "Jews' Hospital" to "Mount Sinai Hospital." The original consulting and attending staff were practically all Gentiles, Drs. Mark Blumenthal and Israel Moses being among the exceptions.

Four years later, in 1872, the hospital made the first of two moves uptown, to Lexington Avenue and Sixty-sixth Street to a new three-and-a-half-story building with a capacity of 120 beds.

The new home of the hospital was typical of the period. Built of the best "Philadelphia brick" and with trimmed marble, its central portion consisted of a garden for convalescents and several smaller buildings.

A favorite charity of Jacob Schiff and other patriarchs, Mount Sinai in later years was enhanced by the generosity of old-line second- and third-generation American Jewish families.

The first separate service for the care of children to be established in any New York hospital was organized at Mount Sinai in 1878. Its creation was made possible by a legacy of $25,000 left to it that year by Michael Reese of California. Moreover, for eighteen years the Mount Sinai staff had counted among its members the doctor who helped establish pediatrics as a separate medical specialty and who held the first chair in the field in the United States, Dr. Abraham Jacobi, attending physician since 1860.

In 1879, an eye and ear service was organized, headed by Dr. Emil Gruening, who in 1888 performed one of the early mastoid operations in America. And in 1881 the School of Nursing, one of the country's pioneer nurses' training institutions, was established.

The growth of the laboratory for scientific and investigative research changed the hospital from a home for the sick to a vital scientific institution. Antiseptic and aseptic surgery were introduced, departments separated, and specialties recognized.

In 1904 the hospital moved from Lexington Avenue and 66th Street to still-larger quarters at 100th Street and Fifth Avenue, now comprising 839 beds.

The participation of the hospital in two world wars, contributing a fully equipped medical unit in each; the establishment of a famous consulting clinic; and the gradual change of the medical staff from voluntary to more and more full-time positions added to the repute of the institution.

Among the prominent physicians associated with the hospital in its formative years were: Dr. Karl Koller, who discovered the use of cocaine as a local anesthetic; Dr. Henry Koplik, who discovered "Koplik's Spots" as a diagnostic sign of measles; Dr. Emanuel Libman, who pioneered in the study of bacterial endocarditis; Dr. I. C. Rubin, who introduced the use of peruterine insufflation of the fallopian tubes for diagnosis and treatment of sterility in women (the Rubin Test); Drs. Arthur Master and Simon Dack, who developed the first cardiac stress test, the Master 2-Step; and Dr. Reuben Ottenberg, who was the first to perform blood transfusion with routine compatability tests and to point out that blood groups are hereditary.

By the mid-twentieth century, Mount Sinai's reputation for the discovery of "medical firsts" was unequalled by any hospital in the United States. Dr. Samuel Rosen was a pioneer in using stapes mobilization operation for alleviation of particular kinds of deafness; Bernard Sachs, internationally famous neurologist, whose name is bracketed with that of Dr. Warren Tay, described "amaurotic family idiocy" now known as Tay-Sachs Disease; Dr. Bela Schick developed the Schick Test for susceptibility to diptheria; Drs. Nathan Brill, Burrill Crohn, Jacob Churg, Lotte Strauss, Eli Moschowitz, and Leo Buerger provided classic descriptions of illnesses and syndromes that bear their names: Drs. A.A. Berg. John Garlock, and Ralph Colp were responsible for outstanding surgical advances in the treatment of digestive disorders; Dr. Moses Swick developed a method for introducing radio-opaque media into the bloodstream for visualization of the urinary tract, the intravenous pyelogram. In 1986, Dr. Richard Berkowitz performed the first blood transfusion into the tiny veins of an unborn fetus. In 1958, Mount Sinai Hospital developed the first practical bipolar coagulator, a standard apparatus for neurosurgical operations.

Nevertheless, as late as the 1950s, local and area medical schools hesitated to accept Mount Sinai (or any Jewish-founded hospital) as one of its major teaching hospitals. Accordingly, Mount Sinai's Board of Trustees decided to establish its own medical school. More than ten years were needed for planning and organization. In the space of that decade, some $150 million additional funds were raised, spearheaded by generous gifts from the Walter Annenbergs, the Gustav Levys, the Guggenheims, Lehmans, Laskers, Klingensteins, Rosensteils, Bronfmans, and other Jewish philanthropists. Except for the United Jewish Appeal-Federation of Jewish Philanthropies drives, it was the largest fund-raising campaign in the history of New York Jewry. Its success in building an internationally acclaimed faculty of over twenty-five hundred physicians and scientists, and graduating some one hundred medical students annually, was all but foreordained as the eminent historian Professor Howard M. Sachar stated in his book *A History of the Jews in America*.

THE FIRST JEWISH PHILANTHROPIST

1854

Judah Touro, the son of Reverend Isaac Touro, the first *hazzan* of the famous Newport Synagogue that bears the Touro name, was the earliest and most generous of American Jewish philanthropists. His extensive fortune was largely accumulated by mercantile, shipping, real estate, and other commercial ventures in New Orleans.

Arriving coincidentally with the outbreak of the American Revolution, Judah Touro was born on June 16, 1775, the day before the Battle of Bunker Hill. Even his death paralleled a great historic period. He died four years after the Compromise of 1850 at the venerable age of seventy-nine.

When Judah was eight years old his father died, and four years later his mother passed away. Judah and a brother and sister, Abraham and Rebecca, became the wards of an uncle, Moses Michael Hays, the wealthy, influential, and public-spirited Boston insurance broker and friend of many leading non-Jews in that city.

Mr. Hays gave Judah the meager education that was considered sufficient at the time. Later, he took his nephew into his counting house and thoroughly trained him for a business career. Here Judah learned at an early age that one could be a devout Jew and yet mingle freely with his Christian brethren, teaching them to respect his faith while at the same time respecting theirs.

After having been forbidden to marry his childhood sweetheart, Catherine Hays, his cousin and daughter of Moses Hays, Judah departed for New Orleans, where he was the first Jewish settler. Groomed for business, he there put into practice the theories of his twenty-eight years. With full confidence in his ability, he opened a store and dispensed "Yankee notions." Old established firms in Boston made him their adviser and shipped large consignments of merchandise to him. For over fifty years he lived there, working every day in his store, opening the place every morning at precisely the same time. A formal, little man, scrupulously honest, he sold his goods at a small profit and then invested that profit in New Orleans property and ships. The Louisiana Purchase, Ely Whitney's cotton gin, and rice crops from the delta country brought prosperity to New Orleans and to one of its most astute merchants, Judah Touro.

Patriotically, when the War of 1812 broke out, he enlisted as a volunteer in the army and fought under General (later President) Andrew Jackson. When struck by a cannonball, wounded and left for dying on the battlefield during the Battle of New Orleans, he was rescued by his Christian friend, the Virginia merchant Rezin Shepard, who procured a cart and brought him to a hospital base, where he received medical attention that saved his life. Rezin Shepard was ultimately an executor and residual legatee of Touro's estate.

After the war Touro returned to private life. His business expanded. He imported, and he invested in real estate; he bought grain and goods of every kind. In short, he became wealthy.

Perhaps because of his share in America's struggle for liberty, Touro was always interested in the Revolutionary War. An effort had been made to erect the Bunker Hill Monument, the site of the first battle of the Revolutionary War, but the movement languished for thirteen years. Then Amos Lawrence of Boston offered $10,000 for the purpose, and Judah Touro of New Orleans subscribed the same amount. His gift for the completion of the Bunker Hill Monument received wide appreciation. In 1843, this, the first public monument in America, was dedicated in the presence of the President of the United States, John Tyler. Daniel Webster delivered the famous oration that has become an American classic. A dinner followed at Faneuil Hall in Boston, and the names of Touro and Lawrence were placed on the platform under the American eagle. These verses attributed to Oliver Wendell Holmes were read:

> Amos and Judah—venerated names,
> Patriarch and Prophet press their equal claims,
> Like generous coursers running "neck in neck,"
> Each aids in the work by giving it a check
> Christian and Jew, they carry out one plan
> For though of different faith, each is in heart a man.

Those who knew Judah Touro personally praised him not only for his princely charitable gifts but for his many acts of kindness. Instead of waiting for an appeal to reach him, it has been said that he actually searched out the unfortunates who needed help. There was the black slave he educated to be self-supporting and sent away to live in freedom and dignity, the aged woman who shrank from entering an almshouse, the business competitor who needed but was too proud to ask for a loan— to these and a multitude more did Judah Touro extend the helping hand of brotherhood.

In 1802, when Judah Touro arrived in New Orleans, it was a struggling Spanish-French village; in 1854, at the time of his death, it had become a great city, and he had played a conspicuous part in its transformation. He built the Touro Free Library, the first public library in New Orleans, which was the first free public library in the world; he founded the Touro Infirmary, the first hospital in the South for both white and slave, later to win renown as one of the South's best hospitals; and he erected the Shakespeare Almshouse for the Poor.

A few cities had special hospitals for slaves, and the larger plantations had sick bays, where slaves were attended by slave nurses or a
physician (frequently the master's own). But there was nothing comparable to the Touro Infirmary, which opened its door to all.

Few happy songs have been inspired by hospitals. *Relaxin' at the Touro*
is a jazz melody (no lyric was ever written) composed by Francis "Muggsy"
Spanier after his recovery from a serious illness at the infirmary.

Judah Touro died in 1854 in his seventy-ninth year. A bachelor, he left a
fortune exceeding one million dollars. His famous will attracted wide attention and became a historic document bearing testimony to his broad humanitarian sentiments. Of that money $250,000 was bequeathed to Jewish
causes and $148,000 to Christian and nonsectarian purposes. He left be-
tween $2,000 and $5,000 for every synagogue in America then in existence.
Hebrew schools, hospitals, and relief societies in America and Palestine
were also bequeathed a share of his great fortune. The money he left to
Mount Sinai Hospital in New York enabled it to complete its first building.
To supplement the work of Sir Moses Montefiore in Palestine, he left the
then unheard of sum of $50,000. He donated a church building to a New
Orleans Christian congregation. His bequests also went to individual rabbis
and Protestant ministers; to individual Christians and Jews; to a fireman's
association, a seaman's home, and benevolent societies; to the Touro Free
Library, the first free public library in the country; to the upkeep of the Touro
Synagogue and the Jewish Cemetery in Newport; to the Legislature of the
State of Rhode Island he left a trust fund for the salary of a minister or reader
to officiate at the Newport Synagogue. He also left money for the purchase
of the "Old Stone Mill," allegedly built by the Vikings of Leif Ericson, and for
the adjacent grounds now known as Touro Park in Newport.

When Judah Touro died, almost all of pleasure-loving New Orleans
went into mourning. *The Bee,* one of the leading newspapers of the day,
reported that Judah Touro's funeral was "the largest assemblage of citizens
we have ever beheld . . . the funeral train was immense, almost every
carriage in the city being filled."

No one had ever given away so much money to so many agencies and
to so many causes up to his time. Truly, then, did he earn the epitaph
inscribed on his tombstone:

By righteousness and integrity he collected his wealth;
In charity and salvation he dispensed it.
The last of his name, he inscribed it in the book of philanthropy
To be remembered forever.

Abraham Touro, the brother of Judah, was a great merchant and
philanthropist in his own right. In addition to his business interests in

Boston, he owned a shipyard in Medford, and his summer home there was the town's showplace. Upon his death in 1822, Abraham left $10,000 to the Massachusetts General Hospital and a $10,000 fund for the care and preservation of the Newport Synagogue. Abraham's bequest was among the earliest in America for the purpose of preserving an unoccupied historic building.

Touro College, founded in New York City in 1970 by Dr. Bernard Lander—a four-year college with business, Judaic studies, health sciences, and liberal arts programs and graduate schools that offer a J.D. degree and a biomedical program leading to an M.D. degree—derives its name from the Touro family—father Isaac and sons Judah and Abraham.

THE FIRST YMHA

1854

The Young Men's and Young Women's Hebrew Associations (YM-YWHAs) or Jewish Community Centers—a type of Jewish community organization providing social, cultural, physical education, and camping activities and Jewish education in an informal setting—had their beginnings in the United States in 1854. True, there were Young Men's Hebrew Literary Associations—which started in the 1840s—antedating the first American Young Men's Christian Associations in 1851. But it was not until 1854 that the first YMHA opened its doors in Baltimore to begin a movement that has contributed immensely to the enrichment of Jewish and American life.

Until the 1930s, the Ys were primarily youth-serving agencies, although in their earliest years they played a significant role in the United States in the adjustment of immigrants to American life. As they broadened their programs to include all elements in the Jewish community, the name Jewish Community Center was more generally adopted, but a few of the oldest and some of the newest continue to favor the older YM-YWHA designation.

By the early twentieth century, YMHAs had proliferated among most major Jewish population centers. Their expansion slowed briefly during the Depression, but by the 1930s the Ys—and, increasingly, Jewish Community Centers—broadened their programs to include activities for all age groups and functioned as a meeting place for Jews of all backgrounds. During the post-World War II years, centers continued to spring up or expand their premises in much the same proportions as did synagogues. They ranged from New York City's vast 92nd Street Y to modest edifaces in communities as small as Wichita or Newport News.

The earliest Y had its start in Baltimore in 1854, and nearly twenty-five such societies came into being in the next twenty years. However, at first, most of them failed to flourish, and it was not until a YMHA was formed in New York City in 1874 that a permanent movement was started. The movement was greatly accelerated upon the formation of a YMHA in Philadelphia in 1875. These two associations are the oldest with a continuous history.

From the single Y in Baltimore where Jews of all viewpoints met as one, the movement quickly developed after the Civil War and came to mean community activity for young and old in the arts and physical education, as well as religion.

The YMHAs and Jewish Community Centers, a distinct product of the American environment, represented a new type of Jewish institution that developed out of the needs of the group and was in harmony with a philosophy of Jewish group life and American institutions.

The first YMHA in New York, founded by German Jewish professionals and businessmen, opened its doors in 1874. Its first meeting was held on March 22 of that year at the home of Dr. Simeon Newton Leo, who was the moving force in the formation of the new organization. His residence was located at 320 West 33rd Street, and meetings were held there week after week, until the number of persons attending necessitated more adequate quarters. For a while the meetings were held at the Thirty-fourth Street Synagogue, then in the Trustees' Room of Temple Emanu-El, until small quarters were rented at 112 West 21st Street with parlors, reading rooms, and a gymnasium. Here an extended program of education and recreation was inaugurated, and many new members enrolled.

In less than two years the association was ready for larger quarters, and in April 1876 a long lease was taken on a building at 110 West 42nd Street. These quarters were retained for ten years, during which time the institution grew and developed.

In the 1880s, the YMHA was transformed increasingly into a vehicle for immigrant Americanization. Its curriculum of night classes henceforth was devoted to instruction in English, civics, and home economics.

In 1886 a small building was rented at 721 Lexington Avenue, where the activities of the association carried on for nine years. From the beginning and throughout this period, the program—in addition to Americanization classes—stressed Jewish interests, which gave prestige and support to the institution. From year to year it offered public lectures and courses on Jewish subjects and celebrated Jewish holidays, particularly Purim and Hanukkah, on such a large scale as to attract considerable interest. These events were held in places like the Metropolitan Opera House, Chickering Hall, and Terrace Gardens.

The infant organization was nurtured with great care by men of prominence in the professional and business life of New York City, including Oscar S. Straus, who served in public life under four United States presidents.

The movement received its greatest impetus from the well-known philanthropist Jacob H. Schiff. He had been in this country barely more than a decade when he saw in the YMHA's programs, among other things, promise of a Jewish awakening among the youth of the city. In 1898 Schiff presented the Y with its first permanent home and funded its broadened program of commercial and vocational subjects. This structure, a small brownstone building at 861 Lexington Avenue, was equipped with classrooms, clubrooms, a library, and gymnasium. The response of the young people who came to this building was so great that it soon became overcrowded. So impressed was Schiff with the growth of the YMHA and its services to the Jewish community that before the year was over, he announced a gift of a much larger building at the corner of 92nd Street and Lexington Avenue, an address destined to become world famous. The movement spread by leaps and bounds in other states.

The name Young Women's Hebrew Association (YWHA) was first applied to a women's auxiliary of the New York association in 1888, and the first independent YWHA was founded there in 1902. Its moving spirit was Mrs. Bella Unterberg, who served as president for twenty-six years. Its first permanent home on Lexington Avenue and 101st Street expanded in 1905 to provide residence space and other amenities for Jewish working girls and students. The YM and YWHAs eventually merged everywhere into single organizations.

As the movement consolidated, it built up places of refuge for Jews who had fled the pogroms in Russia and Eastern Europe before and after the turn of the century. The Ys acclimated the refugees in the New World, and also helped their children attain a view of themselves as Americans in the Jewish community.

By the year 1907, there were more than one hundred YMHAs with a total membership of twenty thousand. The time was ripe for regional organization. By 1910, five regional YMHA associations came into being.

In 1913 the National Council of Young Men's Hebrew and Kindred Associations was formed, uniting 175 YM and YWHAs throughout the United States. This in turn merged with the National Jewish Welfare Board (JWB), founded in 1917 to provide for the religious needs and welfare of Jews in the United States Armed Forces in World War I.

The Jewish Welfare Board, with headquarters in New York City, continues to serve as the National Association of Jewish Community Centers and Ys in the United States. The local centers are autonomous, but the JWB provides important aid in planning and programming; personnel recruitment, training, and placement; and administrative services and publications.

By the mid-1960s, there were more than 275 Jewish Community Centers and Ys in over 240 communities in the United States and Canada. The center movement has now taken root throughout the free world, particularly in Western Europe and in Israel. The associations in some 19 countries are linked through the World Federation of YMHAs and Jewish Community Centers, founded in 1946, with headquarters in Israel.

Today a dynamic force in American life, the Jewish Community Centers Association, a major source of Jewish educational and cultural programming, is the central leadership and service organization of the North American Jewish Community Center movement. Its 275 Jewish Community Centers, YM-YWHAs, and camps in the United States and Canada have a constituency of more than one million Jews. These centers employ more than fifteen hundred professional social group workers and maintain some 275 day camps and over one hundred resident summer camps. Characteristic activities, covering all age groups, include arts and crafts, dramatics, physical and health education, music groups, hobby groups, lectures, and forums. Nursery schools are maintained, as are special Golden Age Clubs for the elderly.

It is also the United States government-accredited agency for serving the needs of Jewish military personnel and their families and Veterans Administration patients through the Jewish Welfare Board's Chaplains Council. Its national president is Ann P. Kaufman of Houston, Texas, a past president of the Jewish Community Center of Houston and of the Jewish Federation of Greater Houston.

The 92nd Street Young Men's and Young Women's Hebrew Association, which was founded in 1874 and celebrated its 120th anniversary in 1994, is the oldest Jewish community cultural center in the United States. It has been at its present location at 92nd Street and Lexington Avenue in New York City since 1900. It has grown into one of the nation's most prestigious cultural institutions and serves over 300,000 people annually from newborns to senior citizens. It is recognized internationally for its performing arts programs, lectures, programs in adult and childhood education, Jewish studies, art education, fitness, and health, as well as for its family and senior adult activities.

One of the 92nd Street Y's most revered traditions and anticipated events is its annual lecture on the State of World Jewry, an examination of the political, social and spiritual condition of the Jewish people. Abba Eban, statesman, diplomat, scholar and writer; Elie Wiesel, Nobel Peace Prize winner; Lucy Dawidowicz, historian and author; Edgar M. Bronfman, president of the World Jewish Congress; and Malcolm Hoenlein, executive vice-president of the Conference of Presidents of Major Jewish

Organizations, have been a few of the prominent personalities who have made their predictions and shared their opinions.

Among noted Jewish Center "graduates" who spent many happy hours of their youth and acquired skills at the YMHAs and Jewish Community Centers are the statesman Bernard Baruch, who used its gymnasium; David Sarnoff, the broadcasting and television pioneer; Eddie Cantor, the actor; Rabbi Abba Hillel Silver, prominent Jewish leader who received the first American visa for the State of Israel in 1948; Dr. Abram Sachar, Hillel Foundations pioneer and founding president of Brandeis University; Philip M. Klutznick, United States delegate to the United Nations and former president of B'nai B'rith; and Rabbi David Hartman, head of the Shlomo Hartman Institute of Jerusalem.

THE FIRST MATZO FACTORY

1854

According to tradition, matzoth, or unleavened bread, must be eaten the entire eight days of the Passover holidays. To relate the story of the arrangements for the baking of matzoth in America is to trace the growth of the American Jewish community.

In the beginning the unleavened bread was baked under supervision of the synagogues. Then, after a transition period from 1830 to the 1840s, synagogue control broke down completely. By the late 1850s matzoth were, for the most part, bought by individuals from baking establishments that operated independently of synagogue supervision.

Non-Jewish bakers seem to have been the earliest in New York City commissioned to bake the traditional unleavened bread. Congregation Shearith Israel would arrange for the matzoth with some baker; a supervisor, generally the *shammash* (sexton or synagogue assistant), would be delegated to look after *kashruth* (food prepared ritually and permissible for usage by pious Jews). Each member then ordered from the appointed baker as large a supply as was needed; in addition, the synagogue itself purchased matzoth and paid for it for its officials and the poor.

In 1819 the bakery of a Mr. Hunter, a non-Jew, was used. It consisted of a black-iron coal stove instead of the more usual brick oven. A committee on the baking of the matzoth considered this newer type of oven "superior to the usual one, cheaper and more conformable to our laws."

In 1838 Congregation Anshe Chesed joined with Shearith Israel in the baking arrangements, and in 1839 with Congregation B'nai Jeshurun. In 1840 some Jews began competing with the non-Jewish bakers. A Mr. Jacobs, "a Yehudi" (a Jew), sent a sample of his product to Anshe Chesed.

Apparently, it did not meet the demands, for the order was given to a Mr. Parr, a Christian baker.

In the mid-forties many bakers found it profitable to solicit matzoth patronage of the several synagogues. As a rule they permitted the synagogue to send one or two of its own men to supervise. In 1846 the newly formed Reform Temple Emanu-el, when approached by a baker for its patronage, refused to give him preference over any other, declaring this a matter for the individual members to decide. Emanu-el's action was the herald of a new day; Jewish matzo bakers sprang up and sold directly to the public.

In the early 1850s machine-made matzoth were first introduced in New York. Before the products of these machines could be accepted, an opinion was sought from religious authorities. Chief Rabbi Nathan Adler of London permitted their use, provided there was no more than a nine-minute wait before the dough was baked. However, Judah Middleman, himself a matzo baker, and others at the Beth Hamidrash Synagogue advocated the use of handmade matzoth only.

By the mid-fifties the change was reflected in the minute book of Congregation Anshe Chesed. The "president called the attention of the board to the usage of arranging a baker for supplying the matzoth to the members and asked whether they would take any action about it this year." Bakers now baked independently of patronage as well as supervision.

The five known matzo bakers in New York City in 1855 were M. Cohen, 288 Front Street; S. Kummelstein, 175 Broome Street; W. Kronenthal, 230 Houston Street; Stern and Weil, 275 Houston Street; and Goldsmith Brothers and Company of 115 Broome Street. In 1855 these bakers were said to have baked 237,000 pounds. In 1859 they baked 374,000 pounds, of which about 100,000 were shipped out of town.

Of this group, the first to use a machine was Moses S. Cohen. In the early fifties Cohen advertised his machine-made matzoth in the *Asmonean* (Volume V, Page 232), using a crude drawing of his machine.

Since that time, machine-made matzo has been serving the needs of the American Jewish community. The Goodman Company, founded in 1865 by A. Goodman, is the oldest matzo factory with a continuous history. It started manufacturing in Philadelphia.

In 1881, Rabbi Dov Ber Manischewitz entered the trade in Cincinnati, Ohio. His reputation for scholarship and piety had already preceded him. He had been one of the pupils of the renowned Rabbi Israel Salanter, a central figure among the religious leaders of Eastern Europe, and was so highly regarded that the *Gaon* (reverential title of head of a Talmudical academy) of Salant had designated Rabbi Dov Ber as his personal *shochet*.

Rabbi Manischewitz was the first to package matzoth for distribution beyond the limits of a single neighborhood. He was among the first to introduce the baking of matzoth in a bright, clean baking plant. Among his other innovations were the use of gas-fired ovens, instead of antiquated black-iron stoves (an important factor in controlling the speed of the baking operation); the development and the use for matzo baking of the now-famous traveling ovens; and the standardization of the matzo quality.

Originally bakers of matzoth exclusively, the B. Manischewitz Company now markets a full kosher food line for Passover and daily use. In addition to the bakery, warehouse and office complex in Jersey City, New Jersey, the company now has a food processing plant in Vineland, New Jersey.

THE FIRST JEWISH MANUFACTURER OF READY-MADE CLOTHING

1854

Back in colonial times and in the early national period, families made their own clothes, employed itinerant journeymen tailors, went to custom tailors, or wore renovated garments. Aaron Lopez—the "Merchant Prince" of colonial New England—produced cheap, ready-to-wear garments for sailors, slaves, and the poor. The total production of such items until the 1830s was very limited. It is possible that as late as the Civil War, the second-hand clothing business in New York, at least, may have been more important than the trade in custom-made clothes.

During the period of the rapid development of the United States from 1830 to 1860, the system of home manufacture of clothing proved inadequate to the needs of unattached men having no homes or wives or sisters who flocked to the growing industrial centers and of the pioneers who "opened up" the West.

In the 1840s immigrant German Jews who were slowly beginning to make their way in the New World began to turn to the retailing and manufacturing of men's apparel, but the industry was to remain predominantly a Gentile one until well after the Civil War. Before and even after the perfection of the sewing machine by Elias Howe in 1846 and Isaac Singer in 1851, these early manufacturers employed the put-out system; the work was done by women who labored at home.

In the 1850s more and more Jews began making clothing for men. The decades witnessed the coming of millions of immigrants who sooner or later would have to be clothed.

For the first time, the census of 1860 recognized the manufacture of clothing as a national industry. Retailers and wholesalers with typical

American enterprise opened retail and wholesale outlets for their goods in different parts of the country.

It was natural for German-Jewish peddlers and shopkeepers, trained to meet whatever demand made itself felt, to include clothing in the stock of their "general stores," as soon as improvements in manufacturing lowered prices. When the community was large, they drifted into specializing in clothing. By 1860 some of the more successful of these earlier clothing shopkeepers in the larger cities had begun to manufacture ready-to-wear clothing. Freedley, who foresaw in the spread of ready-made clothing "a most important and complete revolution . . . in the ancient and respectable occupation of tailoring," in 1854 named Gans, Leberman & Co. and Arnold, Nusbaum & Nirdlinger (Wolf, Arnold & Nirdlinger), both of Philadelphia, in his list of "extensive and respectable clothiers in the United States." Indeed, in an advertisement in 1856, Gans, Leberman & Co. proclaimed itself "the oldest exclusively wholesale clothier in Philadelphia" and announced that its ready-made clothing was "manufactured under the care and superintendence of two of the proprietors who are practical tailors." In 1861, Bishop, in his *History of American Manufacturers*, records two other Jewish firms, Bernheimer Brothers and William Seligman & Co., in a list of fourteen clothing houses of New York enumerated among the largest in the United States.

The Civil War stimulated the production of ready-made clothes, the experience with uniforms demonstrating that certain combinations of measurements occurred with great frequency. For the first time uniform standards and measurements were adopted, and a growing labor pool made possible efficient factory production. As the style and fit of men's ready-made clothing improved, factory production whittled down the custom share of the industry.

During the next twenty years, from 1860 to 1880, a constantly increasing number of Jews became proprietors of clothing factories and wholesale as well as retail clothing merchants. Along with this, Jews became skilled clothing workmen, expert foremen and designers.

The factory production of women's garments developed somewhat more slowly, for most women had been long accustomed to making their own clothes or having better garments made to order. In rapid succession, however, manufacturers of cloaks and suits, shirtwaists and dresses, undergarments and nightwear improved the quality and style of their products, lowering their prices so that even greater numbers of women were pursuaded to purchase their garments ready-made.

By the 1880s, American Jews were well on their way to dominating the nation's apparel industry. So irresistible had the combination of cheap immigrant labor and the newest machinery become that an inspirational pamphlet entitled *Genius Rewarded: or The Story of the Sewing Machine* saluted new arrivals as they landed in New York, "the great mart of Sewing Machines in this country."

Despite the sufferings of the sweatshops, the Orthodox Jewish masses found it most satisfactory to work in the shops maintained by their coreligionists, where the Sabbath and all the Jewish holidays were observed. Only the hardy ventured forth during their early years in the United States to seek employment in the strange world outside the crowded city center.

The sword knife and the slotted table had replaced shears in the cutting room by 1880. The electrically operated knife followed, and advances in electric motor construction led to the perfection of the small portable rotary and reciprocating electric knives. Finally, the adoption of the steam-pressing iron in the place of the gas- or coal-heated irons and the electrification of the sewing machine completed the mechanization of the factory.

Then the manufacture of ready-made clothing, in common with its distribution and sale, became a pillar of the German-Jewish immigrant economy.

Noteworthy were the achievements of the Hart family, arriving in Chicago in 1858 from the Bavarian Palatinate with a brood of eight children. Two of the older sons, Harry and Max, opened a small clothing store in 1872. It thrived with the expansion of the city. In 1878 the brothers turned to manufacture and distribution. Supplied with additional capital by a distant cousin, Marcus Marx, and taking in another relative, Joseph Schaffner, an experienced creditman and bookkeeper, the four partners opened a small workroom on Chicago's South Side.

Hart, Schaffner & Marx was a competant, far-visioned company. The quality of their garments exceeded current standards. Instead of loading its salesmen with huge trunks, it sent them out with swatches. Theirs was the first company to adopt an all-wool policy and to guarantee colorfast-ness. Schaffner developed the advertising, marketing, and distribution techniques that became the norm for the industry. By the turn of the century Hart, Schaffner & Marx emerged as the largest manufacturer of men's clothing in the world.

When the soldiers of World War I were about to embark for home after the Armistice, they were greeted in France by banners assuring them that Hart, Schaffner & Marx would provide them with a good garment for their return to civilian life.

In its time, Joseph Schaffner's recognition of the Amalgamated Clothing Workers was no less spectacular. Any dealings with unions in 1911 were regarded, particularly in Chicago, as treason. In 1910 the entire clothing industry was in the midst of strikes, the Hart, Schaffner & Marx workers being led by Sidney Hillman. With a sharp sense of the value of goodwill, Joseph Schaffner decided to experiment in industrial democ-racy. In 1911 the Amalgamated Clothing Workers of America and Hart,

Schaffner & Marx signed a collective bargaining agreement that was not only steady, unbroken, and progressive but also mutually beneficial. Like Gompers, Hillman became an important national figure.

Although the German Jews did not invent the ready-to wear clothing industry, when once they got the foothold that they turned into control of the clothing manufacturing business, they cheapened the cost of clothing, improved its quality, and made it so practical that ready-made clothing became America's standard outfit for rich and poor alike. In addition to Hart, Schaffner & Marx, Koppenheimer, Hickey-Freeman, Stein-Bloch, and Rosenberg's Fashion Park soon became national symbols for the well-dressed man throughout the land for garments within the pocketbook reach of the masses.

Gradually Russian Jews displaced the earlier immigrants as clothing workers so that by 1897, not only in New York but in all clothing centers, three quarters of the clothing workers were Jews. Figures from the Bureau of Immigration show that by 1925, 362,642 Jewish immigrants were classified as skilled workers in the clothing industry.

After they had learned their trade in the establishments of the German Jews, Russian Jews opened their own shops in such numbers as to make women's wear their own domain. To them is due the credit for the American women becoming the best dressed women in the world and for style having been placed within the reach of the slenderest purse.

THE FIRST JEWISH COMMODORE

1860

Uriah Phillips Levy, one of the most colorful figures in American naval history, was America's first Jewish commodore, the then-equivalent of an admiral. He was the first Jewish officer to chose a life career in the United States Navy.

Born in Philadelphia in 1792 into a distinguished family of United States patriots, he was the grandson of Jonas Phillips of Revolutionary War fame and a cousin of Mordecai Manuel Noah. Uriah ran away to sea when he was ten years old. After two years as a cabin boy, his father apprenticed him to a ship's master. He then studied seamanship in the Naval School in Philadelphia. A second mate at eighteen, he commanded two years later the schooner *George Washington*, of which he owned a third.

At twenty-one he experienced the first real adventure of a life crammed with exciting triumphs and defeats; his crew mutinied, seized the vessel, and left him stranded and penniless on a remote island. Picked up by a British sloop and compelled to work his way, he resisted impressment in the British Royal Navy. Somehow Levy got back home. He raised money, rounded up the mutineers, and had them all brought back to the United States to be tried and convicted.

When the War of 1812 broke out, Levy immediately volunteered for service and was commissioned as sailing master in the United States Navy. Until 1813 he served on the brig *Alert*. Then he went on to the brig *Argus* on a mission of high importance to France and later captured twenty-one British merchant ships. Levy was placed in command of one prize vessel he had taken and rashly attacked a warship in the English channel. The American master and crew were captured and imprisoned in England until the end of the war.

After his release, although he rose rapidly in rank, his years in the Navy were far from untroubled. Some of his friends believed that Uriah's frequent quarrels with his fellow officers were due entirely to their jealousy of one who had served as a cabin boy, while they had received their training at Annapolis. But Levy himself insisted that his troubles were due neither to his humble beginnings nor his fiery temper, but solely to his loyalty to the faith of Israel.

While in Paris he heard a French officer and a civilian hiss the name of President Jackson, so he promptly challenged them both to duels, extracting apologies both to himself and to his country. He was tried six times by court-martial and repeatedly degraded in rank. He insisted on a chance to vindicate himself, had a special commission of inquiry appointed by Congress, proved his complete loyalty and efficiency as an officer, and was reinstated as captain in 1844.

Levy wrote several important observations gleaned during travel and received appropriate replies from the Navy Department.

In 1860, he was promoted to the rank of commodore, the highest title in the American Navy at that time. Given command of the squadron in the Mediterranean, he replaced Lavalette, the commodore who testified against him with all the vindictiveness of a Judeophobe.

As commodore he was one of the first individuals to fight against the barbarous practice of flogging on the high seas as a disciplinary measure, which finally culminated in the passing of a law abolishing corporal punishment in the United States Navy.

Indeed, Levy had long advocated such a change, not only in numerous writings, but during the War of 1812 as captain of the USS *Vandalia*, the first ship to sail with discipline maintained without recourse to the lash. Levy also published a *Manual of Internal Rules and Regulations for Men-of-War*, the first printed guide book for young officers' duties aboard ship, a work that ran into three editions, up to and including the "new age of steam."

Levy was so ardent an admirer of Thomas Jefferson that he donated a fine bronze statue of the president, which stands in Statuary Hall in the Capitol in Washington.

For many years Levy was the owner and preserver of Jefferson's beautiful home, which stands on a magnificent hill just above the University of Virginia. He labored to restore it and preserve it for unborn generations and established it as a memorial to the democratic president. Today it is one of the showplaces of America.

Uriah P. Levy, a religious man, was the first president of the Hebrew Congregation in Washington, D.C., and was also a member of Congregation Shearith Israel in New York City.

When the Civil War broke out, Levy was the highest-ranking officer in the Navy but too old for active duty. It is said that he offered the president his entire fortune for the war effort. Lincoln declined, and Levy subscribed heavily to the War Loan.

Uriah Phillips Levy died in New York two years later, in 1862, and is buried in Shearith Israel's Beth Olam Cemetery in Cypress Hills, Brooklyn, overlooking Jamaica Bay. Over his grave is a statue of him in full naval uniform with the inscription: "Father of the law for the abolition of the barbarous practice of corporal punishment in the Navy of the United States."

On March 28, 1943, the USS *Levy*, a destroyer escort, was named in his memory and launched at Port Newark, New Jersey.

Commodore Levy's name was further memorialized when the Jewish chapel at the Norfolk Naval Base was named the Commodore Levy Chapel. The ceremonies, held in 1959 in conjunction with the naming of the chapel, the Navy's first permanent Jewish chapel, was sponsored by the National Jewish Welfare Board's Armed Services Committee and the Norfolk Jewish Community Council. The Commodore Uriah P. Levy Jewish Chapel is located near the main gate of the historic naval station in Norfolk, Virginia, and is open to the public.

THE FIRST AMERICAN FLAG WITH HEBREW LETTERS

1861

Throughout his life, Abraham Lincoln had numerous Jewish associates and friends. To one of them he expressed his views concerning the bigoted "Know-Nothing Party." He was Abraham Jonas of Quincy, Illinois, who at one time served with Lincoln in the Illinois State Legislature. The Know-Nothing Party, as he wrote Jonas in a letter dated July 21, 1860, opposed Catholics and Negroes, and another time they might oppose Jews. Rather than live under the hypocrisy of American bigotry, Lincoln said he would prefer to live under open tyranny in a country such as czarist Russia.

This courageous stand won for Lincoln warm support of large sections of American Jewry. Influential Jewish political and community leaders rallied to him from all parts of the country. Among the delegates to the 1860 Republican National Convention was Lewis Dembitz of Louisville, Kentucky, a Hebrew scholar and uncle of Justice Louis Dembitz Brandeis. Designated a "Lincoln delegate," Lewis Dembitz voted for Lincoln's nomination as president. From an altogether different milieu came Sigmund Kaufmann of New York City, a popular Jewish publisher of German-language newspapers in that city, who "delivered" to Lincoln the liberal German immigrant vote in 1860. A Philadelphia political supporter was Moses Aaron Dropsie, of the wealthy and prominent Dropsie family, which founded Dropsie College for Hebrew and Cognate Learning a half century later.

Lincoln's concern for the Jews was reflected on the international scene as well as in America. When he took office, he appointed a Jew as consul in Zurich, Switzerland. Lincoln was the first and, happily, the only president ever called upon to revoke an official act of anti-Semitism by the United States government. In response to a petition and repudiating his favorite general, President Lincoln countermanded the notorious Order No. 11, which had been issued by General Ulysses S. Grant in 1862 during the Civil War, expelling Jewish peddlers from selling their merchandise to Union Army soldiers under the jurisdiction of the Department of the Tennessee—one of the military areas into which the country was divided.

Lincoln, recognizing the injustice of the order, issued instructions for its immediate cancellation. "To condemn a class is, to say the least, to wrong the good with the bad. I do not like to hear a class or nationality condemned on account of a few sinners," he wrote.

When Abraham Lincoln took up residence in Washington to assume the office of president of the United States in 1861, he received a gift of an American flag inscribed with Hebrew verses from the first chapter of the Book of Joshua. The inscription read:

Be strong and of good courage;
Be not afflicted, neither be thou dismayed;
For the Lord thy God is with thee, whatsoever thou doest.

The man who sent this gift was Abraham Kohn, a merchant and later city clerk of Cook County in Chicago. Kohn, like the majority of Jews in the United States were strong supporters of Abraham Lincoln in his fight for the emancipation of black slaves. Because of his militant republicanism, Kohn was widely known as "one of the blackest Republicans" and was in the forefront of every political activity. It was during the presidential campaign of 1860 that Kohn met Lincoln. Kohn's popularity and influence was brought to Lincoln's attention by his advisers, who recognized in the Jewish merchant an ally whose acquaintance would prove a valuable asset in the coming election. Lincoln was introduced by Congressman Isaac N. Arnold, who took him to Kohn's store. This meeting inspired Kohn with admiration for the distinguished visitor and a conviction that Lincoln was the designated American Moses and liberator of the slaves then in bondage.

This found expression in his unique message of encouragement sent to Lincoln shortly after the election.

Tribute was paid Kohn in a speech by President William McKinley in 1885 at a Lincoln Anniversary held under Jewish auspices:

> Could anything have given Lincoln more cheer or been better calculated to sustain his courage or strengthen his faith in the mighty work before him? Thus commanded· and thus assured, Lincoln journeyed to the Capital, where he took the oath of office and registered an oath in heaven, an oath to save the Union. And the Lord was with him until every oath was kept.

In appreciation of this gift, Lincoln wrote to Kohn to thank him. The president's letter was sent through a mutual friend, John Scammon Young, a prominent citizen of Chicago, who delayed delivering it until six months after Lincoln's departure from Springfield.

The text of Lincoln's letter has been lost and no copy exists. Nor can the whereabouts of the flag be traced. Years later, Kohn's daughter, Mrs. D. K. Adler, went to Washington and made an exhaustive search but had to abandon the effort. Kohn never saw or communicated with Lincoln again. His last association was in 1865, after Lincoln's assassination, when the mayor of Chicago appointed him to a committee of citizens to escort the train bearing the president's body to Chicago.

Kohn's flag is mentioned by Admiral George G. Premble in his standard work on the American flag, *The History of the Flag of the United States,* which was published in 1894.

In 1951 there appeared Dr. Bertram Korn's book *American Jewry and the Civil War,* which attempts to shed further light on the subject. It is the contention here that the souvenir presented to Lincoln by Kohn was a painting of a replica of the American flag and upon it in Hebrew appears the verses from the Book of Joshua, and not an actual flag as such.

THE FIRST AMERICAN JEWISH INTERNATIONAL BANKER

1862

In 1867 Joseph Seligman passed up the best bargain since Peter Minuit's original purchase of Manhattan Island from the Indians. He rejected an offer to buy all the land north of 60th Street and west of Broadway—up to 121st Street, where Grant's Tomb now stands, including most of what is now West End Avenue and Riverside Drive—for $450,000, a fraction of what a single city block would cost now. Had he decided differently, the Seligmans would today easily be the richest family in the world.

To educate his five sons, Joseph Seligman employed Horatio Alger, the future writer, as tutor. One can easily surmise how Horatio Alger hit upon his pattern of "rags to riches through pluck and perseverance" stories, which he turned out by the dozens.

For many years the Seligmans, who had landed as penniless immigrants, set the tone of German-Jewish society in New York City and were conspicuous as heroes of the American success story.

Joseph Seligman was born in Baiesdorf, Bavaria, in 1819. During a period of reaction and denial of rights, he managed to graduate from the Gymnasium of Erlangen and acquire what was equivalent of a two year college education. The poverty of the Germanic states after the Napoleanic wars and the oppression of all liberal thought prompted him to emigrate to the land of opportunity.

A steerage passenger, he arrived in the United States during the Great Depression of 1837 yet found a job in one of the Pennsylvania stores owned by Asa Packer. Joseph explained that he was good at figures, and the future millionaire and founder of Lehigh University hired him as a cashier-clerk. The salary of $400 a year might have satisfied many a native son, but eighteen-year-old Joseph sensed a better future in business. He turned his savings into merchandise—small jewelry, some watches, rings and knives—and was perfectly willing to set out on foot from village to farmhouse in Pennsylvania, carrying a heavy pack on his back.

A store in Lancaster was the reward for peddling. The store gave Joseph a warehouse where he could expand his line into heavier and more general merchandise—boots and overshoes, brooms, hardware and bags of feed. He was evolving from a foot peddler to a small-town merchant. As he prospered he brought his seven younger brothers to this country— William, James, Jesse, Henry, Leopold, Abraham, and Isaac.

The brothers began as peddlers and then opened stores in Pennsylvania, New York, Alabama, and California. They then became wholesalers and European importers, selling apparel, dry goods, and even cigars in their New York, St. Louis, and San Francisco establishments. By the late 1850s, they turned to the manufacture of clothing.

While Jesse and Henry operated a store in Watertown, New York, Ulysses S. Grant, a young lieutenant stationed at Sackett's Harbor on Lake Erie, came to buy and began a lifelong friendship with Jesse that extended to Joseph and the other Seligmans.

The Seligmans were the first of the German Jews to go into banking. They learned banking fundamentals so well that the firm of J. & W. Seligman & Company was the only New York commercial bank not closed by the Panic of 1857. The example of the Rothschilds pointed to the advantage of concentration and expansion within the family circle. With Joseph at the helm when they had started banking in New York City, the Seligmans prudently held on to the clothing business. This precaution proved fortunate, for shortly afterward, when the Civil War broke out, President Lincoln called for volunteers. Soon the largest mass of recruits ever yet enrolled in the American army were under arms. The Seligmans were equipped to furnish the armed forces with uniforms on a large scale. They received huge contracts and after the war demonstrated their patriotism by carrying the million-dollar debt owed by the Navy for an additional year—an extension highly appreciated by the harassed War Department.

Joseph Seligman virtually created international banking in America. In 1862 he expanded the scope of his New York institution; J. & W. Seligman and Company took on a promising side line. They began to sell American war bonds in Europe, primarily in Germany and Holland. When the federal government's credit needed support in financing the Civil War, the Seligman's succeeded in selling $200 million of government bonds to European investors. This was not an easy job. There was resistance because the United States was still a slave country; slavery was not repudiated until 1863. The Seligmans could do little business as bond salesmen in England and France, for the two world powers looked upon the North as a rival. The Germans and Dutch were more sympathetic. In the course of time they opened branches of their bank in London, Paris, and Frankfurt, as well as in San Francisco and New Orleans.

In 1871 J. & W. Seligman and Company was appointed one of the fiscal agencies of the United States to secure the conversion of its wartime loan, the "five-twenties," into new five percent bonds.

The services of the Seligmans enhanced their prestige in Washington. When Grant became president, he offered the post of secretary of the treasury to Joseph Seligman, who respectfully declined.

In the years following the Civil War, the mergers, bankruptcies, and the organization of railroads were creating an enormous field for stock and bond speculation. by 1869 Joseph Seligman and his brothers had already acquired a working capital of over $6 million, and their firm became the first German-Jewish banking concern to enter the railroad securities field. Joseph Seligman undertook to sell the South Pacific's first bond issue. Meanwhile, he was also helping to finance the Atlantic and Pacific Railroad. In the years to come his investments escalated from three railroads to over a hundred. At times, he himself seemed to be confused by his activities.

The Seligman firm was one of the first to espouse a waterway to connect the coasts of the United States and to this end headed an American syndicate to take over the ill-fated De Lesseps Company, which originally conceived of the idea of the Panama Canal.

In 1877 Joseph Seligman was at the height of his career. Moreover, he had been one of a committee that rescued the City of New York from the corruption of the Tweed ring. Financially successful, socially recognized, politically powerful, Seligman ranked among the nation's great. But neither character, prestige, nor patriotic service would ward off a vicious attack of anti-Semitism.

On June 13, 1877, Joseph Seligman arrived at the Grand Union Hotel in Saratoga Springs, New York, and applied for accommodations but was refused admission on the grounds that the new owner, Judge Henry Hilton, did not want "Israelites." Hilton had been a local New York politician connected with notorious Tweed machine. A power in the courts, Hilton had won over the goodwill of the former owner of the Grand Union Hotel, A. T. Stewart and became the executor-trustee of the deceased man's estate. The Grand Union incident aroused anger and indignation. Discussed in the press, on the pulpit, and in social circles, the snub was considered in political circles a retaliation for Seligman's activities in smashing the Tweed machine.

The Reverend Henry Ward Beecher—outstanding liberal, then America's leading clergyman, and brother of Harriet Beecher Stowe, the author of *Uncle Tom's Cabin*—made the Hilton-Seligman affair the subject of a widely publicized sermon entitled "Jew and Gentile." It was repeatedly reprinted until it became a sort of American classic. From that day on, Beecher became an outspoken and acknowledged champion of the Jews, and his potent voice formulated for many ardent followers their attitudes toward the Jews.

Joseph Seligman continued to serve his country and remained a leader in Jewish communal affairs until his death in 1880. One of the founders of the Hebrew Orphan Assylum (together with his brother Jesse), he was also president of the German Hebrew Benevolent Society, formed to assist oppressed German Jews. Loyalty to Judaism did not preclude his interest in the teachings of Felix Adler. Always the intellectual concerned with ideas, he became the first president of the Ethical Culture Society. He also served as a member of the Board of Education of the City of New York and presided over the first Rapid Transit Commission.

Shortly after his passing, among the many items in the newspapers was the notation that the village of Roller's Ridge, Missouri, through which one of his railroads passed, had voted to change its name and would thereafter be known as Seligman, Missouri, in tribute to the great man's life.

THE FIRST PEDIATRIC CLINIC

1862

Today spread all over the United States there are hundreds of pediatric clinics that treat thousands of children. Doctors learn, practice, and teach in them. But it was not until 1862 that the first pediatric clinic in this country was established. In that year Dr. Abraham Jacobi, a Jewish physician, opened the parent clinic.

Dr. Jacobi was born in Hartum, Westphalia, in 1830 and came to the United States in 1853. In the manner of European students of that day, he had gone from one university to another, from Greifswald to Gottingen and from there to the University of Bonn, from which he was graduated in 1851. He first studied Oriental languages but soon was attracted to medicine through his interest in anatomy and physiology. Meanwhile, the Revolution of 1848 broke out, and the young student was drawn into the struggle. When he went to Berlin to appear for his examinations, he was seized by the Prussian authorities and imprisoned for a year and a half in the fortress of Cologne. Finally, acquitted of the charge of treason, he made his way to Hamburg, where he boarded a ship for England. From England he sailed on a forty-three-day voyage to the United States, landed in Boston, and from there made his way to New York. He set up a medical office at 20 Howard Street and in the first year of practice earned $973 by charging 25¢ for office visits, 50¢ for house calls, and $5 to $10 for obstetrical cases.

A year later he attracted the attention of the medical profession with the invention of the laryngoscope. From then on, for over a period of forty-two years, he was connected with numerous hospitals in New York and taught pediatrics in the New York medical schools. He made significant contributions to the field of infant feeding and inaugurated the first bedside instruction for physicians in America.

When Columbia University's College of Physicians and Surgeons appointed Jacobi Professor of Infant Pathology and Therapeutics in 1860, the first systemized instruction in that field began. Here in 1862, two years later, he established a pediatrics clinic—the first in the country.

Another precedent among New York hospitals was created in 1878, when a separate service for the inpatient care of children was established at Mount Sinai Hospital through a legacy of $25,000, left to the hospital in that year by Michael Reese of California. The need for such a separate service had long been felt. The department in the Dispensary was not adequate to care for the number of children who came.

Dr. Jacobi was the first doctor in America to recognize the importance of boiling cow's milk for infant feeding and recommended it as early as

1877. When diptheria antitoxin was discovered, he was one of the first physicians to apply it in practice.

Dr. Jacobi, a constant contributor to medical journals, was founder and editor of the *American Journal of Obstetrics* (1868). Among his other contributions to medical literature were his books *The Raising and Education of Abandoned Children* (1870), *Infant Diet* (1878), and *Therapeutics of Infancy and Childhood* (1878).

The respect and admiration in which he was held by his colleagues was demonstrated by the honors they showered on him. He was the first immigrant elected to the presidency of many medical societies, including the American Medical Association, and he received honorary degrees from Harvard, Yale, Columbia, and Michigan.

At the age of seventy-two this passionate Democrat told the graduating class at Yale: "The greatest gift America has given to the world is not the realization of the republican form of government—ancient culture exhibited it before and allowed it to perish by political shortsightedness, lust of conquest, and undemocratic jealousy. It is anesthesia!"

Thus, for the first time the monster pain was put in its proper perspective.

Dr. Jacobi died in 1919 at an advanced age after a stirring life as medical practitioner, teacher, author, and distinguished figure in American medical circles. His chief work is the *Collectanea Jacobi*, which was published in eight volumes in 1909.

One of the hospital buildings of the $40 million Bronx Municipal Hospital Center, a teaching center of the Albert Einstein College of Medicine of Yeshiva University in the Bronx, New York, bears Dr. Jacobi's name.

THE FIRST JEWISH CHAPLAINS

1862

Thousands upon thousands of Jewish refugees had crossed the Atlantic to help build up a life of freedom for all. Now in America they found a nation in chains. They rallied behind President Abraham Lincoln to help make America the land of the free, for white men and black men alike.

As soon as the Civil War broke out, Congress passed on July 22, 1861, the act establishing the national defense. And it was provided that each regiment should have a chaplain, as it had been the custom heretofore "to be appointed by the commander on a vote of the field officers of the company." It further provided that the chaplain so appointed must be "a regular ordained minister of the Christian denomination."

This gave rise to widespread comment and agitation that was taken up by the newspapers and many public patriotic societies. The recently organized Board of Delegates of American Israelites, the only one really nationally representative group then in American Jewish life, presented to President Lincoln and to the Senate and to the House of Representatives a memorandum setting forth the facts that the Acts of Congress "be formally amended, so that there shall be no discrimination as against professors of the Jewish faith in the several laws affecting the appointment of Chaplains in the armed services of the United States."

Reverend Arnold Fischel of Congregation Shearith Israel of New York, backed by the authority of the Board, went to Washington to point out the need to President Lincoln and was most instrumental in bringing about the change in the law. In the meantime, without official recognition, he took upon himself the duty of visiting camps and hospitals, ministering to the needs of Jewish soldiers.

On May 20, 1862, the law was changed to include rabbis, and thereupon President Lincoln appointed Rabbi Jacob Frankel of Congregation Rodeph Sholom of Philadelphia hospital chaplain for the Philadelphia area. The second rabbi to be appointed a hospital chaplain was Rabbi Bernard Gotthelf of Louisville, Kentucky. He served in a number of hospitals not only in Louisville but also in southern Indiana. Only one rabbi was what we would call a fighting chaplain. He was Rabbi Ferdinand Sarner, whose pulpit had been in Rochester, New York, and who was appointed chaplain of the Forty-fourth New York Regiment, which fought in the Battle of Gettysburg. He was so badly wounded that he could not go back to active duty. He was told by the doctor in the military hospital that he could not serve anymore and that he would have to be discharged. Not knowing enough about military red tape to realize he would have to wait for his discharge papers, he left as soon as he got well enough. He limped for the rest of his life due to his wound. It took the Army five years to catch up with him, and then they finally discharged him as being AWOL (absent without leave).

There were no Confederate Jewish chaplains during the Civil War because there were not enough Jews in any one unit for them.

In the Spanish-American War, the question of chaplains did not arise as the war was comparatively short.

During World War I, President Wilson appointed six Jewish chaplains and, for the first time, a regimental chaplain—Rabbi Elkan C. Voorsanger. Since Rabbi Voorsanger was already abroad with a hospital unit, he received his commission there on November 24, 1917. He held the first Passover services in the war zone at St. Nazaire, France, in 1918—the first Jewish holiday celebration officially conducted ·by an officer of the United States.

Ultimately twelve rabbis saw active service as regimental chaplains, ten of them abroad. Thirteen others were commissioned first lieutenant chaplains and served in camps and cantonments with the Army in the United States.

The first rabbi appointed a Navy chaplain was David Goldberg of Corsicana, Texas, who entered the service in October 1917.

Just three days after the United States entry into World War I, leaders of American Jewish organizations met and established a board to provide for the needs of Jewish servicemen. A year later, supervised by the military authorities, it formally became known as the National Jewish Welfare Board and helped secure Jewish chaplains, conducted religious service for Jewish soldiers, generally spearheaded recreational activities, and gave whatever aid was necessary. Despite several name modifications over the years, the JWB's Jewish Chaplains Council of the Jewish Community Centers Association, now headed by Rabbi David Lapp, continues to serve as the primary American Jewish agency striving to meet the religious needs of Jews in uniform and in the Veterans Administration Hospitals.

It continued its work during World War II under the direction of Rabbi Aryeh Lev, often going to endless pains to fly chaplains to remote areas for Passover celebrations and other Jewish holidays. The number of full-time chaplains reached 311, of whom 250 saw service overseas; forty-six were decorated for bravery.

During World War II, the arrival in the extermination camps with messages of hope, the rescue of survivors of Nazi savagery, the founding of orphanages and schools, the opening of displaced persons camps, the uniting of families, and the rehabilitation of the scattered remnants all attest to the heroism, compassion, and devotion of the Jewish chaplains who were there.

Chaplain (Captain) Joshua L. Goldberg, U.S.N., Third Naval District Chaplain, was the first Jew to be appointed a district chaplain. A gallant hero in two great battles for freedom, with the Army in World War I, he was credited in participating in five major engagements; for service in World War II, he was awarded a citation with commendation ribbon.

On February 3, 1943, a German submarine sunk the troop ship USS *Dorchester* in the North Atlantic. Chaplain Alexander Goode along with two Protestant chaplains—Lieutenants Clark V. Poling and John P. Washington—and one Catholic chaplain—George E. Fox—went down with the ship after having voluntarily given up their lifejackets to enlisted servicemen. They received the Purple Heart and Distinguished Service Cross posthumously.

In 1948 a Four Chaplains Commemorative Stamp was issued by the United States Postal Service in their memory.

In the Korean Conflict, sixty rabbis saw active service as chaplains.

Rabbi Julie Schwartz was the first female military chaplain on extended duty. She entered the Navy in 1986 upon ordination from Hebrew

Union College-Jewish Institute of Religion, along with her husband, Rabbi Steven Ballaban (thus becoming the first husband-and-wife Jewish chaplain team). She served in the Oakland Naval Hospital in California until 1989.

Rabbi Chana Timoner, an officer in the Army Reserve, became the first Jewish woman to hold a long-term appointment as a chaplain in the United States Army. Rabbi Timoner, who graduated from the Academy for the Jewish Religion in New York City and was ordained as a Conservative rabbi, had completed her course for a doctorate at the Jewish Theological Seminary of America. She began her duties as a chaplain on January 8, 1993, at Fort Bragg in North Carolina, where she served soldiers and their families, directing adult and children's education, arranging holiday celebrations, and conducting religious services. She was responsible for the religious needs of a battalion of six hundred to seven hundred soldiers of all faiths.

Four Army, three Navy, one Air Force, and one Marine Jewish chaplain served in operational roles in the Gulf War. Chaplain Ben Romer, USA, from Fort Stewart, Georgia; Chaplain Maurice S. Kaprow, USN, aboard the USS *Saratoga;* Chaplain Howard Zyskind, USAF; and Chaplain Jon Cutler, USN, who served with the Marines at Camp Le Jeune, North Carolina, were the first Jewish chaplains from their respective branches of service called to action in the Gulf War.

Chaplain Ben Romer, the first rabbi to land on the ground, served in the area over eight months. For his superb efforts he was awarded the Bronze Star, as were two other Jewish chaplains serving there — Lieutenant Colonel David Zallis and Major Ken J. Leinwand.

For more than 130 years, Jewish chaplains have written an extraordinary chapter of dedication to their country, to the Jewish military community, and in the service of all Americans in uniform.

THE FIRST JEWISH STATESMAN

1862

By the time the War of Secession started, the number of Jews in the United States rose to 150,000. Six thousand Jews fought with the North and two thousand with the South. On both sides they served with distinction. The Seligman brothers of New York raised $200 million to finance the Union side of the Civil War. Southern Jews were ardently loyal to the South. They gave their brains, talents, brawn, and life. Judah Philip Benjamin of Louisiana served successively as attorney general, secretary of war, and secretary of state of the Confederacy. Representing the deep South in the United States Senate before the war, Benjamin stood foremost among the defenders of slavery. His loyalty to the system of slavery surprised Jews and Christians alike. The northern "free soil" senator from Ohio, Benjamin F. Wade, who knew of the devotion of Jews to freedom and justice, called Benjamin "an Israelite with an Egyptian heart."

Judah Philip Benjamin was born in 1811 of an old Sephardic family in the British West Indies. His impoverished parents brought their eight-year-old son to Charleston, South Carolina, where with the assistance of a Jewish philanthropist Benjamin received an early education. At the age of fourteen he entered Yale University, where he is accounted one of her distinguished students although he was never graduated from that institution. When he was seventeen, he moved to up-and-coming New Orleans and apprenticed in a lawyer's office, according to the practice at that time. When he was twenty-one he was admitted to the bar. Gifted with rare oratorical powers, in a short time he won an outstanding reputation in the legal field.

A passionate Southerner, Benjamin ran for the Louisiana State Assembly and was elected in 1842. Subsequently, in 1845, he was elected a member of the convention to revise the constitution of his State. His name became associated with celebrated legal cases, and his ability as a jurist became recognized nationally. President Franklin Pierce offered to nominate him to the position of associate justice of the Supreme Court of the United States. He preferred the turmoil of political life, however, and in 1852 was elected to the United States Senate and was reelected four years later. He was the first professing Jew to be elected to the United States Senate. (David Levy Yulee, who was elected to the Senate in Florida in 1845, had converted to Christianity). When Benjamin was senator, he had the reputation of being one of the leading orators of the Senate, a man compared to Daniel Webster and John Calhoun.

In 1855 he warned that secession was inevitable unless a reasonable compromise could be effected between the conflicting interests of the North and South. With the slavery issue in the forefront, Benjamin upheld the principle of state sovereignty. Like many southerners, he long resisted secession, but when the step was taken, he cast his lot with the Confederacy. On February 4, 1861, after Louisiana seceded, Benjamin delivered a brilliant farewell speech to the Senate and resigned his seat. Three weeks later, President Jefferson Davis appointed him first attorney general of the Confederacy. His abilities were soon demanded for secretary of war, a post difficult enough for any civilian who had to impose views and orders on such paladins as Lee, Jackson, Beauregard, and Johnston.

On March 17, 1862, in the face of hostile opinion, Davis promoted his war minister to secretary of state, a position virtually identical with that of prime minister in Europe. Benjamin was the Confederacy's most trusted adviser and was often referred to as "the brains of the Confederacy" because of Davis's reliance on him.

Benjamin's alliance with the Confederacy aroused the ire of many Union leaders in the North. This ire found expression in the form of anti-Semitic attacks. On one occasion when he was referred to as "that Jew from Louisiana" by a Senator in a debate, he replied, "It is true that I am a Jew and when my ancestors were receiving their Ten Commandments from the immediate hands of Diety, amidst thunderings and lightnings on Mount Sinai, the ancestors of my opponent were herding swine in the forests of Great Britain."

As secretary of state of the Confederacy, it was now Benjamin's mission to secure diplomatic recognition and intervention by England and France; this would break the Union blockade. Believing that England would not be able to get along without southern cotton, Benjamin tried to procure her aid, but with this his representative, James Mason, made little headway. Then he turned to France, through his representative John Slidell. Louis Napoleon was swayed, but the lack of communication facilities and the subsequent fall of New Orleans blasted the hope of an early intervention.

The southern armies, after their first brilliant victories, began to falter and retreat; their military failures were blamed on Judah P. Benjamin. A general who was defeated at Roanoke charged he had not been given proper supplies. The Confederate Congress censured Benjamin for his failure to send sufficient guns and ammunition for the Confederate Army. Benjamin did not try to defend himself. His defense, which could not be made public and which he withheld in order not to lower public morale, would have been very simple: He had no supplies to send.

After the Confederacy surrendered in April 1865, a reward of $50,000 was offered for his capture. At the end of the war, penniless and over fifty, Benjamin—after hair-breadth adventures, including a Robinson Crusoe shipwreck at sea—found his way to London. Here he was befriended by Disraeli and Gladstone. He once again resumed his practice of law and began writing books on legal subjects that brought him a fortune. His book *Treatise of Law on Sale of Personal Property,* popularly known as *Benjamin on Sales,* is still recognized in law schools and by law practitioners as a standard textbook in all English-speaking lands. Appearing before the Privy Council of Chancery Court of the House of Lords, he argued cases of the highest importance. Gradually bench and bar began to take note of the foreign Jewish lawyer who started at an age when many contemplate retirement and staged a comeback unequalled, perhaps, in legal circles. In some years he had an income of over $100,000, unprecedented legal earnings for the 1870s.

He became the first American Jew to hold the title of Queen's Counsel, an honor conferred only upon the most distinguished lawyers. (The second American to hold this title was Arthur Goodheart, dean of the law faculty of Oxford University and nephew of Herbert H. Lehman, former United States senator and governor of New York.)

The first public banquet ever given in honor of an American by the Bar of England was tendered to Benjamin upon his retirement. Graced by the Lord Chancellor, the Lord Chief Justice, and other high officials of the British Empire, Benjamin was toasted as the only man "of whom it can be said that he held conspicuous leadership at the bars of two continents."

Yet, Judah Philip Benjamin holds no place of honor in Jewish tradition for he held no contact with Judaism. Never a conscious convert to any other religion, he nevertheless lies in a Catholic cemetery, where his wife had him buried according to the rites of her church.

When he died in Paris in 1884, a contemporary newspaper said of him in a leading article: "His life was as varied as an eastern tale, and he carved out for himself by his own unaided exertions not one but three histories of great and well-earned distinction. Inherent in him was the elastic resistance to evil fortune, which preserved his ancestors through a succession of exiles and plunderings. . . ."

Such was the acclaim with which this strange career came to an end.

Two mansions associated with Benjamin—one his estate in Louisiana, Bellechase, and the other the house near Tampa, Florida, where he found refuge in 1865 during his flight from the country—were designated historic sites.

III

We Pay Our Debt
to America

THE FIRST JEW TO RECEIVE THE CONGRESSIONAL MEDAL OF HONOR

1864

Hundreds of Jewish soldiers gave their lives for the cause of Negro emancipation in the War between the States. Many led campaigns againt the Southern forces. Three foreign-born Jews—August Bondi from Vienna, Jacob Benjamin from Bohemia, and Theodore Wiener from Poland—joined John Brown, the fiery abolitionist, and later all three enlisted in the Union Army. The Seligman brothers of New York raised $200 million to help carry on the war. For centuries the Jew had fought for his own freedom. He was happy now to protect others from oppression.

At least ten Jews attained the rank of general in the Union Army. The highest military rank was attained by Fredrick Knefler of Indianapolis, an immigrant Jew born in Hungary who volunteered as a private in his hometown of Indianapolis and rose to be colonel of the 79th Indiana regiment. He rode with General Sherman on his historic march to the sea through Georgia in 1864. Knefler's highest actual rank was Brigadier General, to which the temporary rank of Brevet Major General was later added.

Three Jews were full colonels and brevetted brigadier generals: Edward S. Solomon of Chicago, Leopold Blumberg of Baltimore, and Philip J. Joachimson of New York, who was district attorney and had secured the first conviction for the inhuman traffic in slaves.

On July 12, 1864, for the first time in American history, Congress authorized the award of the Congressional Medal of Honor for bravery and heroism, the highest award that can be given to an American soldier and the most difficult to obtain. Seven Jews received the Congressional Medal of Honor, the first one going to Sergeant Leopold Karpeles.

Karpeles was born in Prague in 1838 and came to the United States at the age of twelve. Soon after his arrival, he went to Texas to join his brother, whose business was conveying caravans across the Mexican border. When the Civil War broke out, he enlisted in the Army in Springfield, Massachusetts, in the 57th Infantry as a sergeant. On April 17, 1864, the regiment left New England to go South to meet the enemy. They traveled through Washington, where President Lincoln watched them pass in review. By the end of April, they arrived at the Wilderness, Virginia, where General Sherman hoped to make the first step in taking Richmond.

Sergeant Karpeles and his regiment were soon under attack as they fought a bloody three-day battle. It was in the early evening of the third day and the woods were full of smoke and fire when the Confederate forces charged the regiment's lines. The colors entrusted to Karpeles were the only ones visible on the field.

He stood upright, holding up the colors for all to see, and General Wadsworth, observing them, rode up and down the lines, calling on every man in uniform to rally around the flag to check the Confederate attack. The men responded and rallied around the flag, lining up and firing back at the Confederate forces. They stopped the charge.

Sergeant Karpeles was awarded the Congressional Medal of Honor for his act in rallying the men of the 57th Massachusetts Volunteers around the flag and turning a retreat into a victory. The official citation read: "At the Battle of the Wilderness, May 6, 1864, while color bearer of his regiment, he rallied the retreating troops and induced them to check the advance of the enemy."

Karpeles was in many more battles after this engagement. He also saw action at Whitehall, Kingston, Goldsborough, Gum Swamp, and Gettysburg. He was wounded several times, once so badly that he was permanently left with a limp. He was in the Mount Pleasant General Hospital in Washington, D.C., being treated for his badly wounded leg, when he met the woman he was to marry.

Rabbi Simon Mundheim, rabbi of the Washington Hebrew Congregation, his wife, Hannah, and two daughters, Sarah and Henrietta, would go with him on visits to the hospitalized soldiers, where they could read to them or write their letters. It was on one of these visits that Sarah and Leopold met and fell in love. The doctors wanted to amputate his leg, although they felt that if he received the proper care at home, the leg might be saved. The Mundheim family took Karpeles home with them, and he was able to save his leg.

Five years after he married Sarah, she died in childbirth. His sister-in-law, Henrietta, came to take care of the two surviving children. He then married her, and they were blessed with six children.

His son, Dr. Simon Karpeles and his wife, Dr. Kate Karpeles, served with distinction in World War I, and they are buried in Arlington National Cemetery.

Many years later, following World War I, the Congressional Medal of Honor continued to be awarded to Jewish soldiers. Nine governments heaped awards upon Sergeant Benjamin Kaufman, who fought valiantly at Argonne, and his own country gave him its highest award—the Congressional Medal of Honor. For many years Sgt. Kaufman served as National Commander of the Jewish War Veterans of the United States.

THE FIRST HEBREW COLLEGES

1867

The need for a school to train rabbis, *hazzanim,* and Hebrew teachers was not keenly felt in America until the 1840s and 1850s. Rarely did a child attend school beyond the age of thirteen, which marked the year of confirmation and the year in which a boy gave up his formal studies and became apprenticed to a trade or worked in a business establishment. In New York, Mordecai Manuel Noah and S. M. Isaacs made constant mention of the need of a college of higher Jewish learning. In 1852 Sampson Simson tried to organize a Jewish Theological Seminary and Scientific Institute; however, it never progressed beyond the planning stage because he was too busy with other institutions.

Isaac Leeser, spokesman, educator, editor, and self-taught rabbi of Congregation Mikveh Israel, who had seen the need for higher Jewish education in America, had long harped on the subject in *The Occident and American Jewish Advocate.* He founded and opened the first Jewish institution for the rabbinate and other higher Hebrew learning in Philadelphia on October 27, 1867. Maimonides College, as it was called, was maintained by the Hebrew Education Society of Philadelphia and the Board of Delegates of American Israelites. Among the faculty were Marcus M. Jastrow and Dr. Sabato Morais, while Leeser served as president. Leeser died three months after the college was opened, but it carried on until 1873, when lack of funds forced it to close its doors. Five students comprised its first class, three of whom occupied pulpits.

The first Hebrew teachers' training school in the United States was established in Philadelphia in 1897 in pursuance of the will of Hyman Gratz, of the famous early American family of merchants, landowners, and civic leaders. Gratz bequeathed a sum of approximately $150,000 to Congregation Mikveh Israel in a trust fund "for the education of Jews residing in the city and county of Philadelphia." It was thought at first that he intended to project a general college, but since funds were insufficient, Dr. Cyrus Adler, then of the Smithsonian Institute in Washington, suggested that it become a college for the training of teachers for Jewish religious schools. Gratz College, still in existence today, offers a wide variety of undergraduate and graduate programs in Judaic, Hebraic, and Middle Eastern studies.

To provide a theological center from which the beliefs of Reform Judaism might be disseminated, Rabbi Isaac Meyer Wise founded the Hebrew Union College in Cincinnati in 1875 and served as its president until 1900. The first graduation was held on July 11, 1883, at which time Israel Aaron, Henry Berkowitz, Joseph Krauskopt, and David Philipson were ordained. The oldest center of higher Jewish learning in America today, it is now known as the Hebrew Union College-Jewish Institute of Religion and has four campuses, located in Cincinnati, New York, Los Angeles, and Jerusalem. The college-institute trains Reform rabbis, religious school educators, scholars, cantors, and communal workers. Its museums, libraries, and archives are repositories of Jewish art, history, culture that generates research, and publications.

It was the first successful attempt to train American rabbis for American Reform congregations. Through its graduates, Hebrew Union College forged a strong American Jewish consciousness by uniting the American ideal of equality with the Reform movement's vision of social justice.

With the rise of fascism in Europe in the 1930s, the college recognized the need for a political solution to Jewish persecution. Under President Julian Morganstern, the college embarked on a program of rescuing as many Jewish scholars as possible, and the Cincinnati campus became known as the Jewish College in Exile.

In 1948, during the administration of Nelson Glueck, Hebrew Union College became affiliated with the Jewish Institute of Religion in New York, which was founded by Rabbi Stephen S. Wise in 1922 to provide training "for the Jewish ministry, research, and communal service." Men of both Reform and traditional theological persuasion were encouraged to attend. President Glueck then launched the Los Angeles campus and in 1963 inaugurated the first building on the Jerusalem campus, which today includes a School of Biblical Archeology—a center for studies in the fields of Bible, archeology, and the history of ancient Israel.

During the administration of President Alfred Gottschalk, the first woman rabbi, Sally Priesand, and the first Israeli-born Reform rabbis in Jerusalem were ordained. The School of Jewish Communal Service in Los Angeles was founded, programs of study in Jerusalem for all first-year rabbinic and cantoral students were introduced, and the School of Graduate Studies on the Cincinnati campus—which confers Masters of Arts degrees in Bible and Cognate Studies, Masters of Philosophy, and Doctor of Philosophy degrees—was implemented. The school has gained renown for its unique Interfaith Fellow Program for Christian scholars.

The Jewish Theological Seminary of America, the flagship of Conservative Judaism, was created at a pivotal moment in the country's history. Tens of thousands of Eastern European Jews had begun to settle in the United States and Canada. Unlike the largely self-contained Jewish communities from which they had come, America offered an open society where Jewish affiliation was voluntary. Most immigrants wanted to acculturate without assimilating; they hoped to become Americans without giving up traditional beliefs and practices. Anticipating these needs, a small group of Sephardic rabbis, European Jewish scholars, and American

Jewish lay leaders convened in the fall of 1886 to found the Jewish Theological Seminary Association. Led by Dr. Sabato Morais, rabbi of Congregation Mikveh Israel in Philadelphia, he and his cofounders sought to establish an institution that would provide American rabbis with a thorough grounding of Jewish sources while helping them preach effectively in English and understand the social and economic realities of immigrant life. It would be traditional, continuing the centuries-old learning and interpretation of the Bible, Talmud, and medieval commentaries and codes. Yet it would also be modern, drawing on the emerging perspectives from such disciplines as history, philology, literary criticism, sociology, and psychology.

As there was no historical parallel to the situation in American Jewry in the 1880s, so there was no precedent for an endeavor such as the Jewish Theological Seminary. While other religious movements ultimately established professional and scholarly institutions, the reverse was true in the case of the Seminary and the Conservative movement; the institution "spawned" the movement.

In January 1887, the ten students recruited for the first Seminary class met in the vestry rooms of Congregation Shearith Israel. By the fall the students would move to larger quarters at Cooper Union, and in 1892 to a brownstone on Lexington Avenue, near Fifty-ninth Street.

Most students were teenagers who supplemented the rigorous eight-year rabbinical program with high school and college studies, often at Columbia University. In 1891 Columbia instituted its long association with the JTS by extending to Seminary students free tuition at its School of Liberal Arts and Philosophy.

The Seminary president was Dr. Morais who commuted four hours each way from Philadelphia three times a week. It was not until 1894 that the Seminary graduated its first class. Among the new rabbis was the first JTS alumnus who would make a mark on world history; Joseph H. Hertz, later chief rabbi of the British Empire and author of the widely used commentary on the Torah.

Morais's death in 1897 was a severe blow to the institution. His friend Dr. H. Pereira Mendes, rabbi of Shearith Israel, struggled to maintain the Seminary in the face of inadequate funding.

To the rescue came a group of prominent lay leaders and philanthropists. In 1901, at a party in New York at the home of business magnate Isidor Straus, Dr. Cyrus Adler, a Semitics scholar who was then assistant librarian at the Smithsonian Institute in Washington, mentioned the Seminary's financial plight. Among those who heard him was the investment banker Jacob H. Schiff, who promptly convened a group of prominent acquaintances from the worlds of law, business, and commerce, including Judge Mayer Sulzberger, Daniel and Simon Guggenheim, Felix M. Warburg, and

Louis Marshall. They pledged the very substantial sum of $200,000, which assured the Seminary's immediate future. It would never again be on such a precarious financial footing, and with a suitable building presented by Jacob Schiff, it forged ahead.

In 1902 the Seminary Board brought the institution to a new level of academic excellence by recruiting Dr. Solomon Schechter as its president. A reader in rabbinics at Cambridge University, Dr. Schechter had an international reputation both for his exploration of the Cairo Genizah (a storehouse of medieval Jewish documents), his discovery of priceless manuscripts belonging to the Genizah, and his scintillating essays on Jewish thought.

During his term as president (1902–1915), he gathered to the Seminary a faculty of scholars who were leaders in their disciplines. He appointed Dr. Louis Ginzberg as Professor of Talmud. From Europe he also brought Dr. Alexander Marx as Professor of History, Dr. Israel Friedlander as Professor of Bible, and Dr. Joseph Mayor Ashor as Professor of Homiletics. In 1909 Dr. Schechter established the Teachers' Institute, headed by Dr. Mordecai Kaplan, who later founded the Reconstructionist Movement, which defines Judaism as "an evolving religious civilization." The rabbinical school was transformed into a graduate school, and a program of advanced doctoral studies was instituted.

In addition, Dr. Schechter put the Seminary "on the map" by vigorously backing the new Zionist movement, which he predicted would be the "great bulwark" against assimilation. He opened the Seminary to Zionist activity and himself attended the eleventh Zionist Congress in 1913 in Vienna.

Furthermore, Dr. Schechter devoted his energy to community building. The rabbis trained during the Schechter years faced new challenges. Congregants were likely to look to them as models for how one could retain a commitment to *mitzvot* (commandments) while adjusting to the rapidly changing economic, social, and cultural realities of American life.

Dr. Schechter was succeeded as president by Dr. Cyrus Adler (1915–1940), who maintained the Seminary's position of scholarly eminence. The Seminary Library became the home to the most outstanding collection of Judaica outside of Israel. With the founding of the Seminary College of Jewish Studies, later united with the Teachers' Institute, the Seminary expanded to include undergraduate studies. Upon Dr. Adler's death, Dr. Louis Finklestein, a prolific scholar, was inaugurated as the institution's fourth president and in 1951 was named its first chancellor.

During the years of Dr. Finklestein's leadership, the Seminary flourished, growing from a small rabbinical school and teacher training program to a major university of Judaism. Dr. Finklestein also established the Seminary's Cantors Institute and the Seminary College of Jewish Music

(1952) and a West Coast branch in Los Angeles (1947) that later became the University of Judaism.

Interfaith dialogue was also among Dr. Finklestein's major priorities. He established the Institute for Religious and Social Studies, which brought together Protestant, Roman Catholic, and Jewish scholars for theological discussions.

Upon his retirement in July 1972, Dr. Finklestein was succeeded as chancellor by Dr. Gershon D. Cohen, who reorganized the Seminary schools and restructured their curricula. He emphasized close relations between Diaspora Jewry and Israel. He encouraged the formation of the Masorati (Traditional) Movement to promote Conservative Jewish institutions in Israel.

In May 1986, the undergraduate college was renamed the Albert A. List College of Jewish Studies. It offers a full spectrum of courses in Bible, Hebrew, Jewish education, Jewish history, literature, philosophy, and Talmud leading to a B.A. degree in Jewish Studies. It also conducts joint programs with Columbia University and Barnard College, enabling students to receive two B.A. degrees.

Dr. Ismar Schorsch became the head of the Seminary in July 1986. Like his two immediate predecessors, Dr. Schorsch was ordained by the Seminary. A member of its faculty since 1964, he served as the first dean of the graduate school from 1975 to 1979 and as Seminary provost from 1980 to 1984. Under his leadership, the Seminary embarked on a campaign to place Jewish education at the top of the communal agenda.

The Seminary became home to the Melton Research Center for Jewish Education, creator of quality curriculum materials for use in supplementary and day schools and developer of innovative teacher education programs, and the Franz Rosenzweig Lehrhaus, the Seminary's institute for adult Jewish learning.

On October 11, 1994, the Jewish Theological Seminary announced a gift of $15 million from William M. Davidson, a Detroit businessman and majority owner of the Detroit Pistons basketball team.

The world's largest and most comprehensive Graduate School of Jewish Education will open its doors at the Jewish Theological Seminary in September 1996, thanks to Mr. Davidson's gift.

On March 11, 1912, Bernard Revel became the first graduate of Dropsie College as he was awarded the degree of Doctor of Philosophy for his thesis, "The Karate Halakhah (Jewish law) and Its Relation to Sudduceon, Samaritan, and Philonian Halakhah."

In 1915, at the urging of Rabbi Moses Zebulun Margolis, the dean of the American Orthodox rabbinate, Dr. Revel accepted the position of president and Rosh Hayeshiva (head) of the recently merged Rabbi Isaac Elchanan Theological Seminary and Yeshiva Eitz Chaim of New York.

Under his leadership, the merged ÿeshivot developed into a world-famous institution. President Revel reorganized the program of study at the yeshiva and introduced a rabbinic program that was geared to prepare graduates capable of ministering to an Americanized Jewry. In 1922, the yeshiva absorbed the Teachers' Institute of the Mizrachi Organization of America (Religious Zionists). It was the first school of higher learning in this country to use Hebrew as the language of instruction. In so doing, it made Hebrew once again a viable, living language, and students at the institute became proficient in its daily use.

The Teachers' Institute has provided hundreds of principals and teachers for Hebrew schools throughout the United States.

Despite opposition from those who feared that Jewish studies would be undermined, in 1928, Dr. Revel founded Yeshiva College as an extension of the Rabbi Isaac Elchanan Theological Seminary and was its spiritual guide until the time of his death 1941. It was the first college of liberal arts and sciences in America to offer a traditional Talmudic education and a modern course of secular studies on a higher level. In 1945, under the leadership of his successor, Dr. Samuel Belkin, the institution attained university status and came to include a school for graduate studies, a school of social work, the Albert Einstein College of Medicine, and the Benjamin N. Cardozo Law School. Since 1977 it has been headed by Dr. Norman Lamm, a rabbi, philosopher, and author, its first president to have been born and raised in the United States and an alumnus of both of its institutions—Yeshiva University and the Rabbi Isaac Elchanan Theological Seminary.

In 1953 the Ner Israel Rabbinical College, founded in Baltimore in 1933, was given the authority to grant the degrees of Master and Doctor of Talmudic Law from the Maryland State Board of Education. This was the first time in Jewish history—and, indeed, in the history of education—that a doctorate has been authorized purely for the study of Talmud.

The Bureau of Jewish Education of Boston, appreciating the need of providing American-trained teachers for various types of Jewish schools, purchased on December 9, 1920, a synagogue building located at 14 Crawford Street, Roxbury, for the purpose of conducting a Hebrew College.

Dr. Nissan Touroff, formerly the head of the Jewish School System of Palestine, was appointed dean. On November 27, 1921, two classes were opened with a total registration of thirteen students. The number of students grew rapidly. In the spring of 1924 construction work began on a large annex adjacent to the original quarters. Through the influence of the Hebrew Teachers' College, a Principals' Association of Greater Boston was organized in 1923, and a uniform curriculum for all the Hebrew schools of Boston was adopted.

The Hebrew College has evolved into a nationally and internationally recognized college granting bachelor's and master's degrees in

Jewish studies and Jewish education and bachelor's degrees in Hebrew literature. It houses the Hebrew Teachers' and Principles' Institutes, the Jewish Music Institute, a Center for Adult Jewish Studies, and the Wilstein Institute of Jewish Policy Studies.

Its summer camp, Camp Yavneh, founded in 1944, and located in Northwood, New Hampshire, is the first Hebrew-speaking camp to provide regular Hebrew instruction on a daily basis and to conduct all its programs and activities entirely in Hebrew.

The significant successes of its new Shoolman Graduate School of Education, its cross-registration agreement with Northeastern University, its Eli and Bessie Cohen Residential Kerem Summer Institute, and its Elderhostel programs have created concomitant needs for additional classrooms, faculty, library space, office space, and other amenities utilized by an academic institution.

On February 28, 1995, Hebrew College President Dr. David Gordis announced that it will leave its quarters in Brookline's historic Longwood section and will relocate and develop its own campus on land leased or purchased on an undeveloped portion of the Andover Newton campus of Andover Newton Theological School, the oldest Protestant graduate school in the country founded in 1807 as the Andover Theological Seminary.

Although the initial announcement sent shock waves rippling through the Jewish community, Hebrew College Provost Barry Mesch assured that "each institution will function as a separate entity."

The Hebrew College and Andover Newton will maintain their own educational missions, guiding philosophies, presidents, separate and distinct faculties, facilities, boards of trustees, and administrations.

In academic terms, the schools are now contemplating allowing students to take courses from both catalogs and establishing a joint degree program. In addition to the library, the one major area where the schools would share facilities, the schools may set up a new center for common areas in Jewish and Christian studies—women's studies, the history of religion, psychology, the arts, or sociology.

Andover Newton students would definitely have access to a deeper, richer understanding of Judaism. The benefit to the Jewish community of providing this access remains to be seen.

THE FIRST AMERICAN JEWISH SCULPTOR IN THE IMPERIAL ACADEMY

1872

The nineteenth century was hardly an era propitious to the fine arts. America, still a fairly young country that needed forests cleared, houses erected, railroads built, and rivers spanned, had no time for leisure. But strangely enough, there lived at that time a Jewish sculptor of international renown, Moses Jacob Ezekiel, who not only made outstanding statues but perpetuated in bronze, marble, and clay the beauty and noble aspirations of mankind as well as its ugliness and vicissitudes. His unusually distinguished career as an artist included several international medals and knighthoods from both the king of Italy and the emperor of Germany. In 1872 the highest honor was bestowed upon him when he had the privilege of being accepted as a member of the world-famous Imperial Academy of Arts in Rome. He was the first American and the first Jew to receive such a distinction.

Born in Richmond, Virginia, on October 28, 1844, he was the son of Philadelphian-born Jacob Ezekiel. The desire to paint, to sculpt, to model, manifested itself quite early. But the tidal wave of patriotism for the seceded Confederacy soon submerged every other feeling. In 1861 young Moses entered the Virginia Military Academy and enlisted as a cadet in the Confederate Army. He took part in the Battle of New Market during the Civil War and rose to the rank of lieutenant. At the war's end, since there was no art school in America at the time, Ezekiel went to Berlin, Germany, to study sculpture at the Royal Academy of Art. In 1872 he won an award that took him to Rome for further study.

For the next forty-four years, Ezekiel lived and worked in Rome, although he made frequent trips to the United States. In the capital city of Catholicism, he never concealed his Jewishness. Yet the eternal city cast a spell on him. Identification with past Roman grandeur found expression in his famous studio set up in the Baths of Diocletian and later removed to the vaulted Belisarius Tower in the old city walls. Here he assembled the art treasures of many places and periods. To his studio came artists, diplomats, aristocrats, and leading notables of the world, including Garibaldi and D'Annunzio, the great Italian liberators, and even the king and queen of Italy. Among his friends were the celebrated Robert E. Lee, Franz Liszt, and William II, King of Wuerttemberg.

His works were exhibited in art salons of many European cities. For one of his earlier works, his bas-relief *Israel*, he was awarded the Michel Beer Prix de Rome in 1873. He was the first American sculptor to receive this award.

American history was another of his favorite subjects. It was in recognition of his colossal bust of George Washington that the Imperial Academy accepted him into their fold.

Ezekiel's best-known work from the Jewish point of view is his heroic statue *Religious Liberty*. It was commissioned by B'nai B'rith as a gift to the people of the United States on the celebration of the centennial of American Independence and placed permanently in Fairmount Park,

Philadelphia. The first piece of sculpture dedicated to this theme in America, it was unveiled on Thanksgiving Day in 1876. On the front of its pedestal is this excerpt from the Constitution:

> Congress shall make no law respecting the establishment of religion or prohibiting the free exercise thereof.
>
> 1776–1876

Ezekiel chiseled into marble his conception of the Judaic spirit. Among his subjects besides *Israel* and *Religious Liberty* are *Adam and Eve; Cain or the Offering of the Rejected; David; Queen Esther,* which stood in the palace of the Sans Souchi before the Russians took East Berlin over; and the monument to Massarini in the Jewish cemetery in Rome.

American to the bone, Moses Ezekiel was affected by politics, industry, and the history and ideals of his native land. He was also sensitive to the culture of the past, to classic Hellenism, to Roman and Renaissance art, and to modern music. He was deeply attached to the lost cause of his younger days — the fallen Confederacy. His statue of *Virginia Mourning Her Dead* stands in Lexington, Kentucky; the *Stonewall Jackson Monument* graces the State House in Charleston, West Virginia; his *Robert E. Lee Monument,* commissioned by the Daughters of the Confederacy, was dedicated at Arlington National Cemetery by President Woodrow Wilson.

Among his other works are busts of Beethoven, Liszt, Longfellow, Shelley, Jefferson, Isaac Mayer Wise, and Edgar Allen Poe (his last work). His bust of Lord Sherbrooke is in Westminster Abbey.

Ezekiel worked furiously to his last days. The astonishing number of his creations ran into the hundreds. They are to be found in public squares and university campuses, in palaces and state capitols, in art museums and navy yards, and in Washington, Paris, London, Berlin, and Rome.

Rarely had there been more fluctuating estimates of a man's work than the varied appraisals to which Sir Moses Ezekiel was subjected. After Ezekiel's first efforts were scorned, he was recognized as one of the greatest sculptors of the nineteenth century. There followed a period in which he was alternately honored and assailed. For a while his creations, regarded with faint approval, were largely neglected. Then, a few years later, Ezekiel was rediscovered and was compared to Michelangelo.

Ezekiel died in Rome on March 27, 1917. In his will he specified that he be buried in his beloved native land, but because of the war, his body was not returned to the United States until four years later. When the Daughters of the Confederacy, donors of the *Confederate Monument* in Arlington, which he had designed, asked to have him buried at the foot of the monument, his family agreed. Rabbi David Philipson officiated at the burial service, which was held at the Arlington Amphitheater on March

30, 1921. This was the first public service held at the famous structure where the tomb of the Unknown Soldier is located.

The lengthy autobiography, *Memoirs from the Baths of Diocletian*, Sir Moses Jacob Ezekiel left behind at his death abounds in anecdotes and gossip about the upper-class Europe of his day. There is no doubt from a letter in the appendix that he was a proud and conscientious Jew. In this letter he hopes for Jewish colonization in Palestine as a solution to the problems of Russian Jews. He was a Zionist even before Herzl. "There was no reason why Palestine should not flower again like a garden. . . ." he proclaimed in a letter written to his father in 1891. He envisaged a Jewish Palestine secure with all the necessities for independent living, including "education of a military character."

THE FIRST JEWISH ORCHESTRA CONDUCTOR

1873

New York today has one of the finest symphony orchestras in the world under the best conductors, is home of the Lincoln Center for the Performing Arts and the excellent Julliard School of Music, and has evoked much popular interest in music. Throughout the nineteenth century, interest in music was growing, but it was not until 1873 that the first symphony orchestra was formed.

Leopold Damrosch, its conductor, a Prussian-born Jew, came to New York in 1871, and up to the time of his death he was one of the most important musicians in America and one of the most vital forces in the elevation of musical standards in this country.

Born in Posen, Prussia, in 1832, Damrosch displayed an early talent for playing the violin. His parents, however, disapproved of a musical career and insisted that he study medicine. After his graduation from Berlin University, he attempted to practice medicine for a short while but returned to the study of music and violin.

Damrosch was soon touring the less-important cities of Europe, playing the violin as a virtuoso. His performances impressed Franz Liszt, who appointed him first violinist in the famous orchestra he directed for the duke of Weimar. Leopold's reputation grew, and Posen made him director of its City Theater. When he was thirty, he became conductor of the Philharmonic at Breslau and together with Liszt was instrumental in introducing many new works of contemporary composers.

In 1871 Damrosch was invited to come to America to become the musical director of the New York Arion Society, a choral society dedicated to promoting neo-German music in America. This was in a day when Italian opera was dominant. The Damrosch home became a sort of shrine for music lovers and inspired them to go forth as musical ambassadors. With a small circle of friends, mostly amateurs, Damrosch started the Oratorio Society. A decade later, its membership had risen to five hundred and ranked among the world's leading choral groups. At first they met on Saturday evenings in the music hall of Damrosch's home, then, as the group got larger, in Pythian Hall. They engaged in choral singing and played symphonies and other music for their own enjoyment. Damrosch himself led the group and played the violin.

In 1873 Damrosch and his friends also formed the New York Symphony Society (predecessor of the New York Philharmonic), the first organized group in New York devoted to symphonic music. These three societies gave hundreds of concerts until 1926 and did much to raise the standards of and gain appreciation for good music.

As conductor of the Oratorio and Symphony societies, Damrosch was able to assemble a chorus of twelve hundred together with an orchestra of 250 instruments. In the huge Seventh Regiment Armory, he scored unforgettable triumphs with the greatest of all requiems by Berlioz, with Rubinstein's *Tower of Babel*, with Handel's *Messiah*, and with Beethoven's *Ninth Symphony*.

In 1881 Damrosch conducted the first great music festival in New York, unprecedented in scale and scope. He was hailed as one of the two best conductors in America.

When Damrosch accepted the directorship of the Metropolitan Opera House for the 1884–1885 season, he was impelled by the opportunity to bring German opera, chiefly the musical works of his friend Richard Wagner to the American public.

Worship of Wagner, the musical genius, probably blinded Walter Damrosch, as it did many others, from detecting the dangers lurking in Wagner, the racist, who could seldom acknowledge merit in any composer not a German.

A newspaper review of the time, recalling Damrosch's brilliant opera season, says of him: "And together with Anton Seidel he conducted a season of German opera at the Metropolitan Opera House which will remain memorable in the musical annals of America."

Damrosch was also the first to conduct Brahms works in this country. In addition, he carried on the weekly task of training the Arion and Oratorio societies.

His distinguished career came to an end in 1885 when he complained of feeling ill during a rehearsal of Verdi's *Requiem* and was rushed home in a cab. Pneumonia set in, and, weakened by overwork, within a week he died. He was eighty-eight years old.

It was as conductor of the New York Symphony Society that, after inheriting the baton from his father, Walter Johannas Damrosch, son of

Leopold Damrosch, earned for himself the title "Dean of American Conductors." He fell heir to the Oratorio Society and the Symphony Orchestra and managed both successfully for a number of years. He conducted the Metropolitan Opera House and organized the Damrosch Opera Company. He toured the length and breadth of the country with his orchestra. For the first time in America, music of great composers was brought to towns and villages where it had never been heard before. The son was also responsible for the first American performances of many great works and was the first American conductor to go on a tour of European cities.

In 1928 under the instigation of David Sarnoff, chairman of the board of directors of the Radio Corporation of America, Walter Damrosch conducted the weekly "Music Appreciation Hour," which became a regular part of the curriculum in thousands of American schools.

Walter Damrosch composed four operas, but his most popular compositions are the songs he set to Kipling's poems, including *On the Road to Mandalay*. After forty-two years of service, Walter Damrosch resigned as conductor of the New York Symphony Orchestra and joined the National Broadcasting Company as musical director. Perhaps his greatest contribution was popularizing music by broadcasting into the homes of millions who listened on the radio to his lectures on music appreciation.

THE FIRST BLUE JEANS MANUFACTURER

1873

Among the many adventurous men who went to San Francisco in 1853 in the feverish hunt for gold was young Levi Strauss. Just twenty-four years of age and only six years in America, Strauss had no money to buy equipment he needed to join the search for gold in the El Dorado. Instead he brought with him a bundle of heavy fabrics that he hoped to sell for tent covers and wagon tops. Though he was to strike it rich in the West, it was not through a pickax and shovel, but with a pair of pants.

Bavarian-born Levi had come to America in 1847 with his mother and sister. He was preceded by two older brothers who put him to work peddling with them on the East Coast. But it was no life for the young man. In 1853, during the Gold Rush, he bought a ticket to California. After sailing five months on a clipper ship from New York—17,000 miles around South America—Levi finally stepped ashore at a rowdy frontier town aflame with gold fever. Seeing the city's gold-boom economy, Levi Strauss sensed the opportunity for a thriving dry-goods business. He had taken supplies for such a business with him from the East, including canvas for tents and Conestoga wagon covers. But the miners didn't want cloth for their tents and wagons. They were sorely in need of clothes, especially pants tough enough to withstand rough treatment.

Levi Strauss took the cotton duck, a heavy canvaslike fabric, to a tailor and created the world's first jeans. Word of the quality of the pants spread quickly, and he began turning out dozens of pairs. Levi switched to a sturdy fabric (or "serge") that had originated in the Middle Ages in Nimes, France, called "serge de Nimes." Later the name of the fabric was shortened to "denim."

Strauss, however, was not able to solve the problem of the torn pants that the miners would stuff with gold nugget specimens and tools until a Reno, Nevada, tailor, named Jacob Davis took the pants to a harness maker and had the pockets riveted with copper fasteners. Davis discussed this solution with Strauss and together they patented the innovation in 1873. Soon the business grew as word spread throughout the country of the durability of the pants.

Levi Strauss & Co. advertised their riveted clothing as being "so tough even a team of plow horses could not tear them apart." The two-horse logo became one of the company's most famous trademarks. It has been in use longer than any other United States apparel trademark.

Levi did not refer to the pants he manufactured as "jeans." The word "waist-overalls" was the common name for pants of this type. Not until 1960, well after his death, did the company refer to them as "jeans," a word derived from the term for cotton trousers called "genes" by the French which referred to the pants worn by ancient sailors from Genoa, Italy. By the mid-1960s Levi's jeans were being marketed all over the world. Cowboys wore them because they endured the roughness of the saddle and long rides on horseback. Factory workers used them to protect themselves from the grime and grit of their surroundings. Soon movie stars, socialites, and the world of fashion made them the "in" thing to wear.

In addition to overseeing the growth of his company, Levi Strauss devoted his time and resources to charitable and philanthropic endeavors. His community service included membership on the board of the California School for the Deaf and the establishment of twenty-eight scholarships at the University of California. His business advice was sought by many, and throughout his career he served as director of a bank, an insurance company, and a utility. He was a charter member of the San Francisco Board of Trade. He was a devoted member of Temple Emanu-El of San Francisco, remaining faithful to Jewish traditions and observances all his life. He left large sums of money to Jewish, Catholic, and Protestant orphanages.

When Levi Strauss died on September 26, 1902, at the age of 73, flags in the San Francisco wholesale business district flew at half mast. The city's newspapers printed lengthy front-page columns and obituaries. The

San Francisco Call's headline over the obituary read: "His life was devoted not only to fostering the highest commercial conditions but to the moral, social, and educational welfare and development of the young men and women of the state."

Since Levi never married, he left his business to his four nephews, and the oldest, Jacob Stern, became president. Sigmund Stern took over the business when Jacob became chairman of the board of directors. In 1958 Walter Haas, Jr., a grand-nephew of Levi Strauss, assumed the office.

By the mid-1960s Levi Strauss & Co., surpassed one milestone after another. Its employees made more than just Levi's jeans. The company introduced sand-colored denim pants that teenagers dubbed "White Levi jeans." Then came stretch Levi's jeans and corduroy Levi's jeans, followed by Sta-Prest, the revolutionary process that made trousers stay pressed permanently even after machine washing and drying.

The beginning of the 1970s brought new corporate leadership to the company. Peter Haas succeeded his brother as president, and under his guidance growth continued unabated. The rapid expansion required capital to build plants and develop all aspects of the business. To secure it, the Haas and Koshland families sold stock in the company to the public in 1971. Sales hit $1 billion in 1975 and doubled a mere four years later.

When Peter Haas left the presidency of the company in 1981, he was succeeded by Robert Grohman—the first non-family president. Walter Haas, Jr.'s son, Robert, who took over in 1984, is the current chief executive officer and Levi Strauss's great-great-grand nephew. In 1985 relatives of Levi Strauss had restored full ownership of the company to the family by repurchasing the publicly held stock.

In memory of Walter Haas, Sr. the Haas family gave more than $23 million for the establishment of the Haas Schools of Business at the University of California in Berkeley. It was the largest gift in the university's history.

Walter Haas, Jr., together with his brother Peter E. Haas and his sister Rhoda Haas Goldman created the Walter and Elise Haas Promenade which provides a magnificent panoramic vista over the whole of Jerusalem.

Today Levi Strauss & Co. is the world's largest apparel company. Factories, warehouses, and sales offices, more than one hundred in all, have spread across the continent and beyond. A new computerized system being installed at some original Levi's stores allows women to order customized blue jeans. A sales clerk measures the customer using instructions from a computer as an aid. The final measurements are relayed to a computerized fabric-cutting machine at the factory.

To this day one can watch the sewing of the famed Levi's blue jeans, the originals with the copper rivets, manufactured in the historic building at 250 Valencia Street since 1906, when the original factory was destroyed in the San Francisco earthquake. Tours are conducted once a week on Wednesdays for visitors. A contrast to the little clapboard plant is the beautiful redbrick Levi Plaza, world headquarters of the company at 1155 Battery Street in San Francisco.

THE FIRST "ONE PRICE" STORE

1874

Jews have taken part in making American business synonymous with enterprise and achievement. Such a Jew was David Lubin who put into operation a number of innovations that establish him as one of America's merchandising pioneers.

Lubin was born of Orthodox parents in Klodova, Galicia, Russia-Poland, in 1849. When he was an infant four days old, the wick of the Sabbath candle flew off and burnt his face, leaving a scar that lasted a lifetime. His mother cried at the injury done, but the mystical rabbi of the community scolded her for crying on the Sabbath day instead of rejoicing. As for the child, the Zoharite explained, it had received a special mark of Divine favor through the medium of the burnt candle that was blessed. The child was marked for God's service, he declared. He should be named David after the biblical king, and in days to come he was destined to do great things.

When David was just six years old, his parents brought him to America and settled on New York's Lower East Side. At the age of twelve he left school and obtained a job in Attleboro, Massachusetts, polishing the gold plate of cheap jewelry at $3.60 a week. When the Civil War broke out, he ran away to sea and tried to join the Army. From that time on he shifted for himself, doing odd jobs, making a trip across the continent to San Francisco, joining a gold-prospecting expedition to Arizona and getting lost in the desert for two days without food or water, then returning East to his family.

His stepbrother Harris Weinstock, who had $600, induced David to open a dry-goods store with him in San Francisco. But soon David decided to be on his own. In 1874, when he was twenty-five years old, he made a trip across the continent again and landed in Sacramento, which at that time, although the state capital of California, was still a rough mining camp. He rented a small store above a basement saloon. The sign, D. LUBIN-ONE PRICE, showed originality at a time and place when haggling and bargaining were habitual in retailing.

Here for the first time in America was established the principle of selling merchandise at retail with fixed prices marked in plain figures on each item. In a short while Lubin won everyone's respect for honesty and fair dealing. The Mechanic's Store, as it came to be called, became a Sacramento institution. Before the year 1874 was over, he had established and advertised several business principles that today represent fundamental precepts of retailing but then were startlingly new: (1) to sell at one price only; (2) to mark all merchandise with the selling price in plain figures; (3) to never misrepresent merchandise; (4) to buy or manufacture goods at the lowest price possible; (5) to figure out at how low a profit the goods could be sold. The enterprise became not only the largest retail store in Sacramento, when later Lubin added a San Francisco store, he thus founded the first chain of stores in America.

As his business grew and people from near and far came to buy from him, he solved the broader problems of transportation by establishing for the first time in America the mail-order house. (The development of the mail-order house from that time on, especially as expanded by the great philanthropist Julius Rosenwald, founder of Sears-Roebuck & Company, is the saga of the modernization of rural life. Hardly an item for personal or general use was omitted from the huge catalog that the firm distributed annually to over forty million people until 1992.)

In 1884 Lubin made a journey with his devout mother to Palestine. He always considered it the climax of his career. In the Holy Land, his observations led him to conceive of the small land-owning farmer as the basic factor in a democracy. Upon his return to America, his interest in business shifted to farming. He bought a farm in California and set out to master the subject of agrarian economics. He began to study soils and methods by which California farmers could best raise products for the market, a study he felt could apply to the rebirth of Palestine. He soon became owner of the largest fruit-packing company in the state and founder of the California Fruit Growers' Exchange. At this time he was also one of the early sponsors of cheap parcel post.

Convinced that the consumer could buy food cheaper and farmers could get more by-products through cooperation on a worldwide basis, he founded the International Institute for Agriculture. Through this organization Lubin convinced nation after nation of the value of his idea of pooling knowledge to improve the food of the world. Nation after nation saw the feasibility of his plan, and forty-five countries joined in what was the first permanent international cooperative in the world, the precursor of the League of Nations.

Lubin was appointed the first United States representative to the institute and continued in this post for ten years. The institute met in Rome, and the king of Italy, Victor Emmanuel III, gave a splendid building for its use. Nations sent their official representatives and technical experts to cooperate with Lubin, who worked equally for the American farmer and the common man the world over. Farmers from all parts of the globe were sent by their countries to talk with each other about their problems and exchange information about soil and crops.

Some of the institute's experiments were attempted by the New Deal in Roosevelt's administration. In 1946 the International Institute of Agriculture became part of the United Nations Food and Agriculture Organization.

Emphasis on his Jewishness was an outstanding characteristic of Lubin's. Samuel Gompers, in his autobiography, *Seventy Years of Life and Labor,* calls attention to this. "Lubin insisted upon forcing on all with whom he came in contact his pride in his Jewish ancestry. He stated upon any and all occasions that it was his greatest glory that he was a Jew."

On January 1, 1919, David Lubin died in Rome at the age of seventy, overflowing to the last with fiery enthusiasm, never ceasing his untiring labors for his cause.

In 1936, the city of Rome paid posthumous honor to this practical visionary by naming a street for him—the Via David Lubin.

THE FIRST YIDDISH POET

1876

Jacob Zevi Sobel (James H. Sobel) is considered the first Yiddish poet in America, though Yiddish verse had been written here before his time. Of the twenty Yiddish writers of verse of the period, the only one singled out as a writer of literary merit was Sobel. Born in 1831 in Lithuania, Sobel was ordained as rabbi and headed a yeshiva, but influenced by the *Haskalah* (the movement among Russian Jews for secular culture in lieu of exclusive rabbinical learning), he broke with Orthodoxy. In 1876 he arrived in New York, then later moved to Chicago, where he earned his living as a Hebrew teacher. He contributed to Hebrew periodicals in Russia and the United States but also wrote for the Yiddish and American press.

Sobel's first poem in Yiddish in this country appeared in the *Yiddish Gazette* in 1876. It bore two titles in one, one in Hebrew—"The Golden Song of Israel"—and one in Yiddish—"Old Israel." A year later, in 1877, there appeared a small book of his verse with the same titles, which has the distinction of being the first book of Yiddish poetry published in the United States. The volume contains in addition to *Haskalah* motifs lauditory verses in praise of the Hebrew language, a poem entitled *"Der Polnisher Talmud Chochem in America"* ("The Polish Scholar in America"). Sobel describes a European talmudic scholar and his experiences in the new country during his first few days here. The scholar becomes a peddler and thus improves his financial status, but he bewails the ignorance and the lack of spiritual ideals among the Jewish immigrants of the 1870s.

Sobel, who had studied at the world-famous Slabodka Yeshiva in Poland, had contributed Hebrew verses as well to such Old World periodicals as Smolensky's *Hashachar* (*The Dawn*) and also wrote a book of Hebrew poetry, a paean to Jewry, the Hebrew language, and American democracy that condemns the ignorance and spiritual emptiness of Jewish immigrants.

It was not until several decades later that Morris Rosenfeld was to become the first Yiddish poet whose works were translated into other languages by men of letters.

Born in 1862 in the village of Bolkshein, Russia-Poland, Rosenfeld grew up in Warsaw. After learning tailoring in London, he emigrated to New York in 1886 and worked as a presser in the sweatshops whose inferno he later immortalized in his famous poems of the shop entitled *Songs of Labor.* Rosenfeld is revolutionary in the theme and tenor of his song. Reared in the spirit of traditional Judaism, he draws much of his inspiration from the old literary sources, but for form and versification, he is indebted to the English and German masters, especially Schiller and Heine. At the same time he is original in the treatment of his subjects and in the pathos and imagery with which his writing abounds.

His first collection of poems, *Di Gloke* (*The Bell*), appeared in 1888 and was followed by *Di Blumen-Kete* (*The Flower Wreath*) in 1890. During the next decade his reputation grew as his songs were sung by workers in factories and at mass meetings. His collection *Liederbuch* (*The Book of Songs*), published in 1897, was the sensation of the day in Yiddish literary circles. Its translation into English by Professor Leo Wiener of Harvard University introduced him to the larger, non-Jewish world. Rosenfeld probably did more than any other Yiddish poet to bring home to the American reading world the economic tragedy as well as the yoke of serfdom brought about by the industrial revolution.

Rosenfeld also wrote on national and romantic themes. During his lifetime Yiddish poetry developed far beyond his capabilities, but his successors' achievements were made possible only because of his pioneering efforts and stylistic innovations.

Yet even though Rosenfeld was for many years supreme in American Yiddish literature, he found his master and superior in "Yehoash," pseudonym of Yehoshua Solomon Bloomgarden. Born in Vierzbolavo, Lithuania, in 1870, Yehoash as a boy came under the influence of both the yeshiva and *Haskalah*. At the age of seventeen he took his first Hebrew poem to Warsaw, where I. L. Peretz encouraged him to continue writing Hebrew and Yiddish lyrics. The following year Yehoash emigrated to the United States. For a decade he faced severe privations until he contracted tuberculosis in 1900 and went to the Denver Sanitorium for Consumptives to recuperate. There he remained for ten years, maturing as a Yiddish poet, publishing his poems, ballads, and fables in leading newspapers, periodicals, and journals.

Less well-known to the outside world than Morris Rosenfeld, nevertheless Yehoash came forward as a forceful exponent of verse of much that is best in Jewish thought and feeling. He may well be considered the greatest lyric poet Yiddish has yet produced. In his early thirties, he undertook to translate the Bible into modern Yiddish, which would combine scholarly precision with simple idiomatic language, a task to which he devoted the rest of his life. His *Gamelte Liede* (*Collected Poems*, New York, 1910), as well as a later volume *In Sun Un Nebel* (*Through Mist and Sunshine*, New York, 1913), are among the finest collections of Yiddish verse of the twentieth century. He also mastered classical Arabic and translated portions of the Koran and Arabian Tales into Yiddish.

Yehoash is also noted for his piercing humor. His prose is limpid and true as his verse is sublime. He translated into Yiddish Longfellow's *Hiawatha* and the *Rubiat* of Omar Khayyam. His lyrics were reprinted in many anthologies and were translated into many languages.

THE FIRST TALKING-MACHINE INVENTION

1877

To some of us the most wonderful of all the marvelous inventions of which we have so many these days is the talking-machine or phonograph record, no matter by what name we call it. That a black, flat disc covered with tiny grooves should be able to give us the golden voice of a Caruso, a Placido Domingo, or a Luciano Pavarotti; the wonderful tones of a violin in the hands of a master; the full crash of a brass band or the winged words of a great orator seems impossible to believe, yet we know that it is true.

Scientists had known for a long time that it was possible to make a record of the vibrations of sound, and the first practical instrument to do this was patented by Thomas Alva Edison in 1876. By simply reversing this machine, it was found that you could "make it talk." However, the first successful talking-machine record, and the one most of us know today, was patented in 1877 by a German Jew named Emile Berliner who lived in Washington, D.C., in the first decade after the Civil War.

Born in Hanover, Germany, in 1851, Emile Berliner graduated from a German school at the age of fourteen. Eleven children were too many for his father, a small merchant with a Talmudic background, to support. So Emile went to work as a printer's devil and then in a dry-goods store.

While handling fabrics at the age of sixteen he showed an inventive streak by constructing a weaving machine, although he had never had any scientific training.

Hanover, in 1866, was taken over by Prussia. When a visiting family friend from America offered Berliner a job, he eagerly accepted the opportunity to emigrate to the free land across the ocean.

After clerking in a men's furnishing store in Washington, D.C. and then working at odd jobs, he went to New York. He found work analyzing sugar in the laboratory that subsequently discovered the method of manufacturing saccharin out of coal tar. His evenings were spent in the scientific library of Cooper Union, reading books on acoustics and electricity.

Berliner became interested in Edison's newly invented talking machine. Edison had established its feasibility when his half-baked experiment talked back. For several years the Edison Company was selling gramophones (phonographs) that reproduced on soft wax cylinders the human voice in a mechanical, nasal twang. Edison saw the gramophone as primarily for office use to record dictation. Berliner saw the popular entertainment uses of the phonographs that Edison did not.

Discarding the cumbersome cylinder as impractical, Berliner invented the flat disc, which propelled the reproducing stylus or needle in a groove of even depth and varying direction. This disc made of a hardened rubber material could be produced in large quantities and sold cheaply. The moveable reproducer was a great improvement over Edison's fixed machine. The Berliner gramophone developed into the Victor Talking Machine with its logo of a dog listening to "His Master's Voice," the primitive forerunner of today's complex electronics. Victor records became a medium of culture and pleasure in every civilized country and were sold the world over.

As a result of Berliner's foresight, his company grew to dominate the field. The Berliner Gramophone Company introduced the idea of paying royalties to singers and other artists for exclusive recording contracts. It produced and placed on the market a low-priced record player and made the first shellac records in 1897. In the same year it opened—in Philadelphia—the first commercial recording studio and the first record shop in an adjoining building so that what the studio produced the shop could sell.

Emile Berliner thus made possible the modern record industry. His company was eventually absorbed by the Victor Talking Machine Company, now known as RCA.

For Berliner's development of the so-called "lateral-cut method" of recording the human voice, which became the heritage of radio broadcasting, Berliner was awarded the Elliot Cresson Gold Medal of the Franklin Institute in Philadelphia.

In the same way, much of the credit that goes to Alexander Graham Bell for having invented the telephone should also go to Berliner, for it was he who really made it a practical instrument. In its early, formative stage in 1876, the telephone was hardly more than a toy used for the amusement of youngsters listening to each others voices through the walls of their homes. Sound carried imperfectly, and speech needed repeated shoutings for the ear to distinguish words at the other end. Bell's invention lacked a practical transmitter, since it used magnetic induction and the human voice produced only weak, undulating currents. Berliner's invention—patented in 1877 as a telephone receiver—permitted a clear sound of greater volume and resulted in the increase in the distance of communications. The Bell Telephone Company soon bought the rights to the Berliner transmitter, and he was engaged for three years as chief instrument inspector of the company.

Berliner continued to make improvements in telephony and was the first to use an induction coil in connection with transmitters. Without Berliner's contribution, the commercial telephone as we know it today would be inconceivable.

His tinkering with the telephone led Berliner to invent another acoustical device: the microphone. The value of this instrument becomes apparent when one realizes that radio, television, and the recording industries would be silenced without it. The original Berliner microphone now occupies a place of honor in the Smithsonian Institute in Washington.

Berliner's inventive genius reached out and noticeably affected the domains of many other inventions. In 1925 he invented acoustical tile for securing better acoustics in auditoriums. He made the motion picture projector possible, and he added further devices to the telephone.

As early as 1903, Berliner had experimented with helicopters and made some significant contributions. He collaborated with his son, Henry, a graduate of Cornell and M.I.T., in designing three different kinds of helicopters that made successful flights from 1919 to 1926. He also invented the air-cooled engine with revolving cylinder, now still in use extensively in airplanes.

Public health was another of Berliner's consuming interests. Convinced that epidemics of typhoid, diptheria, and scarlet fever were largely traceable to raw milk, Berliner worked to popularize Pasteur's theories. Through his efforts, pasteurization received federal endorsement in 1907.

Having had little formal education himself, Berliner ensured education for others by contributing to Hebrew University in Jerusalem in the early years of its existence. He became interested in the rebuilding of a Jewish State in Palestine. He favored the Jewish pursuit of agriculture and assisted the National Agriculture School in Doylestown, Pennsylvania.

In religion and philosophy, Emile Berliner could be classified as an agnostic, judging from his book, *Conclusions*. Yet, in his later years he came to realize that the differences in religion were not the sole cause of group hatreds.

It was in speaking of him that President Herbert Hoover said: "The German immigrant boy, Emile Berliner, has become one of our most useful citizens."

Active to the end, Emile Berliner died in Washington, D.C., on August 3, 1929 at the age of seventy-eight. His novel inventions made the world more enjoyable, more communicative, and more colorful than it had ever been before.

THE FIRST RED CROSS MEETING

1881

While the Civil War was being fought, the foundation of a great international humanitarian movement was being laid in Geneva, Switzerland. In 1863 a congress of delegates met to found the Red Cross. The movement called for international agreements for the protection of the sick and wounded during wartime without regard to nationality and for the formation of voluntary national societies to give aid on a neutral basis. The United States at first remained aloof, partly because of the sympathy of European nations toward the Confederate cause. During the late 1870s, however, private meetings were held at the homes of Washington, D.C., citizens in anticipation of American adherence to the Red Cross Treaty. One of the principal meeting places was the home of Adolphus Simeon Solomons, a New York-born Jewish publisher who had become prominent in Washington's communal affairs and its philanthropic organizations.

Born in New York City in 1826, he was the son of an English journalist who wrote editorials for New York newspapers. A graduate of City College of New York, Solomons went to work for a firm that imported stationery and fancy goods. He was evidently sent on a business mission to Europe when Secretary of State Daniel Webster appointed him "Special Bearer of Dispatches to Berlin." While abroad he visited a Jewish ward in a hospital in Frankfurt, Germany. He determined to establish a similar institution in New York City, and when he returned home he became one of the founders of Mount Sinai Hospital, first known as the Jews' Hospital.

On June 25, 1851, he married Rachel Seixas Phillips, a descendant of a distinguished colonial family of devoted patriots. They had eight daughters and a son.

In 1859 he moved his own printing plant of Philip and Solomons to Washington, D.C., which for a number of years was the official government printer until the Government Printing Office was established. He added to his plant a book department and a photographic gallery to which many prominent people came.

On the executive committee of the Board of Delegates of American Israelites, Solomons was the most prominent Jew in the capital during the Civil War period.

Solomons was active in Jewish life. In 1862 he was one of a group of Jews that appealed to President Lincoln to rescind General Grant's anti-Jewish military Order No. 11 expelling "Jews as a Class" from his lines on the grounds that their mercantile activity interrupted the movement of his troops in the Union Army's Department of Tennessee—one of the military areas to which the country was divided.

When the District of Columbia was granted self-government, Solomons was elected to their House of Delegates and served as chairman of the important Ways and Means Committee. In 1873 President Grant proposed Solomons as governor of the District of Columbia, but Solomons declined the office because he was a Sabbath observer and felt that the duties necessitated violation of the Sabbath, which he strictly observed.

Throughout his years in Washington, Solomons's name was identified with the establishment of every important social welfare agency. He organized the first training school for nurses and the Washington Night-Lodging House Association that supplied homeless men with lodging. As a leader of the Jewish community he took part in all the presidential inaugural ceremonies from the time of Abraham Lincoln to that of William H. Taft. He was a close friend of Lincoln, and one of the last, if not the very last, photographs of Lincoln was taken in Solomons's place of business.

Perhaps the most significant of Adolphus Solomons's humanitarian efforts were those he devoted to the Red Cross. In May 1881, together with Clara Barton, he issued a call for volunteers to meet in his home at the very first meeting to help organize the American Red Cross. It was here that a proposal was accepted in June 1881 to incorporate in the District of Columbia a society known as the American Association of the Red Cross, and the movement in America officially began. He was one of its two vice presidents and first treasurer.

After the United States ratified the Red Cross Treaty of 1882, President Chester Arthur appointed Clara Barton, Judge Joseph Sheldon, and Adolphus Solomons to represent the U.S. Government at the International Congress of the Red Cross held in Geneva. Solomons was elected first vice president of that congress.

When Clara Barton was absent from Washington in 1883, he conducted the young organization's affairs from its Washington headquarters and was described by Barton as "my good vice president and kind counsellor." Solomons held this office for twelve years. During the Spanish-American War he was still a member of the executive committee of the American Red Cross, which rendered an important service in ministering to the needs of American soldiers. In subsequent war and domestic relief, the Red Cross assumed a role that made it an almost indispensable organization in American life.

In his later years, Solomons became general agent in the United States of the Baron de Hirsch Fund, an influential organization set up to help ameliorate the condition of Jewish immigration from Eastern Europe and to assist in Jewish colonization projects.

Solomons died on March 8, 1910 in his eighty-fourth year. On his death, Louis Marshall, the noted American Jewish leader, summed up the feeling of contemporaries toward Adolphus Solomons with the following tribute: "He believed in the sacred duty of personal service, and he performed that duty as a religious act with cheerful heart, serious mind, and willing hand."

THE FIRST ZIONIST ORGANIZATION

1882

Since the destruction of the Second Temple in Jerusalem in the year 70 C.E., throughout the ages, Jews have always looked in constant prayer and hope for their return to the land and the city of their birth.

Modern Zionism was actually begun and practical work for the rebuilding of the National Jewish Homeland started when the First Zionist Congress was called by Theodor Herzl in Basel, Switzerland, in 1897, almost one hundred years ago. Though Zionism made its first appearance on the American scene almost at the beginning of the world movement, the first Zionist endeavor dated back many years before. Major Mordecai Manuel Noah—who in 1824 declared, "We will return to Zion as we went forth, bringing back the faith we carried away with us"—is considered the first articulate American Zionist. However, his attempt to set up a temporary "city of refuge" for Jews, to have been known as "Ararat" on Grand Island in the Niagara River near Buffalo, New York—the grand scheme of his life—proved a failure. Twenty years later we find him writing a pamphlet in which he advocated Jewish restoration of Zion by Jewish self-effort, demanded support of the Christian world for Jewish resettlement in Palestine, and suggested that the land be acquired through purchase.

Modern Zionism was imported to America with the stream of Russian-Jewish immigrants in the early 1880s, dating from the establishment of the *Choveve Zion* (Lovers of Zion) movement in Russia that was founded by Rabbi Samuel Mohiliver, the head of Bialistok Jewry. Several branches appeared in larger communities in the United States and claimed a few hundred members.

While intellectual personalities joined the movement in its early days, the Russian Jew in America was especially fertile ground for its development. He had the nationalistic sympathy reinforced by the Russia pogroms and, in addition, was building up wealth to support it. In 1892, in New York City, a Russian Jew founded the first *Choveve Zion* group in America. Even in his student days in New York University's Medical School, Dr. Joseph Bluestone dreamed of a Jewish State in Palestine that would serve a spiritual purpose and as a refuge necessary for the persecuted Jews of Europe, whose effulgence would permanently sustain American Jews and keep them safe from assimilation.

Dr. Bluestone's aspirations were translated into a speech he delivered on the Fourth of July 1882, when the poetess Emma Lazarus, in *An Epistle to the Hebrews*, gave voice to the plea and wrote of the need for "a free Jewish state . . . a home for the homeless . . . and a nation for the denationalized."

Dr. Bluestone edited and published *Shulamith*, the first periodical in the United States devoted exclusively to upholding the nationalistic Jewish viewpoint. His constantly growing activities as a physician did not abate his activities on behalf of Zionist matters. He was the first vice president of the New York chapter of the Federation of American Zionists upon its formation in 1897 and three times served as grand master of the Order Sons of Zion (later known as Bnai Zion). He also served as secretary of the American Mizrachi (Religious Zionists) upon its formation in 1909.

There were many other visionaries like him, and the movement began to grow. Another society was organized in Baltimore in 1890 under the name of *Ahave Zion* (Lovers of Zion). In Chicago, Bernard Horwich organized a Zionist society in 1895 that sent Leon Zolotkoff as a delegate to the first Zionist Congress in Basel in 1897.

The first interstate Zionist body in America was charted in Chicago on October 27, 1897, under the name of Knights of Zion. Its leading figures were Bernard Horwich, Leon Zolotkoff, and Max Shulman.

The first national conference of the representatives of the *Hovevei Zion* from New York, Philadelphia, Boston, and Baltimore took place in the spacious study of Professor Richard Gottheil at Columbia University in New York City in 1897. Professor Gottheil, a prominent orientalist and archeologist, served as the first president of the movement that became known as the Federation of American Zionists. It was a loose union of several existing societies, all adhering to Herzl's Basel program, which called for a "publicly recognized" and "legally secured" homeland in Palestine.

Between 1898 and 1900 over fifty Zionist societies were organized throughout the land. Gottheil remained in office until 1904, when he was succeeded by Dr. Harry Friedenwald, a prominent opthalmologist from Baltimore. In 1902 Jacob de Haas, an English Jew who had been Herzl's secretary in London, producing the *Jewish Advocate*, a weekly periodical in Boston, became secretary of the Federation of American Zionists and editor of the *Maccabean*; this monthly was for many years the official Zionist publication, until succeeded by the *American Zionist*. In 1903 Louis Lipsky, a young journalist from Rochester, New York, took over both of these offices. A little later an attempt was made to interest larger masses by establishing a Yiddish organ, *Dos Yidishe Folk* (*The Jewish People*), edited by Abe Goldberg, founder of the first Labor Zionist party in America—Poale Zion—organized in New York City in 1903 and now known as the Labor Zionists Alliance.

By 1900 there were over one hundred Zionist societies in existence. From the very start, the organization worked slowly and quietly. It had special problems of its own, such as the charge of double patriotism, which several leaders answered in special pamphlets. The Zionists had to fight Jacob Schiff, the Reform rabbinate, and the American Jewish Committee on this charge.

American Jews were aroused by the Kishineff pogroms in Russia in 1903 and 1905, which, aided and abetted by the authorities, saw forty-seven Jews slain, hundreds wounded, thirteen hundred houses and shops plundered and wrecked, and two thousand families made homeless. The Zionists took an active part in the relief work for the unfortunates, and the condition of European Jewry began to seem closer. This resulted in the growth of the Zionist movement here. A feeling of closeness was strengthened by the visit of Shemarya Levin in 1906 and later by Nachum Sokolow, leading European Zionists.

Just before World War I, in 1912, Hadassah, the Woman's Zionist Organization of America, was founded by Henrietta Szold to carry on health work in Palestine. It not only introduced modern medical methods but established a new hospital, medical center, and health units, which pioneered in many "medical firsts," opened a nurses' training school, and set up the country's first infant welfare stations. Thus began the great humanitarian project of American Jewish women still going on to heal the sick and strengthen the healthy in the Jewish homeland. (Today it also conducts various educational projects through internationally recognized facilities in Israel as well as other programs worldwide.)

As part of the Federation of American Zionists, Bnai Zion, a fraternal organization, was founded in 1908 on the principles of Americanism, Zionism, and fraternalism. It offered life insurance and other benefits to its members. In the ensuing years the Bnai Zion Foundation began to support various humanitarian projects in Israel and the United States, chiefly the Bnai Zion Medical Center in Haifa and homes for retarded children in Maon Bnai Zion, in Rosh Ha'ayim, and the Herman Z. Quittman Center in Jerusalem. In the United States, it sponsors programs of awards for excellence in Hebrew for high school and college students.

In 1907, the Zionist Federation created Young Judaea as its junior department, seeking to educate Jewish youth toward Jewish and Zionist values. Later it was reorganized and adopted as a project by Hadassah. In 1915 there was also created the Intercollegiate Zionist Association to spread Zionism on the campus.

The Mizrachi Organization of America (Religious Zionists) was established in 1911 by Rabbi Meyer Berlin (Bar-Ilan, in whose memory Bar-Ilan University in Israel was founded in 1955). In time it became the backbone of the World Mizrachi Organization by virtue of its numbers and resources.

By 1914 Zionist sentiment in America was already strong enough for American Zionists to send a delegation of forty to the Eleventh Zionist Congress. This was the first congress with adequate American representation.

When World War I broke out, the American Zionist leaders felt called upon to act in the emergency. In August 1914 an extraordinary conference of all Zionist groups met. It had been called by Louis Lipsky on behalf of the Zionist Federation of America at the instigation of Shemarya Levin, then a member of the World Zionist Executive. A Provisional Executive Committee for General Zionist Affairs was formed with Louis Dembitz Brandeis as chairman and Rabbi Stephen Wise as vice chairman. An emergency fund for institutions in Palestine was also established.

In accepting the chairmanship of the Provisional Committee, Brandeis, a relative newcomer to the cause and already known as the famed "people's attorney," assumed the responsibilities of American Zionist leadership, which in fact involved trusteeship of the world movement and the Zionist institutions in Palestine. He plunged into the work with vigor, drawing into the circle of Zionist action not only men of prestige such as Nathan Straus, Felix Frankfurter, Julian Mack, and Horace Kallen but also great mass support. The Zionist Organization boasted of a membership of over 176,000 and 270 local societies nationwide in 1919, with thousands of others affiliated with the Orthodox and socialists groups. Brandeis headed the American Zionist movement for nearly seven years and made a tremendous contribution to the world Zionist cause, particularly during the years of World War I, when the Jewish community of Europe faced dissolution, and European Zionists were forced to halt their work. Under his able leadership the financial resources of the organization were greatly improved, modern accounting methods were introduced, and substantial aid to the Palestine institutions was furnished. The organization gained steadily in political influence, enabling it to play a decisive role in the events that led to the issuance of the Balfour Declaration on November 2, 1917, in which the British government pledged to facilitate the establishment of the Jewish National Homeland in Palestine.

During this time the movement was reorganized on a permanent basis as the Zionist Organization of America (ZOA), being formed at a convention in Baltimore in 1917. It included all groups except the religious Mizrachi and the socialist Poale Zion and was based on the idea of individual membership organized along geographic lines. Brandeis became honorary president and Judge Julian Mack, president.

At the Pittsburgh Convention in June 1918, the so-called Pittsburgh Program, drawn up by the Brandeis group as the basis of the charter of the Jewish National Homeland, was unanimously adopted and was later carried by the American Zionists to the peace conference. The platform called for political and civil equality of all inhabitants of Palestine; equality of opportunity, with public ownership of land, natural resources and utilities; free education; the cooperative principles of economic development; and Hebrew as the national language.

With the Armistice international, Zionism began to reappear, and contact with Europe and Palestine became a reality again.

At the first Zionist Congress after the War held in Basel in 1946, the moderates were replaced by a bolder leadership—David Ben-Gurion of Israel and Rabbi Abba Hillel Silver of the United States. Under Silver's leadership, the Zionist movement in America lost a certain inhibition against using all available political pressure to attain Jewish national aims. American Zionist pressure began to achieve results when President Harry Truman called for the immediate admission of 100,000 Holocaust survivors into Palestine. President Truman, using his right as president of the United States, single-handedly made the historic decision to recognize the newborn Jewish state eleven minutes after its proclamation of Independence on May 14, 1948.

During the half century between the First Zionist Congress in Basel in 1897 and the establishment of the Jewish state in 1948, Zionism was a major issue in the life of the American Jewish community. Perceiving the need for an independent Jewish state in Palestine, Orthodox, Conservative, Reform, and secularist Jews joined their efforts and raised millions of dollars to assist European survivors of the Holocaust and fighters for the State of Israel.

On May 14, 1948, with the birth of the Jewish state, the Zionist Organization became a faithful ambassador of the Jewish state to the masses of the Jewish people in the Diaspora. The common effort now was concentrated on mass immigration, the rapid absorption of the newcomers, and the upbuilding of the country.

"The first two decades after independence would bring war, hostility, and siege with Arab armies," wrote Abba Eban, Israeli statesman, scholar, and author in *Heritage: Civilization and the Jews*. But within the siege there would be a great eruption of creativity. A million Jews from dozens of lands would join the 650,000 Israelis who laid the foundation of the state. They would bring with them a diversity of skills, devotions, experiences, and talents. Hundreds of cooperative villages and collective farms would spread a green carpet over the expanding landscape. New cities, new schools, universities—above all, thousands of homes—would give Israeli society a new breadth and a new solidarity.

Faced with war, terrorism, isolation, and economic boycott, Israel has not only survived against all odds, it has flourished.

The State of Israel Bonds program in the United States was inaugurated in 1951 by David Ben-Gurion as a major source of investment capital for the young state. By March 1994, $14 billion in bond sales had been raised since its inception. Israel Bonds proceeds have been utilized to build and develop an important array of industrial, agricultural, and technological projects.

The success of Zionism was as great as it was unanticipated. A barren, poverty-stricken land was transformed into a green and pleasant one. There was a revival of the Hebrew language and a culture to go with it. There was construction of more Jewish religious institutions and at a higher level in every field than had ever existed before, or at least for thousands of years. There are more students studying in yeshivot in Israel today than there were in Eastern Europe in its heyday.

An historic handshake shook the world at the outset of the Jewish year 5754 (1993) between Yasir Arafat, chairman of the Palestine Liberation Organization, and Israeli Prime Minister Yitzhak Rabin, and a handshake toward year's end with King Hussein of Jordan stirred great hopes for peace. In between there was anguish, bloodshed, bitter dissent, and recrimination.

Perhaps the most memorable image of that year was a proud President Bill Clinton coaxing a pained Rabin to shake hands with a smiling Arafat on the South Lawn of the White House on September 13, marking the signing of the Oslo Declaration of Principles that has already changed the course of the Middle East.

The document outlines a complex plan for ceding the Gaza Strip and Jericho (lands that biblically and historically belonged to the people of Israel) to the Palestinians, with the prospect of more West Bank territory going over to Palestinian control in the future if both sides keep their agreement. By year's end, Gaza and Jericho were under Arafat's control.

In Israel the opposition to the government's initiative was constant and forceful, fueled by right-wing opposition, Orthodox Jews, and West Bank settlers fearful of their future. There were demonstrations, calls for the government to step down, and rabbinical assertions that soldiers should not take part in removing Jews from the land. But the leader of the Likud opposition, Benjamin Netanyahu, was perceived as not having a credible alternative policy of his own or a counterproposal to the government's initiative other than to say no.

From the start friends and foes of the peace process in the Middle East clashed—one took to the streets, the other to the editorial pages. The Israeli consul in New York, Colette Avital, took to the *Daily News* op-ed page to trumpet the success of her Labor government's peace initiative. "Peace with the Palestinians has resulted in the opening of almost every door in the global village," she wrote.

In the midst of the gloom over the failure of the peace process is the acceptance of Israel among the nations of the world (Gad Yaacobi, Israel's ambassador to the United Nations, cites almost thirty countries that have established diplomatic relations with Israel since the signing of the Declaration of Principles with the PLO). The many accomplishments so far include the secondary boycott of companies doing business with Israel is a horror of the past; the trade ties Israel has forged with Eastern Europe, the former Soviet Union, China, and India, have led to a rise of forty percent in Israel's merchandise exports from 1992 to 1994; active and direct negotiations are underway with Syria; and most important, the signing of a peace treaty with Jordan could not have come about without rapprochement with the Palestinians.

Yet according to a sampling of Israeli newspapers, on one given day, on April 11, 1995, the four largest Israeli dailies all ran editorials revealing a profound skepticism about the prime minister's relentless pursuit of the peace process.

Yediot Achronot, the largest daily, questioned what further Palestinian terrorism Israel could expect if Rabin cedes more territory to the Palestinian authority. The editorial noted that Gaza has become even more of a terrorist base since Israel withdrew from there.

Ma'ariv, the second largest daily, suggested Rabin accept the advice of President Ezer Weizman, telling PLO Chairman Arafat that all implementations of the Oslo Agreement—expanded Palestinian autonomy, elections, Israel's troop redeployment, travel regulations—be immediately suspended until the Palestinian authority gets serious about ending the murderous activity by Hamas and Islamic Jihad.

While each act of terror brings more worry and anger to Israelis and Americans, several media commentators on the Middle East have noted that a complete breakdown of the present peace process could lead to one of two contradictory scenarios.

According to one scenario, the peace process will crumble under the weight of terrorism, and the Rabin government will be replaced by the hard-liners of the Likud bloc.

Under the second scenario, informed observers say, Israel and the Palestinians, rather than see the gains made so far dissolve in the face of terrorism, will accelerate the pace of negotiations and tackle several so-called "final status" issues that were originally intended to be postponed until May 1996.

The slow pace of the Israeli-Palestinian diplomacy is producing new shadings and possibly new alignments within Israeli politics. The constant changing makes it difficult to predict what course Israel is likely to pursue.

While the establishment of the State of Israel marked the fulfillment of the Zionist enterprise, American Zionists understood that basic modification in the movement would have to be made. The leaders never anticipated, however, that within a few years the American Zionist movement would be reduced to a fraction of itself. With the exception of Hadassah, Zionist membership fell dramatically. The woman's organization not only kept its membership but grew, primarily because it had a non-political program that appealed to many people—the providing of quality medical care through the Hadassah Medical Organization and the Hadassah Hospital in Jerusalem and its related international educational program.

Jews who chose not to make *aliyah* could still be considered Zionists and friends of Israel, while those who did settle in Israel fulfilled the Zionist dream.

In the United States today, a coalition of seventeen Zionist groups and four affiliated bodies claim a total of one million members. The agencies all cooperate to some extent under the umbrella of the newly created American Zionist Movement (AZM), which resulted in a restructuring of the American Zionist Federation (AZF), reestablished in accordance with the territorial reorganization adopted by the twenty-seventh Zionist Congress in 1968.

In his presidential acceptance speech in 1992 before the American Zionist Movement, Seymour Reich, a prominent New York City attorney and former chairman of the Conference of Presidents of Major American Jewish Organizations and a former president of B'nai B'rith International, traced the relevance of Zionism to the 1990s. He noted:

> The uniqueness of the Jewish people and its dispersion created a climate that cried out for a central unifying force. The world Zionist movement is that

force. Zionism speaks out to our continuing need for Jewish unity, Jewish continuity, and Jewish security, with the centrality of Israel as its basic tenet.

Israel is the source, the touchstone, of our national "self." Israel is where our traditions first took root; and it is the place from which the rhythm and flavor of Jewish life still draws its essence.

THE FIRST REAL SETTINGS ON THE AMERICAN STAGE

1882

Jews are found in considerable numbers in the theater and motion pictures and on radio and television. They are actors, playwrights, producers, directors, and theater owners. As a rule, they are simply interested in putting on a good show but sometimes a Jewish element enters into their work. At one time there were even sufficient individuals in the performing arts with Jewish interests to organize a Jewish Theatrical Guild of America with two thousand members for the purpose of "perpetuating Judaism in the theater." The Rabbis' Sons Theatrical Benevolent Association was founded by Al Jolson and Harry Houdini and was restricted to sons of rabbis, cantors, and other officials of the synagogue.

Head and shoulders above all pioneers in the American theater were producers like Charles Frohman and David Belasco, who invested their own wealth in scores of their own productions. Belasco, in particular, left an indelible mark upon the American stage. He breathed new life into an old art by bringing naturalism and a modern touch to it. He made actors out of ordinary performers and great actresses out of simple and untrained girls. With his clerical collars and priestly black raiment, the publicity-conscious Belasco set a pattern for the Big Producer—of which the contemporary Hollywood counterparts are pallid copies.

Born in San Francisco in 1853, Belasco came from a Portuguese-Jewish family named Velasco. As a boy in Victorian British Columbia (where his father, a one-time clown, owned a store), he joined a circus. At the age of eleven, David appeared at the Victoria Theater in Charles Kean's production of *Richard III*. At sixteen young David was through with school and trying his hand at show business. For several years he trouped from town to town as actor, manager, and playwright. Working as a stage manager on the Pacific Coast, he devised melodramas with fires and battles and a passion play with real sheep.

Since his short stature and high-pitched voice were handicaps in acting, Belasco soon turned exclusively to directing, producing, and writing for the stage. When work out West ran low in 1879, he went East to tackle the New York stage. Soon his name became associated with sensational scenic effects.

As director, producer, and playwright, he attempted and accomplished what no other figure in the theater had ever attempted to do before. Until Belasco began to produce plays, audiences were satisfied to see a library represented by rows of books painted on the scenery; when Belasco showed a doctor's office on the stage, he not only used real volumes but chose the very medical books a doctor would need. For one production, in keeping with the plot, he constructed a complete Child's Restaurant on the stage and fried eggs.

The first play he produced, Bronson Howard's *Young Mrs. Winthrop* (1882), ran for nearly two thousand performances and made a tremendous impression. Belasco's own *May Blossom* was performed 170 times in Madison Square Garden and altogether more than one thousand times. His original play of western life, *The Girl of the Golden West* (1905), was made into one of the first operas with an American setting. Its premiere was held at the Metropolitan Opera House with Toscanini conducting and Caruso and Amato in the chief roles. Shakespeare's *Merchant of Venice* had in Belasco's staging (1922) the longest run ever remembered on Broadway.

People flocked to see his plays. Yet, the popularity of his productions were not due to literary power alone. No one ever expended more effort and hard work in ironing out the minute details that went into perfecting a performance as he did. He brought realism into the scenery, the furnishings, and the settings.

At the same time, Belasco was contributing many significant features to the theater itself. He was the first to introduce electric lighting on the stage in the 1880s, the new invention of Thomas Edison's. In 1902 he opened the first of two theaters called the "Belasco," where he introduced other innovations such as footlights sunk below stage level.

In the modern theater Belasco holds a high place not only as a playwright, as an original worker especially in the field of stage lighting, but also as the man who discovered and trained a number of leading actors. He established the Lyceum School of Acting and produced successes such as *Du Barry* and *Zaza*. He lavished great care in training his actors to render their lines with intelligence and conviction. The nuances of speech and voice, intonation and inflection were refined to a subtle yet emphatic degree. Mrs. Leslie Carter, a society woman spoiled by leisure and idleness, without any previous experience as an actress, under Belasco's instruction became a star, heralded in America and England. Mary Pickford graduated from his school to become America's sweetheart and a world celebrity. Another, David Warfield, became one of the most prominent Jewish actors of his day.

Belasco produced plays in Europe as well as in various American cities and became a legend in the theater long before he passed away. In all, Belasco produced over four hundred plays ranging from minstrel shows to high tragedy, from fairy tales to musical comedy, from melodrama to pageantry, including some 150 dramas he had written himself.

Little of his fame remains today other than the theater that bears his name. Yet David Belasco was the first to secure for the American theater its recognition as a temple of art, not as a mere place of business.

Charles Frohman (1860–1915) was the first United States producer to become famous outside the country and produced some 125 plays in London. A theater manager and producer, he was for some years a booking agent with connections throughout the United States. As a producer, he scored his first real success with *Shenandoah* in 1899. Frohman managed and developed many stars of the stage of his day; some of the best known were Maude Adams, Ethel Barrymore, John Drew, William Gillette, and Otis Skinner. He also introduced Oscar Wilde and Somerset Maugham to the American public.

His starring of E. H. Sothern and Julia Marlowe produced the finest Shakespeare repertory that the American audiences ever saw up to that time. Yet he was equally painstaking with light musical comedies. If a play was a smash hit in New York, he sent out as many as five companies to delight the public throughout the land. His stock shows, whether the Wallack Theater company or the Ben Green Players or Isadora Duncan's Classical Dances, brought uplift and pleasure to urban and rural America.

Frohman dominated the United States stage in his time, and with his death on the torpedoed *Lusitania* in 1915 an era ended.

The Shubert brothers—Sam (1875–1955), Lee (1876–1953), and Jacob (1877–1963)—a family of theater proprietors and producers, became Broadway's most powerful theatrical dynasty. By 1956 the family enterprise owned or controlled about half the legitimate theaters in the nation, including seventeen on Broadway. The Shuberts produced more than five hundred plays. Jacob was one of the early backers of Florenz Ziegfeld. Among the stars the Shuberts introduced to American audiences were Al Jolson, Eddie Cantor, Marilyn Monroe, Fanny Brice, Ray Bolger, and Bert Lahr.

THE FIRST AMERICAN HOLIDAY INAUGURATED BY A JEW

1882

Labor Day, observed on the first Monday in September, has become one of the most generally celebrated holidays in the United States, ranking along with Washington's Birthday, Independence Day, and Thanksgiving. A large share of the credit for enactment of the law establishing Labor Day as a holiday is given to Samuel Gompers, one of the most distinguished labor leaders of the past century. It was first celebrated in New York on September 5, 1882, with parades held by the Knights of Labor, a mixture of secret lodges, mystical order, fraternal society, and labor federation that disappeared after a generation. In 1894 Gompers succeeded in getting Congress to declare the first Monday in September as Labor Day, a national holiday.

Gompers, who was born on January 27, 1850 of Dutch-Jewish parents in the East End of London, had come to America with his family during the Civil War period. He was one of the founders and for almost forty years president of the American Federation of Labor. It was Gompers who led and helped win the battle against sweatshops and starvation wages. He succeeded in outlawing company unions and labor injunctions and defeated the first Communist attempt to control the American labor movement.

As a small boy in England, Samuel was sent to the Jewish Free School for a general education and to a school at night where he studied Hebrew, the Bible, and Talmud. When he was ten years old, he was apprenticed to a shoemaker, but he preferred cigar making (his father's trade) and was indentured at a salary of one shilling a week for the first year and two for the second. Conditions were bad in England during the American Civil War. Factories unable to secure Southern cotton closed, and much suffering ensued.

With the assistance of the Cigarmakers' Society (Union) of England, which had established an emigration fund to relieve unemployment by ridding England of superfluous cigarmakers, the Gompers family came to America in 1863. They established their home on Houston and Attorney Streets on New York's Lower East Side. Father and son began making cigars at home. Samuel managed to pick up some odds and ends of an education at Cooper Union. At sixteen he went to work in a cigar factory and soon joined a local of the Cigarmakers' National Union and remained a card-bearing member to his last day.

Through the years of depravation, Gompers learned how important it was for workingmen to act together and how much power they had when they did. In 1873 he established another local cigarmakers' union that later became Local 144, which was to make labor history.

In 1877 Gompers and his associates Adolph Strasser and Ferdinand Laurrell led a cigarmakers' strike against the unfair encroachment of labor-saving machinery and unsanitary working conditions. The strike was a failure. Starving workers could not prevail against the rich Cigar Manufacturers Association, but the three leaders held to their ideals. The capabilities, the untiring labors, and the honest devotion of Samuel Gompers was recognized. From that beginning Gompers went on to develop his ideals about the relationship between workers and employers until he had clearly in his mind the objectives to which he was to devote the rest of his life; a large organization of workers who could stand together to improve their working conditions and thereby attain richer and fuller lives.

At the age of thirty-one in 1881, in Pittsburgh, at the first national meeting of labor he attended, he was elected a vice president of the Federation of Organized Trades and Labor Unions of the United States and Canada.

In Columbus, Ohio, in 1886 he formed the nucleus of what was to become the American Federation of Labor out of the remnants of the Federation of Organized Trades and Labor Unions, which had led a nominal existence and which began to expire. He was the first elected president of the new group at the beginning annual salary of $1,000. He held this office from 1886 to 1924 with the exception of a single year. He also edited the official journal of the federation from 1894 until his death.

Beginning in a humble, unfurnished room with a kitchen table for a desk and wooden crates discarded by a grocer for files, the A.F.L. evolved slowly into the most powerful labor organization in the world; its head-quarters, a seven-story building in Washington, D.C., was dedicated by President Woodrow Wilson. As the A.F.L. grew stronger and larger, Gompers came to be acknowledged everywhere as the spokesman of the American worker and labor's most famous champion.

The first great campaign of the American Federation of Labor was the struggle for the eight-hour work day and for legislation protecting workers on dangerous jobs and compensating them and their families in case of injury or death. This was eventually won, but more improvements were sought. Gompers then proceeded to arouse the country's consciousness for decent wages for workers, clean shops, and successful arbitration machinery, all of which he felt could be achieved through the organization of unions. Although he called for the unionization of all workers, he basically accepted the decision of the A.F.L. to concentrate on the skilled and retain the craft basis for organizing, which maintained the position of the existing trade unions.

As a result of Gompers's activities as founder of the A.F.L., the American worker was lifted from the slough of despair and hunger to human dignity and hope.

During World War I, Gompers supported President Woodrow Wilson's war policies and organized the War Committee on Labor. It included representatives of labor and business. After the war Wilson appointed him as a member of the International Labor Legislation, which was founded to make new and better labor laws for all governments of the world.

When Gompers died on December 13, 1924, the American Federation of Labor had grown to a membership of five million and he had lived to see his dream of organized labor come true in the land of the free.

On October 8, 1933, national tribute was paid to the great labor leader when President Franklin D. Roosevelt dedicated the Samuel Gompers Memorial Monument in Washington, D.C. Of bronze and marble, it shows Gompers seated in front of three allegorical figures representing Unionism, Fraternity, and Brotherhood.

In January 1950, on the occasion of the one hundredth anniversary of the birth of Samuel Gompers, one of the first commemorative postage stamps carrying the picture of a Jew, the Gompers stamp, was issued by the United States Post Office.

Other Jewish labor leaders in the American labor movement who came to the United States as poverty-stricken immigrants and then rose to prominence in the nation's labor history include Meyer London, the first Socialist leader to be elected to the United States Congress; Sidney Hillman, under whose leadership the newly founded Amalgamated Clothing Workers Union grew rapidly to become one of the largest labor organizations in the nation and who helped establish the C.I.O.; Jacob Potofsky, who held a succession of important posts in the Amalgamated Clothing Workers Union; and David Dubinsky, president of the International Ladies' Garment Workers' Union.

Their pioneering leadership was responsible for the creation of a successful, continuous arbitration machine that pointed the way to industrial peace. Such innovations as unemployment insurance, labor banking, union housing, adult education programs, and medical care for workers were all developed by these men.

THE FIRST YIDDISH THEATER IN AMERICA

1882

The origins of the Yiddish theater are generally traced to the traditional merrymaking that accompanied the Jewish festival of Purim. This gave rise to the *Purim Shpil* (Purim play), about the deliverance of Jews of Persia from extinction threatened by Haman, the prime minister, through the intercession of Esther, the beautiful Jewish queen of King Ahasuerus. Lighthearted dramatizations of the biblical Book of Esther were first performed in the late Middle Ages by amateurs and yeshiva students and later by traveling troups of actors, and they continued to gain popularity until the eighteenth century.

Other than the cantor, synagogue choir, and *badkhonim* (wedding jesters), the *Purim Shpil* constituted the main force of entertainment among the Yiddish speaking Eastern European Jews. By the mid-nineteenth century the Jews of Europe, having achieved degrees of emancipation, and enlightenment, began to look beyond the limited scope of the *Purim Shpil*, setting the stage for the professional Yiddish theater.

In the early 1860s a group of entertainers, based in the Galician city of Brod and known as the Broder Singers, mimed and clowned their way through the Russian-Polish Pale of Jewish settlement. Their typical act combined the wit of Jewish wedding jesters with the slickness of the Viennese café entertainers.

Modern Yiddish theater was born in a Romanian wine cellar in the town of Jassy in 1876, with a two-act improvisation by the actor, playwright, and composer Abraham Goldfaden. His earlier appearance in the title role of Dr. Solomon Ettinger's *Serkele* (1862) marked the beginning of the illustrious theatrical career of Goldfaden, who starred in many of his own musicals and eventually became universally acknowledged as the father of the modern Yiddish theater.

Goldfaden turned to the glories of the past and composed operettas that would bring back heroic episodes and at the same time move the heart with touching melodies set to uplifting llyrics. Tunes from his plays became accepted as folksongs. His lullaby "Rozhinkes un Mandlen" was sung in many languages by singers of the popular idiom.

When the czarist government of Russia banned the Yiddish theater in 1883, it was forced to move elsewhere. First a major new center for it emerged in London, England, and soon thereafter in the United States.

The first performance of a Yiddish play in America was recorded in 1882. It was, perhaps, the good fortune of Leon and Miron Golubok and their Yiddish theatrical troupe to have left Russia and been stranded in London in 1882 before the influx of the better-known actors to the United States began. They were also lucky to have a brother, Abe Golubok, who had already settled in New York. The American Golubok and a co-worker in the same cigar factory, Boris Thomashefsky, a sixteen-year-old choir singer in a synagogue, persuaded Frank Wolf, the proprietor of a saloon, to finance the visit of the Golubok troupe to New York in the summer of 1882.

On August 18, assisted by local talent and featuring the young Thomashefsky, the actors premiered with Goldfaden's play *Koldunya (The Witch)*. The performance in Turner Hall at 66 East Fourth Street started late and ended in disaster. Some years later, Thomashefsky offered in his memoirs (1935) a glamorized version of the event, including attempted sabotage by some uptown German Jews. It seems, however, that the performance left no imprint in the life of the community, and its importance is primarily that of a historic first.

Thomashefsky was given a singing part in this first production. There was a shortage of women on the Yiddish stage, and with his high falsetto voice, he later often played female parts. He himself arranged numerous stage pieces, produced and acted in sentimental melodramas, and revived Goldfaden's operettas. The pioneering Thomashefsky became a popular figure of the Yiddish theater as actor, playwright, producer, and matinee idol of hardworking young women in the sweatshops, and their glamorous hero of romance.

Thomashefsky brought to the Yiddish-speaking public, often in adaptation, plays like Shakespeare's *Hamlet* (1893) and *Richard III* (1895) and Goethe's *Faust* (1902). He also arranged for the Vilna Troupe to perform in the United States and staged Israel Zangwill's *Children of the Ghetto* in Yiddish under Zangwill's supervision (1905).

By the middle of the 1880s, the American Yiddish stage had become professional—good actors made their appearance, and good dramatists began to write plays by the dozens, catering to the feelings and sentiments of the newcomers. The two most popular writers of the day were Joseph Latteiner, who came to New York in 1884, and Moses Horowitz, who arrived several years later. Latteiner was a garment worker who became America's first Yiddish playwright; Horowitz, the "professor," was an adventurer of dubious antecedents. Both men ground out over one hundred sentimental plays, melodramas, and comedies with songs, dances, and buffoonery. Many of Horowitz's plays were historical, and even such dramas on such timely events as the Homestead strike or the Kishineff massacres could be designated contemporary history. His best-known drama, *Tiza Eslar*, based on the blood libel in Hungary, took two evenings to perform.

With the arrival of Odessa-born, young, and distinguished-looking Jacob Adler in 1880, many successful years followed for the Yiddish theater. Adler was quickly recognized as a dramatic actor of unusual ability. From the enactment of romantic roles to hybrid melodramas, he emerged as a tragedian in plays of a more serious and realistic nature. He acted in the plays of Shakespeare, Schiller, Goethe, and Tolstoy. Under his stimulus, Adler's son, Luther, and four daughters, Celia, Francis, Julia, and Stella, became talented performers. Stella for many years headed the Drama Department of New York University and became an adjunct professor of acting at the Yale School of Drama.

Audiences also showed warm appreciation for the talented and appealing Bertha Kalish, the comedian Sigmund Mogulescu, and David Kessler, the latter whom many experts believed was the greatest actor of them all. It was Kessler who coached Enrico Caruso when the great Italian tenor was preparing his role as Eleazar in *La Juive*.

The arrival in the United States in 1891 of Jacob Gordin, a cultured Jew who edited Russian-language newspapers in the Ukraine, marked the beginning of the "Golden Age" of the Yiddish theater in America. Gordin had literary skill and power. He was a realist concerned with the problems that haunted the family in a modern industrial society. He and other serious writers hoped to make the theater a cultural institution and not merely a place for raucous laughter and passing entertainment. He waged battle against the sentimental melodramatic offerings of *shund* (lowbrow), and championed *kunst* (art) theater, which aspired to higher standards of writing and performance. During his eighteen-year career, Gordin wrote nealy eighty plays including such classics as *Mirele Efros* (1898), *God, Man, and the Devil* (1900), and *The Jewish King Lear* (an adaptation from Shakespeare, 1892).

At its peak, the Yiddish theater was one of the most productive of all theaters and one of the most glamorous. According to historian Moses Rischin, the four major Yiddish theaters—the Thalia, the Windsor, the People's, and the Grand—presented eleven hundred performances annually at the turn of the century for an estimated audience of two million patrons. The theaters, all in the Bowery area, were a far cry from the modest halls of the 1880s. The Thalia was a three-thousand-seat house. The Windsor opened in 1893 and, with thirty-five hundred seats, was the largest playhouse devoted to popular plays. The People's, leased by Thomashefsky in 1900, had a seating capacity of twenty-five hundred and housed the greatest Yiddish hit of its day, Thomashefsky's *Dos Pintele Yid* (*The Jewish Essence*, 1907), a magnificent spectacle that ran for an entire season and was seen by tens of thousands of people. The Grand, managed by Jacob Adler, opened in 1903 and seated two thousand.

By the outbreak of World War I, there were almost a score of these playhouses on Second Avenue in New York City, as well as full-time ones in Philadelphia, Boston, Chicago, Detroit, and Cleveland.

In 1918, Maurice Schwartz and Jacob Ben-Ami, talented Yiddish actors and directors, leased the Irving Place Theater, a former playhouse, and got together a well-balanced company. With Peretz Hirschbein's *Dos Verforfen Vinkel* (*The Forsaken Nook*), a simple play of Jewish life in a Lithuanian village, they scored a great success and moved into the Yiddish Art Theater on Second Avenue and Twelfth Street, once the site of Peter Stuyvesant's estate. This theater prospered and continued producing plays of outstanding merit until 1950. Maurice Schwartz directed almost all the productions while playing leading parts in most of them. Not only were the productions of high caliber, even the stage designs and program notes reflected an extremely sophisticated level of art and decoration.

A later generation of stellar performers included Rudolph Schildkraut, Leo Fuchs, Ludwig Satz, Herman Yablokoff, Zvi Scooler, Seymour Rexsite, Miriam Kressyn, Ida Kaminska, and Jenny Goldstein.

Molly Picon, a musical-comedy star who rose to stage fame during this period under the sponsorship of her husband, Jacob Kalich, director, play adaptor, and occasional playwright, made the most noteworthy contribution to Yiddish musicals, both by her acting and by the general quality of the productions in which she appeared.

The Yiddish theater has not confined itself but has brought to its crowded houses—in addition to Shakespeare and Moliere—Oscar Wilde, George Bernard Shaw, Feuchtwanger, Ibsen, and Strindberg. But the main strength of the Yiddish theater has always been authors whose genius is rooted in the phenomenon of Jewish life. Its leading spirits have been: Sholom Aleichem, who gave the theater *Tevya, Hard to Be a Jew, Wandering Stars,* and *Stempenu;* I. L. Peretz, who wrote *Der Golem, Der Nier Nigun (The New Tune),* and others; I. J. Singer, whose *Yoshe Kalb* is an extraordinary landscape of movement and form and who is responsible for the great epic chronicles *The Family Carnovsky* and *The Brothers Ashkenazi.* Also influential in its development were the works of Sholom Asch, Leon Kobrin, David Pinski, Peretz Hirschbein, and H. Leivick. Its most famous composers include Achron, Chernyavsky, Olshenetsky, Rumshinsky, and Sholom Secunda.

In 1951 the New York City Opera Company decided to produce S. Ansky's *The Dybbuk,* one of the most famous of all Yiddish plays. This play holds the highest box-office attendance of Yiddish theaters in this country. A folklore drama with supernatural overtones, it was translated into many languages and recast into an Italian opera.

By 1966 the number of Yiddish theaters in New York City had dwindled to two, one in Manhattan and one in Brooklyn. Membership in the Hebrew Actors' Union had decreased from 1,500 in the 1920s and 1930s to 240.

The decline began with silent films and motion pictures offering entertainment and serious drama at low admission prices. This caused such capable actors as Muni Weisenfreund (Paul Muni), Edward G. Robinson, Joseph Buloff, Menashe Skulnik, Herschel Bernardi, and others to seek wider fields on English-speaking stages. But the foremost cause of the atrophy lay in the gradual dying out of the generation that spoke Yiddish as its primary language.

Today, a renewed interest in Yiddish and Eastern European Jewish culture has made New York City the center of a revitalized Yiddish theater. Indicative of this resurgence is the continued viablity of the Folkbienne (founded in 1915), the oldest Yiddish theater company in existence in the United States, and the Joseph Papp Yiddish Theater, which launched a successful opening season in the fall of 1988. Since then, the Joseph Papp Yiddish Theater, named for the creator of the Public Theater in New York City who first brought the works of Shakespeare to Central Park, has conducted workshops at the Yivo Institute for Jewish Research and presented Yiddish plays at the Riverdale YM-YWHA in New York.

THE FIRST CHIEF RABBI OF AMERICAN ORTHODOX JEWRY

1888

In 1888 under the leadership of the Beth Hamidrash Hagadol, the oldest and largest synagogue of East European Jewry in New York City, the Association of American Hebrew Orthodox Congregations—composed of seventeen synagogues, large and small—united to secure a prominent rabbi from Russia for the newly created office of chief rabbi of the Orthodox community. In April of that year a call was issued in Hebrew and English to its member congregations to join the association in the search.

The Russian-Jewish immigrants feared the negative effects of the American milieu upon their faith. A *Gaon* (reverential title for a genius) as *Rav Ha-Kolel* (chief rabbi) of New York would have precedence over the other Orthodox rabbis, including the imposing minister of Congregation Shearith Israel, the Spanish and Portuguese Synagogue, the oldest in America. Furthermore, a chief rabbi from Russia would raise the status of East European Jews in the eyes of the uptown Americanized German-Jewish Reform community.

The association acted quickly. It announced that to keep the next generation faithful to Judaism, Rabbi Jacob Joseph of Vilna, the "Jerusalem of Lithuania," had been chosen as chief rabbi. A *Beth Din* (religious court) under his leadership was to be formed to meet the religious and judicial needs of the Jewish community. An appeal was made for proper support, and congregations and organizations were summoned to organize and contribute financially and "show the world that Orthodox Judaism has zealous followers."

Rabbi Joseph, who was born in Kovno, Russia, in 1848, studied at the world-famous Yeshiva of Volozhin. He gained considerable renown as a student of Talmud and became famous as a preacher. He was rabbi of several smaller communities when, in 1883, he was appointed *Maggid* (preacher) of the Jewish community of Vilna. In 1889 he published *Lebeth Yaakov*, a collection of homilies and notes to his rabbinic writings of which a new Warsaw edition appeared in 1900. He was to be the first and only chief rabbi American Jewry would ever have.

On early Saturday morning, July 7, 1888, the ship *Aleer* docked at the port of Hoboken, New Jersey. Rabbi Jacob Joseph remained aboard until sundown. After evening services were over, delegates of the association crossed the river by ferry to welcome their chief rabbi with symbolic offerings of bread and salt, reciting the traditional benedictions upon seeing a sage. The chief rabbi responded in a brief address, calling for unity and cooperation to carry on the holy work. The procession set out from Hoboken to the rabbi's residence on the Lower East Side, and when it reached the house on Henry and Jefferson streets, thousands of Jews were waiting to welcome him.

Soon after his arrival, Rabbi Jacob Joseph founded the Bes Sefer Yeshiva Tifereth Jerusalem in 1900. It marked the beginning of the Jewish Day School movement in America.

Everything seemed to augur well for Rabbi Joseph to fulfill the expectation of his sponsors when a misstep upset the era of good feeling and prepared a tragic end to the experiment.

The Kosher system of slaughter and preparation of meat and fowl has an importance in rabbinic Judaism altogether incomprehensible to non-Jews and even to some non-Orthodox Jews. Its significance to the pious is linked with the preservation of Jews and Judaism. The preparation of koshering meat becomes an intricate ritual, requiring organized supervision. Thus, when the association leaders saw the respect their rabbi evoked, they concluded that such veneration would succeed in bringing about the enforcement of *kashruth*. The association aimed to reorganize the system and place *kashruth* under strict surveillance. But all organizations involve expenses. So the leader decided to impose a penny tax on every fowl slaughtered by the *shochet* (the one who slaughters cattle or fowl in accordance with Jewish law). The association instructed housewives not to buy slaughtered chicken unless it had attached to it a tag with the imprint: *Rav-ha-Kolel Jacob Joseph* (Chief Rabbi Joseph). The income from the one-cent tax would be used to pay the cost of supervision. Rabbi Joseph objected to the procedure, but he was overruled by practical businessmen who maintained that it was the approved American practice of meeting overhead.

Immediately the storm broke. Opponents of the chief rabbi joined forces. Prominent among the dissenters were those rabbis who had not been consulted about setting up a chief rabbinate in New York. The butchers opposed to supervision organized as the "Hebrew Poultry Butchers Association." They were joined by radical elements, the socialists and anarchists, who seized any occasion to expose the "gouging methods of clerical exploitation."

With devastating effect the opposition exchanged angry words about the term *Karboka*, the tax imposed by the czar's government upon Kosher meat, a tax that was often used for anti-Jewish purposes. Identification of the chief rabbi's penny tax on poultry with *Karboka* brought back memories of the evils and humiliations in Russia and served as a propaganda slogan to exasperate the masses. Rabbi Joseph refused to utter a word of bitterness against his detractors, but went on preaching in the synagogues of the association, all the while attempting to bring reforms in *kashruth*. He did, however, criticize those who, because of a penny, chose to buy non-Kosher meat.

The chief rabbinate itself became an object of scorn when another group of synagogues chose Joshua Segal as chief rabbi and proceeded to compete with the Association of American Orthodox Hebrew Congregations in supervision of *kashruth* and in operating a *Beth Din*. It became quite obvious that there could be no limit to the number of "chief rabbis" who might be selected by several congregations banding together in New York or in any other large city.

Conditions took a serious turn for the worse in the spring of 1895. The retail butchers banded together, rejected Rabbi Joseph's authority, and dispensed with his supervision. He still held the title of chief rabbi, but it was obvious to him, as to everyone else, that his mission in the United States had failed. He bore the humiliation of his decline and neglect with stoic dignity. Nor did financial distress help to ease his pain. Eventually, the unfortunate rabbi was forced to move with his family to a squalid tenement flat, for he was left without any income. Soon confined to a bed, he spent his remaining years on a "mattress grave."

After suffering a series of paralyzing strokes, Rabbi Jacob Joseph died on July 28, 1902, at the age of fifty-four. His funeral was attended by ten thousand mourners. As the procession passed the printing-press factory of R. H. Hoe and Company on the Lower East Side, workmen and apprentices from the upper floors overhead began jeering and throwing buckets of water, bottles, metal bolts, and screws on the marchers. This precipitated a riot in which many of the mourners were injured and mistreated. The police arrived but evidently were not overzealous in identifying the assailants. The country was shocked at the desecration, and Mayor Seth Low ordered an investigation. The facts were established and the anti-Semitic elements were removed from the police department.

Thus closed a unique episode in American Judaism. Never again was the idea of a chief rabbi reinstated. A chief rabbinate successful in Great Britain or France seemed unsuitable to conditions in America. In America, the synagogue was to be independent of communal dictation. The Association of American Hebrew Orthodox Congregations failed to distinguish the basic differences in the structural form of religious life in America. The next generation attempted to bring order into Orthodoxy by creating the Union of Orthodox Jewish Congregations of America.

Today the Orthodox Union is a major representative of Orthodox Jewry in Washington, D.C., throughout the country, and throughout the world. Unlike many organizations, the union is multifaceted, making significant contributions in areas ranging from politics to social and educational programs and *kashruth* supervision.

From time to time rabbis of exceptional caliber and influence stood out in different cities, men like Rabbis Bernard Levinthal in Philadelphia; Aaron Mordecai Ashinsky in Philadelphia; Eliezar Silver in Cincinnati; the wise and witty Jacob Vidrovitz, known as the "Moscover Rov"; Moses Z. Margolies in New York; and others. Some were called chief rabbis, but the title was only complimentary.

Controller Joseph's son, the great-grandson and namesake of Rabbi Joseph, enlisted in the United States Marines in 1938 after graduating from Columbia University and became a captain in the Solomon Islands, the scene of furious fighting during World War II. He was probably the youngest officer of that rank in the Marine Corps. He was killed in action in June 1942, the very day his father was leaving home for an appointment in Washington with Lieutenant General Thomas Holcomb, Commander of the United States Marine Corps, to discuss joining the service himself.

THE FIRST AMERICANIZATION CLASSES FOR IMMIGRANTS

1889

The lot of the Jew in czarist Russia was not a happy one. In 1881 there began a hideous nightmare of oppression, rioting, and bloodshed as dreadful as the orgies of the Spanish Inquisition. Jews were persecuted and expelled, and thousands of them fled in the wildest exodus of Jewish history to Germany, France, England, and Palestine. Between 1881 and 1901, 1,562,800 Russian and Polish Jews came to the United States. The same harsh treatment befell the Jews of Austro-Hungary and Romania, and from these countries as well came large numbers of refugees.

The problems arising from the influx of these newcomers in the early 1880s became intense because of the lack of existing societies capable of coping with the situation. In 1882 the Young Men's Hebrew Association of New York established a downtown branch, the first neighborhood center for immigrant groups.

Baltimore, Maryland, also received many of the refugees of the Russian pogroms. The home of Rabbi Benjamin Szold, one of its prominent and erudite spiritual leaders, was constantly filled with the haggard men and women asking for advice. To help the newcomers, Henrietta, the first of his eight daughters, to whom he had given a sound Jewish and Hebrew education, came up with the idea of evening classes where immigrants might be taught the rudiments of English as well as many other practical subjects to enable them to better adjust themselves to the cultural and economic life of America. She rented a room above a store in the impoverished section of town and began classes for thirty pupils. It was the first night school devoted specifically to immigrants. During the first semester more than fifty heads—young and old, often father and son—touched each other over the primer, together learning their ABCs.

Henrietta's work routine from 1889 to 1893 would have her arising at 4:30 AM to prepare assignments for her night teachers, then conducting her own daytime classes in a private girls' school in Baltimore, then teaching her night classes until 11:30 P.M. The heartthrob of it warmed Henrietta's body and soul on the cold wintry nights in the long rides of the horsecars from the Baltimore slums to her father's home. Soon other immigrants learned about the night school and came to join.

After more than five thousand pupils proved the worth of her pioneering efforts, in 1898 the municipality of Baltimore took over the evening school. The superintendant of schools saw that the evening classes for immigrants was the answer to a great problem, and soon, too, the public school systems throughout the country incorporated the program. The immigrants adapted to their new environment. Their children, now grown to adulthood, differed from their fellow Americans only in the traditionally acceptable American differences that leaves to each man the free exercise of his religion.

Many years later, in 1935, at a reception given in honor of Henrietta Szold's seventy-fifth birthday in New York's City Hall, Mayor Fiorello LaGuardia gave her the key to New York City, and said that it was Americanization work such as hers and that of the YMHA that had made possible his own ascent to the mayorality and had saved America from a new slavery perhaps worse than the first.

From Baltimore, where Henrietta Szold was born in 1860, to Jerusalem, where she died in 1945, her passionate dedication to her people was expressed again and again. One of the pioneer builders of Jewish culture in America, she is gratefully remembered as the tireless editorial secretary of the Jewish Publication Society of America, a position she held from 1893 to 1916.

Besides her secretarial duties, she translated a dozen books from Hebrew and German into English, including Graetz's monumental *History of the Jews*. From 1904 to 1908 she edited the yearly edition of the indispensable *American Jewish Yearbook*, which is still being published today by the American Jewish Committee. She collaborated on the compilation of the *Jewish Encyclopedia*, which appeared in 1905. She assisted Professor Louis Ginzberg, the Talmudic scholar, in the research and organization of his multivolume *Legends of the Jews* at a time when English was still a new language for him.

Nevertheless, her greatest achievement was her work in Zionism—for Hadassah, the Women's Zionist Organization of America, of which she was the founder, and for Youth Aliyah, an organization through which she saved thousands of young Jewish lives from the inferno of Nazi Germany and other lands of danger and brought them to the safety of Palestine.

Drawn from the seclusion of her scholarly interests, Miss Szold became involved in the dynamic Zionist movement that was emerging at the turn of the century. She imbibed it from her father, one of the founders of the original Federation of American Zionists. After visiting Palestine in 1909, she wrote, "I am more than ever convinced that if not Zionism, then nothing–then extinction of the Jew!" When she returned to America, a woman already in her fifties, she was determined that something had to be done to provide medical help for the Jews and Arabs in Palestine. She had seen the ravages of malaria and trachoma and the absence of elementary hygienic standards, and she sensed that this was the challenge she had been awaiting all her life.

In New York City on February 24, 1912, a group of thirty-eight women in a Jewish study circle met with Henrietta Szold in Temple Emanu-El and formed the first chapter of Hadassah. Since the meeting was held on Purim, the festival honoring Queen Esther, the charter members chose for their group the Hebrew name of the Queen, which is Hadassah. The quotation from the prophet Jeremiah on their seal expressed their purpose: "The Healing of the Daughter of My People." The dual purpose of the society was to establish and maintain a district system of nursing in Palestine and an educational program to foster Zionist education in America. Henrietta Szold was elected first president of the new group. Soon afterward, she pursuaded the philanthropist Nathan Straus to help underwrite the cost of sending two nurses to Jerusalem to set up a welfare station for maternity care and the treatment of trachoma for a five-year trial period.

In 1916, during World War I, an urgent appeal came to Hadassah for medical help in Palestine, where there were few doctors and drugs to cope with the epidemics that were rife throughout the Middle East. A complete medical unit organized by Hadassah set sail for the Holy Land, consisting of forty-four physicians, nurses, and public health specialists and equipment for a fifty-bed hospital.

The Henrietta Szold-Hadassah School of Nursing–the first in Palestine–opened with thirty students in 1918. Throughout the Holy Land Hadassah established hospitals and clinics and turned them over to the local municipalities to serve the sick without regard to creed or nationality.

In 1939, the Rothschild-Hadassah-Hebrew University Hospital, the first teaching hospital in Palestine, opened atop Mount Scopus in Jerusalem, thus beginning a series of medical "firsts" for the region.

Hadassah's responsibilities for tens of thousands of adults and children alike became a sacred cause for American Jewish women, sixty thousand of whom were enrolled by 1939. Since that time Hadassah has grown into an organization of 385,000 members in the United States and Puerto Rico to become the largest Jewish women's organization and the largest Zionist body in the world.

If, as she was to glowingly describe Hadassah many years later, it became "a marvelous flexible, well-oiled machine," it was because she built it with unprecedented precision and skill.

She also saw in Hadassah's major medical and health programs in Palestine an opportunity to build a bridge between the Jews and the Arabs. In a letter to her sister, Bertha, prior to the establishment of the Jewish State in 1948, she wrote: "We hope for friendship with our Arab neighbors, we want to develop the country for the good of both the Jews and the Arabs."

Like many people, Henrietta Szold, who settled in Palestine in the 1920s, had believed that the year 1918 marked the end of all wars, but the rise of Nazism changed her thinking. Early in the 1930s, soon after Hitler rose to power, she felt the coming tragedy and left immediately for London and Berlin to lead the Youth Aliyah project. She mobilized the Yishuv (population of Palestine) and the Jews in the Diaspora to participate in the rescue of youth from the inferno of Nazi Germany, White Paper restrictions, and Moslem oppression and bring them to the safety of Palestine. Their housing, their health, problems of adjustment, and education were all her concern. Often she would meet the boats at the port of Haifa to welcome the new arrivals. On many occasions she would accompany them to their new settlements to see if they were properly installed. She discussed their problems with them on her frequent visits to the settlements and in some special cases invited them to come to Jerusalem to talk with her. She was then in her seventy-fourth year.

In the years 1933 to 1945 that Henrietta Szold was head of Youth Aliyah, thirteen thousand orphans from thirteen different countries who otherwise would have perished in the concentration camps were saved. By 1948, thirty thousand children had come under the care of the program. She who had no children of her own and who never married had indeed become a mother to her people.

Henrietta Szold's seventy-fifth and eightieth birthdays were widely celebrated, both in Palestine and in America. Honors were lavished upon her, and the love and esteem in which she was universally held were manifested on all sides. Her eightieth birthday was a public holiday in Palestine, particularly for the children.

She was eighty-four when she died on February 13, 1945, in the Hadassah Hospital in Jerusalem. An entire generation of Jews mourned her. She had long become a legend; her last breath enshrined her in history.

Two postage stamps honoring Henrietta Szold were issued in December 1960, the centenary of her birth. The first, issued by the State of Israel, was one of several commemorations to mark "Henrietta Szold Year." The second was issued by the United States Post Office. The

Szold stamp shows the founder and first president of Hadassah in the foreground and the Hadassah-Hebrew University Medical Center in the background.

To pay further tribute to the memory of Henrietta Szold, the Board of Education of the City of New York dedicated a Lower East Side public school in her name. This was the first time that a public school was named for a Zionist leader.

THE FIRST GRAND OPERA PRODUCTIONS IN ENGLISH

1889

For a long time the citizens of New York had been listening to opera. The Metropolitan Opera House had been functioning season after season, but always at a loss.

Closely associated with the development of opera and the popular theater in the United States was Oscar Hammerstein. Born in Berlin in 1847, he ran away from home, reached New York in 1863, and found work in a cigar factory. He soon became an important and wealthy figure and later rose to financial leadership on Broadway.

A self-made man, he displayed capacities in many fields: invention, building, speculation, journalism, music, and theater. A profit of $1,600 in one week made Oscar a real-estate speculator for life. He had a hunch that far away Harlem offered a good field for realty speculation. He bought land and built a block of apartment houses there. Long a lover of music, he had composed musical comedies, opera, and music for the ballet. To attract tenants, he thought it a good idea to build an opera house on his block. With this in mind, he erected the Harlem Opera House in 1889, where for the first time in America he introduced the singing of opera in English. The completed theater lacked a box office, yet the acoustics were excellent. The first season—an artistic success, to be sure—left a large hole in Oscar's pocket. Hammerstein's first theater, the Harlem Opera House, has long since become world famous as the Apollo Theater.

He then built another theater in Harlem, the Columbus, afterward known as Proctor's; this was a vaudeville house where everything from grand opera to circus freaks was presented.

He went on to build theater after theater; in the next ten years he built and operated seven. The citizens of New York flocked to the large, handsome buildings to see artists who could act as well as sing, using the language that was familiar to them all. He was by no means always successful, and once when one of his theaters, the Olympia, was lost by foreclosure, he had to borrow money for food.

The most prosperous of his theaters was the Victoria, built in 1899. It was on Times Square, then known as Longacre Square, in a neighborhood considered too far uptown but afterward the center of the theatrical district. The Victoria was run like a continental music hall and for many years was supposed to be earning a quarter of a million dollars annually. It was said along Broadway that it was the goose that laid the golden egg from which Hammerstein's opera singers were hatched.

Hammerstein showed acumen in discerning the public taste and would search the ends of the earth for talent that would startle, entertain, and excite.

In 1906, against the strong objection of both of his sons, William and Arthur, he diverted the profits from the Victoria to erect the Manhattan Opera House just five blocks away from the Metropolitan Opera House. From Europe he brought such renowned singers as Melba, Bonci, Calve, and Renaud and proceeded to gather a young, fresh chorus, together with a competant orchestra under Campanini as conductor. Starting from scratch, he equipped the new building with scenery, costumes, sets, and decorations befitting this regal form of entertainment. The paint was still wet as the workmen were leaving for the opening night before an overflow house with crowds struggling to gain admission. A new chapter in the history of opera began with the astounding spectacle of two rival houses in one city producing the best of musical drama in a land not particularly noted for operatic appreciation.

Each house intrigued behind the scenes and attempted to lure each other's artists. But Hammerstein scored heaviest in giving excellent performances freed from the restraints that standarized and devitalized opera. With Mary Garden he demonstrated some revolutionary concepts that streamlined opera with good acting, trim figures, and teamwork in the cast. He brought over new works such as *Louise, Thais, Electra, Le Jongleur,* and *Pelleas et Melisande,* all ignored by his rival. The new techniques demolished the standard notion that a heavyset diva could act the part of a 16-year-old Juliet, if she merely possessed a magnificent voice. He demonstrated for the first time that the "singing actress" was more appealing than the massively proportioned prima donna.

During a four-year period of operation, Hammerstein produced forty-nine different operatic works in 463 performances. The Metropolitan Opera House was startled by his success. They purchased his project outright in 1910 at the price of $1,250,000. He had to turn over all scenery, costumes, and contracts on singers and operas and agree not to stage opera in the United States for ten years. This settlement was negotiated by the Metropolitan's chairman of the board, the capable banker Otto H. Kahn. After this sale Hammerstein, who was regarded as a dangerous opponent to be bought off at a high price, continued to infuse his own personality in the company's policy and grand opera ever after was rendered more popular and exciting.

Scientific as well as musical all his life, Hammerstein is said to have taken out over one hundred patents for inventions in the cigar trade. In addition to discovering a method of stripping tobacco, he also invented a way of applying air suction to the manufacture of cigars. As a result of his invention, cigar making became a factory process; it practically put an end to the manufacture of cigars in tenements and did much to improve conditions in what had been an unhealthy trade.

While still a young man, before his first invention, Hammerstein left the job of packing cigars for the more congenial one of reporting on a paper for the trade. By 1874 he owned his own paper, *The United States Tobacco Journal*, considered the best in the field of trade journalism and widely read outside the tobacco business for the spice with which Hammerstein flavored it.

But opera was his first love. In 1919 he conceived the plan of having a municipally owned opera house in every American city. He offered to help build them if cities would operate them on the popularly devised Carnegie Library Plan, the matching gift technique whereby he would match every sizable gift with an equal one of his own. However, his plan was cut short by his death.

In all, he gave an opera house to Philadelphia, to London, and another, the Lexington, to New York. He supplied David Belasco with a theater where the playwright-director would produce unhampered by any competative theatrical combine.

Hammerstein's son Arthur, as producer and inventor, followed in his father's footsteps.

Oscar Hammerstein II, the grandson, was for many years America's most popular librettist and played an important part in developing the "musical play" into an integrated dramatic form. By 1920 he had produced the books for three musicals. Subsequently, he collaborated with Richard Rodgers on such record-breaking Broadway musicals as *Rose Marie* (1924), *Desert Song* (1926), *Show Boat* (1927), *Oklahoma* (1943), *South Pacific* (1949), *The King and I* (1951), and *The Sound of Music* (1959). With a style and form of his own, he was in part responsible for such hit songs as "The Last Time I Saw Paris," "Some Enchanted Evening," and "Lover Come Back to Me."

THE FIRST READY-MADE CLOTHING FOR CHILDREN

1889

Children's clothing made by machine has become a permanent fixture in American homes and constitutes big business. Yet, until comparatively recently, even while clothing manufacturers were developing the art of ready-made suits for men and dresses for women, little attention was given to clothing for children. It was still thought that every mother with a needle and thread could put together a garment for her child. The situation did not undergo change until a poverty-stricken Yiddish-speaking Jewish immigrant, Louis Borgenicht, coming to America from a small Galician village in Poland and, beginning as a peddler in the New York ghetto, saw his opportunity in 1889 and had the foresight to start a new American industry.

His story was first the ordinary account of the poor alien struggling for a foothold amid his new surroundings. Prompted to pushcart merchandising, he sold pots, pans, socks, and stockings. He tramped all over the Lower East Side, surveying the marketplace and taking notes. He discovered that no one made children's aprons—then an essential part of a child's wardrobe. Without any capital but with the aid of his wife and a few second-hand sewing machines, he began to manufacture children's aprons, which he peddled from house to house.

From the making of aprons he began turning out children's dresses, meeting with even greater success. He came to the conclusion that ready-made clothing for children would save mothers endless work, the material and sewing would be better than homemade, and the prices would be lower than that of similar mother-made garments. Since he and his wife had twelve children, it was appropriate on all counts.

Although when Borgenicht started, there were three other New York manufacturers making children's clothing in a limited way—one an East Side tailor and two other enterprises that turned out expensive garments—his creative energy made him by far the pioneering leader. His shop created classically styled dresses that made girls feel like little girls and not like little women. Observing his triumph, others undertook the manufacture of children's clothes—dresses, knee pants, and double breasted-jackets.

With a leap and a bound, America became clothes conscious in those ending days of the nineteenth century. As Borgenicht kept ahead of the rest, he became known as "King of the Children's Dress Trade," and his business grew into many millions of dollars. Ready-made children's clothing appeared from Maine to California. He had created a modern miracle business—an American industry designed to make American home life easier, more colorful and more dramatic—and exceeded a billion dollars a year.

Pioneering the mass production of reasonably priced, decent-quality clothing, immigrant Jews in large numbers made their fortunes by helping to obliverate the more visible external distinctions between rich and poor, employer and employee, master and servant.

Before the American advent of the German Jew and later the Russian and Polish Jews, and their progress here from peddler to storekeeper to merchant to merchandise jobber and finally to manufacturer or department store proprietor, there was such a wide difference between the dress and living standards of the rich olegarchy of aristocrats and the American proletariat that class distinction made itself apparent wherever people assembled. It has been well said that the genius of the German Jew as a garment manufacturer and distributor of merchandise helped make democracy work in the United States. These Jews abolished that class distinction in dress that, before they had taken hold of clothing America, from colonial days had always enabled the haves and the have-nots to be told apart. Their garment factories, replacing in large measure what had originally been a handicraft producing made-to-order clothing for men, developed into one of the early mass-production systems in the country. Although they did not invent ready-to-wear clothes, when once they got the foothold that they turned into control of the clothing manufacturing industry, they cheapened the cost of clothing, improved its quality, and made it so practical that ready-made clothing became America's standard outfit for rich and poor alike.

The progress of the German Jew from peddler through his various stages of advancement had tremendous influence in lowering prices and bringing greater variety and a wider range of choice of merchandise available to the masses in cities, towns, and villages across the land. Their competition and unbounded energy, their imaginative daring, business sagacity, and merchandising ability made them important factors in cutting down the costs of merchandise distribution and in providing expanding markets for mills and factories developing the American system of mass production. The end result was to create the best-dressed working class with the highest standard of living in the world.

As the cycle swung and Jews from Eastern Europe—mostly Russian Jews—toward the last quarter of the nineteenth century dominated American Jewry, they took over the garment trades where the German Jews left off. Soon fashions of the minute were available to the purse of the shopgirl as well as the society queen, and the clerk was apt to set the pace for the boss in the latest style for men.

THE FIRST SEMITIC MUSEUM

1889

The Semitic Museum of Harvard University, founded in 1889 and located on Divinity Avenue in Cambridge, Massachusetts, is America's first Semitic museum. Home of Harvard University's Department of Near Eastern Languages and Civilizations, it was established "to gather, preserve, and exhibit all known kinds of materials illustrating the life, history, and thought of Semitic peoples and to increase the knowledge of the Semitic past in exploration of Semitic countries and ruins."

The museum building, designed by Alexander Wadsworth Longfellow, nephew of the poet, was the gift of Jacob Schiff, the noted philanthropist and patron of Jewish learning and the arts.

The Museum collections include glass of all types, ceramic wine and oil jugs, lamps, arrowheads, jewelry, amulets, and ancient tombstones. There are also beautifully shaped pots thousands of years old and mummy cases that send shivers down the spine. The museum's various objects are from civilizations where the Semitic languages are spoken—Israel, Jordan, Egypt, modern day Iran, Iraq, Syria, Lebanon, and Turkey. From time to time, the Semitic Museum publishes its results of its investigations to show the Semitic contributions to civilization.

Early Semitic Museum activities included participation in the first United States expedition to the Near East in 1889, the first scientific excavations in the Holy Land at Samaria from 1907 to 1912, and important excavations at Nuzi (northern Iraq) and the Sinai, where the earliest alphabet was found.

In the early 1990s the collections continued to grow; thousands of clay tablets, huge models of the Temples of Solomon and Herod and the Tabernacle, and scale models of the Hills of Zion were added.

During World War II the museum was relegated to the basement when first the Army and then the Navy moved into the building. After the war, the Center for International Affairs took over the top floors. The museum work remained underground physically, and most of the collection was dispersed for safekeeping.

In 1970 the accidental discovery of an extraordinary cache of twenty-eight thousand prints, lantern slides, and negatives—nineteenth century views of Middle East landscapes, architecture, and figures—coincided with the museum's efforts to emerge from the basement. The museum's archeological collections were inventoried, the facilities were refurbished, and new expeditions were launched. The photographs have since become an important tool in documenting the cultural heritage of the modern Middle East.

The museum emerged from the underground in 1982 with the exhibit *Danziq 1939; Treasures of a Destroyed Community*. The shows that followed—*Remembrances of the Near East; The Photographs of Bonfils, Crossroads of the Ancient World; Israel's Archeological Heritage*, and *Mounumental Islamic Calligraphy from India*—continued to increase public awareness of the rich heritage of the Semitic world.

For Harvard University's 350th anniversary in 1966, the Semitic Museum staged *The Jewish Experience at Harvard and Radcliffe*. In this context the museum itself was a significant part of the story being told.

One of the Semitic Museum's most exciting archeological finds was recently unearthed in the ancient port city of Ashkelon in southern Israel by the Leon Levy Expedition. In the summer of 1990, the Ashkelon excavation dig found a four and a half inch long, three-thousand five-hundred year-old metal calf and the cyclindrical pottery jar that protected it. The calf is believed to be an idol connected with the worship of a Canaanite god, either El or Baal. Its bronze body was sheated in silver. The silver calf of Ashkelon, as it is already widely known and celebrated, was found in the outskirts of the city, and it is speculated that merchants, approaching the city might have stopped to make an offering at a Canaanite sanctuary.

After several months of celebratory exhibition, the idol was returned to Israel.

THE FIRST PASTEURIZED MILK STATIONS

1892

Jews have never felt that their charitable duties were discharged by providing for the needs of fellow Jews only. The Talmud goes beyond the Bible in its insistence on generosity. Always motivated by the humanitarian teachings of their religion, Jews have wholeheartedly borne the philanthropic burden of the general community. Into this picture fits Nathan Straus, member of the famous Straus family, whose benefactions and gifts to humanity earned for him the name of "the great giver."

Lazarus Straus, his father, was a Rhineland Bavarian who often spent time as an itinerant vendor of general merchandise on the plantations of Georgia. He had settled in that state, in Talbotton, as the keeper of a general store when Nathan was six years old. There he remained until the end of the Civil War, when he moved North. He took his family to New York City in 1866 and started a business in crockery and glassware, while Nathan, now in early manhood, was sent to business college. Nathan later joined his father's firm and proved to be an extraordinary salesman. Under his management the business prospered.

One day in 1874 Nathan called on the New York City firm of R. H. Macy and Company with two porcelain plates under his arm. The clever salesman interested Mr. Macy so much that he arranged for the firm of Lazarus Straus to rent the basement of the Macy store for a crockery department.

In the same year that Nathan Straus was twenty-six, he and his brother Isidor became partners in the Macy firm, and by 1887 they were the sole owners of the business. With their investments and joint partnership, a new era in Macy's history began, and department store retail trade began growing.

By 1893 they crossed over to Brooklyn and bought an interest in the store known thereafter for the next one hundred years as Abraham and Straus.

Nathan Straus became one of the wealthiest merchants in the world but seemed glad to retire so that he might devote all his time to his hobby: philanthropy. The most famous of his many philanthropies, which saved the lives of many thousands of babies and has preserved the health of children in our own day, was the Straus Milk Fund.

In 1892 dairies lacked adequate milk inspection. Milk often became infected and brought sickness and even death to those who drank it. Nathan Straus lived with his family on his country estate; he prided himself on his fine herd of cattle. One day his livestock manager explained that his family could no longer have milk from their own cows because one had died of tuberculosis. Mr. Straus then began to think of what danger his family had been in and what danger there was present everywhere from the milk that people drank. He believed that the milk of a tubercular cow might transmit the disease to human beings unless the milk was treated in some way that would kill the germs of disease.

Thousands of babies were dying each year, but no one knew why. Straus began an investigation of the dairies of New York. Many of them were very dirty. He found them breeding places for sick cows. Soon he became convinced that impure milk was the leading cause of fatality among children.

In 1892 Straus attended a congress of physicians and scientists in Brussels, where the great French scientist Louis Pasteur demonstrated that the harmful bacteria in milk were killed when treated with heat by the Pasteur method. He returned to America determined to educate the country in the advantages of purifying milk by pasteurization, as the process was called.

Beginning in 1892, at his own expense, he set up, pasteurization laboratories where milk could be treated and made safe to drink. He then established the Straus Milk Fund, which distributed pasteurized milk at less than cost to needy people. In the first year alone thirty-four thousand bottles were given out. Prior to this treatment of milk, 241 babies out of a thousand died before their first birthday. After pasteurization, during a four year period, four babies died.

Meanwhile Straus began his great campaign for adequate milk inspection by the state. He withstood attacks and ridicule by many businessmen who sold milk and did not believe in the process he installed. Straus would not give up the battle and triumphed in the end. Twenty years passed and at last he was able to close his private pasteurization laboratories, for in every state throughout the country pasteurization became a law.

During the Panic of 1893–94, he initiated a chain of groceries to distribute coal and food to the needy and later served as president of the New York Board of Health.

In 1923 the people of New York acclaimed him their greatest benefactor in the field of social welfare. President Taft said of him: "Nathan Straus is a great Jew and the greatest Christian of us all."

Nathan Straus was a devoted Zionist and carried his benefactions to Palestine. He established a domestic science school for girls in 1912, a health bureau to fight malaria and trachoma, the dreaded eye disease of the Middle East, and a free public kitchen. He opened a Pasteur Institute, child welfare stations, and the Nathan and Lina Straus Health Centers in Jerusalem and Tel Aviv for Jews and Arabs alike. He also established a factory there for the making of buttons from mother of pearl. Nathan Straus had in the early days provided funds to pay for the passage of the first two American-trained Hadassah nurses who set up welfare stations for maternity care and who brought hope and healing in the treatment of the ravages of malaria and trachoma. His equally generous wife, Lina Straus, had sold her jewels to aid the cause, believing that the work must go on.

On January 31, 1928, on Straus's eightieth birthday, Natanyah, a city in central Israel on the Sharon coast, was established by the B'nai Benjamim Association and named in his honor.

Nathan Straus, who invested not only money, time, energy, and skill in the service of mankind, died on January 12, 1931 at the age of eighty-three. The death of the Grand Old Man of American Jewry called forth tributes from high and low, from far and near. He had given large sums for the relief of those who had suffered from the ravages of the First World War. His death spared him the knowledge of the horrors of the Hitler persecutions and of another conflict even more terrible.

THE FIRST VISITING NURSES

1893

One hundred years ago, a frightened, tearful child stood in the doorway of a tenement room on New York's Lower East Side and sobbed to the nurse inside who was conducting a class on home care for the sick, "My mama's sick. Please won't you come home with me?"

Instantly the nurse dismissed her class and hurried with the child to where the sick mother lay. Thus she began the first visiting nurse service in history.

Lillian Wald, trained nurse, opened a new chapter in humanitarian service when she answered the little girl's call for help. Stemming from the Visiting Nurses' Service and the Henry Street Settlement, which she founded and which became the "heart" of her activities, this chapter is filled with stories of improved health conditions; clean, safer homes; and the saving of many lives.

Lillian Wald's greatest achievement was in the field of public health nursing, and she may well be remembered as the ultimate pioneer in this type of social welfare.

The daughter of Minnie and Max Wald, she was born on March 10, 1867 in Cincinnati, Ohio. Her family came to the United States from Germany in the migration that followed the rebellion and defeat of the freedom fighters of 1848. They soon moved to Rochester, New York, the nation's center for the optical profession, her father's business. As a youngster, Lillian was an avid reader and curious about the world around her. It was her sister's illness that aroused her interest in nursing. She had long conversations with her sister's nurse and was fascinated by her knowledge of anatomy, medical terminology, and therapeutic techniques.

When she was twenty-two, Wald enrolled in the New York Hospital Training School for Nurses. Following graduation two years later in 1891, she became a nurse in the New York Juvenile Asylum. Always dispensing more help and attention to her patients than the hospital authorities deemed necessary, she was constantly at odds with her superiors. She left and enrolled in the Women's Medical College in 1892 but did not complete her training. Asked to teach a class in home nursing, she encounted an area in New York's Lower East Side in which hundreds of thousands of immigrants lived in extreme poverty. Shocked, but not frightened, she began her work of nursing the poor with great love and compassion.

Wald's visit to the sick woman's apartment turned out to be the "baptismal of fire" that fueled her lifelong commitment to serving the disadvantaged.

Moved by the absence of hygienic and nursing facilities in the slum flats on the Lower East Side, she instituted classes to teach folks how to care for sickness in the home. She had seen through kind, sympathetic eyes how sickness frightened people and made them helpless, and she was the first to plan some method to overcome this fear.

Together with her friend Mary Brewster, who was also a nurse, she went to live on New York's Lower East Side, where the people needed her help the most, and with financial aid from Jacob Schiff began a nurses' service, the first visiting nurses in the world. This service grew and ultimately became the Visiting Nurses' Service, which is the largest non-profit provider of home and community health care in the United States. Little did Lillian Wald realize that less than fifty years after its inception, there would be an army of more than twenty thousand visiting nurses in the United States.

Soon after her nursing service began, Wald saw that her quarters were not nearly large enough to care for the throngs that came for her help. Therefore, in 1893 she moved to 265 Henry Street, to the settlement that became so important that one little boy said he thought "God must live there."

When Wald saw the noisy and littered streets that served as the only playgrounds the Lower East Side children knew, she turned the backyard of the settlement into a little park where grownups and children might play safely away from the busy and dangerous streets and rest in the fresh air and sunlight. Thanks to the fine example set by her, city playgrounds have been established all over the United States.

In 1902 Lillian Wald organized the first city school nursing program in the world, and the United States became the first country to start regular medical care for school children. She also started the first "bedside school" for handicapped children.

Wald went to insurance companies to sell them the idea of providing free visiting public health nurses to their policy holders. The Metropolitan Life Insurance Company was the first one to do so in 1903. Before long other insurance companies followed.

Sickness and tragedy received another blow when she urged authorities to organize a Federal Children's Bureau, which was established by Congress in 1912.

During the Depression of the early 1930s, before public relief was taken over by the federal government, the Henry Street Settlement issued thousands of food tickets and directed relief regardless of race, color, or creed.

Many outstanding figures in America came to support Lillian Wald's work, including President Theodore Roosevelt. Prime ministers, poets, and dignitaries from overseas, too, came to see for themselves the miracle that Lillian Wald had created.

By 1913 the Henry Street nursing service had grown to include over ninety women, who were making about two hundred thousand visits a year.

Over the years Wald was an important member of most of the leading social reform organizations of the day and worked as well in the Women's Trade Union League, women's suffrage, and peace movements, thereby becoming a pioneer of American feminism. It was largely through her initiative that a Department of Nursing and Public Health was established at Teachers' College, Columbia University.

The exemplary service performed by her and her associates was adopted by municipal governments, public schools, the Red Cross, and industry.

Known throughout her lifetime as "the angel of Henry Street," Lillian Wald retired in 1933. Her seventieth birthday was celebrated nationally. She died in her home in Westport, Connecticut, on September 1, 1940. Her death evoked tributes from the leading figures in the United States.

Lillian Wald was the author of *The House on Henry Street* (1915) and *Windows on Henry Street* (1934), two autobiographical works that are important volumes in the library of American public health and social work literature.

In 1976 the buildings in which the Henry Street Settlement was founded were declared national historic landmarks.

The Henry Street Settlement's innovative programs have become models for similar efforts in countless municipalities across the nation. Many Henry Street initiatives have led to major state and federal legislative changes, as well.

THE FIRST UNIFORMS FOR WOMEN

1896

The history of Jews in nineteenth-century America is marked by their development of the clothing industry. Starting in the 1830s, with factories that produced crude, cheaply made clothing, they developed the industry so well that by the end of the century, suits for men and dresses for women of good quality and cut were being produced in such quantities that their price was within the reach of most people. These entrepreneurs eliminated the differences in dress that perpetuated class distinctions from colonial days; in this they helped to democratize American society.

Into this picture fits Henry Dickstein, who came to America in 1892 at the age of forty-two from the small poverty-stricken village of Poltava in the Ukraine, changed his name to Dix, and had the foresight to start a new branch in women's wear: the manufacture of uniforms.

Soon after his arrival in America, Dix and his wife, attracted to the clean and cheerful little village of Millville, New Jersey, decided to capitalize on their experience as shopkeepers in Russia by opening a dry-goods store. They supplemented their shopkeeping by peddling through the countryside, selling the rural population "Mother Hubbard" wrappers for everyday wear and "tea gowns" of flowered sateens for Sunday wear, produced in New York sweatshops. One day they came to the conclusion that if they themselves could produce something that was better looking and cost no more, women would prefer to buy such garments.

With no knowledge of manufacturing and with no acquaintance with dressmaking or tailoring, husband and wife designed and made their first gowns. Then they found a youth who had worked in a Philadelphia dressmaking shop and hired him at twelve dollars a week as mechanic and designer. The village girls were hired as operators. Thus they began their manufacturing in a modest way as they journeyed forth to put to test the work of their hands. Their garments improved steadily, and before long they were turning out something that was far better than anything else at the price on the market.

From the very first, Dix insisted that every garment should be marked "Made by Henry A. Dix" and that it should be simple in style, of good material, and carefully stitched. In competition with "job lot" cheap wrappers and house dresses, he emphasized quality—"not how cheap, but how good"—his merchandise could be for the price.

In 1896 he remodeled his store into a workshop, office, and stockroom, where all the family worked to meet the demands of an increasing business.

Dix built slowly but on a sure foundation, only gradually expanding the business of Henry A. Dix and Sons into the neighboring villages of Bridgeton and Somerville. Finally he had three factories, all rather modest in size, run under his personal direction and working full time throughout the year, each turning out goods of the same high standard that he had set for his merchandise.

Then came the second development in his business: a change to the making of uniforms for working girls so that help in hotels, waitresses in restaurants, maids in households, and saleswomen in shops might have simple, neat costumes. Up to that time the working girl on her job made use of any old second-best dress.

The same Dix standard of quality, taste, workmanship, and fair prices applied to "Dix Uniforms." They became a popular success from coast to coast. A new branch in the women's-wear industry was created.

From such a start, making uniforms for nurses was a natural advance. Soon no hospital was considered up to date unless its nurses were properly uniformed. In 1917, when the Red Cross adopted a nurse's hospital uniform, it turned to Dix to design it. Then the Dix Red Cross uniform took its place as international insignia and became recognized in whatever corner of the earth required the ministrations of that noble institution. Soon thereafter the United States Government appointed Dix to design and supply Army and Navy nurses' uniforms.

In 1922, looking back over his seventy-two years, long years of struggle without an idle day, Henry A. Dix, essentially a man of simple taste, grown rich, faced the problems of the future. As the year grew to a close, he turned his business over to his employees. Newspapers acclaimed the first incident of its kind in American history:

Man Who Gave Workers $1,000,000 Business Calls It Merely Justice . . . Dix never had a strike in a quarter of a century. He has made all he wants—declined big price for plant so his employees could have a chance.

But that was not all that Dix did. He converted his large estate in Mount Kisco, New York, into a home for working girls and donated a maintenance endowment of $100,000, paying rent for the part of the estate he used for his own purposes. Dix also established a trust fund of $100,000 for the maintenance of the Federated Jewish Charities of New York and similar funds for the Young Women's Hebrew Association; in addition, he gave $50,000 for the erection of an administration building for the latter institution.

The Dix story ends in 1938, the year in which he died at the age of eighty-eight, but after him lives the industry that he founded and his ideas, which transmuted the garment in which working women toiled into the insignia of self-respecting service.

THE FIRST AMERICAN JEWISH COPPER KINGS

1898

Early in 1848, Simon Guggenheim, who had wearied of the cruel conduct and economic oppression of his townsmen, left his native Switzerland with his family of fourteen souls and set off for America. Their ship took the customary two months to cross the Atlantic, entered the mouth of the Delaware River, and deposited them all in Philadelphia. Simon was then fifty-six; his oldest son, Meyer, was twenty. Father and son set out peddling in the anthracite country. By 1898, Guggenheim enterprises were producing nearly half of the world's copper supply.

What may have been the greatest single fortune in America, outweighed only by that of John D. Rockefeller, began very modestly.

After a few years of incredible hardships, father Simon Guggenheim plodded the streets of Philadelphia offering shoelaces, ribbons, needles, and such articles as were not usually in the small shops off the main business section. Adding a much-used polish for iron stoves, Meyer trudged the open highways from hamlets to farms carrying the heavy knapsack on his back.

Profits enabled Meyer to attempt other lines of business. During the Civil War all kinds of goods were in demand. The United States Army gladly bought his essence of chicory and coffee beans, roasted, boiled, and bottled, that was relished by the soldiers.

Meyer Guggenheim's business acumen constantly perceived new frontiers of opportunity and sources of revenue. He dealt in pepper, condiments, and spices from the West Indies brought by clipper ships from Amsterdam. The Pennsylvania Salt Company enjoyed a monopoly on lye used by families in the making of soap out of the fat saved from food. Meyer picked up an option on English caustic alkali that, when melted, was equivalent to the lye and sold much cheaper. The Guggenheim product proved such competition that the salt company bought the lye business and paid a heavy profit. Meyer loaned extra cash to friends and received mortgages secured by real estate. He also did some speculating in the stock market.

One day Meyer received a consignment of embroidery from his wife's uncle in Switzerland. A letter explained that Uncle Myers had started a factory that would embroider lace cheaply by machine, a process hitherto done expensively by hand. He had produced more than he could sell in Europe and believed that the lace would go well in America. His price was but a small coverage of cost.

The alert Guggenheim sensed new possibilities immediately. The lace came at the right time. Meyer had been wondering what to do with his older sons, who showed no disposition for school but keen interest in business. He formed a partnership, Guggenheim and Pulaski, with offices in Switzerland and later in New York. Daniel Guggenheim, only seventeen but the shrewdest of the boys, went with Morris Pulaski to Switzerland to finish his education and learn the lace embroidery business. While the business prospered, there intervened an incident that ultimately brought the Guggenheims—for a time, at least—into the category of the Rockefellers, the Morgans, the Fords, and the Du Ponts.

Losing money after the Civil War, Charles Graham, a dignified Quaker from Germantown, Pennsylvania, attempting to retrieve his fortune by investing his remaining $2,000 in some Leadville, Colorado, silver-lead mines, applied to Guggenheim for a loan. The map of the gulch and the Quaker's promotional enthusiasm forced Meyer to proclaim, "If the mine is as good as all that, I won't lend you a penny. I will take a partnership." The partners traveled to Leadville, but all Meyer could see on the hill was a deep shaft filled with water. The manager seemed confident of a big strike if he had the necessary machinery for pumping out the water and enough funds to continue digging.

Meyer returned to Philadelphia not overconfident. During the next few months more and more of Meyer's money was needed to keep the pumps going. Nervous irritation increased with each telegram asking for another $1,000. One day a messenger brought in a telegram from Leadville that read: "Rich strike—mine yielding fifteen ounces silver sixty percent lead—Harsh." Excited, he grabbed a pencil and computed that fifty tons a day would produce $1,000 in silver. He was indeed a millionaire. Thus the firm of M. Guggenheim's Sons embarked upon the mining and smelting business at a time when these industries were in their infancy. From that day in 1881, the spice business and even the profitable lace-embroidery firm seemed a mere trifle. Mining meant big business worthy of smart men's efforts.

He set up a smelting plant that refined his own metals and served others. The embroidery firm was sold, and his three older sons went wholeheartedly into mining and smelting. By 1882 Meyer's holdings were large enough, according to his biographer, to "enlist and hold the attention of all of his sons," who had been working for him all along. Meyer formed M. Guggenheim's Sons for this purchase, in which each of his sons was an equal partner. He began lending his sons money to go out and buy and build smelters. In 1888 the boys bought their first smelter in Pueblo, Colorado, for $500,000, and soon they had another in Mexico. The profits they divided were enough to hold anyone's attention. In 1890, one mine alone was worth $14,556,000. A year later the Guggenheims had made so much money that they decided to form a trust of their own, consolidating about a dozen of their refining operations under the name of the Colorado Smelting and Refining Company.

In the rise of trust building, H. H. Rogers and the Rockefellers formed the American Smelting and Refining Company, which monopolized the smelters' industry. They invited the Guggenheims to enter on attractive terms.

At a critical time, the Guggenheims endeared themselves to labor, to miners, and to the general public by complying with the Colorado eight-hour labor law, by paying a better price for gold and silver ore, by advancing loans to hard-pressed miners, and by keeping open during the shut down ordered by the Smelters' Trust. In 1901, the trust capitulated on the terms of the victor, and the Guggenheims took over the Smelters' Trust. The family received $45,000,000 in stock and became the majority stockholders of the American Smelting and Refining Company, perhaps the most remarkable deal in Wall Street history.

Within a generation the Guggenheims stood out as the world's copper kings. They refined silver and extracted lead and zinc. They developed tin mines in Bolivia and dug gold in the frozen Yukon. The Guggenheim Exploration Company sent forth engineers to roam throughout the world, searching for profitable mines and ores, minerals and metals. At the invitation of Belgian King Leopold II, they became partners in the diamond fields of Angola and the Congo. They extracted nitrate in Chile and drew rubber from plantations in the Belgian Congo. They monopolized the mining industry of Mexico and controlled the Smelters' Trust through the American Smelting and Refining Company. They initiated and launched such gigantic enterprises as Kennecott Copper Corporation, Nevada Consolidated, the Esperanza Gold Mine in Mexico, and the Chile Copper Company.

The highest point in Guggenheim wealth and power came with the First World War. No one was better prepared for the role of purveying essential metals, first to the Allies and later to his own country, than

Daniel Guggenheim. The Guggenheim Corporations were geared to their top efficiency in production and distribution. In fact, it was difficult to envision an Allied victory without their resourceful organizations. All the sons threw their energies into the war effort. The younger generation enlisted in the armed forces, and their fathers worked selling Liberty Bonds, helping the American Red Cross, and serving on war boards that directed phases of the conflict.

Meyer Guggenheim and his sons distinguished themselves by their benefactions to philanthropic and humanitarian causes. For six years Simon Guggenheim represented Colorado in the United States Senate. As a memorial to his son who died April 26, 1922, he established the $10 million John Simon Guggenheim Memorial Foundation, which since 1925 has given thousands of fellowships to further the development of scholars and artists by assisting them to engage in any field of knowledge and creation in any of the arts or sciences, under the freest possible conditions and irrespective of race, color, or creed.

On New York City's Fifth Avenue between 88th and 89th streets stands the Solomon R. Guggenheim Museum, a mecca for art lovers and home to one of the world's finest collections of modern and contemporary art. The famous spiral building itself is a masterpiece. Designed by Frank Lloyd Wright and opened to the public in October 1959, the building is the youngest ever to be designated a New York City landmark.

The Murray and Leonie Guggenheim Dental Clinic cared for the needs of thousands of schoolchildren free of charge on East 72nd Street in New York City for a period of thirty-six years before it was closed in 1967, having been supplanted by federal and state legislation.

Several years before Charles Lindbergh startled the world with his solo flight across the Atlantic, Daniel Guggenheim—instigated by his son Harry, subsequently ambassador to Cuba—began contributing funds to various universities for research in the study and promotion of aviation as a safe and useful means of transportation when the new art of flying was in the doldrums in the 1920s. He then set up the Daniel Guggenheim Fund for the Promotion of Aeronautics with an initial $2,500,000 for loans to commercial companies for landing fields, beacon lights, and air markings. By taking up where he left off, and following the methods he established, the Daniel and Florence Guggenheim Foundation has been able to aid materially in bringing about greater safety, reliability, speed, and range in air transportation and to help speed the progress of flight in space. Daniel's son Harry was one of the chief supporters of the rocket and astronautic experiments of Dr. Robert Goddard.

In the course of seventy years, of the many grants made since 1924 by the Daniel and Florence Guggenheim Foundation, a large number have also been in support of civic, educational, religious, medical, cultural, and other causes and for the relief of victims of disaster and for research in the criminal justice system. Among the organizations aided have been the United Jewish Appeal, the Federation of Jewish Philanthropies, the Hebrew Orphan Asylum in New York City, the American Jewish Committee, the National Council of Jewish Women, and the American Jewish Joint Distribution Committee, among others.

For many years Daniel Guggenheim was a trustee of Temple Emanu-El in New York City. In 1901 he was one of the incorporators of the Jewish Theological Seminary of America and continued as a director from 1902 until the time of his death in 1930.

The French government made Murray Guggenheim an officer of the French Legion of Honor for erecting in Paris a dormitory for 320 students in recognition of French-American friendship.

THE FIRST HEBREW LETTER ISSUED BY THE UNITED STATES GOVERNMENT

1902

In 1900 Romania was hit by an economic crisis, and its more than a quarter–million Jews, who, as a result of repression, living on the verge of poverty even in normal times, were reduced to appalling destitution. Thousands of them—men, women, and children—set out on foot for the ports of Western Europe, where they embarked for the United States. Between 1900 and 1906, some seventy thousand of them left the country. The stampede created a sensation in Europe. In America, neither the Jews nor the U.S. government, which found its country at the receiving end of so much misery, could remain indifferent to it.

In 1902, John Hay, the scholarly secretary of state in the cabinet of President Theodore Roosevelt, took diplomatic action of an unprecedented character. On August 11 of that year he dispatched a long note to the representatives of the United States in France, Germany, Great Britain, Italy, Russia, and Turkey, the signatories of the Treaty of Berlin, for the attention of the governments of those countries. It was a scathing indictment of Romania's policy, which made paupers and fugitives of those whom she had promised in a solemn international undertaking to emancipate and protect. The United States, the note claimed had the right to denounce the policy because it forced those upon her shores a great many "outcasts, made doubly paupers by physical and moral oppression in their native land," whose immigration lacked "the essential conditions which made alien immigration either acceptable or beneficial."

That, however, was not the only grounds for protest.

The note took occasion to recount in some detail the numerous disastrous disabilities that reduced the Jews of Romania "to a state of wretched misery." It cited "their exclusion from the public service and learned professions, the limitation of their civil rights, and the imposition upon them of exceptional taxes," and it stressed the fact that they were "prohibited from owning land, or even from cultivating it as common laborers." Barred from the rural districts, they found that "many branches of petty trade and manual production [were] closed to them in the over- crowded cities where they [were] forced to dwell and engage, against fearful odds, the desperate struggle for existence."

Hay's note made a deep impression throughout Europe, and the Jews in America were gratified by the castigation administered by the great republic of the West to the persecution of their coreligionists in Romania; their leaders had doubtless played no small part in the event.

The first Hebrew letter issued by the United States government was sent by Secretary of State John Hay in 1902 to Rabbi Marcus Dobov, spiritual leader of Congregation B'nai Moshe of Evansville, Indiana. Rabbi Dubov had written earlier to express his gratitude to Secretary Hay for his efforts on behalf of Romanian Jewry. The letter signed by Secretary Hay was prepared by a Mr. Thomas, official translator of the State Department who knew Hebrew well. This is the first and only time Hebrew was used in an official document of the United States government.

The letter in English translation reads as follows:

Man of God, I received the letter and was glad that my work for the persecuted brethren of the kingdom of Romania found favor in thy sight. Peace be to thee and the Congregation B'nai Moshe.

I pray that the Lord our God may bless all of thy brethren in Evansville in all their efforts, physically and spiritually, and that the God of Peace may be with thee forever. I will remain thy friend,
    John Hay

The note proved a barren victory. It brought no amelioration to the lot of the Jews in Romania, nor is there any indication that the government to whom it was addressed bestirred themselves on their behalf. Such action by Russia was out of the question. Her zeal in persecuting Jews was no less keen than that of her neighbors. The other signatories of the Treaty of Berlin discovered that their economic and political interests in Romania made it unwise for them to risk the displeasure of her government. Hay's note of 1902—which, of course, had the unqualified approval of his chief in the White House, President Theodore Roosevelt—was no doubt a chival- rous gesture, but it remained only that.

The first time Hebrew was officially used in international diplomacy was in 1951, when Abba Eban, then the youngest delegate at the United

Nations, representing Israel, then the youngest state on earth, signed the Genocide Convention Treaty in the language of the Bible.

THE FIRST SONNET ENGRAVED ON A STATUE

1903

For almost a century many millions of immigrants to America, visitors from far and near, newcomers, tourists and native-born Americans read the glorious lines engraved on the base of the Statue of Liberty at the entrance to New York Harbor.

Perhaps the most poignant expression of the concept of America as the "mother of exiles," they were written in 1883 by a young poetess of Sephardic ancestry, Emma Lazarus, a native and resident of New York City.

The imposing figure of the gigantic Bartholdi statue of *Liberty Enlightening the World* recalled one of the seven wonders of the ancient world, the famous Colossus of Rhodes, so Lazarus called her sonnet "The New Colossus."

As the writer of the famous sonnet, Emma Lazarus has been universally acclaimed as the champion of American liberty and democracy, just as the statue itself has become the symbol of liberty. Lazarus will always be remembered for her immortal lines:

Not like the brazen giant of Greek fame,
With conquering limbs astride from land to land;
Here at our sea-washed, sunset gates shall stand
A mighty woman with a torch, whose flame
Is the imprisoned lightening, and her name
Mother of Exiles. From her beacon-hand
Glows world-wide welcome; her mild eyes command
The air-bridged harbor that twin cities frame.
"Keep ancient lands, your storied pomp!" cries she
With silent lips. "Give me your tired, your poor,
Your huddled masses yearning to breathe free,
The wretched refuse of your teeming shore.
Send these, the homeless, the tempest-tossed to me.
I lift my lamp beside the golden door!"

Yet this paean to America as the haven of the oppressed, the first sonnet engraved on the base of a statue, almost went unwritten, and once written was almost forgotten.

In 1883, when the Republic of France decided to give the United States the Statue of Liberty as a gift to celebrate the one hundredth anniversary of American independence, there was no pedestal at the selected site on which to place it, due to the failure of Congress to appropriate funds for the purpose. It was not until Joseph Pulitzer adopted the cause in one of his earliest crusades after the founding of the *St. Louis-Post-Dispatch* and the *New York World* that $300,000 was obtained to complete the base. Pennies, nickels, dimes, and quarters were raised in a nationwide campaign from 120,000 contributors.

Another means of adding to the fund was an art and literary auction. The most famous writers of the day were invited to contribute an original manuscript or sketch, the contributions to be auctioned off.

Walt Whitman, Mark Twain, and Bret Harte were among those who submitted manuscripts. Emma Lazarus was asked to contribute a poem for this occasion. At first she refused, saying she "could not possibly write verses to order." Constance Cary Harrison, who was planning to publish the manuscripts and artwork in a souvenir portfolio, finally persuaded Lazarus to change her mind by writing her: "Think of the Godess of Liberty standing on her pedestal yonder in the bay and holding the torch to those Russian refugees you are so fond of visiting in Ward's Island" (predecessor of Castle Garden and Ellis Island).

Two days later Mrs. Harrison received Emma Lazarus's contribution, a fourteen-line sonnet called "The New Colossus." The auction was held in 1883, and Emma's sonnet brought in $1,500 for the pedestal fund, an unheard of amount for a short piece of poetry.

When the Statue of Liberty was dedicated on October 28, 1886, by President Grover Cleveland, Emma Lazarus's sonnet had apparently been forgotten for it wasn't mentioned. In 1903, sixteen years later, a New York artist, Georgiana Schuyler, found a copy of Mrs. Harrison's portfolio in a New York bookstore. The artist was so impressed by Lazarus's inspiring lines that she had them inscribed on a bronze tablet and obtained permission to have them affixed to the base of the Statue of Liberty.

Part of Emma Lazarus's sonnet is now one of the first things a new arrival to the United States sees when he comes by air. Etched into a large marble block that faces the entrance to the International Arrivals building at Kennedy International Airport in New York are the last four lines from "The New Colossus."

The family into which Emma Lazarus was born on July 22, 1849, was one of the best-known and oldest Sephardic families in New York City. The gently reared daughter of Nathan Lazarus, a wealthy sugar merchant, and Esther Nathan Lazarus was herself a fourth-generation American whose grandparents had been married in New York during the American Revolution. Emma had been educated in private schools and by private tutors at home, as was the custom among wealthy American families.

At an early age she had shown talent for writing poetry. At seventeen her published book of poems *Poems and Translations* received wide acclaim and brought her to the attention of Ralph Waldo Emerson and other literary lights of the day.

But then, in 1881, something happened that gave purpose to her life. Almost overnight she became an inspired spokesperson for the Jewish people and for all the persecuted and downtrodden. She was brought to a forceful awakening of her Jewish soul. Newspapers blazed forth the awful tidings of the Russian pogroms, and hundrds of Jewish victims were hurled to the shores of the New World. Emma saw them in Ward's Island; she saw their poverty and distress but also their pride and devotion to their ancient faith. From then on she seemed to be reborn for the remainder of her all-too-short life and belonged, as one of her heroines termed it, "wholly to her people."

Realizing she was greatly deficient in Jewish knowledge, Emma began to study Hebrew, which she mastered well enough to begin translating the classic Hebrew poems of the great literary figures of Spain's golden age, including the works of Judah Halevi, Ibn Ezra, Ibn Gabirol, and others. A number of her beautiful translations have found their way into the prayer book. She began to study the history of her people. She thrilled at the heroism of the Maccabees and wrote "The Banner of the Jew," which is still recited in Hebrew schools. She read about the Black Death of 1349, when the entire Jewish community of Norhausen, Germany, was faced with the choice of conversion or death at the stake. For them there could be only one choice: men, women, and children danced into the scorching flames while singing the praises of God. Lazarus put this tragedy into a poetic play called *The Dance to Death*. It appeared in her volume *Songs of a Semite* (1882). Lazarus dedicated the play to George Eliot, author of *Daniel Deronda* (1876) as follows: "This play is dedicated in profound veneration and respect to the memory of George Eliot, the illustrious writer who did most among the artists of our day towards elevating and enobling the spirit of Jewish nationality."

With missionary zeal, the frail poetess undertook to defend her people against all detractors and defamers. When an article in *Century Magazine* in April 1882 written by a Madame Z. Ragozin appeared, called "Russian Jews and Gentiles: From a Russian Point of View," which justified the terrorist attacks of the Russian mobs against their Jewish neighbors, Lazarus rushed into print. In the next issue of the *Century*, her powerful polemic rejoinder, "Russian Christianity Versus Modern Judaism," was a devastating attack on the apologists for the pogrom. This was a new voice and a new tone in America and American Jewish literature.

Long before Zionism became a contemporary force and when Theodor Herzl was still a university student, she was the first to appeal for funds to colonize the Jews in Palestine and dreamed and wrote about the Return of the Exiles. The poetess, once shy and sensitive, was now busy calling meetings of Jewish leaders. Her program of land buying anticipated the Jewish National Fund. On her desk lay the plans for the Hebrew Technical Institute of New York and schools to be established in the Near East. And then she turned to her major and most sustained prose work, *An Epistle to the Hebrews*, which was originally published in fifteen sections in the *American Hebrew* from November 3, 1882, to February 23, 1883. In it she expounded her prophetic views on the future of Palestine, which would become a "home for the homeless, a goal for the wanderer, an asylum for the persecuted, a nation for the denationalized."

She spent four months between May and September 1883 in England and France for the sole purpose of calling attention to the unhappy conditions of the Jews in Russia and Romania.

Her fame as a leader among Jewish intellectuals and idealists of her day spread abroad. Laurence Oliphant, the British diplomat and non-Jewish pioneer of Zionism, contacted her that she should secure American governmental support for his Gilead project. This was to be a bold political-economic plan to open the Transjordan region north of the Dead Sea for mass settlement of Jews.

Emma Lazarus did not live to see even an initial success of her pioneering work in Palestine. At the height of her literary and organizational activities, she fell seriously ill. She died of cancer on November 19, 1887, at the age of thirty-eight. All the synagogues of New York held services for her, an immortal American and prophetic champion of Israel who had written:

> The spirit is not dead, proclaim the word,
> Where lay dead bones, a host of armed men stand!
> I open your graves, my people, says the Lord
> And I shall place you in your promised land.
>
> (From "The New Ezekiel")

"A great princess is fallen in Israel," wrote the poet Stedman. John Greenleaf Whittier said of Emma Lazarus's passing: "Since Miriam sang of deliverance and triumph by the Red Sea, the Semitic race has had no braver singer. . . . Among the mourning women at her grave, the sympathizing voice of Christian daughters will mingle with the wail of the daughters of Jerusalem."

Her tombstone stands in Shearith Israel's Beth Olam Cemetery in Brooklyn, overlooking Jamaica Bay where she found rest beneath the cypress trees she so often described.

In 1949 the centenary of Emma Lazarus's birth attained worldwide attention.

THE FIRST JEWISH MUSEUM

1904

The Jewish Museum founded in 1904 in the Library of the Jewish Theological Seminary of America, is the first, the oldest and the largest institution of its kind in the world outside Israel devoted entirely to Jewish culture.

In 1904, Mayer Sulzberger, a prominent judge, included twenty-six objects of art as part of a gift of books and manuscripts to the Jewish Theological Seminary of America. These works of ceremonial and fine art were donated "to serve as a suggestion for the establishment of a Jewish Museum." Subsequent gifts and purchases have helped form the Jewish Museum's collections and develop the concept of the institution, whose mission is to collect, preserve, interpret, and present Jewish cultural history through the use of art and artifacts.

It was in 1925 that the Jewish Museum installed its first major acquisition with the Hadji Ephraim Benguiat Collection of Jewish Ceremonial Objects, a gift of Felix Warburg, the prominent banker, and his father-in-law, the noted patron of Jewish learning Jacob H. Schiff. This distinguished private collection of Ashkenazi and Sephardic art was primarily assembled during the nineteenth century by Benguiat, the son and grandson of dealers in antiquities from Smyrna (Izmir), Turkey, who had undertaken a "self-imposed family task to preserve . . . Jewish memorials of interest."

Years later it was Warburg's widow and Schiff's daughter, Frieda Schiff Warburg, who gave the museum its own home when she donated the family mansion on Fifth Avenue and 92nd Street to the Jewish Theological Seminary to house its Judaica collection. Located along New York City's Museum Mile, this elegant fifty-four-room family mansion has been the home of the Jewish Museum since 1947.

Moving the collections and installing them in the Warburg mansion was undertaken by the first curator of the museum in its building on Fifth Avenue, Stephen Kyser. From 1945 to his departure in 1962, he directed the development of over eighty exhibitions, the acquisition of approximately six thousand objects, ongoing research on the collections, and an impressive traveling-exhibition program.

A sculpture court outside the mansion was added in 1959, and the Albert A. List Building was added four years later to provide additional space for exhibitions and programs of large-scale, contemporary work.

In the early 1970s, when Joy Ungerleider-Mayerson became director, the museum expanded its focus to encompass all of Jewish culture, including the development of an ancient Israelite archaeology collection and exhibition and the establishment of an education department. Since 1981, director Joan Rosenbaum has reinforced that identity while greatly expanding the museum's program to include large temporary and permanent exhibitions of an interdisciplinary nature.

A major renovation and expansion program begun in 1990 and completed in 1993 has provided the museum with an additional thirty thousand square feet, effectively doubling the exhibition space, creating an education center, and providing many more public amenities. For the first time in its history, the museum is able to present a comprehensive interpretive exhibition on Jewish culture from antiquity to the present, drawn primarily from its own collections.

After a fund-raising drive that raised $36 million and two and a half years devoted to renovations, architect Kevin Roche has doubled the size of the building, extended the original limestone facade, and preserved the mansion's original style both outside and in. It still looks, as it originally did in 1908, like a Gothic French chateau when it was designed by architect Charles P. H. Gilbert.

The centerpiece of the expanded Jewish Museum is a permanent exhibition on the Jewish experience that conveys the essence of Jewish identity—the basic ideas, values, and culture developed over four thousand years. Occupying two floors on the expanded galleries, *Culture and Continuity: The Jewish Journey* showcases a significant portion of the Museum's collection of twenty-seven thousand works of art, antiquities, ceremonial objects, and electronic media materials.

Moving from the biblical period to the present, one encounters four principle themes that are later reiterated: Covenant, Exodus, Law, and Land. One exhibit on the fourth floor, *Forging an Identity: Antiquity (1200 B.C.E.–600 C.E.)*, describes the transformation of Israelite to Jew and the evolution of the Jews as a people with distinctive customs, rituals, and institutions. *Interpreting a Tradition: The Middle Ages and After (800–1700)* explores the vitality and diversity of Jewish life in the Diaspora with objects from each area where Jews have interacted with people of host countries. *Confronting Modernity (1700–1948)* considers the recasting and renewal of Jewish concerns and identity in the context of modernity. A final section, *Realizing a Future*, brings the visitor to the present with a look of contemporary issues confronting Jews and Jewish identity.

Culture and Continuity: The Jewish Experience features among its settings a gallery devoted to the ancient synagogue, with a hand-painted, one-third-scale replica of the western wall of and original ceiling tiles from the third century C.E. synagogue at Dura Europa (present-day Syria).

Dramatically displayed are also original artifacts that decorated ancient synagogues throughout the Mediterranean. The adjacent gallery explores the important study and interpretation in Jewish life, and enables visitors to gain a sense of the Talmudic process through an original computer program that explores issues of contemporary relevance to peoples of all cultures.

In another gallery reaching up two stories, objects illustrate cultural styles shared by Sephardic, Ashkenazic, and Eastern European Jews and house intricately carved and painted Torah arks, decorative ceremonial metalwork, elaborately embroided ritual textiles, and the finest collection of menorahs (Hanukkah lamps) in the world.

A semi-enclosed space, devoted to the *Shoah* (Holocaust) is given over to George Segal's plaster sculpture of figures of concentration camp inmates called *The Holocaust*. White ghostlike figures lie in a heap inside barbed wire, where they form a Star of David. A lone figure – the survivor (symbolizing hope) – stares out at the viewer and stands upright clinging to a fence. Another entire corner displays objects belonging to individuals and communities that personalize and memorialize this tragedy in Jewish history.

The final section, *Realizing a Future,* contains important art works that reflect the artists' individual perspectives on a wide variety of critical issues, such as Jewish identity, realities of life in Israel, and the quest for spirituality.

Adjacent to *Realizing a Future* is a Resource Center with listening and viewing stations offering selected television and radio programs from the collection of the museum's National Jewish Archives of Broadcasting, which contains the largest and most comprehensive body of electronic media materials on twentieth-century Jewish culture in the world.

Six thousand objects in the Jewish Museum's collections were gathered and donated by Dr. Harry G. Friedman, an art collector with a profound Jewish and aesthetic knowledge. Dr. Friedman's gifts to the museum encompass objects from every place that Jews have lived and range from examples of folk art produced by anonymous Jewish artisans to elaborate ceremonial works executed by some of Europe's finest silversmiths.

Besides the richness of its own collections, over the years the Jewish Museum has originated and hosted a large number of diverse and provocative temporary exhibitions with definite historical reference. For example, *From Seder to Stella: The Art of Passover in the Collections of the Jewish Museum; Golem! Danger and Deliverance in Art; The Dreyfus Affair: Art, Truth and Justice; Gardens and Ghettos; The Art of Jewish Life in Italy; The Circle of Montparnesse: Jewish Artists in Paris, 1905–1945; Robert Cappa: Photographs from Israel: 1948–1950; The Art of Memory; Holocaust Memorials in History;*

Jewish Life in Tsarist Russia; A World Rediscovered; and *Art, Politics and Change: Jewish Artists in Russia, 1890–1990.*

The Jewish Museum's collection of three thousand coins and medals from all over the world is the most distinguished of its kind. Assembled and donated between 1935 and 1948 by Samuel Friedenberg and his son, Daniel Friedenberg, the collection continues to grow. Today it contains over eighty percent of all known coins and medals illustrating Jewish history and culture. These medallions of illustrious men and women in Jewish civilization, artistically and systematically arranged, demonstrate beyond a doubt that Jews and Judaism have always played an active and significant role in the development of civilization.

THE FIRST BUILDER OF JEWISH INSTITUTIONS

1905

Jacob Henry Schiff was one of the nation's most powerful and influential bankers. He was also one of its greatest philanthropists and the first and most remarkable builder of Jewish institutions there has ever been among American Jews. Many of the institutions that are thriving today owe their existence or their establishment to his philanthropy.

Born on January 10, 1847, in Frankfurt, Germany, the son of Moses and Clara Nidenhofheim Schiff, Jacob Schiff was the descendant of a distinguished family of rabbis and businessmen who could trace their ancestry back to the fourteenth century. He studied in the neo-Orthodox school of Samson Raphael Hirsch and never forgot the lessons of his student days nor quite lost the spirit generated in that atmosphere. Nevertheless, he chose a business career, and after acquiring the rudiments of banking in Frankfurt, he departed for America at the age of eighteen.

In New York he went to work as a bank clerk in the brokerage business. At twenty he had sufficient knowledge of the field to form a brokerage firm of his own under the name of Budge, Schiff and Company. Later he met and fell in love with Theresa Loeb, daughter of Solomon Loeb, head of the private banking firm of Kuhn, Loeb and Company. They were married on May 6, 1875, and he was invited to join her father's firm.

Schiff's remarkable business acumen was recognized when he was named head of Kuhn, Loeb in 1885, upon his father-in-law's retirement. Schiff's firm soon became one of the two most powerful private banking houses in the United States. In this capacity, as head of the firm, he loaned hundreds of millions of dollars to business enterprises, foreign governments, trust companies, bankers, and railroad builders such as Edward H. Harriman and James Hill, who opened up the empire of the West to settlement. He was closely associated with Hill in the building of the Great Northern Railway, which united the vast uninhabited regions of the Northwest. He floated huge loans for the Pennsylvania Railroad and assisted in realizing the dream of A. J. Cassatt to build the Hudson Tunnel under the Hudson River and Pennsylvania Station so that trains could penetrate the heart of New York City. His firm was engaged in financial operations that also assisted such railroads as the Baltimore and Ohio and the Chicago and Northwestern. His outstanding project was the rehabilitation of the Union Pacific Railroad, which, toward the close of the century, had become "battered, bankrupt, and decrepit."

To Jacob Schiff, financial operations meant more than commissions for floating bond issues. He felt equal responsibility for the investor's money as toward the companies he assisted.

His operations were not confined to railroads. He financed a number of various undertakings unrelated in character such as Western Union, Armour and Company, American Telephone and Telegraph, Anaconda Copper, Westinghouse Electric, American Smelting and Refining, and United States Rubber. He did more than market their securities. He investigated thoroughly the prospects, the difficulties, and the problems of these corporations and often helped with sound advice and suggestions.

Deeply angered by the anti-Semitic policies of the czarist regime in Russia, Schiff was delighted to support the Japanese war effort. In 1904–1905, during the Russo-Japanese War, his firm loaned huge sums of money to Japan. For floating a bond issue of $200 million for the Japanese government, the most outstanding achievement in international finance since the inception of America, he was awarded the highest decoration ever given to an American, and became the first private Westerner to be received by the Emperor of Japan.

It was said that "nothing Jewish was alien to his heart." Personally devout and proud of his religious heritage, Schiff used his immense personal wealth and influence on behalf of his coreligionists. During the Russian pogroms of 1903–1905, Schiff helped organize a committee to raise the unprecedented sum of $1,750,000 for the relief of the victims of the massacres. The following year he sponsored the American Jewish Committee, the first American Jewish organization concerned with the civic and religious rights of Jews both here and abroad. Schiff was equally interested in the promotion of Jewish learning. A roll call of the Jewish educational instutions that owe their existence or sound establishment to him would include many of the major undertakings of Jewish learning such as: the Rabbi Isaac Elchanan Theological Seminary (Orthodox), later to become the rabbinical component of Yeshiva University; the Teachers' Institute and Library building of the Jewish Theological Seminary of

America (Conservative); and the establishment of the Hebrew Union College (Reform). He made possible the building of the Semitic Museum of Harvard University. He contributed generously to the Jewish Publication Society and underwrote its great English translation of the Bible, published in 1917.

The important twelve-volume *Encyclopedia Judaica* of 1905 was also made possible by his generosity. In 1897 the New York Public Library was the recipient of a gift from Schiff for the purchase of Semitic literature, which later became the Jewish Division of the Library. To the Library of Congress he gave one of the world's greatest collections of Hebraic books, manuscripts, and documents. Although this library had been collecting works in Semitic languages and civilizations from its inception in 1800, it was not until 1914 that a separate Hebraic section was established by an act of Congress. Schiff's original gift consisted of nearly twenty thousand books which he later enlarged with ten thousand additional volumes.

In presenting these landmarks of Jewish learning, Schiff was guided not only by personal reverence for the traditions and culture of the Jewish people but a deep desire to find a means of revitalizing that culture. It was this motivation that prompted him at the very beginning of his career as a patron of Jewish learning to come to the support of Jewish agencies dedicated to the education of Jewish youth. During its first two decades the New York YMHA found it difficult to gain community support, but when Schiff came to its rescue, it soon reached a significant place on the Jewish scene. Schiff was also a factor in the formation of the National Jewish Welfare Board.

New ideas in social service would also claim his attention. Thus, when Lillian Wald unfolded her idea of a settlement house with trained nurses visiting the sick among the poor, Schiff became enthusiastic in his support and joined this idealistic woman in founding and then enlarging the Henry Street Settlement on New York's Lower East Side.

Proud of his Americanism, Schiff contributed generously in time and money to civic activities and philanthropies. He was also interested in general education. When Barnard College was founded, he gave more than $1 million to the new college. At Columbia University he founded a department of social economics and provided scholarships for students in that field. His war contributions to the American Red Cross, Knights of Columbus, the YMCA, and the Salvation Army were magnanimous. He served on the New York City Board of Education, was vice president of the Chamber of Commerce, and participated in several special mayoral commissions.

Although a good deal of his far-flung philanthropy was anonymous, none of his gifts went out carelessly. He sat on the board of many institutions, continuously made inquiries about the welfare of those concerned, and talked with their workers.

Intensively involved in health care, Schiff supported the Montefiore Home and Hospital in the Bronx, New York, named in honor of the British philanthropist, Moses Montefiore, who devoted most of his life and millions to assisting his fellow Jews everywhere. Schiff spent many hours conversing with Montefiore's patients, eating the regular fare with them, not only helping them from the outside but trying to see the world from the angle of their poverty and misery. He knew all the permanent inmates personally and seldom missed a Sunday visit or a board meeting. He took pride in its dignified synagogue and kosher kitchen. Elected president of the institution in 1885, he held that office until his last day in 1920.

Yet a blind spot marred an otherwise faultless career. Jacob Schiff opposed the idea of a Jewish state. His devout faith was repelled by the secular attitude of the early Zionists, who discarded messianic prophecies for direct action. The massacres in the Ukraine after the war and the growing hostility in Poland opened his mind to the dire need for a Jewish commonwealth. Disagreement with Zionism did not prevent practical assistance to the colonists in Palestine. Schiff was interested in the cultural and economic development of Palestine and donated $100,000 for the founding of the Haifa Technion. A few weeks before his death, Schiff corresponded with Sir Herbert Samuel, the first British High Commissioner. He believed it was possible to finance a Palestine Project then underway and that the country could be rebuilt in accordance with the terms of the Balfour Declaration. His death, unfortunately, put an end to this work.

Jacob Henry Schiff died in New York City in 1920 at the age of seventy-three. The next morning the *New York Times* devoted its lead story and its entire second page to the story of his life and career.

"The funeral was an extraordinary affair," writes Stephen Birmingham in *Our Crowd: The Great Jewish Families of New York,* "not for its pomp and grandeur, though there was plenty of that, and not for the weight of the testimonials that poured in from heads of state, government officials, the public, and the press. It was remarkable for the sheer power of the emotion that gripped the thousands of mourners throughout the ceremony. Jewish survivors of the pogroms of Russia felt they owed their lives directly to him. To millions who had never laid eyes on him, who knew him only as the founder of the American Jewish Committee and the guiding spirit behind the Joint Distribution Committee, his name stood for salvation.

"There was the usual speculation in the press about the size of his estate. Estimates ranged from fifty to two hundred million dollars. Actually, his estate amounted to some forty million. It was clear that he had given away more than that amount in his lifetime."

THE FIRST JEWISH PRESIDENTIAL CABINET MEMBER

1906

American Jews have achieved fame as public servants and gained respect for their ability. They have occupied almost every public office in the land, not always in proportion to their numbers but certainly enough to prove their patriotism and loyalty.

In 1906 President Theodore Roosevelt chose Oscar Solomon Straus to serve in the newly created Department of Commerce and Labor. For the first time in American history, a Jew occupied a presidential cabinet post. The choice of Straus was singularly apt, for some twenty years earlier, in 1887, he served his first Turkish ministry post. In Turkey he succeeded in reopening American schools, which had been closed for six years, and in securing permission for the American Bible Society to distribute Bibles. He enjoyed good relations with the sultan and arbitrated a major railroad dispute for him. Straus performed his difficult and trying mission in Constantinople with such success that in 1890, 1897, and 1909, when affairs in Turkey were in a critical state, three succeeding presidents drafted him for the same post.

Straus, born in 1850, was the son of Lazarus Straus of Talbotton, Georgia. Impoverished by the Civil War, the family moved to New York, where the elder Straus was eventually to become head of R. H. Macy & Company.

Oscar Straus attended Columbia College and Columbia Law School in New York City. At the age of twenty-three he entered private law practice and was associated for a time with the law firm of James A. Hudson. He liked the strenuous work but decided to leave the profession. In 1881 he joined the family business in their ever-increasing mercantile ventures. From that time on his career was rapid and brilliant in law practice and business, in scholarship, authorship, and finally in public service.

Oscar S. Straus began his forty-six-year career of public service when, as a young lawyer, he served as secretary of the committee to reelect William R. Grace, mayor of New York. Grace defeated his Tammany opponent, and Straus was on his way.

His devotion to his country led Straus to make a special study of its institutions and of the men who laid the foundations of the republic. This resulted in the publication of two notable books. One, *The Origin of the Republican Form of Government in the United States* (1901, 1925), was the first attempt of its kind to trace with skill and scholarship the rise of American democracy from the ancient Hebrew commonwealth under the judges as it was expounded in the Bible and interpreted by the early Puritans in New England. The second, entitled, *Roger Williams: Pioneer of Religious Liberty in the United States* (1896), earned for him the honorary degree of L.H.D. from Brown University. He later wrote several other books, including his autobiography that he called *Under Four Administrations* (1922), referring to the four presidents under whom he held public office: Cleveland, McKinley, Roosevelt, and Taft.

After his return from his second mission to Turkey in 1902, Oscar Straus was one of the four American representatives to the Permanent Court of Arbitration at the Hague and was reappointed three times by Presidents Theodore Roosevelt and Woodrow Wilson, holding the position for twenty-four years, from 1902 until his death in 1926. He worked with President Wilson in Paris in 1918–1919 to make the covenant of the League of Nations part of the Versailles Treaty. It was a deep disappointment to Oscar Straus that the United States did not rise to its historic duty and responsibility in bringing about a permanent peace through the League of Nations. Straus also served as a public service commissioner of the State of New York and arbitrated many labor disputes and either settled or prevented more than a dozen important strikes during the year and a half of his incumbency.

President Theodore Roosevelt frequently called Oscar Straus to Oyster Bay or Washington to ask his advice on diplomatic or political questions. In fact, when in December 1906 President Roosevelt asked him to accept the post of secretary of Commerce and Labor in his Cabinet, he did so with the words: "I have a very high esteem of your character and ability. There is still a further reason: I want to show Russia and some other countries what we think of Jews in this country."

Straus served with distinction to the end of the administration in 1909. The Department of Commerce and Labor prospered under the attention of its new secretary. Hardships and injustices attending the arrival of immigrants in this country—a matter then under the supervision of his department—aroused Straus's concern. He devoted much time to the improvement of regulations governing the arrival of newcomers to the United States. He emphasized the interest of the public in the clashes between capital and labor, and like Theodore Roosevelt he advocated cooperation with business and regulation of trusts.

At the end of the administration, Roosevelt requested Straus's presence in Cairo. There the ex-president unfolded his plan about forming a third party to run against Taft. After Straus resigned, he joined Roosevelt in organizing the Progressive Party, known also as the Bull Moose Party. He ran on this ticket for governor of New York and although defeated in the three-corner race, he actually polled more votes in New York than Roosevelt did.

At the height of the anti-Jewish persecutions in Russia when the civilized world was shocked by the Kishineff massacre in 1903, Oscar Straus headed a committee to collect funds for the stricken and persecuted. Three years later, in 1906, he participated in forming the American Jewish Committee with Jacob Schiff, his brother Nathan, and others to safeguard the rights of Jews everywhere. Oscar Straus was also a founder of the American Jewish Historical Society and served as its first president from 1892 to 1898. These were not his only Jewish activities. As early as 1874 he had been a charter member and leader in the formation of the New York YMHA. He was a governor of Dropsie College for Hebrew and Cognate Learning in Philadelphia, and a trustee of the Jewish Publication Society of America. He was actively engaged in the administration of one of the largest Jewish charities in New York, the Hebrew Orphan Asylum. From 1893 to 1912 he was president of the Educational Alliance in New York, one the best-known Americanization centers in the country.

Straus supported the Zionist movement, and after World War I he used his influence to help win guarantees of the rights of Jewish minorities in several European countries.

A loyal Jew, lawyer-diplomat, and patriotic American, Oscar Straus was one of the outstanding men of his generation. He carried his ideas to the world, writing books, delivering lectures, working with private organizations and public offices to bring about a reign of understanding and peace on earth.

He died on May 3, 1926, at the age of seventy-five.

A memorial to him at the Department of Commerce building in Washington, D.C., was dedicated on October 26, 1947, by President Harry S. Truman. The following words are inscribed on the memorial: "Our liberty of worship is not a concession nor a privilege but an inherent right."

THE FIRST ORGANIZATION CONCERNED WITH JEWISH RIGHTS

1906

From Peter Stuyvesant's day onward, Jews have been quick to react against injustices to Jews. From the first two hundred years of Jewish settlement in this country, individual Jews like Asser Levy and Mordecai Manuel Noah spoke out. In 1859 Isaac Leeser founded the Board of Delegates of American Israelites, the first Jewish representative and defense organization. The board played a credible part in the campaign against the discriminatory treaty with Switzerland and asserted itself on a number of occasions during the Civil War, when issues arose that touched the fair name and welfare of American Jewry. This group soon merged with and became part of the Union of American Hebrew Congregations as Reform Judaism's social action agency, a function now carried forward by the group's Commission on Social Action.

The American Jewish Committee, the oldest Jewish defense organization in existence today in the United States, was founded in New York City in 1906 primarily by a group of concerned "uptown" Jews "to prevent the infraction of the civil and religious rights of Jews in any part of the world." It was a response to the vicious Kishineff massacres and the general persecution of Jews in czarist Russia, issues about which the Eastern European Jewish immigrants, crowded into ghettos in major American cities, were continually agitated.

In her history of the American Jewish Committee, *Not Free to Desist* (1972), Professor Naomi W. Cohen points out that "organization was in the air," and had the patrician stewards not founded a major organization to address itself to the problem, the frustration of Eastern European immigrant Jews would have expressed itself in less acceptable ways. They decided on a more-active leadership role, not only out of genuine concern with the fate of Russian Jewry but also out of fear that more unruly, often socialistic-oriented immigrants would employ radical methods of protest rather than respectable behind-the-scenes activity—which they were convinced was more effective in the long run.

Thus, in the early years of this century, a group of America's leading Jews were stimulated to create the American Jewish Committee. Using their prestige and wealth to influence government officials—the president, secretary of state, and others—they sought to bring the growing power of American policy to persuade the czar's government to desist in its persecution of Jews.

Louis Marshall, a leading New York constitutional and civil rights lawyer, took the lead in creating an organization to help alleviate the suffering of the victims and to speak for the Jews in such crisis.

It was felt that an organization of Jews in America capable of coping with emergencies similar to that created by the Russian massacres was essential. Accordingly, following several conferences participated in by such men of distinction as Jacob Schiff, Cyrus Adler, Mayer Sulzberger, and Oscar and Nathan Straus, it was agreed that it was "advisable and feasible to establish a general committee in the United States for the purpose of cooperating with various national Jewish organizations in this country and abroad on questions of national and international moment to the Jewish people."

On November 11, 1906, the first general meeting of the committee of fifty was held in Jacob Schiff's home to create such a central communal organization. What emerged from the proceedings was the organization called the American Jewish Committee. Judge Mayer Sulzberger of

Philadelphia presided at the conference and was its president during its first six years.

The committee was most effective in mobilizing the friendship and support of the American government on behalf of Jews in Europe and the United States. For seventeen crucial years, from 1912 to 1929, Louis Marshall was president of this group. During his tenure in office, Marshall demonstrated a highly developed talent for shrewd and tactful negotiations. He launched a vigorous campaign for Jewish rights wherever they were being threatened. This led him into activities as diverse as defending Leo Frank, wrongfully accused of the murder of a young girl in Atlanta, Georgia; courageously attacking the Ku Klux Klan, a masked organization opposing not only Jews but also Catholics, blacks, and the foreign-born; condemning the establishment of quotas in colleges; and deploring the release of movies that he felt strengthened anti-Jewish stereotypes.

The committee in 1912 prevailed upon our State Department to abrogate the century-old commercial treaty between America and Russia in protest against Russia's refusal to grant entry visas to American Jews carrying American passports.

After the outbreak of World War I, the American Jewish Committee, in cooperation of the Zionist Organization of America, sent emergency aid to the Jews of Palestine who had been cut off from communication with other Jewish communities. In October 1914 Marshall set up the American Jewish Relief Committee, the largest American Jewish relief body, which was soon thereafter merged with other relief organizations into the Joint Distribution Committee for extending relief to Jewish war sufferers and displaced persons in other countries. By the end of the year it had distributed $16 million received from various sources.

After the war, the American Jewish Committee sent delegates to the Versailles Peace Conference and helped secure guarantees of minority rights for Jews in the newly created states of Eastern Europe.

The committee welcomed the Balfour Declaration in 1917 that supported a Jewish homeland in Palestine but underscored the provision that it would in no way prejudice the liberties of Jews in other lands.

Louis Marshall's post-war correspondence with Chaim Weizmann led in 1929 to an enlarged Jewish Agency composed of Zionists and anti-Zionists for the purpose of building up the economy of Palestine.

Hailing the establishment of the Jewish state in 1948, the American Jewish Committee was the first American Jewish organization to open a permanent office in Israel.

Fighting anti-Jewish discrimination in the United States became the American Jewish Committee's major priority in the 1920s. Louis Marshall persuaded the uninformed industrialist Henry Ford to cease publication of his newspaper, *The Dearborn Independent*, and repudiate the numerous articles on "The International Jew" and the insidious *Protocols of the Elders of Zion.*

After World War II, under the professional leadership of executive vice presidents John Slawson and Bertram Gold, the American Jewish Committee became heavily involved in intergroup relations work. Active in the movement for civil rights, the agency also developed programming in Jewish-Christian relations and in interethnic understanding. Its legal staff presented numerous amicus briefs to appelate courts on First Amendment questions, concentrating especially on preserving the separation between church and state. The American Jewish Committee distinguished itself in the field of research with its sponsorship of social scientific studies of anti-Semitism and prejudice. Concerned about the possible internal erosion of American Jewish life, the committee initiated programs to enhance the Jewish knowledge and identity of its members. In addition, its research staff collects information relating to the Jewish population, its attitudes and occupations.

Today the American Jewish Committee, headquartered in New York City, has fifty thousand members in its thirty-two chapters across the United States and national members in nonchapter cities. In addition, it maintains a Washington, D.C., office that deals directly with government officials and representatives of foreign governments. It also continues to maintain an Israel office. The agency works through four program departments: international affairs, interreligious affairs, national affairs, and communal affairs. The committee also cooperates with the Jewish Publication Society of America in the publication of the annual *American Jewish Year Book.* Another of its outstanding publications is its monthly journal of opinion, *Commentary,* which, like its *American Jewish Year Book,* has achieved international renown.

During World War I, the American Jewish Congress emerged at first for the purpose of securing rights for Jews in the peace treaty that would end the war but later as a voice for Jews of East European origin. The American Jewish Committee also continued its labors in these matters, and through active contact, cooperation, and parallel action with European organizations aided in safeguarding these rights. As the committee and congress evolved, each began developing its own viewpoint, symptomatic of its leadership. The committee, long led by Louis Marshall, preferred to work somewhat quietly behind the scenes, educating people in power and molding public opinion. The congress, eventually led by Rabbi Stephen S. Wise, preferred mass publicity and public rallies to rectify wrongs.

In February 1990 the American Jewish Committee's board of governors tackled long-standing budgetary problems by cutting back on programs. Concluding that the American Jewish Committee's focus had become unclear because it had branched off in too many areas, the board decided to concentrate on combating anti-Semitism, safeguarding Israel, supporting human rights, promoting intergroup relations, and influencing American policy in the areas of civil rights, immigration, and the separation of church and state.

In 1993 the American Jewish Committee named as its executive director David A. Harris, a forty-three-year-old staff member and expert on international affairs.

On August 15, 1994, Phil Baum became the American Jewish Congress's executive director after fifteen years in the number two spot, behind Henry Siegman, and after forty-five years with the organization.

In 1994 the separation of church and state continued to be a major focus of the American Jewish Congress, which has a long tradition as a defense organization and a feisty one that is willing to take on all organizations and issues—particularly in the courts.

THE FIRST AMERICAN JEWISH NOBEL PRIZE WINNER

1907

On November 27, 1895, a year before his death, Alfred Nobel, the Swedish engineer, inventor, and philanthropist, signed his famous will that stipulated that the major part of his estate, more than thirty-one million Swedish kroner ($4.4 million), should be converted into a fund and invested. The income from the investments was to be "distributed annually in the form of prizes to those who, during the preceding year, have conferred the greatest benefit to mankind." The five fields in which he wished to stimulate progress as outlined in his will were physics, chemistry, physiology or medicine, literature, and fraternity (peace) among nations. In 1968 the Bank of Sweden instituted an Alfred Nobel Memorial Prize in Economic Sciences and placed an annual amount at the disposal of the Nobel Foundation.

While Jews make up less than two percent of the world's population, they have been awarded thirteen percent in the six categories. In 1907, Albert Abraham Michelson, professor of physics at the University of Chicago, was the first American Jew and the first American scientist to become a Nobel laureate. For a number of years the only other physicists in the United States to receive the award were students or associates of his.

Albert Abraham Michelson was born on December 19, 1851, in the little Prussian town of Strenlo, the son of Samuel and Rosalie Przlubska Michelson. His parents emigrated to the United States when he was two years old, settling first in Nevada but moving fifteen years later to San

Francisco, where the boy attended high school. In 1869, the year the railroad from coast to coast was completed, young Michelson journeyed from California to Washington, D.C., to seek an appointment to the United States Naval Academy at Annapolis. Although there was no vacancy, President Ulysses S. Grant was so impressed by the lad's ability that he made an exception and appointed him.

Four years later, in 1873, Michelson was graduated from the United States Naval Academy and commissioned a midshipman of the United States Navy. After the required two-year midshipman cruise at sea, he became an instructor in physics and chemistry at the Naval Academy until 1879. During those years he developed a fascination for physical problems, particularly the measurement of the velocity of light which in 1878, at the age of twenty-six, he computed to be 186,508 miles per second. As a result, Michelson won international renown as a physicist and was summoned to the Nautical Laboratory of Professor Simon Newcomb in Washington to assist him in his experiments on the speed of light.

Since research rather than teaching was Michelson's major interest, shortly after this investigation was completed, he applied for and obtained leave of absence from the Navy to go to Europe for further study. For two years he listened to lectures, attended seminars, and worked in the laboratories of eminent European physicists—Helmholtz in Berlin, Quincke in Heidelberg, and Cornu and Lippman in the College de France in Paris.

Physicists had long been asking themselves whether the ether surrounding our earth remained fixed in respect to the heavenly bodies through it, or whether the earth in its motion through space dragged the ether with it, much as a moving vehicle might carry a quantity of air with it in its motion. Michelson had devised an instrument known as the interferometer that was capable of measuring more minute distances than the most high-powered microscope. He began his famous "ether-drift" experiments in Berlin, in an attempt to answer this question. But the results were unsatisfactory due to jarring of the sensitive instruments by city traffic.

Michelson returned to the United States as professor of physics at the Case School of Applied Sciences in Cleveland, Ohio. Here he continued his experiments on the independent motion of the earth and the supposed "ether," partly in collaboration with Edward William Morley, professor of chemistry at Western Reserve. The conclusion of the experiment indicated that light travels with the same velocity in any direction under any circumstances, and the implication was that the ether did not exist. This brilliant discovery made by Michelson subsequently became one of inestimable value to the development of the science of optics and furthermore served as an incitement for the considerations that ultimately led to Einstein's Special Theory of Relativity.

From the Case School, Michelson went to Clark University in Worcester, Massachusetts, remaining there from 1889 to 1892, when he became professor of physics at the University of Chicago and head of the Ryerson Laboratories there, appointments he held for thirty-seven years until shortly before his death.

By using the interferometer in astronomy, scientists were able for the first time to measure the diameter of stars. A formula was eventually evolved so that the star's diameter could be computed. This method was used at Clark University to measure the diameter of Jupiter's satellites. In 1920, at the Mt. Wilson Observatory in California, Betelgeuse was the first star to be measured, probably the greatest single mass in the universe.

Another instrument that Michelson devised was called the echolon spectroscope, one of the earliest instruments powerful enough to give the eye evidence of molecules in vibration when a substance is heated.

This same almost miraculous gift for accuracy led Michelson to measure the rigidity of the earth. A pair of pipes six inches in diameter and five hundred feet long was placed horizontally six feet underground, one in an east-west direction, the other north-south. Each pipe was half-filled with water, and the tidal rise measured; the whole tidal range in these pipes was only one one-thousandth of an inch. By subtracting the exact measurement of this tidal pull from the theoretical maximum arrived at by the computations of the earth's size and that of the moon and sun, the results proved that the earth's interior was rigid as steel and in an elastic condition.

At Sèvres, France, there is a meter stick that is the standard of measurement for the whole world. Scientists were concerned over its possible deterioration or destruction, so Michelson was asked to substitute the speed of light as a unit of terrestrial measurement. This work took a year to complete. Using the radiations from cadmium (a metallic chemical element), Michelson was able to correlate the meter distance with the speed of a light ray. Thus we have now an indestructible and constant standard of linear measurement.

Michelson's profound scientific achievements were recognized throughout the world. He received honors from learned societies in various parts of the globe, particularly in England, France, Germany, and Italy. American universities conferred honorary degrees. He was president of the American Association for the Advancement of Science in 1910 and the National Academy of Sciences from 1923 to 1927. The Royal Society of London, the oldest scientific society in existence, awarded him the Rumford Medal in 1889, elected him a foreign member in 1902, and bestowed on him its highest award, the Copley Gold Medal. In 1907 he was awarded the Nobel Prize in physics from the Swedish Academy of Science. The citation read:

For his optical precision instruments and the spectroscopic metrological investigations carried on with their aid.

Albert Abraham Michelson, pure experimentalist, designer of instruments, refiner of techniques, drove the refinement of measurement to its limits and by so doing showed a skeptical world what far-reaching consequences can follow from that sort of process and what new vistas of knowledge can be opened up by it.

In 1929 Michelson retired to Pasadena, California, still conducting his work. He died two years later, on May 9, 1931, and was mourned as one of the greatest scientists of modern times. Gifted with deep insights and breadth of view, he also had strong artistic leanings. Like Einstein, he was an accomplished violinist, and his paintings attracted attention.

His major publications include *Light Waves and Their Uses* (1903) and *Studies in Optics* (1927). The first represents his Lowell Lectures delivered in 1899; the second consists of a condensed summary of his most important researches.

No scientist has ever left his lifework in a more complete form. No physicist has ever made more exact measurements or shown more skill in the design and manipulation of scientific apparatus.

The proving of his revolutionary theory of the absolute speed of light under any conditions has become the underlying principle of modern physics, astronomy, and cosmology and is considered to be perhaps the one absolute natural law in the universe.

THE FIRST AMERICAN PORTRAIT COIN

1909

The first coin bearing the portrait of the head of a president of the United States, the Lincoln penny, issued by the Treasury Department on August 2, 1909, was designed by a Jewish artist, Victor David Brenner, whose initials, VDB appeared on the first twenty-eight million of these coins. This was the first portrait coin ever used in American currency.

Brenner, born in Lithuania in 1871, came to the United States in 1890. As a young man he obtained employment as a die cutter and engraver of badges in an Essex Street shop on New York City's Lower East Side. At night he attended classes at Cooper Union and later at the National Academy of Design and Art. In 1893 he set himself up as a die cutter for jewelers and silversmiths and sent for his family.

One day while Professor Ettinger, on the faculty of the City College of New York and a well-known coin collector, was browsing around the Lower East Side, he entered Brenner's shop and was attracted by a plaque of the head of Beethoven that Brenner had done for a musical society. His interest in the young immigrant resulted in an introduction to the Numismatic Society, through which Brenner won the commission to design a medal that brought him into prominence. He was able to study in Paris under Louis Oscar Rotz, ranking medalist of Europe, and Alexander Charpentier, member of the Rodin group. Under these influences Brenner's work developed in scope. As a result he won a bronze medal at a Paris exhibition and several other awards in American cities.

After extensive travel throughout Europe, Brenner came home to throw himself at once into the battle then being waged by the Numismatic Society for better American coins. The movement met with the hearty approval of President Theodore Roosevelt, whose head was being modeled by Brenner for the obverse side of the Panama Medal awarded to every workman who put in two years of labor on the canal.

During one of the sitting sessions, Brenner showed President Roosevelt a design for a Lincoln plaque he had made that so impressed the president that he urged the Treasury Department to adopt it as the first step in reforming United States coinage. But to Brenner, this was more than a chance commission. He expressed the desire that the design be used on a one-cent piece in order that it have the widest circulation possible and thus familiarize even the most humble with President Lincoln's face.

Brenner also designed numerous medallions, plaques, and tablets, many of them symbolic of social activities and interpretive of American types. His mastery of portraiture in bas-reliefs was shown in the heads of John Hay, the diplomat; of Emerson, the philosopher; of Huntington, the railroad builder; of Swasey, the telescope maker; and a score of others.

In 1910 Brenner wrote *The Art of the Medal*, a leading book in the field. He achieved further prominence with his bust of Charles Eliot Norton, which is in the Fogg Museum at Harvard University. His famous bas-relief of George Washington may be seen today in the Federal Building in Pittsburgh.

THE FIRST FEATURE-LENGTH MOVING PICTURE

1913

Ever since 1894, when the Holland brothers opened up the first penny arcade and peep show on Herald Square, the citizens of New York could not stay away from the kinetoscopes or nickelodians. The pictures they saw were only a few minutes long—"Broncho Billy" chasing a train and falling on his face, a boxing match, a boy kissing a girl, or a couple of drunks running away from each other.

In 1896, a fourteen-year-old boy, who had been born in poverty on August 27, 1882, in the Jewish section of Warsaw, Poland, came to the United States. Little did Samuel Goldfish, as Samuel Goldwyn was then called, realize that he was destined to become America's first and foremost motion-picture producer. Little is known of his family background, but he was the son of poor parents who died young. At the age of eleven, the boy left Poland. After spending two years in England, he emigrated to Gloversville, New York, where he took a job sweeping floors in a glove factory.

The youth already had a drive for which he was to become noted in Hollywood. By the time he was seventeen, he was foreman of one hundred workers in the glove plant, and at nineteen he went out on the road as a glove salesman. Four years later he became a partner in the company, and before he was thirty, he was making more than $15,000 a year.

It was almost by accident that he got into movie making. In 1910 he married Blanche Lasky, whose brother Jesse was a vaudeville promoter. Lasky, at the urging of a theatrical lawyer, Arthur S. Friend, toyed with the idea of filmmaking and tried to interest his brother-in-law in such a venture. Goldfish, who had moved to New York, was cool to the idea until one cold day in 1913, when he stepped into a Herald Square nickelodian to warm up and only incidentally saw a Western starring Broncho Billy Anderson. He was impressed not only with the "flicker" but also with the flow of nickels the management was raking in. He had an idea that full-length stories and plays could be made into motion pictures.

In those pioneering days, all motion pictures were made in the East, mostly indoors. Samuel Goldfish, full of enthusiastic plans for picture making, wanted to find a more suitable place with a good climate for the making of outdoor movies the year round. He went West and found such a place – a nondescript little Southern California village. It turned out to be Hollywood, now the foremost world center for movie making.

By 1913 Goldfish had left his successful business career to produce the first feature-length moving picture made in Hollywood, an epic of American Indians and London high society called *The Squaw Man*. The picture was produced in a rented stable near the present intersection of Sunset Boulevard and Vine Street. At night coyotes came down from the hills to prowl around the building. Cecile B. De Mille, an unsuccessful playwright turned director, shot a couple of them and nailed their skins to the wall.

De Mille, who had never worked on a movie before, was one of Goldfish's partners in this pioneer enterprise. So was Lasky, who started as a coronet player and became one of America's best-known vaudeville and cabaret impresarios in America. Arthur S. Friend, Lasky's theatrical lawyer, was the fourth member of this group.

With the enthusiasm that was typical of him, Goldfish took up the idea of forming a film company of his own. He and Lasky each put up $10,000 and between them and Mrs. Goldfish and Mr. Friend pledged the rest of the $26,500 capitalization for the Jesse L. Lasky Feature Pictures Player Company. Another $15,000 in stock was set aside for general sale, while $5,000 more went to Dustin Farnum as salary for playing the lead in *The Squaw Man*. At the last moment Farnum backed out of the stock deal and demanded his $5,000 in cash. He got his money, but three years later the stock he had refused was worth over $1 million.

De Mille and Lasky kept their stock and eventually became millionaires. For many years they were prominent producers and leading figures in the Hollywood motion-picture industry.

The company's initial success resulted in a sudden interest in it from Goldfish's partners, which, as it turned out, was exactly what he didn't want. The partners battled constantly, and Goldfish seemed to be in a permanent rage. Shortly after the company merged with Adolph Zukor Famous Players Company, Goldfish sold out his shares for nearly $1 million.

In 1917 Goldfish joined forces with Edgar and Archibald Selwyn, who as Broadway producers had built up a library of plays that might make good films. The new organization was called the Goldwyn Pictures Corporation, a name derived from the first syllable of Goldfish and the last syllable of Selwyn. The more Goldfish saw and heard the name Goldwyn, the more he liked it, and he legally annexed it for his personal use.

In 1922 Goldwyn became an independent producer, convinced that he would never be able to get along with partners or boards of directors. A year later he converted his interest in Goldwyn Pictures to form Metro-Goldwyn-Mayer with Louis B. Mayer, but soon he dropped out and again made pictures of his own.

From the time he became an independent producer, Goldwyn was noted for the reverence in which he held creative talent. He coddled actors, writers, and directors, but when he felt they were not producing what he had expected of them, he switched tactics and heaped invective on them.

Goldwyn always believed that the story was the thing that made good movies, and he spent lavishly on scripts written for him by writers such as Rupert Hughes, Mary Roberts Rinehart, Moss Hart, Lillian Hellman, and Robert E. Sherwood.

Among the stars Goldwyn discovered were Tallulah Bankhead, Robert Montgomery, and Gary Cooper. He remained the only producer whose name on a theater marquis meant as much as the star's.

His quest for excellence became known in the motion picture industry as the "Goldwyn touch." Goldwyn films won dozens of Oscars in several categories: direction, writing, scenic design, music, color, and acting.

For over fifty years he made the finest motion picture in the world and produced many screen classics such as: *Street Scene, Arrowsmith, Wuthering Heights, Dodsworth, The Dark Angel, The Little Foxes, Stella Dallas, Hans Christian Anderson, The Pride of the Yankees,* and *The Best Years of Our Lives.* The latter, produced in 1946, was acclaimed the best picture of the year and received an unprecedented total of nine Academy Awards.

Goldwyn came out of semiretirement in 1959 to make his last film, *Porgy and Bess,* based on the George Gershwin folk opera. Although he was already seventy-eight years old, he held his chesty, six-foot-tall body erect, and his swinging walk seemed as always to be jet propelled as he strode through his studio streets. His eyes, deep set in his rather plain face, could still flash with anger, and his Polish-accented voice had lost little of its deep vibrancy.

To the general public he was known for his "Goldwynisms," the malaprops, mixed metaphors, grammatical blunders, and word manglings that included the now classic: "include me out," "I'll tell you in two words: 'im-possible,' " "an oral agreement isn't worth the paper it's written on," and "this bomb is dynamite."

Samuel Goldwyn, whose name became a household word, died on February 1, 1974 at the age of ninety-one. While other early producers of motion-picture fame retired on their earnings and prestige, he continued to turn out the best pictures he knew how to make, and each year the industry looked to him to set the pace.

Other Jews brought to the industry the talents so essential for theatrical undertakings. Their stories of individual success have become American legends. Adolph Zukor, a furrier from Hungary, put together Paramount Pictures Corporation, which owned the largest chain of theaters in the world. Carl Laemmele, a bookkeeper, successfully challenged the old Motion Picture Patents Trust and came to the San Fernando Valley to build Universal Pictures on the biggest movie lot in the world. Harry Cohn, a former song plugger, transformed a marginal film business on Hollywood's "poverty row" into one of the major studios. William Fox, a garment maker, named his company after himself and was one of the most powerful men in the industry until the financiers forced him out, and then he merged his company with Twentieth Century. Harry, Jack, Albert, and Sam Warner gambled on sound and revolutionized the industry. Louis B. Mayer, who had worked for his father as a junk dealer, took a chance and bought local distribution rights to a film called *The Birth of a Nation,* founded his own company, and became the highest-paid executive in the

United States with a salary in seven figures. He and his brilliant production chief, Irving Thalberg, shared an uncanny knack for discovering stars. By the 1930s, when a merger with Samuel Goldwyn created Metro-Goldwyn-Mayer, he could boast of having "more stars than there are in the heavens." In 1939, David O. Selznick, the son of a family in the film industry who rose rapidly to the front ranks of Hollywood producers, produced *Gone With the Wind*, then the most expensive and successful film yet made. This small group of Jews built a series of entertainment empires that straddled the globe and whose appeal was universal. For many years, seventy-five percent of screen time around the world was devoted to their product.

By the end of the 1920s, silent pictures reached their apex. The business world no longer looked down on the $1,250,000,000 film industry. In fact, movie bonds had become a favored investment, recommended by bankers to conservative clients. The industry itself had become the fourth largest in the United States.

In the last decade of twentieth-century America, movies are the most popular form of entertainment. They provide employment to hundreds of thousands of people and play an increasingly important role as an educational tool, as an agent of social change, and as a prime influence on popular taste.

With the announcement made on October 13, 1994, that three of Hollywood's giants, Stephen Spielberg, the most successful director in movie history; David Geffen, a billionaire record impresario, investor, and producer; and Jeffrey Katzenberg, former chairman of Walt Disney Studios, have come together to launch a new multibillion-dollar studio venture, Jews continue to play a preeminent role in the film industry today.

THE FIRST JEWISH GOVERNOR

1915

Many American Jews have taken part in municipal, state, and national affairs. Some have risen to high public office. Four western states, which have very few Jews, have elected Jews as governors, the highest office Jews have obtained in popular elections.

In 1801, David Emanuel, of Jewish birth but a convert to Presbyterianism, became governor of Georgia after having been president of the state senate. Emanuel County was named for him. In 1870 Brigadier-General Edward S. Solomon, famous hero of the Civil War, was appointed governor by President Ulysses S. Grant of the territory that later became the state of Washington.

The first Jew to be elected a governor in the United States was Moses Alexander, governor of Idaho, whose term ran for four years, from 1915 to 1919. He was the first foreign-born Jew to hold the gubernatorial office in the United States.

Alexander's family had emigrated to the United States from Bavaria, Germany, in 1868 and settled in Chillicothe, Missouri. Here young Alexander grasped the rudiments of the English language and continued his schooling. While he was still at an early age, family circumstances forced him to leave school for a position as a clerk in a clothing store. He studied nights and perfected his English while learning the Constitution of his adopted land. A few years later he became owner of the store in which he held his first job.

It was then that he showed an interest in local politics and in 1886 and 1887 served on the City Council of Chillicothe. In recognition of his record, he was elected mayor in 1888 and then saved the municipality from bankruptcy.

In 1891, because of ill health, Alexander was forced to leave Missouri and went to Boise, Idaho. He opened a clothing store there that soon developed into a thriving chain-store business with branches in Lewiston and Pocatello.

Again he entered the political arena. When the Reform Party invited him to be its mayoral candidate, he accepted and was elected in 1897. Alexander declined to succeed himself, but his reelection on a coalition ticket in 1901 made him a leader in the Democratic Party. Defeated in his first try for governor in 1908, he ran again in 1914 in a campaign that made political history.

When he took office in 1915 in Idaho's twenty-fourth year of statehood, he had to contend with a hostile legislature. Nevertheless, he gave the state a businesslike administration that won him many friends and, as one writer put it, "more enmities than any man has a right to expect." At the end of his first legislative session, he was faced with a huge stack of bills. When asked what he was going to do with them, Alexander riffled through the pile and replied, "I think I'll sign the thin ones and veto the thick ones."

He was reelected in 1917, this time with a Democratic legislature, and pushed through legislation that gave the state the first worker's compensation law; paved the way for a state highway system; created much-needed irrigation, reclamation, and waterway projects; and established prohibition. He retired from public life at the end of his second term in 1919 but was prevailed upon to run again for office in 1922, only to be defeated.

Alexander contributed regularly to Jewish charitable organizations in this and other countries and was a president of Congregation Beth Israel of Boise.

The town of Alexander, Idaho, is named for him.

The year Alexander became governor of Idaho, another Jew, Charles Himrod, was mayor of Boise, and two others, Max Mayfield and Leo Greenbaum, were Boise councilmen. Shortly afterward, Simon Bamberger, a Jewish merchant from Salt Lake City, was elected governor of Utah. He was the first Democrat and non-Mormon to become governor of that state. The only railroad named for a person, the Bamberger Line of Utah, was founded by and named for him.

When President Franklin D. Roosevelt took office in 1933, there were four Jewish governors in the United States. They were Herbert H. Lehman of New York, Henry Horner of Illinois, Julius Meyer of Oregon, and Arthur Seligman of New Mexico.

Lehman won his first elective office as lieutenant-governor of New York in 1928, as the running mate of FDR. Later, when Roosevelt went on to the White House, Lehman was elected governor by an unprecedented plurality of close to one million votes over his Republican opponent. Reelected for four more terms (1934, 1936, 1938, and 1940), his administration was marked by a sympathetic application of the New Deal in legislation for New York State.

Many of the measures he sponsored—particularly laws regarding social and religious discrimination, labor reforms, and protection of the aged and youth—helped make New York one of the most socially progressive states in the Union.

After serving as governor of New York for four terms, in 1949 Herbert H. Lehman was elected to the United States Senate and thus achieved the distinction of being the first Jew to be elected to the Senate by popular vote. Other Jews in the Senate had been appointed or elected by the several legislatures before enactment of the Seventeenth Amendment, which called for election by the people.

Henry Horner began his public career as a probate judge and was reelected four times. During the two terms of his gubernatorial office in Illinois, he successfully combated corruption and fought for social reform. He had a great interest in Lincoln and owned the world's most extensive collection of Lincolnia, which he donated to the Illinois Historical Society.

Julius Meier, the son of an Oregon pioneer, had promoted industry, agriculture, and aviation in Oregon, contributed to the state's highway system and served as director of the Council of National Defense before he was elected governor of Oregon. He effected important administrative and social reforms.

Arthur Seligman's occupancy of various political posts, including six years as mayor of Santa Fe, New Mexico, was characterized by stabilization of finances and modernization of life. His election of the governorship in 1930 was a personal triumph, overthrowing traditional Republican strongholds. He was reelected in 1932 and died while in office.

Ernest Gruening became territorial governor of Alaska from 1939 to 1952, in which capacity he was a strong proponent of Alaskan statehood. When Alaska was admitted to the Union, Gruening was elected a United States Senator (1958) and was reelected in 1962.

The seventh elected Jewish governor was Abraham Ribicoff of Connecticut, who served in office from 1955 to 1961 and who resigned to join the Cabinet of President John Kennedy as secretary of Health, Education, and Welfare.

When President Bill Clinton took office, Bruce Sundlin, a Democrat, was governor of Rhode Island, having been elected in 1990 and reelected in 1992.

On March 30, 1995, Senator Arlan Specter of Pennsylvania, the son of Jewish immigrants from Russia, announced his candidacy for the 1996 Republican presidential nomination. He thus became the first Jewish candidate to enter the race for the highest elective office in the land. Dr. David Gordis, president of Hebrew College and director of the Wilstein Institute of Jewish Policy Studies in Brookline, Massachusetts, noted that the lack of an automatic embrace for Specter "suggests a certain level of confidence among the Jewish community" and a sense of "at homeness" in American politics.

THE FIRST JEWISH SUPREME COURT JUSTICE

1916

Both in private practice and on the bench American Jews have risen to high eminence in the law profession.

When Woodrow Wilson was elected president of the United States in 1912 on a platform of the New Freedom, he turned to Louis Dembitz Brandeis for counsel in translating ideas of political and social reform into the framework of legal institutions. In their frequent meetings afterward, Brandeis rapidly became the president's unofficial counsel on antitrust and financial legislation.

For twenty years Brandeis had fought and won legal battles against the nation's corporate giants. As a corporation lawyer, he had inveighed forcefully against the establishment of his day, for its callousness, its exploitive practices, and its mad scramble for power and profit. He was a militant crusader for social justice whomever his opponent might be.

It was on January 28, 1916, that President Woodrow Wilson made the precedent-breaking appointment that saw the first Jew in history nominated to the position of associate justice of the Supreme Court. The nomination surprised and shocked Washington, and it provoked a furor of press commentary and debate across the nation. The Senate confirmation ran into heavy weather, and it took four months.

At the Senate subcommittee hearings, witness after witness sought to besmirch Brandeis's reputation and character. Seven former presidents of the American Bar Association, including Elihu Root, former secretary of state, and William Howard Taft, former president of the United States, petitioned the Senate to reject Brandeis's appointment. Although a drawn battle was fought between the reactionary and progressive forces in America before the Senate confirmed the appointment, Wilson insisted that he knew no one better qualified by judicial temperament as well as legal and social understanding.

Conscious of an anti-Semitic undercurrent in the attack, Brandeis wrote to his brother, "I suppose eighteen centuries of Jewish persecution must have inured me to such hardships and developed the like of a duck's back."

Brandeis had, of course, made numerous friends and gained many distinguished enemies before the Senate finally confirmed his Supreme Court nomination on June 1, 1916, by a vote of forty-seven to twenty-two.

Louis Dembitz Brandeis was born on November 13, 1856, in Louisville, Kentucky, the youngest of four children of an immigrant couple, Adolph and Fredricka Dembitz Brandeis. His parents had left Bohemia for the United States with the "Forty-eighters" who fled Europe after the collapse of the liberal movement there. His maternal uncle, Lewis Dembitz, was a member of the National Republican Convention that nominated Lincoln for president and was well-known as a scholar and writer on Jewish topics.

His father prospered in Louisville as a plantation owner and grain merchant so that Louis was able to spend his early years in an atmosphere of comfort and culture.

As a young man Brandeis studied law at Harvard Law School and completed the course before his twentieth birthday with an academic record unsurpassed in the history of the school. In 1878 he formed a law partnership with Samuel Warren, a Harvard classmate, and set up the first really modern law office that Boston had ever had. Within an eight-year period he became the leading barrister in the city. By representing liberal causes before the court and the "little man" against great corporations before the turn of the century, he became known as "the people's attorney."

Brandeis's practice as a public-cause attorney brought him cases concerning the privacy rights of individuals, municipal corporations, labor retaliation, and abuse in state-run facilities for the indigent. He helped secure passage of legislation that fixed minimum wages and hours of employment. He worked out such splendid projects as the Massachusetts system of savings bank insurance and pensions for wage earners. He often took up the cause of those considered defenseless at reduced fees and frequently at no fee.

In 1910 a widespread strike broke out in New York in the garment industry between employers and workers, many of whom were Jewish immigrants from Eastern Europe. Brandeis was called to New York to serve as mediator of the strike, the largest New York had ever seen. It was on this occasion that he had his first encounter with East European Jews, most of whom spoke Yiddish and many of whom declared themselves to be Zionists. He came to admire them for their passionate interest in the welfare of their coreligionists.

At the age of fifty-four, Brandeis began to read Jewish history and made inquiries about the then newly formed Zionist movement launched by Theodor Herzl at the First World Zionist Congress in Basel in 1897. An early Zionist leader, Jacob de Haas—an English Jew producing *The Jewish Advocate*, a periodical in Boston, who had been Dr. Herzl's secretary in London—helped influence Brandeis's thinking, too.

In the course of time, Brandeis announced that he was a Zionist, explaining, "My approach to Zionism is through Americanism. In time, practical experience and observation convinced me that Jews were by reason of their tradition and their character particularly fitted for the attainment of American ideals. Gradually, it became clear to me that to be good Americans, we must become Zionists. Jewish life cannot be preserved and developed, assimilation cannot be averted unless there is established in the fatherland a center from which the Jewish spirit may radiate and give to the Jews scattered throughout the world that inspiration from the memories of a great past and the hope of a great future."

When European Zionist leadership was isolated as a result of the First World War, Louis Brandeis was elected chairman of the Provisional Committee for General Zionist Affairs. Four years later he was named honorary chairman of the Zionist Organization of America, and in 1920, after peace had been restored, he received the same distinction from the World Zionist Organization, convened to implement the Jewish National Home in Palestine. Although Brandeis resigned from this body one year later after differences with its president, Chaim Weizmann, he remained a staunch supporter of the Zionist movement for the rest of his life. He played a dominant role in obtaining American approval of the Balfour Declaration, which gave international recognition to Zionist aims.

A businesslike Zionist, Brandeis stressed the practical aspects of rebuilding a Jewish Palestine. He helped found the Palestine Economic Corporation and played an important part in the encouragement of the investment of private capital in Palestine.

When President Wilson appointed Brandeis to the Supreme Court in 1916, he was head of the Provisional Zionist Executive Committee.

Brandeis's judicial career on the Supreme Court spanned more than two decades—to 1939. During much of his tenure as associate justice, Brandeis found himself, along with Justice Oliver Wendell Holmes, in a minority, continually challenging outworn concepts. But this minority opinion eventually reshaped the law and American thinking.

Brandeis was a great scholar as well as a jurist of unusual intellectual power. But it was his overwhelming sense of social justice and his keen perception of the hopes and needs of his time that strongly colored his thinking. He was unique in his appraisal of the social problems raised by the development of the machine and of the big corporations and their relations to human liberty and the general welfare of the American people. A "subtler civilization," he believed, was upon us, and "the law must still protect a man from things that rob him of his freedom, whether the oppressive force be physical or of a subtler kind." He was against conformity. The needs of the individual, his uniqueness, diversity, and creativeness, occupied a large part of his faith. In that respect, Brandeis was in close accord with the spirit of his forebears. He once said: "The twentieth-century ideals of America have been the ideals of the Jew for twenty centuries."

In the popular mind, Brandeis won fame as a dissenter. His dissenting opinions are significant because, in many instances, he stated the law as it was to be interpreted in the future. Prior to his retirement, he saw his beliefs and prophecies welded into the framework of the law.

One winter, at the age of eighty-three, Brandeis suffered a serious illness and couldn't seem to recover his strength. With a curt one-line note he retired from the Supreme Court. He continued to take an active interest in Zionism and called on President Roosevelt to solicit help for the refugees from Nazi barbarism. Nor did he slacken his attention to national and international affairs. He died two years later, on October 5, 1941, shortly before his eighty-fifth birthday. He left to his wife and family, to the Zionist movement, and to many public causes a large legacy. He left to humanity an even richer and more permanent legacy.

In Palestine a *kibbutz* (a communal agricultural settlement), *Ein Hashofet* (Spring of the Judge), was named for him, and in Waltham, Massachusetts, not far from Boston, where he began his career, a university bears his name.

Today, Brandeis University, founded in 1946, the first nonsectarian Jewish-sponsored liberal arts institution of higher learning in this country, welcomes students of all races and religions and takes its place as a preeminent member of the American family of universities.

Louis Dembitz Brandeis's brilliant record on the Supreme Court made it easier for two other Jewish lawyers, Benjamin Nathan Cardozo and Felix Frankfurter, to follow him. Indeed, during the six-year period between 1932 and 1938, Brandeis and Cardozo sat on the Supreme Court simultaneously.

While each of these men rose to that high office on his own merits, the continuous presence of at least one distinguished Jewish jurist on this country's highest court took on a symbolic importance to the American Jewish community and the society at large.

THE FIRST DIAGNOSIS OF CORONARY THROMBOSIS

1916

American Jews have made notable contributions to medicine in many of its branches. Several have won Nobel Prizes in physiology or medicine. Large numbers are engaged in medical practice, medical research, and as medical laboratory technicians.

The recognition, diagnosis, and treatment of coronary thrombosis and many other forms of heart disease was one of the big question marks of medical science until Dr. Samuel Albert Levine turned his mind to answering it. Before his time a "coronary" was not recognized as such until the patient died and an autopsy was performed; if he lived, it was assumed he had not had a coronary attack, for it was thought to be incompatible with survival and he was suffering from a digestive disorder.

Today, because of Dr. Levine's research, a great deal is known about cardiovascular disease. Tens of thousands of people who suffered serious heart attacks have been properly diagnosed and are alive because of his findings.

Dr. Levine's investigations in cardiology started in 1916. In that year, as a twenty-five-year-old house officer on the staff of the Peter Bent Brigham Hospital in Boston (which in 1993 merged with Massachusetts General and Women's Hospital), he made an antemortem diagnosis of acute coronary thrombosis (narrowing or blockage of one of the coronary arteries that supply blood to the heart muscle due to a thrombosis or clot). This resulted in his publication in 1918 in the *American Journal of Medical Science* of one of the first papers to appear on the clinical recognition of coronary thrombosis. The only one who had previously described the condition was Dr. James Herrick of Chicago, and his work was known to but a few physicians.

In his early work, Dr. Levine established that coronary thrombosis was a complete entity that could be recognized clinically. He described many of the detailed and electrocardiographic features of the disease that permits its early recognition and described its complications. He also showed that loud systolic murmurs are always associated with some form of cardiovascular disease. After that, Dr. Levine made equally great advances, diagnosing and devising the treatment of one form of heart disease after another.

In later years he showed for the first time that chair rest, instead of bed rest, aids the recovery of patients suffering from coronary thrombosis—a departure from the long-accepted practice of keeping coronary patients in bed for many weeks—and that chair rest is preferable to bed rest in the treatment of many other types of heart disease. His studies in digitalis therapy and his recognition of hyperthyroidism, which masks itself as heart disease, are also milestones in the care of the cardiac patient.

Dr. Levine wrote what was for many years considered the outstanding textbooks on heart disorders. *Coronary Thrombosis*, which first appeared in 1929, still remains a classic. *Clinical Heart Disease*, originally published in 1936, also became a standard work in the field. Dr. Levine also wrote over 250 articles on various phases of heart disease, many of them "firsts" in content that are widely quoted in international medical literature.

One of the country's foremost exponents of simplification of "medical diagnosis," Dr. Levine stressed the diagnostic value of clinical bedside methods, especially auscultation (the detection and study of sounds arising from various organs, chiefly the heart and lungs). He always insisted on the importance on the use of the stethoscope and bedside examinations, noting that a cardiogram should be used to supplement trained ears.

He stimulated considerable discussion among doctors by propounding the theory that heart disease was far less frequent in China because of the diet and philosophical view of life.

Born on January 1, 1891, in Lomza, Poland, Samuel Albert Levine rose to prominence in the field of medicine from humble beginnings. His parents emigrated to the United States and settled in Boston when he was three. A child prodigy, he reached the sixth grade in elementary school at the age of eight. He sold newspapers on the streets of downtown Boston as a member of the Newsboys Union in his school days prior to his graduation from high school.

He became a recipient of the Harvard College scholarship set up by the Newsboys Union. After graduating from Harvard College in 1911, he set his mind on a medical career. He attended Harvard Medical School, obtaining his medical degree in 1914 at the age of twenty-three. He was the first medical student to work at the then newly opened Peter Bent Brigham Hospital in Boston as a volunteer worker in the Out-Patient Department. Following his graduation, he became a member of the early medical staff of the hospital, embarking on his long association with that institution as physician and consultant in cardiology that was to continue for the next fifty years. He also did additional graduate work at Harvard Medical

School and in 1930 was appointed to the faculty as an assistant professor of medicine. He was named clinical professor of medicine at Harvard, a post he occupied from 1948 to 1958, when he became professor emeritus.

Although Dr. Levine gained a reputation as one of the world's finest cardiologists, he prided himself on being an astute and experienced internist. Of his numerous publications, one of his favorites was a monogram on pernicious anemia that was the first to describe gastric achlorhydria (the absence of free hydrochloric acid in the stomach) as an integral part of that disease. He was also an expert in the diagnosis of poliomyelitis, having been involved in a goodly number of epidemics of this disease. Indeed, it was he who first made the diagnosis of polio in President Franklin D. Roosevelt, who was initially treated for a cerebrovascular accident.

Dr. Levine conducted a summer postgraduate course in cardiology for thirty-six years, from 1920 to 1956, the longest in the history of Harvard Medical School. These lectures in the Brigham amphitheater every July were attended by physicians from all over the world.

In 1954, the Samuel A. Levine Professorship in Medicine was established with a grant of $450,000 at Harvard Medical School by a grateful patient and personal friend, the New York investment banker Charles E. Merrell. At that time this was the largest endowment for any single chair in the history of the school.

When asked what seemed to him the most significant in his long and distinguished career, Dr. Levine replied: "My work as a teacher. I love to teach. If I know anything, I want everyone to know it."

Dr. Levine's greatest talent was his ability to make clinical observations and share those observations with others. Many of the postgraduate students and house staff who trained with him became the leaders of American academic cardiology in the 1950s and 1960s.

In 1956, the Samuel A. Levine Cardiac Center was opened at Peter Bent Brigham Hospital (now known as Brigham, Massachusetts General, and Women's Hospital). The center is an intensive care unit for patients who have suffered acute coronary occlusions. Using sophisticated electronic instrumentation, a team of specially trained physicians and nurses continuously monitor vital body functions during the first few critical days following a coronary attack.

Dr. Samuel A. Levine was honored by many universities and medical and scientific organizations. He received the Gold Heart Award of the American Heart Association and an honorary Doctor of Humane Letters degree from Yeshiva University in 1959. He was also the recipient of the American-Israel Freedom Award in 1960.

Dr. Levine died on March 31, 1966, at the age of seventy-three. His special gifts to relieve others of suffering and prolong their lives will reach deeply into the future and into many lives.

IV

We Continue Pioneering after the First World War

THE FIRST JEWISH PIONEER OF RADIO AND TELEVISION

1919

David Sarnoff, who became commercial manager of the Marconi Wireless Telegraph Company in 1919, was one of radio and television's earliest pioneers. By his hard work and relentless drive, he rose from a job as office boy to chairmanship of the giant RCA Corporation, formerly the Radio Corporation of America. While serving in various executive positions with RCA, he led the company's entry into radio broadcasting and reception in the 1920s and into black-and-white and color TV broadcasting and reception in the 1940s and 1950s.

Sarnoff's life story reads like a Jewish version of a Horatio Alger tale. He was born on February 27, 1891, in Uzlian, in the Russian province of Minsk, the son of Leah and Abraham Sarnoff, a desperately poor itinerant tailor.

When David was five, his father left for the United States to earn enough money to later send for the family. The boy was put in care of an uncle, a stern Orthodox rabbi who insisted that he try to learn two thousand words of the Talmud daily in preparation for a rabbinical career. Four years later, the Sarnoffs arrived in America to join their father, traveling steerage and carrying their kosher food for the journey in a market basket.

On the Lower East Side of New York, David sold newspapers and ran errands for a butcher. On Jewish holidays he picked up extra money by singing in a synagogue choir. In 1905, when he was fifteen, his voice changed—and along with it the capacity to earn money singing. Then his father died, so the youth had to become the family's main support. He left school and landed a job as a messenger for the Marconi Wireless Telegraph Company. While working, he saved up enough money to purchase a simple telegraph key and soon taught himself Morse code. He was fascinated by reports of the new means of communication known as "wireless," as radio was first called. He sensed that here lay a major new field of endeavor, and he strove to become part of it.

When he was seventeen, Sarnoff seized the opportunity to become a telegraph operator in a lonely station maintained by the Marconi Company on Nantucket Island, off the Massachusetts coast. The station's excellent library was an added attraction to the sixty-dollar-a-month pay. Then, too, at that station he had an opportunity to communicate with some of the operators on trans-Atlantic liners.

Before long he went to sea on the SS *Beothic* as the ship's first wireless operator on a seal-hunting expedition to the Arctic ice fields. One day they picked up a message about a sailor on a ship one hundred miles away who had suffered internal injuries. Sarnoff immediately notified the ship's doctor, who prescribed treatment via wireless, and the man recovered. The Marine Medical Service is generally regarded to have been established as a direct outgrowth of this incident.

Eagerness for more study led Sarnoff to request a transfer to the Marconi Station at Sea Gate, New York, not far from Pratt Institute in Brooklyn, where he enrolled for evening classes in electrical engineering.

While attending Pratt Institute, Sarnoff became a wireless operator at the Marconi Station atop John Wanamaker's Department Store in New York City. On the night of April 14, 1912, Sarnoff was alone on duty when the SS *Titanic*, the biggest steamship afloat, enroute to New York on her maiden voyage from Southampton, England, struck an iceberg in the icy waters of the Atlantic and sunk. Only 706 passengers were saved out of 2,223 on board. Sarnoff picked up the first shocking message of the tragedy. He remained at the post for seventy-two continuous hours, relaying the names of the survivors to an anxious world. President Taft ordered every other wireless station along the Eastern coast silenced so as not to interfere with Sarnoff's reception. Overnight, both Sarnoff and wireless were brought to the attention of the nation and the world.

The Marconi Wireless Company rewarded Sarnoff by making him an instructor and inspector at their institute.

In 1919 the Marconi Company was absorbed by the newly formed Radio Corporation of America. RCA board chairman Owen Young, somewhat awed by Sarnoff's knowledge of wireless and his vision of the future of communications, appointed him commercial manager.

Four years earlier, in 1915, Sarnoff had proposed a "radio music box," predicting that it would bring music, entertainment, lectures, and reports of national events into the American living room. In the confusion of World War I, Sarnoff's memorandum had been put aside. Now he dug it out. Sarnoff's boss was enthusiastic, but Sarnoff was granted only $2,000 by his superiors to invest in developing radios for home use. Sarnoff arranged for the radio broadcast of the blow-by-blow account of the Dempsey-Carpentier championship boxing match of 1921. The broadcast was a sensation, with two hundred thousand people listening in. A huge demand for radio sets developed. Sarnoff became vice president of RCA in 1922, and within three years the company's radio receiver sales totaled $83 million.

It was Sarnoff who paved the way for the establishment of radio networks. He started the first radio chain, the National Broadcasting Company (NBC) in 1926 with only twenty-four affiliated stations, but under his guidance it grew to include over two hundred stations. In the late 1920s Sarnoff successfully drove the acquisition of the Victor Talking Machine Company, putting down objections by saying, "We'll combine radio and phonograph in the same set."

In 1930 Sarnoff became president of RCA, and in 1947 he was named chairman of the board. Owner of a large share of its stock, he became one of America's wealthiest men.

Sarnoff foresaw a future for television as early as 1923, the same year Vladimir Zworkyn invented the iconoscope, the electronic eye of the television camera. When Zworkin joined RCA in 1930, Sarnoff said he wanted an all-electronic TV system rather than one that used a mechanical scanner. Nine years later, after at least $20 million had been spent on all-electronic television development, Sarnoff appeared before a TV camera at the New York World's Fair in 1939, noting, "Now we add radio sight to sound – this miracle of engineering skill brings the world to your home."

During World War II at the age of fifty-three Sarnoff achieved wide recognition for his efforts in military communications and was assigned as special consultant on communications to General Dwight Eisenhower, commander of all Allied military forces in Europe. While on duty on December 6, 1944, he was elevated to the rank of brigadier general. Thereafter, he was addressed as "General."

After the war he pumped millions of dollars into the development and successful acceptance of color TV sets that could receive black and white as well as color transmissions.

The first postwar television receiver set was introduced by RCA in September 1946. By late 1958 there were 180 television stations in the United States and RCA had produced its ten millionth television receiver.

As a radio and television pioneer, David Sarnoff was a man of many "firsts." It was because of his efforts that the first national political convention was broadcast and televised, as was the first college football game and the first major league baseball game. He introduced radio's first classical music appreciation hour and arranged for the first broadcast of an opera from the Metropolitan Opera House. He also laid the groundwork for today's extensive radio and television news coverage.

The Television Broadcasters Association, in recognition of his work in introducing and developing television in the United States, conferred on General Sarnoff the title of "the Father of American Television" and in 1944 awarded him its highest citation of distinction.

In 1951, on the occasion of his forty-fifth anniversary in radio, the Princeton Laboratories of the Radio Corporation of America were dedicated as the David Sarnoff Research Center. A bronze plaque was unveiled, reading: "David Sarnoff's work, leadership, and genius comprise radio's permanent record of the past, television's brilliant performance of the present, and a rich legacy in communications for the future."

At the age of seventy-five, Sarnoff would have been more than justified if he had retired, but he remained "too fascinated with the future." Although he relinquished his title as chief executive officer, he spent much of his time at RCA's David Sarnoff Research Laboratories. He was still the "General" and no major decision was reached at RCA without his approval.

Sarnoff was honored by the governments of the United States, Italy, France, Poland, Japan, and Israel, the latter conferring its Medallion of Valor and Commendation Award on him in 1960. Twenty-six American colleges and universities and countless industrial and social service agencies paid tribute to him for his work and contributions to the advancement of mankind, among them the Jewish Theological Seminary of America, the B'nai B'rith, the YM-YWHA, the American Technion Society, the American Committee for the Weizmann Institute, and the National Conference of Christians and Jews.

David Sarnoff died in New York City on December 13, 1971, at the age of eighty. The immigrant boy who sold newspapers and delivered messages was universally honored for opening an entirely new world of communications that changed the face of the globe and altered beyond recognition the relations between men and history.

THE FIRST ARTIFICIAL LIGHTNING

1921

Charles Steinmetz was a grotesque little man barely four feet tall with an enormous head and a hump on his back. He was born in Breslau, Germany, on April 9, 1865, into a family that had a long history of inherited deformity. Yet his contributions to science benefited in a practical way all Americans and the entire world.

It was evident early during his school days that he had a brilliant mind. When he completed his course in the gymnasium (high school), his father, a poor railroad clerk, willingly sent him to Breslau University instead of apprenticing him to a trade. From the very first he selected difficult, technical subjects. Beginning with mathematics and astronomy, he expanded his scientific studies so that in his sixth year he was taking theoretical physics, chemistry, electrical engineering, and specialized work in higher mathematics.

In 1888, like many young people at the time, he became involved with a socialist movement that wanted to see better working conditions for the poor. Because of his political views, he was obliged to flee Germany to avoid arrest and in doing so forfeited the doctoral degree he was to have received that year. He escaped to Switzerland and registered at Zurich's Polytechnical School. There he was befriended by a young American student who persuaded him to go to the United States.

Steinmetz sailed steerage on the spur of the moment for the United States, financed by his new friend who accompanied him. They landed in New York City on June 1, 1889. Within a year, Steinmetz mastered the English language, applied for citizenship, and joined the American Institute of Electrical Engineers and the New York (later the American) Mathematical Society.

When Steinmetz received his American citizenship in 1889, he added the middle name of "Proteus," a character in Greek mythology who like himself was a hunchback.

His first job with an electrical firm in Yonkers, New York, brought him twelve dollars a week as draftsman. From then on his career was meteoric.

When the factory he worked for in Yonkers was bought out by the newly formed General Electric Company in 1892, he accepted a position working in General Electric's large factory in Lynn, Massachusetts, not because he was eager to earn more money, but because he was convinced that he would be able to create important new inventions in a large, well-equipped laboratory. He quickly impressed his co-workers by his amazing mathematical wizardry and taught them how to accept his odd appearance by playing pranks and harmless jokes on them.

Three years after his arrival in the United States, Charles Proteus Steinmetz proceeded to revolutionize the field of electrical engineering with his discoveries. Until his Law of Hysteresis Loss was formulated, it was not known how to measure the amount of wasted current from heat build-up in the iron magnetic rings of machines using alternating current. This law helped to determine such wastage, and its principles are still used today in designing efficient machinery.

Before he was thirty years old, Steinmetz was head of GE's vital calculating department. When GE moved to Schenectady, New York, Steinmetz went along and was told by the president of the company that he could do anything he wanted. "Sit and dream all day, if you wish—we'll pay you for your dreaming."

In time Steinmetz developed a way to transmit electrical power at high pressure without damage. He invented numerous motors and worked out the modern method of substations for generating plants to furnish electrical power. He made possible cheap car lighting, quick elevator service, and discovered how to harness electricity to power the telephone lines of this nation.

Steinmetz also developed a new type of electrical street lighting, using magnetite (a black iron oxide) as a filament (the fine wire of a bulb).

The practical advantage of this type of illumination was found in the extreme length of time (two hundred hours) that the metallic electrode could burn without recharging, contrasted to the life of seventy hours in the carbon arc used before this time. The crowd in Schenectady cheered when the new streetlight came on, for at that moment theirs was the brightest corner on earth illuminated with artificial light.

As electrical transmission lines spread all over the country, lightning became more dreaded and protection from lightning more imperative. In an effort to learn more about lightning and its behavior, Steinmetz made a systematic study of the general equation of the electrical current and of "transient electric phenomena," as lightning is scientifically called, publishing the results periodically from 1907 onward for the rest of his life. This work was collected and gradually put into a book entitled *Theory and Calculation of Transient Electrical Phenomena and Oscillations*.

In the summer of 1921, in the course of his studies on the effects of lightning on electrical installations, a bolt of lightning struck and completely demolished a large mirror in his summer home in Schenectady. Steinmetz decided to solve several problems caused by this natural phenomena. He collected the broken pieces, glued them together, and wondered how the lightning caused the damage. He built various model buildings and produced bolts of artificial lightning to strike them. These experiments, which earned him the titles of "Modern Jupiter" and the "Thunderer," enabled him to reveal aspects of lightning hitherto unknown to man and to invent and build electrical devices such as the lightning generator that arrests the damage done by lightning to houses and buildings.

But this does not mean that his investigation was completed. In reality, it was never completed. A large new laboratory was in the course of construction at the General Electric works in Schenectady to enable him to prosecute it with vigor. Steinmetz was still busily at work on it when he died.

The importance of Steinmetz's work was not understood at first, and he tried to simplify his explanations. For this reason he focused his attention on the education of future engineers. In addition to his consulting work at GE and his writing, he taught electrical engineering courses in the evening from 1903 to 1913 and electro-physics courses from 1913 to 1923 at Union College in Schenectady, and he lectured on various electrical subjects throughout the country.

Steinmetz was an ardent believer in education and found the time to serve as president of the Schenectady Board of Education for two years and became president of the national association of corporation schools.

He wrote several books in addition to those mentioned above, among them *Theory and Calculation of Alternating Current Phenomena* in three volumes (1897), *General Lectures on Electrical Engineering* (1908), and *Elementary Lectures on Electrical Discharges, Waves and Impulses and Other Transients* (1914), all of which went through several editions and have been the accepted textbooks in colleges, laboratories, and workshops everywhere.

The greatest scientists of the time came to ask his advice—men such as Einstein, Marconi, and Edison. Steinmetz worked with Edison, often communicating with him by Morse code since the American inventor was hard of hearing.

Steinmetz was honored by a large number of learned societies, scientific organizations, and universities. In 1902 Harvard University presented him with an honorary degree citing him as "the first electrical engineer of the United States and of the world."

Steinmetz never married and died at the age of fifty-eight in 1923. He was still working in his laboratory, making discoveries, experimenting, and teaching. His inventions, the basic principles he formulated, the mathematical equations he devised, helped bring electricity to the home, the factory, and the workplace. He changed electrical power from a plaything and a curiosity to a powerful tool that could be harnessed by man for the betterment of his life.

THE FIRST JEWISH NOVELIST TO WIN THE PULITZER PRIZE

1925

Jews have made many and varied contributions to American literature. Their numbers include many novelists, critics, poets, and playwrights. By the 1920s some of the better-known contemporaries were Edna Ferber, Fannie Hurst, Lillian Hellman, Louis Untermeyer, Robert Nathan, Waldo Frank, and Ludwig Lewisohn. Of this group, Edna Ferber, whose name betokens storytelling magic, gained a place among the most popular women writers of this country. Her book *So Big* won the Pulitzer Prize in 1925 and became the runaway best-selling novel of the 1920s.

Edna Ferber was born on August 15, 1887, in Kalamazoo, Michigan. When she was a small girl, her father, a Hungarian Jew, gave up the struggle of operating a store in Kalamazoo and for a year lived in Ottumwa, Iowa, before trying again in Appleton, Wisconsin. It was in Iowa and Wisconsin that Edna Ferber spent her childhood, where she was to learn to know and love the Midwest and the hardy Americans about whom she was later to write in her novels. While still in her teens, her father went blind. To help the family finances, young Edna accepted a position as a local reporter on the *Appleton Crescent* for three dollars a week.

Before long a new city editor discharged her, and she went to work in Milwaukee, where she obtained a somewhat better position on the *Milwaukee Journal*. When her father died four years later, her mother and two sisters moved to Chicago where Edna landed a job on the *Chicago Tribune*. Her stories fascinated her readers with her condensed, almost conversational idiom. In her spare time she tried her hand at creative writing. She completed a novel entitled *Dawn O'Hara* but did not like it and cast it aside. *Dawn O'Hara* told of life as she saw it while a newspaper reporter in Milwaukee, describing among other things the boarding house where first she stopped. Her mother rescued it from the dustbin and sent it to a publisher. Recognized as a masterpiece, it was published in 1911 and sold over ten thousand copies. A great career was under way.

From that time on, many stories, novels, and plays poured from the fertile mind of Edna Ferber. Her short stories appeared in the leading magazines of the day and were later published in four volumes the best liked, perhaps, being *Buttered Side Down* (1912), which told of a delightful and witty traveling woman "salesman" of petticoats named Emma McChesney. The first American businesswoman of fiction, Emma McChesney quickly became a household figure in America. A play entitled *Our Mrs. McChesney* (1915), of which Edna Ferber and Victor Hobart were the playwrights and starring Ethel Barrymore, had a long run on Broadway.

In 1917 Ferber again turned to the writing of a novel. In *Fanny Herself,* the old rabbi was drawn from life, the hard-working, self-sacrificing Jewish mother was the novelist's own mother. *Fanny Herself* is still considered one of the best fictional portraits of the Jew in small-town America.

Later novels included *The Girls* (1921), which gives a most interesting picture of the life of three generations in Chicago, extending from Civil War days to the First World War.

In 1925, Edna Ferber received the Pulitzer Prize for *So Big,* awarded for the leading novel of the year. It was the story of a boy whose mother spent her life working for him in a truck farm outside Chicago. *So Big* sold three hundred thousand copies in its first season. It served as the basis of three motion pictures, one silent and two "talkies," and a radio program that lasted for six years. It was required reading in high schools and was published in book form in at least fifteen foreign countries.

In 1926 came *Show Boat,* a sweeping panorama that embraces four decades (1887 to 1926) and whose fabulous career on Broadway, in Hollywood, on radio, and on television made this work one of the most widely known and best loved in the history of American fiction. Originally produced on Broadway in 1927 with music by Jerome Kern and lyrics and book by Oscar Hammerstein II, the story concerns the *Cotton Blossom,* a Mississippi River showboat whose crew perform in port towns up and down the river. This great American musical revolutionized musical theater with its sensitivity to plot, characterization, perfection of scoring, and dazzling melodies. *Show Boat* is by far the oldest of America's handful of regularly revived classics as well as being the first musical treating race relations and dysfunctional marriage.

Harold Prince's recreation of *Show Boat* opened on Broadway on October 2, 1994, in the George Gershwin Theater and incorporated elements from the musical's various theatrical presentations and motion-picture adaptations during the past sixty-six years. In 1995 *Show Boat* won five Tony Awards and four Outer Critics Circle Awards, including the Most Outstanding Revival of a Musical. Harold Prince, who won his first Tony Award in 1955 as producer of *The Pajama Game*, won his twentieth as director of *Show Boat*.

Show Boat was about the South. Edna Ferber soon began to write novels with other American backgrounds. *Cimarron* (1929) was about the story of pioneer days in Oklahoma, including the land rush of 1889; *American Beauty* (1931) had its setting in the Connecticut Valley; *Come and Get It* (1935) told the story of lumber kings in the Wisconsin north woods. *Saratoga Trunk* (1941) was a novel of high society and railroad wars ranging from Creole New Orleans to Saratoga Springs in the 1880s. *Giant* (1952), Edna Ferber's eleventh novel was, according to the author, "not only a story of Texas today but, I hope, Texas tomorrow." *Ice Palace* (1958) was a novel about the factions warring for Alaska's riches—those who wanted to keep it a territory to exploit and those who fought for democratic statehood. The novel was given much credit for the admission of the territory of Alaska as the forty-ninth state.

In 1939 Edna Ferber's autobiography, *A Peculiar Treasure*, appeared. It was the story not only of her American Jewish family and its place in a free land but also a powerful indictment of the anti-Semitism that had destroyed Europe and threatened an unwary America. Her second autobiography, *A Kind of Magic* (1963), includes her impressions of the State of Israel.

As a playwright in collaboration with George S. Kaufman, she won over Broadway with such outstanding hits as *The Royal Family* (1921), *Dinner at Eight* (1932), and *Stage Door* (1936).

Edna Ferber received many honors as one of America's leading literary figures, among them membership in the National Institute of Arts and Letters and an honorary Doctor of Letters degree from Columbia University.

Her stories are trenchant and highly readable. Her plots turn on the development of the characters as they meet the vicissitudes of life. Without preaching, she drove home lessons and championed the cause of those who have had a less than fair share of life—the uncomplaining supporters of selfish wives, the women who are compelled to become breadwinners, the old father who is no longer able to work, the immigrant, and the homely girl. She felt, however, that many readers missed the special message her writings contain. They are such easy reading that one scarcely expects the undercurrent of seriousness. Yet, as William Allen White has said: "The historian will find no better picture of America in the first three decades of this century than Edna Ferber has drawn."

Edna Ferber had an unabashed lifetime love affair with all—or most—of America. Her prime importance lies in her exploration of the American literary frontier, for she discovered and chartered an entirely new domain. What she accomplished is not only expressed in the broadly democratic character of her novels—which palpitate with vigor, customs, fears, dreams and hopes of these states—but is reflected in the native works of others following her.

Edna Ferber died on April 16, 1968, widely acclaimed and mourned as one of the best-read novelists in the nation.

THE FIRST PIANO CONCERTO CREATED IN JAZZ

1925

American Jews have shown unusual aptitude for the theater and music. One of the first to be drawn into the stream of popular music was a Jewish boy by the name of George Gershwin. He was to prove himself one of the most brilliantly creative musical geniuses American had yet produced. Before his tragically premature death at the age of thirty-nine, George Gershwin had not only changed the pattern of popular music in this country but had quickened the pulse of music throughout the western world.

George Gershwin was born in Brooklyn, New York on September 26, 1898, the son of Morris and Rose Brushkin Gershwin, Russian-Jewish immigrants. It was by pure accident that Gershwin, who stemmed from a family lacking in musical talent, became a song mill, who carefully converted his own vitality and love of life into a series of carefully written scores, all jazz, the only music he wanted to write.

As a boy, George was typical of big-city youth. He was athletic, played baseball, and was roller-skating champion of his neighborhood. Then when the Gershwins were residing on Second Avenue in Manhattan, Mrs. Gershwin bought a second-hand piano so Ira, George's older brother, could take lessons. In a few weeks, George had crowded Ira away from the instrument. Only thirteen, he begged his mother to get him a piano teacher. A few months later he was learning about Chopin and

Debussy from Charles Hambitzer, who taught him the fundamentals of piano technique and playing.

With the world of music suddenly open to him, George began to haunt the music halls. He listened to the tunes of Irving Berlin, Jerome Kern, and the classics. Everything he heard he soaked up like a sponge.

At sixteen he left school and went to work as a song plugger for a music publishing firm in Tin Pan Alley, the Broadway section of New York where popular songs are born. When they refused to listen to the tunes he wrote himself, he went to the Catskill Mountains as a resort pianist. He played piano all day and later traveled to nearby cities to accompany song pluggers.

Gershwin got his first song published on May 15, 1916, by Harry Von Tilzer when he was eighteen years old. He earned all of five dollars for it. At the age of twenty-one he composed the entire score for a musical comedy, *La, La, Lucille*. Then in 1919 he wrote a number called "Swanee" and became rich and famous overnight when the singer Al Jolson rocked the country with it, singing it in *Sinbad*, the show he was currently starring in.

Now Gershwin began to turn out song hit after song hit. He insisted that "jazz is American folk music" and was to prove to the world that popular songs could be planned as carefully as more formal compositions and could be as musically artistic.

Following the success of his second Broadway musical production, *The George White Scandals*, in 1920, he was asked by Paul Whiteman, leader of the country's finest dance orchestra, to compose a jazz symphony with the piano part to be played by him, accompanied by the Whiteman band. Thus came to be written *Rhapsody in Blue*, the emotional melody with a variety of moods that was forever to dispel prejudice against the use of jazz in symphonic music. Everyone talked about it. It became an American trademark. Nothing ever composed in the United States was so universally performed.

In 1925 Gershwin continued to make musical history when he was commissioned by Walter Damrosch, conductor of the New York Symphony Orchestra, to write a concerto in which the piano played the solo part accompanied by the orchestra. This major composition—the first piano concerto ever created in jazz—Gershwin's *Concerto in F* was orchestrated by Gershwin himself and presented for the first time in Carnegie Hall on December 3, 1925, with the composer playing the piano part. For thirty minutes Gershwin poured forth music full of enchanting tone subleties with a sincerity that moved the audience to tears and cheers.

By the time Gershwin was thirty, he had become internationally famous, and a nation sang and whistled his immortal tunes such as "I Got Rhythm," "Somebody Loves Me," "Maybe," "Liza," and "Our Love Is

Here to Stay." All these numbers bristled with his brother Ira's gleefully ironic lyrics. Before his untimely death in 1937, he had composed the music for *An American in Paris* (1928), *Girl Crazy* (1930), and *Of Thee I Sing* (1931), the first musical comedy to be published in book form and to receive the Pulitzer Prize for the best musical play of the year.

The appearance of *Of Thee I Sing* signaled the tone of the thirties. A marvelous story, serious and funny in a way no show had ever been before, glorious songs perfectly integrated into the scheme, sharp and brilliant lyrics and a highly American subject, it marked a point of culmination in the history of American musical comedy.

In the fall of 1933 Gershwin began sketching what was to be his last and greatest achievement, a folk-opera, *Porgy and Bess*, based on Du Bose Heyward's adaption of his impressive novel of the same name.

The story of a little group of Charleston blacks who live in poverty in "Catfish Row," with the crap-shooting Porgy as its central figure, the libretto, written by George's brother, Ira, was at once earthy, poetic, and profoundly moving. The music was broad in its scope, dramatic, and powerfully conceived with extraordinary contrasts of comedy, tenderness and tragedy. It had its first performance in Boston with an all-black cast. Ultimately, it was performed the world over, achieving recognition as a great American masterpiece.

Before Gershwin had reached his mid-thirties, he had written nearly thirty musical comedies for stage and screen. With the development of sound films Gershwin added a mastery of its form to his proficiency in musical comedy composition. Among his motion picture scores were *Delicious* (1931), *Shall We Dance* (1936, starring Fred Astaire), and *Damsel in Distress* (1937, also for Fred Astaire). He and Ira were in California and happily at work on his fourth film, *The Goldwyn Follies*, when the headaches began. An alarmingly developed growth on his brain was discovered. An emergency operation was performed, but he failed to survive. He died in Beverly Hills on July 11, 1937, at the age of thirty-nine.

In 1940, a few years after Gershwin's death, the great English conductor Albert Coates listed the fifty best musical works of the generation. Only one American composition was included and but one American composer: George Gershwin and his *Conterto in F.*

Gershwin's memory is still verdant, and his music continues to enjoy enormous popularity, not only in his native land but also in countries of several continents. An American production of *Porgy and Bess*, officially blessed by the State Department, opened early in 1952 in Vienna and was received ecstatically. It then moved on to Berlin, where it was the highlight of the September Festival of Arts put on by the Western powers. In 1956 it pierced the Iron Curtain and was presented for the first time in Russia.

On July 12, 1953, the first jazz concert ever held in Florence, Italy, took place in the city's five-hundred-year-old Pitti Palace. The main item on the program was Gershwin's *An American in Paris,* played by the Florentine Municipal Orchestra.

Six decades after his death, George Gershwin's music is performed more often and is more widely acclaimed than ever.

Record companies ransacked his old scores for forgotten numbers, and songs that had not been heard in fifty years were not only redis- covered and revived but attained new popularity. It was now conceded that besides creating a vivid musical vocabulary, George Gershwin had performed a valuable and unprecedented function: he had broken down the barrier between popular and classical music. He had set the tone and tempo of his age; he had given music a new and racy speech and, for the first time in history, an American accent.

Today all-Gershwin musical programs are annual features of Lincoln Center concerts given by the New York Philharmonic Orchestra, and millions of theaters, concert halls, and homes are constantly playing his rich and colorful melodies.

THE FIRST STAR OF "TALKIES"

1927

American Jews are to be found in considerable numbers on the stage, screen, radio, and television and are known and loved as entertainers. Famous as he was as a popular singer for the masses, Al Jolson will always be remembered as the first star of the talking motion picture.

When the experiment of changing from silent films to sound was considered, Warner Brothers wanted the strongest star of film and stage to lead the way. Al Jolson, one of the greatest names in the theater, was chosen to take the plunge. His first talking picture, *The Jazz Singer,* revolutionized the industry and brought "talkies" to every screen all over the world.

Born Asa Yoelson in St. Petersburg, Russia, in 1886, Jolson was the son of a poor cantor who himself represented the sixth in a direct line of cantors. It was his father's hope that his son would follow in his footsteps and become a cantor, too. But when he brought seven-year-old Asa to America, the boy took to singing on the streets, and his taste seemed to lean to ragtime. Imbued with a deep sense of adventure and having learned to sing under his father's guidance, he ran away to join various groups of players. Struck with the lure of stage lights, he got into vaude- ville with the famous Dockstader minstrels, sang in cafés and saloons, and followed circuses. Although his father invariably found him, Asa had already made up his mind to become a singer and actor in his own right.

He made his first stage appearance in 1899 at the Herald Square Theater in New York as one of the mob in Israel Zangwill's *Children of the Ghetto*. By 1910 Asa Yoelson, now Al Jolson, was already a headliner at Oscar Hammerstein's Victoria Theater. Even at that young age he was a polished performer. He would stop in the middle of a show and come downstage and ask the audience if they wouldn't rather hear some of his own favorites instead of the songs in the show—and more often than not they agreed. The newspapers noted the innovation, as did the audiences, and Al Jolson's performances became very popular. This crowd-pleasing technique was made into a permanent attraction when Shubert's Winter Garden Theater began Sunday afternoon concerts where Jolson could sing whatever song he chose.

Jolson achieved major stardom in a musical series of productions known as the *Winter Garden Shows* in which he was often referred to as "Gus," the blackface character. He had many black friends and from them he learned their expressions and accent. He was particularly famous for his blackface act in which he would sing while kneeling on one knee. Various stories have circulated about this, one saying that he painted his face black to overcome his bashfulness, another that an infection in an ingrown toenail made standing extremely painful. Whatever its origin, this technique proved very successful, and he adopted it as his trademark.

Jolson wrote some of the songs he made famous, notably, "California, Here I come," "Rock-a-Bye Your Baby With a Dixie Melody," "Toot, Toot, Tootsie Goodbye," and "April Showers."

Jolson was the first singer to use African-American themes for his songs. He composed the majority of them himself, often using the image of mother and child, as in *Mammy* and *Sonny Boy*. His were sad, touching songs, full of truthful sentiment and did much to introduce the elements of original African-American music into the cultural life of America. It is strange to realize that it was a Jew who pioneered the neglected music of African-Americans and who gave them a permanent voice and place in the world of song.

In 1919 Al Jolson heard George Gershwin play "Swanee" at a party. That same week Jolson used the song at one of his Sunday afternoon concerts at the Winter Garden Theater. It was very well received, and because of the favorable audience reaction, Jolson interpolated it into the show in which he was currently starring, *Sinbad*. "Swanee" became a huge success, selling more than two million records and one million copies of sheet music in a year. It was Gershwin's first and greatest song hit.

A few years later, in 1925, the Warner brothers, a family of Jewish immigrants who had first established themselves as producers and distrib-

utors of motion pictures of the nickelodian type, and then headed up
their own studio, were the first to sense the possibilities of the use
of sound as applied to motion pictures. After witnessing the demonstration of a new device, they acquired the Vitaphone and in 1927 in Hollywood produced the first full-length musical talking film ever made in
America, *The Jazz Singer*. It was also the first successful film to portray the
Jewish immigrant saga. It was based on Jolson's struggle for a career,
dramatizing the plight of the singer torn between his own desire to be in
show business and his father's plan to perpetuate a long line of cantors.
On the evening of *Yom Kippur*, the Day of Atonement, the holiest day in the
Jewish year, when his elderly father is lying on his deathbed, the wayward
son returns to chant *Kol Nidre*—the most sacred of Jewish melodies. Jolson,
in the starring role, caused a revolution in the motion-picture industry.
Before the showing of this film, "talkies" were only an experiment. After
its release, it proved beyond a doubt that sound films were to be a
permanent feature.

Bringing to the industry the talents so essential for theatrical undertakings, Jolson also starred in *The Singing Fool*, *Mammy*, and *Sonny Boy*, the
next three "talkies" made.

From stage and film, Jolson went on to win great fame in radio. He
was the star of the first radio program in which running monologue was
interspersed with song. His voice, with its characteristic richness of
sound, his special style and manner, made him a popular and beloved
performer. He was probably the most imitated singer and artist in the
performing arts in America.

With *The Jolson Story* in 1947 and *Jolson Sings Again* in 1949, two great
Hollywood motion pictures produced by Sidney Skolsky, who also inspired the production of *The Eddie Cantor Story* at a later date, Jolson
skyrocketed to even greater heights. An unknown actor, Larry Parks, was
found to play the role of Jolson. Even though Parks was a singer, Al Jolson
sang all thirty songs in each of the films.

When Jolson sang, something happened to audiences. He had a
spirit, a quality, that brought him close to every person that saw and heard
him. Audiences felt what he felt. When he was sentimental, audiences
wept—and frequently Jolson cried himself. When he shot onto a stage
bursting with vitality and happiness, audiences suddenly grew happier. It
was that quality that made him probably one of the most popular and
successful entertainers in American history.

His record album of old songs sold over a million copies, and he
earned over $3 million from his film rights alone.

He was over sixty years old when the film *Rhapsody in Blue*, devoted
to the memory of George Gershwin, was produced. Jolson appeared in
the picture as the minstrel singer, and although very ill at the time insisted

on finishing the movie dedicated to his friend. This was Jolson's last appearance on the screen.

Jolson died on October 23, 1950, in San Francisco. He had just returned from Korea, where he had given performances for soldiers. Twenty thousand persons jammed Hollywood Boulevard for his funeral. President Harry S Truman sent a message that began: "We have lost our Al."

Jolson left behind a will in which he gave nine-tenths of a $4 million estate to charity, the money divided among Jewish, Catholic, and Protestant causes.

To perpetuate Jolson's memory, the movie industry established the Al Jolson Award, which is given annually to the showman who has contributed most during the previous year toward the entertainment of servicemen. In 1952, the first Al Jolson Award, a gold medal, went to Bob Hope, America's beloved movie, radio, and television star.

THE FIRST LIBERAL ARTS COLLEGE UNDER JEWISH AUSPICES

1928

In 1897 Rabbis Moses Matlin, Yehuda David Bernstein, and David Abramowitz, who came from Eastern Europe, founded a small yeshiva for the advanced study of Torah and Talmud at 44 East Broadway on New York City's Lower East Side. They named it the Rabbi Isaac Elchanan Theological Seminary (RIETS) to perpetuate the name of the revered rabbi of Kovno, Lithuania, who was one of the outstanding rabbinic scholars of the nineteenth century.

The Rabbi Isaac Elchanan Theological Seminary was the first yeshiva for higher-level Torah and Talmudic learning to be established on the North American continent. While the use of the designation "yeshiva" in America dates back to 1728 when Congregation Shearith Israel opened its school under the name Yeshibat Minhat Areb, that school as well as the second-known yeshiva to be established here, the Machazike Jeshibat Eitz Chaim, founded in 1886, were elementary schools for children that provided instruction in general or secular subjects along with Jewish studies.

In 1904, the Rabi Isaac Elchanan Theological Seminary obtained its own building at 156 Henry Street and held its first *Semikah* (rabbinical ordination ceremony) at 13–15 Pike Street, with ordination granted to three graduates.

In 1915, the board of directors of RIETS and the Yeshiva Eitz Chaim decided to merge and moved to 9–11 Montgomery Street to meet the growing needs among East European immigrants for expanded facilities for maximum Jewish education. Dr. Bernard Revel, an Eastern European-trained Orthodox rabbi, was called in to preside over the merged institutions. A young and prosperous man, he embodied in his own person the synthesis of Jewish learning and general culture that the institutions were designated to inculcate. Known as an *ilui* (prodigy) in the European yeshivot where he studied, he earned a Ph.D. degree in semitics from Dropsie College, a Jewish post-graduate institution, only five years after his arrival in the United States. One of his initial acts was the establishment of the first academic high school under Jewish auspices, to make it possible for students to continue simultaneously their Hebrew and secular studies in a school administered by the yeshiva. In 1919 with the chartering of the Talmudical Academy High School by the board of regents of the University of the State of New York, the Yeshiva High School became a full-fledged secondary school with a staff of competent instructors drawn from the New York City high schools.

In 1921, the Mizrachi Teachers' Institute, founded by the Mizrachi Organization of America (Religious Zionists) in 1917 to train Orthodox teachers, supervisors, and administrators of the then-thriving afternoon Talmud Torahs, became an integral part of the seminary. In addition to being one of the first teachers' training institutions in the United States, it was also the first to use Hebrew as the language of instruction. By so doing, it made Hebrew once again a viable, living language, and students at the institute became proficient in its daily use.

Due to the increased student body and expanded activities, the institution began to outgrow the new quarters in a few years. At the same time, a large number of yeshiva students were simultaneously continuing their general education at the college level in the evening under hardships. Their many difficulties helped emphasize the advantages of establishing as part of the institution a college of liberal arts and sciences wherein students of the yeshiva and ultimately other qualified students might pursue their academic studies in an "atmosphere harmonizing the age-old truths and rich treasures of Jewish culture with the fruits of modern knowledge."

Foreseeing the increasingly important role America was to play in the activities of world Jewry, Dr. Revel was determined to prove that it was possible to practice Orthodox Judaism in the midst of western civilization. Jewish knowledge could be based on the Torah as the hub from which all knowledge would radiate, with scientific knowledge as one of the spokes. Furthermore, a dynamic and creative Torah life, clothed in the habiliments of science and humanistic learning, could prevent the slow demoralization of the Orthodox community by a mechanistic scientific environment. It was his dream to open an institution that provided *Torah V'Madah* (religious study along with secular knowledge).

Despite strong opposition from those who feared that Torah study would be undermined, Dr. Revel founded Yeshiva College as a parallel institution of the Rabbi Isaac Elchanan Theological Seminary. The foundation for the transforming the yeshiva into a degree-granting institution was laid on March 24, 1924, when its charter was amended by the regents of the University of the State of New York. The authority to offer courses leading to Bachelor of Arts and Bachelor of Science degrees was granted it. On December 20, 1924, the Yeshiva College of America Fund was launched. Dreams and means were pooled, and on May 1, 1927, the cornerstone of the Main Center of the institution in the Washington Heights section of Manhattan was laid. This building, which was erected at a cost of $2,500,000, was dedicated on December 8, 1928, in the presence of hosts of Jews from all over the United States.

In September of that year Yeshiva College opened its doors with a full-time faculty and distinguished associate faculty consisting of eminent Jewish and non-Jewish professors. For the first time in history a yeshiva was housed and equipped in a manner that compared favorably with the facilities generally provided for the better public and private educational facilities.

In 1935 Dr. Revel realized his ambition to organize a graduate department in advanced Judaic studies leading to Master of Arts and Doctor of Philosophy degrees. (After his death, the graduate school was named in his memory—the Bernard Revel Graduate School).

In September 1932, the first issue of *Scripta Mathematica*, a quarterly journal devoted to the philosophy, history, and expository treatment of mathematics, edited by Professor Jekutiel Ginsburg, appeared. Subsequently in the early years, three other publications were launched. *Horeb*, a semiannual in Hebrew devoted to original studies in Jewish history, edited by Dr. Pinkhos Churgin, dean of the Teachers' Institute and later founding president of Bar-Ilan University in Israel; *Talpiot*, a Hebrew quarterly devoted to source materials in Jewish law and ethics, edited by Dr. Samuel Mirsky; and *Sura*, an annual journal in Hebrew designed to serve as a bridge between Jewish life in Israel and the Diaspora, also edited by Professor Mirsky.

In 1943 Dr. Samuel Belkin, a Talmudic authority and Semitic scholar, succeeded to the presidency of Yeshiva College left vacant by the death of Dr. Revel in 1940. Under Dr. Belkin's leadership, the institution's progress was considerable. In 1945 the college became Yeshiva University—the first in America under Jewish auspices—and was empowered to grant the additional degrees of Master of Hebrew Literature, Master of Science, and Doctor of Philosophy. Several programs of advanced study were instituted and new divisions opened, including the David J. Azrieli Graduate Institute of Jewish Education and Administration (1945), the Wurzweiler School of Social Work (1957), the Ferkauf Graduate School of Psychology (1957), and the Benjamin N. Cardozo School of Law (1976)—the nation's first law school established under Jewish auspices. It also established a cantorial training institute (1954) and a special program for Sephardic Studies—the Jacob E. Safra Institute—to prepare religious leaders for the Sephardic community.

In 1954 an initial gift of $500,000 made by Max Stern, a prominent New York City industrialist, enabled Yeshiva University to open Stern College for Women, the nation's first college for women under Jewish auspices, which provides liberal arts and sciences curricula and preprofessional programs.

Meanwhile, Yeshiva College, having achieved university rank during Dr. Belkin's administration, added still another "first" to its record of achievements. In 1950 its charter had been amended to authorize granting the degrees of doctor of medicine and dental surgery. In 1951 an agreement between the university and the City of New York allowed the future medical school to provide the professional care of all the patients in the fourteen-hundred-bed Bronx Municipal Hospital Center. Students at the school were to utilize all the clinical materials available in the various medical services of the center.

The Albert Einstein College of Medicine of Yeshiva University opened in the Bronx, New York, in September 1955. Today, a world-renowned medical complex, it is historically significant as the first medical institution that catalyzed the dissolution of discriminatory practices in admission of students and faculty appointments among medical schools in the United States.

Dr. Samuel Belkin was president of Yeshiva University until 1975 and the university's first chancellor from 1975 until the time of his death in 1976.

Since 1976 the institution has been headed by Dr. Norman Lamm, its first American-born president and an alumnus of both the Rabbi Isaac Elchanan Theological Seminary and Yeshiva University. A noted rabbi, philosopher, and teacher, he is known for his writings that interpret Jewish law in relation to science, technology, and philosophy in today's society. Dr. Lamm launched a far-reaching program of academic and physical expansion that further enhanced Yeshiva University. Today the diverse schools, incuding the Jacob Burns Institute for Advanced Legal Studies (1987), the Sy Syms School of Business (1987), and the Philip and Sarah Belz School of Jewish Music (1983), are part of the university.

For more than a century Yeshiva University, with its well-respected undergraduate and graduate schools, has provided professional training and credentials for Orthodox Jews and has produced spiritual leaders for the modern Orthodox community.

Yeshiva University currently operates with an annual budget of $315 million for its 16 undergraduate, graduate, and professional schools and affiliates, which enroll 7,000 students (59 percent men and 41 percent women) at four centers in Manhattan, the Bronx, and its affiliated campuses in Los Angeles and Jerusalem. In addition to the Yeshiva University Press, which publishes scholarly books written by its faculty and alumni, publications are issued by the university's schools and programs in such disciplines as Holocaust studies, medicine, law, and social work. It is home to a network of libraries for student and scholarly use, with complete holdings of some 977,000 volumes, and houses the Yeshiva University Museum (1973), a teaching museum that presents exhibits reflecting Jewish life through art, architecture, music, history, literature, science, and anthropology.

Honorary degrees, which the university has been authorized to grant, have been bestowed on such men as Albert Einstein; Harlan Fiske Stone; Herbert H. Lehman; Benjamin N. Cardozo; Earl Warren; Bernard Baruch; Abba Eban; Meir Rosen; Teddy Kollek; Yitzhak Shamir; Shimon Peres; Esther Wachsman, mother of Israeli soldier Nachshon Wachsman, who was slain by Arab terrorists in 1994; Herman Branover, world-famous physicist, head of the Liquid Metal MHD Laboratories at Ben Gurion University; and others.

On September 23, 1986, a postage stamp honoring Dr. Bernard Revel, the institution's first president, was issued by the United States Post Office. The thirty-fifth stamp in the "Great Americans" series, it was the first to cite a Talmudic scholar.

The largest gift in the 107-year history of Yeshiva University—a $40 million bequest from the estate of Rachel Golding—was announced at the university's sixty-ninth annual Hanukkah dinner held on December 5, 1993. The bequest was made by Mrs. Golding in memory of her husband, Samuel H. Golding, a New York banker and realtor.

Under the Goldings' names, students will pursue various studies at the Samuel H. and Rachel Golding Center for Judaic Studies; the Golding Center for Molecular Genetics and the Golding Center for Developmental Neurobiology, which will be housed in a new building bearing the Golding name; the Golding Distinguished Scholars Program, providing financial assistance to Yeshiva University's most outstanding students; the Golding Institute for Biomedical Education; and the Golding Endowment for the Rabbi Isaac Elchanan Theological Seminary, a scholarship and fellowship program.

As Yeshiva University expands, so the name of its founder, Bernard Revel, becomes enshrined even deeper in the historical scene of American Judaism.

THE FIRST OFFICIAL HEBREW COURSES IN THE PUBLIC SCHOOL CURRICULUM

1930

The revival of Hebrew as a spoken language may well be regarded as one of the miracles of our age. That Hebrew has permanently taken its place among the living languages of our time can no longer be disputed. The use of Hebrew as the language of daily speech in Israel, the growth of the Hebrew press and theater, and the rebirth of modern Hebrew literature bear eloquent testimony to this fact.

Although the study of Hebrew in this country goes back to the colonial era, when the first colleges taught Hebrew as one of their required subjects, it was not until 1930 that modern Hebrew was officially introduced into the public high school curriculum. In that year the New York City Board of Education, not certain of the response of the students, had the language taught on an experimental basis in two high schools that had a majority of Jewish students. The first ninety-five boys and girls admitted to the classes were warned that they might not receive any credit. There were no up-to-date books and few qualified teachers. However, with the help of organizations such as the Hebrew Culture Council of the Jewish Education Committee of Greater New York, whose director from its inception was Judah Lapson, these needs were supplied. The experiment proved successful. In 1932 Hebrew was officially adopted as a course of study. Eight years later Hebrew was being taught in eleven schools in New York City, and by 1957 it was included in the language program of more than seventy-eight secondary schools in thirteen American cities, with an annual enrollment of over five thousand. In all these schools, Hebrew was given as an elective course, with high school, regents, and college-entrance credit.

The official course of study for the Hebrew classes set down the objectives: "To develop to the point of enjoyment the ability to read Hebrew, and to instill an appreciation for Hebrew culture and civilization."

The course of study today includes several thousand basic Hebrew words, expressions, and idioms, as well as a grounding in grammar. While religious material is excluded, the curriculum provides the student with a bird's-eye view of all of Jewish history and literature, an acquaintance with Jewish folkways and customs, and an orientation in the life and problems of the reborn State of Israel. The geography of Israel, as well as its folk songs and dances, is also studied. The outline of this course covering four years of instruction was formalized in a syllabus published as an official document by the Bureau of Curriculum Development of the

Division of Secondary Education of the New York State Education Department in Albany, New York, in 1948.

In 1950 the pattern of consultation and services established by the Hebrew Culture Council was extended to communities in other sections of the country interested in teaching Hebrew in their schools by the Hebrew Culture Service Committee for American High Schools and Colleges.

Through the efforts of the Hebrew Culture Council and the Hebrew Culture Service Committee, instruction in Hebrew in secondary schools as an accredited subject gave impetus to the study of modern Hebrew in a number of colleges and universities. By 1989 the National Association of Professors of Hebrew had identified 152 permanent instructors in ninety-three modern Hebrew programs in United States colleges and universities.

Today in New York City colleges and universities alone, two thousand students are taking Hebrew courses. In five colleges under supervision of the Board of Higher Education, Hebrew is taught. It is listed in the catalogs not as an ancient, but as a modern language. In addition, every major college in the city has a well-established Hebrew department with courses on all levels.

In 1944 the first Chair of Modern Hebrew was established at New York University under the director of Dr. Abraham Katsh, enabling students to pursue a course of study leading to baccalaureate, master's, and doctoral degrees majoring in Hebrew or Jewish education.

To foster a knowledge of spoken and written Hebrew in the wider community, the Histadruth Ivrith of America (the Hebrew Language and Culture Association) was founded in 1916.

During the 1930s, the organization fostered the Hebrew youth organization, Histadrut Hanoar Haivri, which published the literary journal, *Niv (Expression)*, and encouraged activities in the fields of choral work, dramatics, and dance. These activities led to the establishment of the Hebrew Arts Foundation, which in 1952 founded the Hebrew Arts School in New York.

Today Histadruth Ivrith represents a multitude of programs spanning all age groups that includes magazines in Hebrew; Ulpanim, a method for the study of the Hebrew language introduced in Israel; and Shavua Ivri, a Hebrew week that takes place annually during the month of July in a country setting with all activities and lectures conducted in Hebrew.

Its biweekly publication, *Hadoar (The Post)*, which celebrated its seventy-third year in 1994, is edited by Shlomo Shamir and Dr. Yael Feldman. The vocalized *Lamishpacha (For the Family)*, which began publication in 1963 edited by Dr. Vered Cohen Raphael, is the latest in a long series of publications that began appearing in 1916.

THE FIRST PROFESSOR OF JEWISH HISTORY ON AN AMERICAN UNIVERSITY FACULTY

1930

One of the twentieth century's most prolific and brilliant scholars of Jewish history was Salo Wittmayer Baron, who was the first historian on an American university faculty to teach Jewish history. His affiliation with Columbia University for close to four decades set a precedent for the establishment of Jewish studies departments on college campuses throughout the United States, many of which were directed by Baron's former students or students of his students.

The Salo Wittmayer Baron Chair in the Study of Jewish Society, Culture and Institutions at Columbia University was established in 1973 to honor the scholar who taught there from 1930 until his retirement in 1963.

Professor Baron wrote thirteen books on Jewish history, many of them multivolume efforts. He edited four other books and produced hundreds of articles and addresses. They include studies on Jewish historiography and historians, studies on the Jewish population of biblical Palestine, some of the medieval spiritual masters, the Jewish question in modern international relations, the history of the Jews in America, and the impact of anti-Semitism and nationalism on Jewish history.

His magnus opus is *A Social and Religious History of the Jews*, which began as a series of lectures on the relationship between society and religion and turned into a three-volume overview of Jewish history, published by Columbia University Press in 1937. It finally grew to include eighteen volumes that presented a broad synthesis of the entire sweep of Jewish history. This indispensable guide, together with his other books and articles, made his name omnipresent in bibliographies and practically synonymous with Jewish history in the English language.

In addition to his enormous knowledge, Baron brought very distinctive views to his scholarship. He inveighed against what he termed the "lachrymose conception of Jewish history" sometimes identified with Heinrich Graetz, an eminent nineteenth-century Jewish historian who found the main element of Jewish experience through the ages to be suffering and Jewish scholarship.

Baron always fought against the view of Jewish history as "all darkness and no light" and labored mightily to restore the balance.

Jewish history was for him the understanding of what was happening to the Jews as an enormously creative and important element within the context of larger historical forces from which Jews learn and to which Jews contribute. Moreover, Baron found the roots of Jewish emancipation not in ideologies nor in the change of heart toward the Jews, but instead in the logic of the eighteenth- and nineteenth-century revolutions. When legal privilege and autonomous corporate groups were abolished in favor of equal rights, they had to apply to Jews as well.

Salo Wittmayer Baron was born on May 26, 1895, in Tarnow, Galicia, the southern region of Poland that then belonged to the Austro-Hungarian empire. His parents, Elias and Mina Wittmayer Baron, belonged, by the right of both ancestry and wealth, to the Jewish aristocracy of Galicia. Elias Baron was a private banker and investor who stood at the head of the local Jewish community, which numbered roughly fifteen thousand persons.

As a small child, Salo quickly made his talents evident, learning to play chess at the age of three, writing Hebrew poetry at twelve, and adding Yiddish, Hebrew, French, and German to his first language, Polish. Eventually, he learned twenty languages and lectured—as he always did without notes—in five.

In secondary schools he was outstanding in physics and mathematics, but his interests lay between Polish nationalism, religious Orthodoxy, and Zionism.

Baron left Tarnow for Vienna in 1912 to attend its university and rabbinical school. He was ordained at the Jewish Theological School of Vienna in 1920 and earned three doctorates at the University of Vienna—in history in 1917, in political science in 1922, and in jurisprudence in 1923.

By 1920 he had already gained recognition as an insightful and original scholar on contemporary issues. His first major published work—*Die Judenfrage auf Dem Wiener Kongress*—explored the Jewish question as it was raised at the Congress of Vienna in 1882, which proposed vast restrictions on Jewish rights, later compounded in subsequent congresses.

After teaching at the Hebrew Teachers' Seminary in Vienna in 1926, at the invitation of Rabbi Stephen S. Wise, he came to the United States as professor of Jewish history and librarian at the Jewish Institute of Religion, which Wise had founded in New York City to provide rabbis for "forward-looking, progressive American congregations."

In 1930 Professor Baron began to teach at Columbia University in the newly established Miller Chair of Jewish History, Literature, and Institutions. It was the first chair in Jewish history at a secular university in the western world. There was some question first about which academic department the new professor would be affiliated with, since the existence of Jewish history as a genuine field was gravely questioned. Academic habit suggested that the small department of Semitic languages where Hebrew was taught was the suitable place; as a historian, however, Baron wanted to be in the History Department, of which he would later become the first Jewish tenured member.

It was late in the 1940s, at the midpoint of his career, that Baron began to work on a new, enlarged edition of his *Social and Religious History of the*

Jews. This project was to set the course of the rest of his life. He planned seven volumes: two on ancient times, two for the Middle Ages, and two on the modern age, with a final volume for bibliography and index. The first two duly appeared in 1952. In his introduction to volume three, which appeared in 1957, together with volumes four and five, he announced that the medieval section, covering the centuries from 500 to 1200, would be expanded to take account of the vast increase in published source material. These three volumes deal with Jewish economic, political, and social life. Volumes six to eight, which appeared in 1958, take up the magnificent cultural accomplishments when the Jewish people were living mainly under Moslem rulers. The period from 1200 to 1650 is covered by the final ten volumes the author lived to produce. Altogether, Baron's *History* is one of the most immense historical projects ever undertaken by one man alone.

Well into his nineties, Professor Baron labored on volume nineteen, and he had projected at least two more volumes carrying the account of Jewish life through 1650.

Alongside this unparalleled production of books were still other publications. Thus Baron produced such studies of Jewish life in America as the three-volume *The Jewish Community: Its History and Structure to the American Revolution* (Philadelphia, 1942); *The Jews in the United States: 1790–1840: A Documentary History,* which was coedited with a Columbia University colleague, Dr. Joseph I. Blau (New York and Philadelphia, 1963); and *Steeled in Adversity: Essays and Addresses on American Jewish Life,* edited by his wife, Jeannette Meisel Baron (Philadelphia, 1971). With Blau he coedited *Judaism: Post-Biblical and Talmudic Period* (Philadelphia, 1954). In 1972 his *Ancient and Medieval Jewish History: Essays* appeared, edited by Dr. Leon Feldman (New Brunswick, New Jersey). Baron also wrote *From a Historian's Notebook: European Jewry Before and After Hitler* (New York, 1962) and *The Russian Jew Under the Tsars and Soviets* (New York, 1964 and 1976). In addition, Baron served as consulting editor of the *Encyclopaedia Judaica* (Jerusalem, 1972).

Besides pursuing his scholarly work at Columbia University, Professor Baron was active in organizational efforts to maintain and strengthen the Jewish community both before and after World War II. He was the leading spirit of the American Academy for Jewish Research and served as its president from 1940 to 1943, 1958 to 1965, and 1968 to 1973, and was honorary president thereafter. He was president of the American Jewish Historical Society from 1953 to 1955 and cofounder with Morris Raphael Cohen of the Conference on Jewish Social Studies and its president from 1941 to 1955. For over four decades he served as editor of *Jewish Social Studies,* a quarterly journal devoted to contemporary and historical aspects of Jewish life.

Following World War II, he organized the Commission on Jewish Cultural Reconstruction, which worked in identifying and reclaiming millions of Jewish books and other cultural treasures stolen by the Nazis and returning them to their rightful owners, to Jewish museums, libraries, and other institutions.

On April 24, 1961, Professor Baron set the historical framework for the Israeli prosecution's case against Adolph Eichmann. In a manner both learned and passionate, he testified at the arch-murderer's Jerusalem trial about anti-Semitism and the condition of European Jewry both before and after the Holocaust.

Baron's prodigious achievements gained him worldwide recognition, including awards, medals, and honorary degrees from universities in the United States, Europe, and Israel.

Baron retired from his professorship in 1963 but remained director of its Center for Israel and Jewish Studies, which he founded in 1950, until 1968. Both before and after his retirement, he lectured and taught in many universities at home and abroad, including Israel. Upon his retirement from Columbia, the university took the rare steps of conferring an honorary degree on a member of its own faculty and of creating a new chair in Jewish history named in his honor (now held by a former student of his, Yosef Hayim Yerushalmi).

Dr. Arthur Hertzberg, professor of religion at Dartmouth College, another former student of Salo Wittmayer Baron's, in summing up his career, wrote in *Midstream* magazine in May 1990: "Salo Wittmayer Baron can be rightfully considered the archaeologist of Jewish history. He not merely recorded the episodes, incidents, fragments, and minutiae of the life process of the Jewish people, but provided a coherent and consistent materialistic methodology with which to probe the laws of causality of that process."

Dr. Baron's pioneering efforts to bring Jewish studies at Columbia University into the mainstream of humanistic scholarship have been credited with contributing to Columbia University's present stature in the field.

THE FIRST AMERICAN JEW TO RECEIVE TEN HIGHER ACADEMIC DEGREES

1934

Dr. Hirsch Loeb Gordon is the first American and the first Jew to receive ten higher academic degrees, all through actual study.

Born on November 26, 1896, in Vilna, Lithuania, son of the eminent rabbi and author Rabbi Elijah Gordon, he was from his early childhood a prodigious student of Talmud in the yeshivoth of Slabodka, Lidda, and Volozhin and grew up to obtain prominence in diverse scientific fields.

Dr. Gordon made his professional debut as lecturer on Talmud at the Rabbinical College of Florence, Italy in 1915 at the age of nineteen, the youngest teacher in the history of the institution. The next four years found him in Palestine whence he was exiled by the Turkish government to Egypt with most alien Jews. Before the year was over, he joined the Zion Mule Corps, also known as the Jewish Legion, with Trumpeldor in World War I. The first voluntary armed Jewish fighting force since the rebellion of Bar Kochba in 135 C.E., it was organized to fight with the Allies to liberate Palestine from the Turks.

In 1915 Hirsch Loeb came to the United States and two years later entered the graduate school of Yale University. His first doctorate came in 1922, when Yale awarded him a Ph.D. in Semitic languages and literature with highest honors. In the next twelve years were to come nine more academic degrees, as well as teaching positions in history, philosophy, philology, and psychiatry.

In all, his degrees were as follows: 1923, a doctorate in Egyptology from Catholic University in Washington, D.C., the first degree of its kind given in the United States; 1924, a master's degree in international law from the American University in Washington, D.C.; 1926, a master's degree in educational psychology from Teachers' College, Columbia University; 1927, a master's degree in Religious Education from the Jewish Theological Seminary of America; 1928, a doctorate in Hebrew Literature from the Jewish Theological Seminary of America; 1928, a master's degree in Fine Arts from New York University; 1931, a doctorate with high honors in Classical Archeology from the University of Rome—first time awarded to an American—for the first book on the history of the basilica and stoa; 1934, a doctorate in natural sciences from the University of Rome; and in 1934, a doctor of medicine degree, also from the University of Rome. The latter three degrees marked the first instance of three doctorates being presented to a foreigner by an Italian university.

With Dr. Gordon's return to the United States came appointments to the medical staffs of various hospitals and serving the government as neurologist and psychiatrist. He was on the staff of the neurology clinic of New York's Mount Sinai Hospital in 1935 and later with the Maimonides Hospital in Brooklyn; Pilgrim State Hospital in Brentwood, Long Island; and Bellevue and Kings County Hospital. During World War II, he was a major in the Army Medical Corps, then chief psychiatrist of the Veterans Administration Hospital in Florida, neuro-psychiatric consultant with the Surgeon-General in the United States Army, and Senior Surgeon in the United States Publc Health Service with the rank of Commander (Chief) in the United States Marine Hospital in Staten Island, New York.

In addition to his many writings on Jewish and medical topics in English, Yiddish, Hebrew, German, and Italian, Dr. Gordon was noted as medical editor of the *Universal Jewish Encyclopedia* (New York, 1941). He was a contributing reviewer to the *American Journal of Psychiatry* and *The American Journal of Psychotherapy*. He also wrote articles in Yiddish for *The Jewish Morning Journal* and in Hebrew for *Hadoar* (*The Post*), both in New York City.

Dr. Gordon was the author of numerous books. Among these are *Shock Therapy* (1934), *Psychiatric Concepts in the Bible, Talmud, and Torah* (1935), and *The Maggid of Cairo* (1952), a psychiatric study of genius and mysticism based on the life of Joseph Cairo, author of the *Shulchan Aruch*, the authoritative code of Jewish law. In 1958, he translated from the Arabic *The Preservation of Youth*, a medical work by Moses Maimonides. It was the first English translation of one of the unique medical works of Western culture.

Apart from his academic degrees, Dr. Gordon was a fellow of many learned societies. Among these were the American Psychiatric Association, the American Medical Association, the Association of Military Surgeons, and the Electric Shock Research Association. He was also a member of the New York Academy of Medicine and president of the American Hebrew Medical Society, which was composed of Hebrew-speaking physicians.

When Dr. Hirsch Loeb Gordon died on January 19, 1969, at the age of seventy-two, the Jewish community lost a great son who had made an important contribution to personality development and shed new light to a better understanding in the fields of history, sociology, and the science of religion.

THE FIRST MAJOR HASIDIC SECT TRANSPLANTED TO AMERICA

1940

Hasidim (literally, "pious ones," adherents of an ultra-Orthodox sect founded in eighteenth-century Eastern Europe by Israel Baal Shem Tov) had emigrated to the United States with the great Jewish migration of 1880 to 1925. They formed part of a body of pious immigrant Jews and frequently established *shtiblekh* (separate synagogues) of their own. They seemed to have been less successful than non-Hasidic immigrant Jews in transmitting their style of religious life to the next generation. Apart from their *tzaddikim* (righteous ones), also called rebbes, or grand rabbis, who were their supreme religious guides, they were apparently at a loss to perpetuate the Judaism they knew. The American Jewish religious atmosphere was not yet ripe for the movement. After World War I several *tzaddikim* settled in the United States, including the Twersky dynasties from the Ukraine. They gathered followers but lacked the means and fervor to establish a Hasidic movement.

This enervation ended with the arrival from Russia (via Poland) in 1940 of Rabbi Joseph Isaac Schneersohn, the Lubavitcher rebbe, and the general revival of Orthodox Judaism in the United States began from that date. A network of schools, institutions, and activities was founded under the direction of Rabbi Schneersohn and his successor, Rabbi Menachem Mendel Schneerson, and the unprecedented practice was initiated in the late 1950s by Lubavitch Hasidim of vigorously evangelizing Jews to return to Orthodoxy and to live in full accordance with the Torah-true way of life.

The momentum was first picked up in 1941, particularly with the expanding programs of Rabbi Menachem Mendel Schneerson. Born in Nikolaev, the Ukraine, in 1902, the great-grandson of the third Lubavitch rebbe, Menachem Schneerson in 1929 married the daughter of Joseph Isaac Schneersohn, then the sixth Lubavitch rebbe. He fled Europe in the early 1940s as the Nazis engulfed the continent. Menachem Mendel was a rabbi, a scholar-philosopher fluent in ten languages. He had studied at the University of Berlin and the Sorbonne in Paris, where he received a degree in engineering—the first rebbe in history to do so.

Upon his arrival in the United States, Menachem Mendel was appointed by his father-in-law, Rabbi Joseph Isaac Schneersohn, to the position of chief executive officer of Merkos L'Inyoney Chinuch, the group's educational division; of Machne Israel, the all-embracing social-service organization of the Lubavitch movement; and of the Lubavitch publishing arms.

The day school was becoming a choice for many children of Orthodox Jewish parents, and Lubavitch was opening Jewish day schools, summer camps, and youth groups in cities and states across the country.

It was in the 1950s that Rabbi Menachem Mendel Schneerson began publishing his own commentaries about numerous treatises on Hasidic and Talmudic texts and *responsa*—literature amassed down through the centuries from the questions and answers to religious law.

In 1950, when Joseph Isaac died, Menachem Mendel inherited the "throne." From that time for a period of forty-four years, from headquarters in the Crown Heights section of Brooklyn, Menachem Mendel served as spiritual leader in the phenomenal spread of the religious activist movement of Chabad-Lubavitch, a Hebrew acronym of the words *chochma, bina,* and *da'at*—or wisdom, understanding, and knowledge.

Rabbi Menachem Mendel Schneerson presented a New Deal for Hasidic culture with the motto "*Ufaratzto,* and you shall spread forth in the West and East and to the North and to the South," as God commanded the patriarch Jacob (Genesis 28:14). The rebbe was going global. He taught that Jews could hasten the arrival of the Messiah if they practiced the traditions laid out in the Hebrew Bible and as interpreted by the rabbis in the Talmud and other classical texts.

Without leaving the United States – or rarely even his own Eastern Parkway headquarters in Brooklyn – Schneerson attained mystical significance as younger Lubavitchers, including many who had joined the movement in their teens or twenties, participated in an aggressive campaign to draw non-observant Jews or those who otherwise lived observant lives but did not subscribe to Orthodox traditions.

Perhaps never before had there been a rebbe who saw the entire world as his flock and who translated that premise into programs. Eventually tallying an estimated three hundred thousand followers worldwide (many who believed him to be the Messiah), the rebbe acquired adherents from Thailand to Chile, from Australia to Zaire, from Hong Kong to Venezuala, and from Budapest to Casablanca.

Starting with little more than one Brooklyn synagogue and several refugees clusters in Europe and Israel, the rebbe transformed Chabad-Lubavitch into an international conglomerate of Jewish activity in over one thousand five hundred outposts in thirty-five countries on six continents as well as in virtually all of the fifty states.

Rabbi Menachem Mendel Schneerson was the first Jewish spiritual leader to sense the potential of satellite television hookups, mass publishing, full-page newspaper advertisements, broadcasting in dozens of languages, and penetrating the secular world with toll-free telephone numbers to bring vast public awareness to the Hasidic model of Judaism as he battled alienation, intermarriage, and assimilation.

Schneerson led an empire that raised most of its $250 million annual budget, which was reinvested into educational programs, from non-Hasidic and even non-religious Jews who appreciated what the rebbe was doing and who hung his photo in their homes and offices.

Rabbi Menachem Schneerson's *farbrengen*, stirring Hasidic gatherings marked by mystical discourses, modest drinking, and exuberant singing of Hasidic melodies, became increasingly popular even to non-Hasidic visitors in the block-long Lubavitch synagogue under 770 Eastern Parkway, the local Brooklyn address that became formally known as the Chabad-Lubavitch world headquarters.

On Sundays he would hand out crisp dollar bills along with a blessing to people who lined up for hours to see him. The bills were supposed to be given to charity, but many kept them as souvenirs.

The rebbe, who modified the Lubavitch stance from anti-Zionist to non-Zionist was himself a major political force in Israel, both in the Knesset and among the electorate. Although he never set foot in the

Jewish state, he could alter the course of Israeli politics with a few sentences. Almost every candidate who ran for major political office in New York over the past several decades traveled to Brooklyn seeking his support. Regarding national issues the rebbe spoke out on a moment of silence in schools and on the public display of religious symbols. Not only are Hanukkah menorahs now lighted in public centers around the world from the White House to Champs Elysees, from Central Park to Melbourne, because of the rebbe's brash brand of Judaism, a Hanukkah menorah was lit in space during a recent space mission. But by far his most significant accomplishment has been to take a persecuted 250-year-old Hasidic sect from the town of Lubavitch in Belarus, southeast Russia-Poland, and turn it into a global movement. Today, three thousand *shluchim* (emissaries) leave Brooklyn and set up outreach centers wherever the rebbe said there was a Jewish soul in need.

In some places the Chabad house or school is the only Jewish institution where Jews can study, pray, receive social services, and learn about Judaism.

For the past twenty-five years, "Mitzvah Tanks" or Lubavitch vans have been a familiar site in bustling downtown neighborhoods and on college campuses in many cities across the United States as they travel on recruitment drives and vie for the hearts and souls of Jews. The movement has also been known to seek out newly arrived Jewish immigrants from Russia, Iran, and North Africa to bring these people for the first time in their lives the feeling and spirit of Judaism.

There is Kfar Chabad (Chabad Village) of five thousand just east of Tel Aviv that was founded in 1948 that is the center of the Lubavitch movement in Israel. Kfar Chabad has become an educational center for thousands of Jewish youth. Aside from the yeshivos for students of all ages, it offers several types of vocational training such as printing, woodworking, sheet metal, and agriculture. Besides Kfar Chabad, Lubavitch followers are also concentrated in B'nai B'rak, Jerusalem, and Petach Tikvah, as well as in hundreds of smaller Chabad outposts in Israel.

Chabad Lubavitch is credited with changing the course of modern Jewish history by getting masses of largely secular Jews to increase their Jewish identification and observance.

By virtue of Rabbi Schneerson's knowledge, aura of piety, charisma, and administrative talent, Chabad Lubavitch became a major factor in American Jewish life.

The rebbe remained vigorous well into his eighties, although a heart attack prompted him to curtail his public audiences that had gone on for years until the early morning hours.

Grand Rabbi Menachem Mendel Schneerson, the Russian-born scholar who studied mathematics and science in Berlin and engineering at the Sorbonne, fled the Nazis in 1941, immigrated to the United States, and rebuilt the Lubavitch movement from the ashes of the Holocaust, died on June 12, 1994, after suffering a massive stroke. He was ninety-two. His passing made front-page news around the world. New York City's four major newspapers devoted multiple pages to the story of his life, and it led the newscasts, as well.

The institutions he built spanned the globe. Indeed the movement's resiliency is exemplified by the fact that in the last two years of the rebbe's medically constricted leadership, the institutions nevertheless grew by more than twenty percent. A dozen new buildings were erected from Florida to Bangkok. Ground was broken for sixteen new Lubavitch schools and centers. Over $100 million in capital building projects were undertaken in 1995 alone.

Lubavitch added thirty-five new locations to its long roster of places to which it sends emissaries to conduct outreach work. Seventeen new institutions of learning were established, from a yeshiva in Detroit to a women's institute in London. And most telling, one hundred new couples joined the ranks of the already three thousand Lubavitch emissaries around the world.

Though he died in June 1994, the charismatic Hasidic leader still receives a daily torrent of more than 1,000 faxes, letters, and hand-delivered notes (kivitlach) requesting intervention and blessing.

And now Lubavitchers have made commuting to the rebbe ever easier. In February 1995, Lubavitchers purchased a house fronting the old Montefiore Cemetery in Cambria Heights, Queens, New York, with a back door less than one hundred yards from the rebbe's grave, a majestic twenty-square-foot mausoleum with an open roof. The Lubavitchers believe that his soul rests above the grave.

In the house, two fax machines churn through nearly a case and a half—7,500 sheets—of paper each week, all requests to the rebbe for blessing and intercession with the Divine. (It is probably the first graveside fax service in the United States).

Letters requesting blessings still come in the mail or are brought in person by the one hundred or more persons who visit the grave each week day.

So massive is the amount of paper that fills the area within the three-foot-high containing walls that the grave would appear to be a mini landfill were it not for the imposing tombstones of the rebbe and his predecessor, Rabbi Joseph Isaac Schneersohn, who died in 1950.

Reportedly, the rebbe himself designed the small, open-roofed mausoleum. The number of visitors rises to more than five hundred on Sundays.

Still another Hasidic sect is that of the Satmar Hasidim, who are bent on retaining a way of life free of the influences of the modern world. It was an extended family of adherents .that had originated in the eighteenth century amid an entanglement of mystical folklores in the Jewish community of Satu Mare, a backward, ethnically fractured corner of Transylvania. Developing rapidly into the most fanatical subcommunity in the Hasidic world, the Satmar by the twentieth century generated relentless animosity to Zionism and later to the State of Israel, for they believed that it was a sin to create a Jewish State until after the Messiah comes. Although two-thirds of them perished in the Holocaust, the disciples of the Satmar rebbe, Moshe Teitelbaum, who "reigned" from 1908 until his death in 1941, and then of his son, Rebbe Joel Teitelbaum, who held the community of his faithful together, had spread to all parts of Eastern Hungary. Some fifty thousand of them had survived the war. So did Reb Joel Teitelbaum himself, who came to the United States in 1947 and built his domain of synagogues, schools, and a yeshiva with the primary purpose of promoting Jewish education in the spirit of Torah-true Judaism among all Jews regardless of background. Over the years the followers of Satmar in Williamsburg and Borough Park in Brooklyn, in Monsey and in Kiryas Joel—a village near West Point, New York—numbered as many as fifty thousand to sixty thousand and had become an establishment of the Empire State.

The Teitelbaum rebbes and others like them, including Rebbe Moses Teitelbaum, who became grand rebbe after his uncle's death in 1979, came to New York primarily from Hungary and Romania and sought to reestablish their communities exactly as they were in Europe. They tried to preserve the dress, the Yiddish language, and customs of Eastern Europe. As such they were successful. They built up a Kosher food industry that continues to flourish. Not all were anti-Zionist as the Satmar subcommunity.

The Bobover rebbe, Rav Shlomo Halberstam, who traces his dynastic roots to Rav Chaim Halberstam (1795–1876) of Tarnogrod, Poland—known to the Hasidim as *Divrei Chaim*, after escaping brutal persecutions in Western Galicia—came to New York after World War II and began the task of rebuilding the House of Bobov. With the aid of his followers, Halberstam opened his headquarters in Crown Heights, Brooklyn, and gradually developed a network of institutions there. Later, these synagogues, schools, and yeshivas were shifted to Williamsburg, Borough Park, and Monsey. The institutions have continued to expand and attract people of different backgrounds.

New Square, New York—the village whose name is anglicized from Skvera, the village near Kiev where the Hasidic dynasty of Skver was founded in the early 1800s—was founded in 1954 and incorporated within the town of Ramapo (Rockland County) in 1961. Its five thousand members are all Skverer Hasidim. New Square, the first entirely Orthodox municipality in the United States, is essentially a transplanted village from the Ukraine.

Rabbi Yaakov Twersky, a Holocaust survivor who came to Brooklyn after World War II, established New Square on a former dairy farm near the heavily populated Orthodox community of Monsey to escape from New York's urban distractions as a haven for Hasidim, who stress individual spiritual growth. The community has grown in four decades from twenty families to seven hundred, with another one hundred on the waiting list.

New Square is a self-contained community with its own large, stone-faced yeshivas for children and adults; a large central synagogue and a new one under construction; a small co-op grocery; a modest medical clinic; *mikveh* (ritual bath); and cemetery. Many residents never step out of its 130 acres.

Inspired by New Square, the Satmar and Vishnitz Hasidic groups have established similar communities in upstate New York.

Still additional Hasidic sects have developed subcommunities of their own, among them conventicles from Ger, Belz, Stolin, Tzelem, and Pupa—all deriving their names and identifying their dynastic rebbes from their Hungarian, Romanian, Polish, or Ukranian towns of origin.

Ultimately, by the early 1990s the Hasidic communities throughout Brooklyn, Rockland County, Sullivan County (the Catskills), and Union City, New Jersey, comprised over 150,000 members. They grew in numbers and strength *not* because of the unique opportunities of the American economic system. Williamsburg, New Square, and the other Hasidic communities became what they were because of the idealism of its people, the strength of their convictions, and their high birth rate.

THE FIRST WONDER DRUG DISCOVERED IN AMERICA

1943

For twenty-eight years, Dr. Selman Waksman pored over test tubes in his cluttered little laboratory in the Rutgers University College of Agriculture, searching for microorganisms in the soil that would prove beneficial to mankind.

It was the theory of this microbiologist that "there are probably more different kinds of tiny plants and animals in the soil than there are on the top of it." And that there is a continuous civil war in the earth between these countless microorganisms, with each type using its own chemical weapons to kill off the others. And that scientists could isolate these chemical weapons, for which he coined the name "antibiotic," which he defined as a chemical substance produced by a microbe that has the capacity to inhibit the growth of and even to destroy other microbes.

Those twenty-eight years were filled with disappointments for Dr. Waksman, but at the end of them, in 1952, he won the Nobel Prize in physiology and medicine "for his discovery of streptomycin, the first antibiotic effective against tuberculosis."

He set out to find an antibiotic that would kill man-harming microbes without itself doing harm to man.

This meant testing and retesting one microorganism after another. Some, like actinomycin and streptothricin, produced by microbes of the streptomyces type—which he found in soil taken out of the Rutgers University campus in New Brunswick, New Jersey—looked promising but proved to be worthless in the treatment of human diseases. Others, like gramacidin, produced by a soil bacillus—which one of his former students, René Dubos, found in a mixture of different soils—had disease-killing potentialities but turned out to be injurious to man.

And continually there were obstacles. The story is told that in 1941, a university official urged that Waksman, who was earning $4,620 a year, be dismissed. "For economy," the official said, arguing there was no possible future for Waksman's research. Providentially, Rutgers did not follow his advice.

Then in 1943 a local poultryman brought a sick chicken to the Rutgers College of Agriculture for diagnosis. The poultry pathologist saw something unusual in the culture that he took from the chicken's throat and sent it to Waksman.

Waksman nurtured the culture and ran some experiments with it. He saw that the culture (and one very similar to it, which he and his assistants isolated from the highly fertilized soil) produced very effective antibiotics.

Both organisms, he found, were strains of streptomyces griseus, but unlike the old one that he first isolated with Curtis in 1915, these new isolates were deadly germ killers. In the test tube they were effective not only against the gram-negative bacteria resistant to penicillin but against "mycrobacterium tuberculosis," the tuberculosis germ.

But would they do as much in humans?

At Waksman's suggestion the antibiotic that he named streptomycin (designated after the microbe that produced it) was tried on the most desperately ill patients suffering from tuberculosis at the Mayo Clinic in Rochester, Minnesota. It proved of immediate value. For the first time, mankind had a genuinely effective weapon against the "white plague." It was soon apparent that streptomycin was effective against virulent forms of pneumonia, meningitis, whooping cough, dysentery, typhoid, gonorrhea, and many other infections resistant to or not responding to penicillin and other sulpha drugs.

Although thirteen years had elapsed between the discovery of penicillin and its introduction to medical practice, only three years separated the discovery of streptomycin, the new wonder drug, and its emergence as a prescription medication.

More than thirty drug companies in this country and abroad are now turning it out, and it is reputed to be saving more lives than were lost in the Napoleonic wars.

From the discovery of streptomycin, Waksman continued to isolate new antibiotics. A steady stream of new discoveries—like acetinomycin, neomycin, candicidin, and many others—issued from his laboratory to a grateful world.

Selman Abraham Waksman, the man who started it all, was born on July 2, 1888, in Priluka, a small town in the Ukraine, not far from the city of Kiev, the son of Jacob and Fradia London Waksman. His father, a businessman and artisan who made copper kitchenware, wanted him to study industrial chemistry, but young Waksman was far more interested in biology. After graduating in 1910 from the college-type Fifth Gymnasium in Odessa, at the age of twenty-two he left Russia for the United States. He planned first to study biochemistry at a medical school but instead chose soil microbiology and enrolled in the Rutgers College of Agriculture in New Jersey. He received his bachelor's degree in 1915 and became a naturalized citizen the same year. He was then appointed research assistant in soil microbiology at the New Jersey Agricultural Experiment Station under Dr. Joseph G. Lipman, also Russian-born, and continued his graduate work at Rutgers, obtaining his master's degree in 1916. He was then appointed research fellow at the University of California in Berkeley, where he received his Ph.D. under the famous biochemist Brailsford Robertson in 1918. This was followed by an invitation to return to Rutgers, where he received appointments as microbiologist at the Experimental Station and as lecturer in soil microbiology at the university. He was appointed associate professor in 1925, and made full professor in 1930. In 1931 he was invited to organize a division of Marine Bacteriology at the Woods Hole Oceanographic Institute and was there appointed marine bacteriologist, where he served until 1942. When Rutgers organized its Department of Microbiology in 1940, he became professor of microbiology and head of the department. In 1949 he founded and was named director of the multimillion dollar Institute of Microbiology, one of the most unique institutions of its kind in the world.

While teaching and writing extensively for scientific and popular publications, he played a leading role in the development of the study of American soil microbiology, which proceeded from a mere collection of unconnected observations to the stature of a scientific discipline.

In 1932 Waksman was asked by the American National Association Against Tuberculosis to investigate the process by which the tubercle bacillus is destroyed in the soil. He concluded that antagonistic microbes were responsible. By 1939 Waksman had decided to embark on a research project to apply his work on soil microbiology to the treatment of human diseases. Another motive for the research work was World War II, then looming on the horizon, which pointed to a need for new agents for the control of various infections and epidemics that were expected to arise.

Waksman's great scientific achievements were recognized throughout the world with honorary degrees, awards, and memberships in scientific societies. In 1952 he was decorated by the emperor of Japan with the Order of Merit of the Rising Sun. The Academy of Medicine in Torino, Italy, conferred upon him the St. Vincent Award for Medical Sciences in 1954. In 1950 he was made commander of the French Legion of Honor. He was elected president of the Society of American Bacteriologists in 1941. In 1937 he was elected corresponding member of the French Academy of Sciences and in 1958 foreign associate of that academy. He won the Nitrate of Soda Research Award, the Passano Foundation Award, the Emily Christian Hansen Medal, the Award of the Calsberg Laboratories in Denmark, and the Leewenhoek Medal from the Netherlands Academy of Sciences. In the course of the next few years he was given not only the Nobel Prize but also the Lasker Award of the American Public Health Association and the New Jersey Agricultural Society Medal.

Dr. Waksman published more than four hundred scientific papers and wrote—alone or with others—fifteen textbooks on microbiology. Among them are: *Enzymes, Principles of Soil Microbiology, The Soil and the Microbe, Humous, The Actinomycetes,* and *Soil Microbiology.* In 1954 he produced his autobiography, *My Life With The Microbes,* a literary best-seller.

Dr. Waksman was assisted in his investigations by numerous students who came from all parts of the world to work under him. In 1950 he acknowledged in a court dispute that Dr. Albert Schatz, a graduate student of his at the time of the discovery of streptomycin, was "entitled to be credited legally and scientifically as co-discoverer." Dr. Schatz as well as fifteen other scientists and twelve laboratory assistants received financial compensation for their contributions.

In September 1958, at the age of seventy, Dr. Waksman retired as director of the Rutgers University Institute of Microbiology but maintained an office and laboratory there. For many years he remained dean of American soil microbiologists, writing and lecturing about antibiotics throughout the United States.

He became deeply interested in scientific research in Israel soon after the establishment of the new state in 1948, and an institute devoted to industrial microbiology was established in his name at the Technion-Israel

Institute of Technology in Haifa with the long-term goal of utilizing microbes in industrial experimentation and development.

In his latter years he spent long periods addressing various scientific groups in Israel, urging young researchers there to press forward with their work and not become discouraged, just as he had not given up for a period of twenty-eight years.

He died in Hyannis, Massachusetts, on August 16, 1973. He was eighty-five years old. During his lifetime he had donated ninety-two percent of all royalties from his discoveries to Rutgers State University's Research and Endowment Foundation.

THE FIRST AMERICAN JEWISH ARMY NURSE TO DIE IN BATTLE

1944

Never before in American history have Jews risen to the ranks they attained in the Second World War. At least sixteen Jews were generals or admirals. More than six hundred thousand Jews—men and, for the first time, women—fought on the various fronts of the war. They served their country in every branch of the service—in the air, on the land and on the sea. From Sergeant Meyer Levin, who put a Japanese battleship out of commission early in the war—its first recorded act of heroism—to Major General Maurice Rose, commander of the Third Armored Division—the first army commander since Napoleon to invade the Reich from the West—Jews in the lowest to the highest ranks of the armed forces made the supreme sacrifice for a country whose basic principles are so consistent with the ideals of their religious faith.

They fought and died in Europe and Asia, on the Pacific and the Atlantic. They went down with their ships and in burning planes and in blazing tanks. Doctors died in forward dressing stations, like Dr. Jacques Saphier, who met death while caring for wounded Marines in Guadacanal. Chaplains met their deaths, like Rabbi Alexander Goode and three Christian chaplains who went down with their ship, the SS *Dorchester*, on February 26, 1943, in the icy waters off Greenland after having given up their life preservers to enlisted men. Reporters died in action, like Morris B. Penner of the *San Antonio Express*, killed when his plane exploded like a meteor while flying over England.

The first American Army nurse killed on the Western Front in World War II was Lieutenant Frances Y. Slanger of the United States Army Nurses Corps, a Bostonian Jewish girl who died of wounds received in Belgium.

Slanger, a Polish-born Jewess, emigrated to Boston as a youngster and was raised in Dorchester, Massachusetts. She was a 1937 graduate of Boston City Hospital's nurses' training program. On August 1, 1943, she was commissioned a Second Lieutenant in the U.S. Army Nurses Corps and went ashore at Normandy on June 10, 1944, four days after D-Day (D-Day plus four). She was stationed near the thickest of the fighting.

It is estimated that she treated over three thousand Allied casualties before she was killed in a hospital tent in Belgium on October 21, 1944. From the day she waded ashore in Normandy and helped set up a field hospital to the last four months she spent in a front-line tent, she grew to love the American soldier for his gallantry, courage, and sportsmanship.

At two o'clock in the morning of October 21, 1944, just before she was killed, she wrote a letter to *Stars and Stripes*, the newspaper for GIs, pouring forth her love, devotion, and admiration for the American soldier. That night her unit was the target of a German artillery barrge, and one of their shells burst near her. She and three other nurses were hit by shell fragments. While she lay there dying, she never uttered a word of complaint.

Her letter was published by *Stars and Stripes* fourteen days later and magnificently symbolizes the noble, womanly, American and Jewish qualities of Frances Y. Slanger. Her letter reads:

I'm writing this by flashlight. The GIs say we rough it, but we in our little tent can't see it. We wade ankle deep in mud. You have to lie in it. We are restricted to our immediate area, a cow pasture or hay field, but then who is not restricted? We have a stove and coal. We even have a laundry line in the tent. Our GI drawers are at this moment doing the dance of the pants, what with the wind howling, the tent waving precariously, the rain beating down, the guns firing . . . Sure we rough it. But you, the men behind the guns, driving our tanks, flying our planes, sailing our ships, building bridges, and the men who pave the way and the men who were left behind—it is to you we doff our helmets. To every GI wearing the American uniform, for you we have the greatest admiration and respect.

Frances Y. Slanger is buried in the Pride of Boston Cemetery. Over her grave is the Star of David, telling the world that here lies a Jewish heroine who died fighting for her country.

In Boston, Jewish women veterans of World War II formed an all-women's post of the Jewish War Veterans and named it the Lieutenant Frances Slanger Post in memory of the first nurse to give up her life in World War II.

The B'nai B'rith organization has contributed $2,000 to the nation-wide campaign for the erection of a national Nurses Memorial Home in

Washington, D.C., in honor of nurses who lost their lives in the war and where Americans for generations to come may learn to know of Lieutenant Slanger and honor her and her kind.

In 1950 the former Italian luxury liner *Saturnia* was renamed the *Frances Y. Slanger* in memory of the first American nurse killed in the European theater of war. It became queen of the Army's "mercy fleet." Early in that year the ship left the New York Port of Embarkation on its first mission as the world's largest and fastest floating hospital.

THE FIRST ATOMIC WEAPONS

1945

It has been previously stated that every American war has been marked by some new invention. The Civil War was the first time in which the railroad was a significant factor. In the Spanish-American War, the steam-propelled Navy ship was outstanding. The First World War was the first one in which an airplane was used. The Second World War was marked by the introduction of atomic weapons.

On October 11, 1939, Albert Einstein, one of the greatest scientists of all time, sent a two-page letter to President Franklin D. Roosevelt, pointing out that "the Germans are working on atomic fission, and the United States must start research at once or all civilization will perish." As author of the relativity theory and the equation relating mass to energy to which all atomic development could be traced, Einstein was the logical person to take the initiative.

The President acted. The United States government's program on atomic research was set in motion. Some two billion dollars of the American taxpayer's money was risked on the Manhattan Project. An advisory committee on uranium was appointed. Research was carried on simultaneously in many American universities on the development of a fission weapon. The most significant was the first "atomic chain reaction pile," achieved on the squash courts of the University of Chicago on December 2, 1942, and directed by Enrico Fermi and his working team of physicists, including George Leon Weil, who pulled out the final control rod, foot by foot, thus activating the atomic furnace and causing the neutron counters to click even faster and louder amid the greatest wartime secrecy. Meanwhile, at the United States atomic power development program at Los Alamos, New Mexico, the most sensational scientific undertaking of modern times, was placed under the direction of Dr. Julius Robert Oppenheimer, a thirty-eight-year-old Jewish physicist.

Born in New York City in 1904, Oppenheimer was the son of a German-Jewish immigrant who became a prosperous textile manufacturer. By the time he was ready to enter Harvard University, Robert Oppenheimer had a full and intimate knowledge of Greek and Latin, wrote sonnets in French, and was engrossed in mathematics and the sciences. He graduated from Harvard in three years summa cum laude and went on to study in Cambridge, England, with Lord Rutherford in the famous Cavendish Laboratory and later with Professor Max Born in the University of Gottingen, Germany, where Oppenheimer obtained his doctorate at the age of twenty-three.

Having developed into a master physicist, he returned to America to become a professor at the University of California at Berkeley and, simultaneously, at the California Institute of Technology in Pasadena in 1929. There he created the most outstanding schools of theoretical physics the world has ever known.

Then World War II broke out. Though he was purely a teacher and theoretician, the United States government turned to him to direct the design and production of the first atom bomb in history. By 1943 he had recruited at Los Alamos, where the bomb would actually be built, perhaps the most outstanding scientific talent in America. Jewish refugee physicists, among whom were several Nobel Prize winners, formed the core of that talent—Leo Szilard, Eugene Wigner, Enrico Fermi, Edward Teller, Victor Weisskopf, and Stanislaw Ulam. In the secret $60 million atomic bomb laboratory created in the isolated desert of New Mexico so many European Jews overflowed the mesa that "bad English" was the prevalent language.

For over two years, Oppenheimer struggled with the great task to produce the first atom bomb, and under his leadership a controlled nuclear reaction was achieved, and the technical difficulties of constructing the atom bomb were overcome.

At 5:30 A.M. on July 16, 1945, the skies over the desert lands of New Mexico were rent by a terrifying explosion. Its dazzling burst of light was brighter than any noonday sun; its heat melted the desert sands and rocks together. A great volcano of dust and debris churned from the desert and seethed high into the sky.

The series of scientific discoveries made both at the University of Chicago and at "Site Y" at Los Alamos underwent the test of fire—fire such as the world had never seen. The experimental bomb—perhaps the most important single experiment attempted by man—was a success. The key to release the almost limitless power within the atom had been found. Mankind had entered the age of atomic energy. It was to split history forever into the preatomic and atomic era.

The first bomb to be used in warfare was dropped on Hiroshima, Japan, on August 5, 1945. More than four square miles, or sixty percent of Hiroshima, was blown off the face of the earth. The Second World War ended.

By dropping the atomic bomb the United States spared a million Americans and Japanese from certain death had America been forced to invade Japan to end the war in the Pacific.

Following the use of the atomic bomb against Japan, Oppenheimer became one of the foremost proponents of civilian and international control of atomic energy. The success of the Los Alamos project filled him with despair. "In some crude sense," he said after the war, "which no vulgarity, no humor, no overstatement can quite extinguish, the physicists have known sin, and this is a knowledge which they cannot lose."

Named chairman of the General Advisory Committee of the Atomic Energy Commission, Oppenheimer continued to influence policy. He strongly opposed the development of the hydrogen bomb on "moral" grounds and became embroiled in the controversy with Edward Teller, father of the hydrogen bomb and its chief protagonist, and Lewis Strauss, chairman of the Atomic Energy Commission. This resulted in his suspension from the Atomic Energy Commission as a security risk. The case aroused wide controversy, with the right-wing press denouncing him as a villain and the liberal press calling him a martyr to the hysteria in the Cold War period and the Joseph McCarthy witch hunt.

Oppenheimer requested and received a secret hearing, which lasted from April 12 to May 6, 1954, during which time distinguished scientists and public officials testified on his behalf.

The issue was even dramatized on the stage.

Notwithstanding all this controversy, Oppenheimer was absolved of the charges and in 1963 was the recipient of one of the government's highest awards, the Fermi Award, for his contribution to nuclear research. On receiving the award, he said, "Most of us look to the good opinion of our colleagues, and our government. I am no exception."

President John Kennedy, aware of the callous injustice done to Oppenheimer by the previous administration, showed his disapproval of the treatment by inviting him to a White House dinner honoring American Nobel Prize winners.

Oppenheimer resumed his activities as director of the Institute of Advanced Studies at Princeton, a position he held until the time of his death in 1967.

Mankind was now faced with the greatest challenge of all time: Would we use this power to blast civilization from the Earth, or would we apply it usefully in all fields of endeavor in a world where each of us is the next-door neighbor to everyone else? Today, the world has good reason to hope that atomic energy will be a powerful weapon for good.

In 1954, it was a Jew, Hyman G. Rickover, head of the nuclear propulsion division of the United States Navy, who first turned atomic energy to nondestructive purposes with the construction of the world's first atomic-powered submarine. It will rank with the first steam engine, the first electric motor, Morse's first telegraph, and Edison's first electric lamp. Already diagnosis, prognosis, therapy, and surgery have begun to make use of radioactive isotopes, the peacetime components of the atom bomb. New materials by the score—metals, fabrics, wood, and glass—are being added to the hundreds of synthetics and plastics on the market.

V

In the Mainstream of American Life

THE FIRST NATIONAL SHRINE OF JUDAISM

1946

Roger Williams, founder of the colony of Rhode Island, believed in religious liberty. His own banishment from Puritan Massachusetts had convinced him that religious intolerance was a threat to civil peace and a barrier in the search for the truth. So he used his influence in Rhode Island to shape a new kind of civil government, one that assured freedom of religion and liberty of conscience.

Ships from Rhode Island's busy ports soon carried the glad tidings across the sea. Among those whose hopes were rekindled at this news were the Sephardim—Jew of Spain and Portugal. Some, called Marranos, had become Christian converts to escape persecution. Others had been driven from Spain and Portugal and now resided elsewhere in Europe, in South America, or the West Indies.

Rhode Island's first Jewish settlement was founded by a group of these Sephardim. They came to Newport as early as 1658. Soon they founded a congregation according to their Orthodox religious tradition.

For over one hundred years they had lived in freedom and tolerance and had worshiped God in their own fashion. The members of the Jewish community had prospered, and they decided to build a temple of praise to the Almighty. One of the finest architects of the day, Peter Harrison, was called in to design their synagogue.

In 1760, bricks were imported from abroad, and the erection of the building began. Finally, on December 2, 1763, the synagogue building of Congregation Jeshuat Israel (the Salvation of Israel) was dedicated. The Reverend Isaac Touro, who had studied at the rabbinical seminary of Amsterdam, was asked to be its first *hazzan*. He led the congregation until 1780. During the Revolutionary War, when the British occupied Newport, many of the Jewish residents left for other parts. Reverend Touro lived for some time in New York City and then left for Kingston, Jamaica, where he died in 1783 at the early age of forty-six.

Many members of the congregation took part in our nation's early struggles for liberty. They included soldiers, businessmen, shipping magnates, and financiers. When the two sons of the Reverend Isaac Touro, Abraham and Judah, who had amassed considerable fortunes as a result of their business enterprises, died, each left a liberal provision in their wills for the care and preservation of the Newport Synagogue, also known as the Touro Synagogue, where their father had ministered to the congregation.

During George Washington's visit to Newport in 1781, a town meeting was held in the synagogue. In 1790 Washington was the recipient of an address by Moses Seixas, warden of the synagogue. In reply, Washington sent the famous letter "To the Hebrew Congregation in Newport, R.I.," which since has become the classic expression of religious liberty in America. In this letter Washington wrote, "For happily the Government of the United States which gives to bigotry no sanction, to persecution no assistance, requires only that they who live under its protection should demean themselves as good citizens in giving it on all occasions their effectual support." The original letter is on exhibit in the B'nai B'rith Building in Washington, D.C. The words "to bigotry no sanction, to persecution no assistance," were not original with Washington. They were included in the letter that Moses Seixas addressed to him. But Washington was obviously so impressed by them, for they seemed to express very forcibly the ideals that he espoused for America, he incorporated them in his letter.

The Touro Synagogue building that houses the Jeshuat Israel Congregation in Newport is the oldest synagogue now standing in the United States. A splendid example of colonial architecture, it has been carefully preserved. Like a little treasure island among the colonial buildings that surround it, it still stands in perfect condition after 230 years. Its woodwork, in its original state, is hand carved. The masonic plan of the structure is similar to the famous Sephardic synagogue in Amsterdam erected in 1675. Twelve Ionic columns representing the twelve tribes of Israel, each made from a solid tree trunk, support the women's gallery. Above these rise twelve Corinthian columns supporting a domed ceiling. From the roof hang five massive bronze candelabra. Two were the gift of Jacob Rodriguez Rivera, given in the name of his son Abraham, and bear the date 1765. Another, dated 1760, was presented by Naphtali Hart Myers, and the fourth, the gift of Aaron Lopez, was made in 1770. The large candelabra before the altar bear an inscription that they were the gift of Jacob Pollack in 1769. The Ner Tamid (Eternal Light) is inscribed as the gift of Samuel Judah in the year 1765, and the beautiful brass candelabra on the rail before the Ark carry the inscription, "Enoch Lyon, 1766."

Among the silver ornaments for the decoration of the Torah scrolls are two sets of rimonim, which are the work of Myer Myers, the famous pre-revolutionary silver craftsman and artist.

Another striking feature of the synagogue is the underground passage that starts beneath the reading desk. At one time this tunnel supposedly had an exit to the street at the side of the synagogue. Some unromantic historians believe the tunnel was merely a storage area. Others say the passage was probably built because the early settlers wished to have a symbol by which they could remind their children of the persecution of their ancestors at the hands of the Inquisition in Spain and Portugal, when Jews worshiped in secret underground rooms. In fact, the tunnel may have been nothing more than a precaution—an unfinished channel of escape provided by men still haunted by the terror and persecution of the past, who felt safer with an escape route that might be used in the event sudden flight became necessary.

On March 5, 1946, the government of the United States, recognizing that Congregation Jeshuat Israel of Newport, the Touro Synagogue, had lived through the history of this country and survived as the oldest synagogue building in America, designated it a historic site, the first national shrine of Judaism in this country.

Although the National Park Service of the Department of the Interior aids in the caring for the synagogue, the ownership of the building remains with Congregation Shearith Israel of New York, guardian of the ancient structure and its burial grounds where so many of the ancestors of its early members had worshiped and were buried.

Though Touro Synagogue was occasionally used for worship or special services in the 1820s, it was not permanently reopened until 1883. By that time new immigrants from Central and Eastern Europe had again brought Jews to Newport.

In 1954 a Restoration Committee was formed by the Society of the Friends of Touro Synagogue to undertake the restoration, preservation, and the refurbishing of the historic edifice. On Hanukkah, December 15, 1963, two hundred years after it was erected, rededication exercises were held in the restored Touro Synagogue.

Today the Touro Synagogue continues to be used daily as a place of worship. Its spiritual leader for the past seven years is Rabbi Chaim Shapiro. Services reflect both the current Eastern European influence and the synagogue's Sephardic past and include some traditions of each.

Since its designation as a National Historic Site in 1946, the synagogue has been a magnet for dignitaries, historians, and authors. Thousands of visitors from all parts of the United States and many foreign countries have made pilgrimages to Newport to see this beautiful ediface that is the religious heritage of the Jews of America in colonial days. Individuals and groups of all faiths have been inspired and impressed by the simple yet majestic beauty of this historic house of God. Protestant ministers and Catholic priests, university students, Jewish and Christian children, and people from all walks of life have listened to the story of the historic background of Touro Synagogue by guides who are on hand to lead the synagogue tours.

For over two centuries, Congregation Jeshuat Israel, the Touro Synagogue, has testified that men may seek eternal truth in their own particular ways without hindrance from the civil government that embraces them all.

THE FIRST TO RECEIVE THE JEWISH WAR VETERANS ORDER OF MERIT AWARD

1947

The first Order of Merit Award ever given by the Jewish War Veterans of the United States was presented in 1947 to Bernard Mannes Baruch, America's "unofficial president" and oft-hailed "apostle of peace." Engraved on a bronze plaque, the order cited Baruch as an outstanding citizen and the "world's foremost humanitarian."

That this honor should be bestowed upon Baruch was not unusual. As one of the great financiers in this country and also as an adviser, confidante, consultant, and close friend of nine presidents of the United states throughout the regimes of Woodrow Wilson to Lyndon Johnson, his unselfish deeds made him a living American legend. During America's two World Wars and the Korean Conflict, he was the one individual—though not an official of any government agency—called upon to help solve a nation's crisis. When peacetime problems supplemented those of war, President Truman summoned Baruch to help work out a way of life for the American people. Hailed as America's "elder statesman," he was an individual whose advice was eagerly sought by all the Washington agencies, cabinet officials, congressional leaders, and the people at large.

Adviser to the mighty and friend to the little man, Bernard Baruch, the second of the four sons of Dr. Simon and Belle Wolfe Baruch, was born in Camden, South Carolina, on August 19, 1870. On his mother's side there were seven generations of American Jews of Spanish ancestors so that he was a lineal descendant of Sephardim. His renowned father, who served in the Confederate Army as a surgeon for three years, was a German Jew, partly of Polish descent, who emigrated from his native Posen, Prussia, to America in 1855.

When, in 1881, Bernard was eleven years old, his father decided to move with his family from Camden to New York City. Soon after his arrival, Dr. Baruch was appointed first chairman of the Medical Board of Montefiore Hospital in the Bronx and became one of the most important medical men in the city. To Dr. Simon Baruch goes the credit for first diagnosing and successfully operating on a patient with a perforated appendix and for the development of surgical techniques in appendectomy. He was also a pioneer exponent of hydrotherapy in the United States. The two books he wrote on the subject became medical classics. *Uses of Water in Modern Medicine* was published in 1892 and *Principles and Practices of Hydrotherapy* in 1898. It was due to his efforts that free municipal baths were established, first in Chicago, then in New York, and later in more than one hundred other cities.

Bernard Baruch was sent to the College of the City of New York, from which he was graduated in 1889 and which in later years was renamed the Baruch College of Business and Public Administration. Today it is the nation's largest business school—private or public.

Baruch's father wanted him to become a doctor like himself, but the young man at first decided on the Army as a career. Although he passed the entrance examinations to West Point, an accident that left him deaf in one ear disqualified him from military life. Instead, following graduation from college, he entered the Wall Street brokerage firm of A. A. Hausman as a clerk for three dollars a week. With his modest earnings in addition to six hundred dollars borrowed from his mother, he began to buy and sell stocks. By 1896 he was made a partner in the firm and for a number of years following was a highly successful member of the New York Stock Exchange.

Bernard Baruch became a lifelong member of New York City's Reform Temple Shaarey Tefila and always spent Yom Kippur there in fast and prayer. On one such Day of Atonement, when he was in the synagogue for the entire day, an aide rushed in and whispered to him that there was a crisis in the stock market and that he should come at once and decide what steps to take. Baruch refused to budge. He said he could not desecrate the holiest day of the Jewish year. As things turned out, because he had not taken any action in the market on Yom Kippur, Baruch discovered to his amazement that his fortune had increased considerably.

Some of Baruch's business associates, respecting his judgment, persuaded him to investigate conditions for them in the West; and while on a trip there, he bought the Liggett and Myers Tobacco Company outright. At the age of thirty-two, he became known as America's most fascinating financier. By means of his financial wizardry and careful market research into raw materials such as gold, copper, rubber, and sulfur, Baruch had amassed a fortune of over $3 million.

His chance to serve the government first came when, as an advocate of economic as well as military preparedness, he was appointed by President Wilson to the Advisory Committee of National Defense in 1916. This in turn led to his role as chairman of the War Industries Board, with power to virtually mobilize the American wartime economy. The most powerful of all government agencies, this board had full command over American production and had the authority to decide what materials manufacturers were to save for the war effort and the quantity they could produce.

As chairman, Baruch devoted his energies to this job sixteen hours a day. He managed to get materials needed for the war effort just in time and arranged for the production of TNT even before the Army understood its importance in warfare. Always economizing, he bought nitrogen from Chile at half the market price, iron from Sweden, and pack mules from

Spain. It was his know-how in this capacity that enabled America to defeat Kaiser Wilhelm.

When the War Board was dissolved after the Armistice, Baruch was selected by Wilson to serve on the Supreme Economic Council at the peace conference in Versailles, where he also made important contributions. For his public service, for which he never accepted any payment, President Wilson awarded him the Distinguished Service Medal.

After World War I, Baruch advised Presidents Harding and Hoover on economic problems. As adviser to President Roosevelt, he helped plan much of the New Deal legislation and the formulation of the National Recovery Act of 1933.

During World War II, whether it was the broad problems of defense, the rubber shortage, the manpower squeeze, lagging airplane production, or factory reconversion, Presidents Roosevelt and Truman summoned this man of many facets to devise escape from the bewildering tangles.

In 1946, upon reaching the three score and ten mark, for nine long months Bernard Baruch began the most important job of his career. As United States representative to the Atomic Energy Commission of the United Nations, Baruch grappled with the most dreaded and mightiest force man had ever unleashed: atomic power. He was the author of the first official United States policy on international control of atomic energy, which he proposed in a speech on June 14, 1946, before the United Nations. His plan called for the creation of an International Atomic Development Authority empowered to universally control all dangerous uses of atomic energy.

The Wall Street wizard who made, lost, and remade several fortunes gave away over $3 million to charity.

In 1944 he created the Baruch Committee on Physical Medicine honoring his father, Dr. Simon Baruch. The work of this committee, which functioned until 1949, laid the basis for modern concepts of physical medicine and rehabilitation. In 1948 the specialty was formally recognized by the creation of the American Board of Physical Medicine and Rehabilitation.

Baruch subsidized many research projects, including a study of the causes of war. The other projects he espoused had far-reaching programs for education and social amelioration such as the Williamstown Institute of Politics.

Many honors piled up. France, Belgium, and Italy decorated him. Seven universities bestowed their honorary doctorates on him. Groups of all sorts tripped over each other trying to do him honor.

On August 19, 1960, in Washington, D.C.'s Lafayette Park—the leafy square across the street from the White House—there was dedicated a "Bernard Baruch Bench of Inspiration." It marked the ninetieth birthday of the park-bench statesman. For many years, it had been a common sight to see him conferring there with top officials, discussing affairs of government, and with bestarred generals, foreign ambassadors, and the "Who's Who" of the world. He had a park-bench "office" in New York City's Central Park, too.

He died on June 20, 1965, a few months before he was to have celebrated his ninety-fifth birthday. To the end of his days, he continued to write letters to newspapers and made his views known on many topics, which he believed to be for the good of the people. Baruch felt that the greatest contributing factor to the increased lifespan of the average American today was "private enterprise."

The subject of several full-length biographies, Baruch wrote his autobiography, *My Own Story* (1957), and its sequel, *The Public Years* (1960), which recounts his public service for four decades. Looking back at his experiences, Baruch interweaves his philosophy of government, service, and values.

Although he was a synagogue member and worshiper all his life, the public record of Baruch's legendary career reveals only a few instances of his direct involvement in Jewish affairs. In 1919 he intervened with a Polish statesman on behalf of suffering Jews in that country, and in 1946 he delivered an address at a dinner of the United Jewish Appeal in New York City.

Baruch did not agree with the Zionist program of rebuilding the Jewish homeland in Palestine for the stateless and persecuted Jews of seventy lands. Instead, he thought that refuge could be found for them and for all victims of persecution in Uganda and advocated a "United States of Africa." His brother, Herman, served as American ambassador to Portugal and the Netherlands.

THE FIRST AMERICAN JEW TO GIVE HIS LIFE FOR THE STATE OF ISRAEL

1948

At four o'clock on the afternoon of May 14, 1948, David Ben-Gurion read to a small audience in the Museum of Art in Tel Aviv: "We . . . hereby proclaim the establishment of the Jewish state in Palestine to be called Israel."

In the proclamation of Israel's independence, the country was described as the

land where the Jewish people came into being. In this land was shaped their spiritual, religious, and national character. Here they created a culture of national and universal import and gave to the world the eternal Book of Books. . . . The State of Israel will be open to Jewish immigration and the ingathering of the exiles.

After centuries of persecution and wandering, after inhuman suffering and superhuman sacrifice, the ancient hope was fulfilled. A people breathed the air of a free land, a land where it could be itself once more. Dr. Chaim Weizmann, world-famous chemist and early Zionist leader who was instrumental in the issuance of the Balfour Declaration, was named Israel's first president.

It is a strange thing. Many years before, the leaders of the American Revolution proclaimed the doctrine: "Resistance to tyrants is obedience to God" (Book of Maccabees). These founding fathers of America found inspiration in the Bible story of the Jews in ancient Palestine. In our own day the Jews of Palestine found inspiration for their struggle for independence in the story of the founding of America and the fight necessary to obtain its liberty. In Palestine, Jews showed they were willing to give of "their lives, fortunes, and sacred honor," as our own Declaration of Independence puts it.

American Jews who had just taken off their uniforms following World War II could not stand idly by. They could not read of the suffering of Jews in the concentration camps or of a tyranny whose word could not be trusted from day to day. They had not fought a war for such a solution.

Dov Seligman of the Bronx, New York, was one of the many Americans who went from uniform to uniform. The war was somehow not to be counted finished unless the last concentration camp inmate was provided with an address. In January 1942, Dov, a two-hundred-pound six footer, had enlisted in the United States Army. In 1944 he was sent to the Pacific Theater as a sergeant in the ground crew of an air transport command. In 1946 he was mustered out and promptly transferred to Palestine in a settlement owned and operated by Shomer Hatzir, a Zionist youth organization. Early in 1948, while driving a tractor on a collective settlement, he was ambushed by Arabs and killed. This announcement followed by two days the disclosure that another American, Moshe Pearlstein, a Brooklyn youth, had been slain by Arabs in the Holy Land while leading a food convoy to a settlement of Hapoel Hamizrachi, the Religious Zionists.

October 10, 1948, was set aside to honor another fallen American hero who fought and died in Israel's War of Independence. It was called "Colonel Marcus Day" in memory of Colonel David "Mickey" Marcus, a veteran of World War II, who was killed on June 11, 1948, while leading Israeli troops near Jerusalem. In an almost incredible confluence of ironic circumstances, like Stonewall Jackson of American Civil War fame, Mickey Marcus was accidentally shot down by one of his own men.

Marcus had devoted to Israel less than half a year of an action-filled life that was snuffed out so haphazardly at the age of forty-seven. His teachings and example continued their impact through the later, brilliant stages of the Israeli Independence War and even at Sinai eight years later.

David "Mickey" Marcus, the son of Romanian Jewish immigrants, was born in Brooklyn, New York, on Washington's Birthday in 1901. A fine student and athlete in high school, Mickey graduated from West Point in 1924 but resigned from the Army after two years to study law. He was at various times intercollegiate welter-weight champion, Commissioner of Corrections under Mayor Fiorello La Guardia, commander of the Ranger's Training School in Hawaii, volunteer paratrooper in Normandy, and Pentagon legal adviser to two presidents.

When World War II erupted in 1941, Marcus went back to the Army as a lieutenant colonel and served in the Pacific on the staff of General George C. Marshall. Appointed a divisional judge advocate and later division commander, he attended meetings of the "Big Five" in 1943. He accompanied President Franklin D. Roosevelt to Yalta and Teheran and later went to Potsdam on the staff of President Harry Truman. When the Allies decided to invade Normandy, Marcus volunteered to join the D-Day airborne assault. With no previous training, he joined the paratroopers and parachuted into Normandy.

In the closing weeks of the war, he helped draw up the surrender documents for Italy and Germany. He outlined the program of military government for the occupied areas, and was with the American column that first liberated the Dachau death camp. By V-E Day, Marcus was promoted to the rank of full colonel.

His ten military decorations included the Distinguished Service Cross and the Bronze Star, both for gallantry in action and British decorations.

The crowning point of his career came in Palestine. Shortly after his return to civilian life in 1947, the Jewish Agency sought his help and smuggled him into Palestine. From the moment of his arrival there on February 2, 1948, serving as Ben-Gurion's military adviser under the name of Mickey Stone, he immediately perceived the special spirit and condition of the Haganah, the Israeli Army, which was emerging from the underground.

In a few short weeks, Mickey Marcus had written out in longhand the four-hundred-page Military Manual that became the basis of officer's training in Israel. It was translated into Hebrew and became the first military manual ever to be published in the Hebrew language. He set up officer's training schools, advised the Haganah on the purchase and use of military equipment, and helped to develop a fighting spirit within the Army. He had a major hand in planning three offensives against Jordanian-held Latrun, the key to Jerusalem.

A measure of Israel's esteem for him was that in their time of greatest peril, soon after the State of Israel was proclaimed on May 14, 1948, they entrusted this foreigner the unifying supreme command over all of the elements on their central front. With it they designated Marcus the first *aluf*, or brigadier general, in modern times. He was the first to hold such rank in Israel's modern army, and the first in the Holy Land since the time of Judah Maccabee in 167 B.C.E.

It was as an *aluf* that Marcus was appointed commander of the Jerusalem front, one of the most crucial areas of the fighting that erupted between Arabs and Jews in May and June 1948.

Between the memorable battles against the Arab Legion at Latrun, Colonel Marcus constructed the Israeli "Burma Road," the incredible cliff-hurdling highway that decisively shattered the enemy stranglehold on Jerusalem.

On June 11, 1948, just a few hours before the first Arab-Israeli ceasefire became effective, he was accidentally shot and killed by an Israeli sentry while making an inspection round in the dark outside the perimeter fence of his military headquarters. Of this tragic event, Ben-Gurion proclaimed, "We lost the best man we had."

Colonel David Marcus had fallen within a hundred feet of the spot where many centuries before the immortal warrior-king for whom he was named had danced and sung in praise of the Lord.

The perfect accolade for this hero came from President Harry Truman, who wrote that the life and death of Colonel Marcus "symbolizes all that is best in the unending struggle for liberty."

Colonel Marcus is the only American killed fighting under a flag other than the Stars and Stripes who is buried in the venerable cemetery of the United States Military Academy at West Point. His epitaph reads: "Colonel David Marcus – A Soldier for All Humanity."

In 1962 Doubleday and Company published *Cast A Giant Shadow* by Ted Berkman, a biography of Colonel David Marcus, the American war hero who, as Supreme Commander of Haganah, broke the Arab siege and saved Jerusalem. This book was the basis of a film of the same name, starring Kirk Douglas as Marcus.

Mishmar David, a housing development for Israeli Army veterans, was named after him.

THE FIRST JEWISH STAR OF TELEVISION

1948

Having distinguished themselves on the American stage, in motion pictures, and on radio, it was only natural for gifted Jewish entertainers to make their mark in the world of television. That they did so with astounding success is apparent by the merest glance at the listing of television programs in daily newspapers and in *TV Guide*.

When in June 1948 Texaco announced its first Television Star Theater, Milton Berle was just one of a number of masters of ceremonies originally planned for the show. But within three weeks it was not a variety hour; it was the Milton Berle Show. Eight out of ten homes usually tuned him in. The magazine *Variety* indisputably dubbed Berle "Mr. Television of 1949."

Milton Berle was born Milton Berliner on July 12, 1908, in a five-flight walk-up at 68 West 118th Street in New York City, the next to the last of five children. His father, Moses Berliner, was a housepainter, salesman, and nightwatchman, who moved from job to job, with the ever-elusive goal of setting up his own business. Milton was raised in Harlem—in those days an Italian, Jewish, and Irish as well as black community for the working class and small tradespeople.

Milton had his Bar Mitzvah (confirmation) at the Mount Zion Temple on West 118th Street, where just down the block among his neighbors were Cantor Yosele Rosenblatt, the world-famous *hazzan*, and the comic George Jessel.

Although Harlem, with its tree-lined streets and sturdily built apartment houses, was regarded a better community than the teeming ghetto of the Lower East Side, it was still viewed with disdain by the affluent residents of Morningside Heights. Berle recounts in his autobiography that he remembers trips taken as a child to the Imperial Nickelodeon at 117th Street and Lenox Avenue with his three brothers. They carried their money tied into the corner of a handkerchief. Admission was a nickel— and patrons got a rebate ticket good for a penny's worth of candy inside.

When Milton was five, his mother entered him in a Charlie Chaplin look-alike contest. She siezed upon his natural stage talent as the economic salvation of the family. He won—and so began his career. His mother, who called herself Sandra, was the archetypal stage mother: laughing and clapping loudly on cue, thrusting her son into the limelight at every occasion—haunting the theatrical agencies and silent film studios with a reluctant tyke in firm tow.

Milton's first job was as Buster Brown—which meant a Dutch-boy haircut that made him an object of ridicule on the block. He would set out with his mother at the crack of dawn for the Fort Lee Ferry at 125th Street to go to the Pathé Film Studio in then-rural New Jersey.

Milton played dozens of children's parts in the silent movies. His mother guided, pushed, and steered the boy onto the stage—but his own natural enthusiasm grew. He practiced by putting on shows in tenement back yards for his pals. Charging a penny admission, he'd tell jokes and sing songs. Kiddie song-and-dance acts were a big thing in vaudeville, and young Milton won a place in E. W. Wolf's troupe, wearing a knickerbocker tuxedo and singing "Take Me to the Land of Jazz."

Berle soon played vaudeville houses all over the United States and Canada, escorted by his mother, living in boardinghouses, and taking his schooling on the run. In Manhattan he played in houses up and down the West Side: the Colosium Theater at 181st Street and Broadway, the Regent at 116th and Seventh Avenue, and the Century at 61st and Central Park West (where he played his first role in musical comedy). He would ride the Broadway trolley to rehearsals every day.

In the late 1920s, after an appearance on national radio, Milton was ready for his own one-man act, "Milton Berle—The Wayward Youth." His first booking was at B. F. Keith's Riverside Theater at 96th Street and Broadway. He was the youngest MC ever to work there.

He entertained troops in World War I. Slowly his fame as a jokster grew. In 1936 he was headlining on Broadway. He became a performer in many legitimate theatrical productions including *Life Begins at 8:40*, a ninety-seven-week run in the Ziegfeld Follies; *See My Lawyer*, his first dramatic endeavor; and more. Then followed radio programs for CBS and NBC. He made movies such as *Tall Dark and Handsome* and *Sun Valley Serenade*. One of the first to realize the effectiveness of sight gags, he took childlike and disarming glee in dressing up. He appeared as Superman, L'il Abner, a cowboy, an Easter bunny, and even as a four-year-old. Then along came television and the Texaco Star Theater.

Berle was originally only one of several Texaco hosts but quickly made the show his personal showcase. When he started only five hundred thousand television sets had been sold in the entire country. By mid-season, the number of sets in use had doubled, with more than eighty percent of them tuned every Tuesday night at 8:00 P.M. to the madcap Berle. Apartment parties would be held to watch him prance about. Soon he was attracting every name guest in the business from Harpo Marx to the new act of Dean Martin and Jerry Lewis.

Berle was television's first astounding phenomenon, working seven days a week as producer, director, and co-writer of the show. Parents became concerned about the new disruption in family life, so the star assumed the reassuring role of Uncle Miltie, telling children to go to bed right after the show.

By 1952 Mr. Television was discovering that he was not alone anymore. His competition ranged directly from Bishop Fulton J. Sheen's weekly homilies to, elsewhere on the schedule, new variety hits like "Your Show of Shows." The format of the Berle show switched from broad vaudeville to sketch comedy, foreshadowing today's sitcom. The star became less frantic, and his ratings climbed back into the top ten, just below "I Love Lucy." In 1955, however, buffeted by the new popularity of westerns, he ended the show's run, although he retained a lucrative contract with NBC.

Despite Berle's failure to make a comeback on television, his seven-year run as "Mr. Tuesday Night" from 1948 to 1955 marked him as possibly the most powerful influence on the new medium. He would continue to have a substantial career on television, including appearances on the *Kraft Music Hall*, and in movies like *It's a Mad, Mad, Mad, Mad World*. He would win many awards and honors. But the highlight of his eighty-year show business run will always remain those astonishing, trail-blazing years in early television.

On March 26, 1978, NBC honored him with a special, "A Tribute to Mr. Television." *TV Guide* (March 31, 1978) summed him up succinctly in its listings the week of the show: "What Henry Ford did for the automobile, Milton Berle did for television."

Berle has always given of his time and energy to help others. One day he sat down with a dozen telephones, hundreds of assistants, and a determination to raise a million dollars for the Daymon Runyon Cancer Fund. When he signed off the air he had received pledges for $1,040,616. He aided the United Jewish Appeal of New York with a similar marathon performance on television. As master of ceremonies, he introduced dozens of stars and spoke by telephone to thousands of Americans who called to pledge contributions. He also helped the March of Dimes and B'nai B'rith.

When the Citation for Service of B'nai B'rith for advancing worthy causes was given to Milton Berle in 1950, Frank Goldman, the organization's president, called the entertainer "a faithful worker in the field of human relations who has contributed to causes without regard to race, color, or creed."

On June 24, 1994, the eighty-five-year-old Berle joined a host of famed female impersonators at New York City's Town Hall for "Charles Busch's Dressing Up," a giant festival. He was the one in heels.

THE FIRST WOMAN RABBI

1950

The list of women who have made contributions to the development of the Jewish people and to the cause of humanity is a long and glorious one. In secular life they have distinguished themselves in art, literature, music, acting, painting, and science and have entered the medical, legal, and teaching professions.

With one exception in Great Britain, where for a period of nineteen years from 1899 to 1919 Mrs. Lilian Helen Montague of London had been acting as spiritual leader of a Reform Jewish congregation, an exceptional history-making event in the practice of Judaism occurred in the United States in 1950 with the appointment of a woman to serve as spiritual leader of a Jewish congregation.

The woman was Mrs. Paula Ackerman, widow of Rabbi William Ackerman of Temple Beth Israel of Meridian, Mississippi. Although Mrs. Ackerman lacked official ordination from a recognized rabbinical school, a requisite of Orthodox, Conservative, and Reform Judaism for men, her succession to the post of her husband was made possible by a ruling in Reform Judaism. She had the full powers of a rabbi, and the State of Mississippi gave her permission to perform marriages.

At the time of her appointment Mrs. Ackerman was fifty-seven years old and had a lifetime of experience as a rabbi's wife in attending to the affairs of a congregation. As such she was a preacher, psychologist, teacher, and manager. Her appointment was unique and opened a new channel of special appeal to spiritual women whose preachments to that date had been limited to families and friends.

Throughout the ages Jewish women had manifested more than their share of humanitarianism and scholarship. Prior to Mrs. Ackerman's appointment, Helen Levinthal Lyons had the distinction of being the first woman to have graduated from a recognized rabbinical school, the Jewish Institute of Religion, founded by Rabbi Stephen S. Wise, now known as the Hebrew Union College-Jewish Institute of Religion. Although she successfully completed the regular course of study prescribed by the rabbinate in 1940, ordination was not conferred upon her because of her sex. She was the descendant of many generations of illustrious rabbis, including her father, Dr. Israel H. Levinthal, rabbi of the Brooklyn Jewish Center, and her grandfather Rabbi Bernard L. Levinthal of Philadelphia, one of the founders and first president of the Union of Orthodox Rabbis of the United States.

Following Helen Levinthal Lyons, the nearest to a woman rabbi in America for many years was Dr. Trude Weiss-Rosmarin, an author, editor and lecturer on numerous Jewish subjects. Born in Germany in 1908, she emigrated to the United States in 1931. Trained as a scholar in the Judaic field, she directed the School for Jewish Women in New York City, taught Jewish history at New York University, and edited the monthly journal *The Jewish Spectator.* Though she was without a pulpit or congregation, she was a prototype of the new breed of women now engaged in serious Jewish study, in research, in teaching, and in the rabbinate in the United States.

The problem of ordaining Jewish women as rabbis became actual in 1922, inasmuch as the nineteenth amendment to the Constitution, granting the vote to women, had been adopted in 1920. The question was raised in Reform groups: Could Jews be more conservative than the United States government and deny equality to women? The issue was exacerbated by the fact that Martha Newmark (later Mrs. Henry Montor) was studying at the Hebrew Union College and would soon be ready for ordination. Confronting this problem in 1921 and 1922, the college faculty and the Central Conference of American Rabbis (the Reform group) reluctantly decided that "women cannot be denied the privilege of ordination." The final ruling, however, rested with the board of directors of the college, which in 1922 limited ordination to males. Martha Montor stayed on until 1925, when she left the school. Her class was to graduate in 1926. In 1972, fifty years later, after the faculty and the Central Conference of Reform Rabbis agreed to accept women in the rabbinate, Sally Priesand (age twenty-five) was ordained a rabbi. Shortly thereafter in the same year, she began her work as an assistant rabbi of New York City's Reform Stephen S. Wise Free Synagogue and then as an associate rabbi there. She thus became the first female rabbi in the United States. She was also the first woman to become the head rabbi of a congregation, having eventually secured a modest congregation in Tinton Falls, New Jersey. When asked why she wanted to become a rabbi, she answered:

> I believe basically in four things—in God, in the worth of the individual, in Judaism as a way of life, and that Judaism is worth preserving for the future. Being a rabbi, in my opinion, is the best way that I can perpetuate these beliefs.

By 1982, some fifty women rabbis were being graduated by the Hebrew Union College and by Philadelphia's small Reconstructionist Rabbinical College, and almost one third of those institutions' current student bodies are women.

Today, most of the 221 female Reform rabbis and fifty-five female Reconstructionist rabbis say that they are accepted as rabbis, not as "women" rabbis.

Progress was rather slower within the Conservative movement. Indeed, over the years, increasing numbers of Conservative synagogue boards of directors already had countenanced women's participation in *minyans* (the minimum of ten required for communal prayers) and in Sabbath Torah readings. In 1973 the Rabbinical Assembly, the organization, at that time, of one thousand Conservative rabbis around the world, lent the practice its "official" endorsement. Yet four more years passed without movement on the issue of ordination. In the interval, Jewish women's *havurot* (study groups) were formed to exert pressure on the assembly. The liberalized practices of individual Conservative synagogues also made their impact. In 1978, the assembly petitioned the Jewish Theological Seminary to study the ordination issue. The school's chancellor, Dr. Gershon Cohen, responded affirmatively. He appointed a faculty committee, which then conducted a nationwide poll of individual congregations. Two more years passed before the committee members issued their report. The document was favorable.

In 1983 the faculty voted to accept women into the regular ordination program. A year after that, Amy Elberg became the first woman to receive ordination at the Jewish Theological Seminary of America and was the first woman to serve as a rabbi in the Conservative movement.

The admission of Rabbi Elberg followed a change in the organization's constitution that was passed by a vote of 636 to 267. "The vote," said Rabbi Alexander M. Shapiro, who was president at that time of the Rabbinical Assembly and who was a leader of the successful effort to ordain women, "demonstrates that we accept the notion that all human beings are created in the image of God and have an equal right to preach and teach the word of God."

The great majority of Conservative rabbis and lay people accepted the change calmly. By the end of the decade, a fifth of the Seminary's student body were women, a dozen had been graduated, and half had secured employment in established congregations, although usually as assistant or associate rabbis.

Over seventy-two women have been ordained as Conservative rabbis in the twelve years since the historic decision to admit women to the Rabbinical School of the Jewish Theological Seminary of America.

Rabbi Shohama Wiener became the first woman to head a rabbinical seminary after her inauguration on November 20, 1994, as president of the Academy for Jewish Religion in New York City. The academy is the only seminary in the United States whose mission is to prepare men and women to serve as spiritual leaders committed to pluralism within Judaism. Rabbi Wiener had served as an executive dean and spiritual director of the academy for seven years before the board of trustees unanimously chose her to be the president.

Rabbi Wiener was ordained at the Academy for Jewish Religion, which combines Jewish scholarship with exploration of a wide range of Jewish religious and spiritual practices. She also earned a Doctor of Ministry degree from the New York Theological Seminary.

While the Reform, Conservative, and Reconstructionist movements ordain women, the Orthodox do not.

THE FIRST JEWISH WOMAN TO OCCUPY A HIGH FEDERAL POST

1950

American Jews have recognized that equality of all citizens under the American Constitution imposes civic duties and responsibilities. They have taken part in municipal, state, and national affairs. They have been elected and reelected—often for decades—as mayors, aldermen, city council members, congressmen, state and federal senators, and judges of municipal, county, and district courts. Jewish women, too, have made their way into politics, and many municipal, state, and federal offices, both elective and appointive, are held by them.

On November 15, 1950, for the first time in American history, a Jewish woman, Anna Lederer Rosenberg, was appointed to the high federal office of assistant secretary of defense. Her task was to direct the Defense Department's manpower, which hitherto had been divided among many different agencies. Known widely for her skill in dealing with troubled labor conditions, Mrs. Rosenberg—who was summoned at the request of Secretary of Defense George C. Marshall—presided firmly if not placidly in what was probably the most important public task ever entrusted to a woman.

"Aunt Anna," as she was affectionately called in Pentagon circles, knew her business and learned from experience with life and practical affairs.

Anna Rosenberg was born in Budapest, Hungary, in 1902 to Charlotte and Albert Lederer. Her mother was a talented author and illustrator of children's books; her father was a successful furniture manufacturer. When, in 1912, a large order for furniture was canceled and her father lost his business, the family emigrated to the United States and settled in the Bronx, New York.

The day that she entered high school, Anna became involved in social and economic issues. As a junior in Wadleigh High School for Girls in New York City, at the outbreak of World War I, she took a personal interest in the fight against Prussian militarism. She served as a volunteer at the debarkation hospital in Manhattan and sold Thrift Stamps and Liberty Bonds for the war effort. One week her street corner sales totaled $2,580 for Thrift Stamps and $5,700 for Bonds. It was here, too, that she settled her first strike. When two thousand students went out on strike against military drilling during hours they considered undesirable, she called a meeting and talked the strikers into cooperating with school authorities.

A wife at eighteen (she married Julius Rosenberg, an infantry veteran who had just returned from the war), a mother at twenty, the little girl who left Budapest at ten found herself running a successful business as a labor consultant when she was only twenty-three.

Anna Rosenberg became involved in politics in the early 1920s. As a suffragette, she astounded Tammany Hall by the results she obtained from a visit to "Old Jim" Hagan, a typical Tammany boss. Anna asked Hagan's support of votes for women. Hagan ignored her. "With that attitude," she exploded, "it's no wonder you can't carry your district." Hagan answered the young suffragette by making her his protege. She learned the political ropes and soon gained enough prestige with Hagan to manage his son's campaign for election. Young Hagan was elected.

Becoming active in Manhattan's Seventh Assembly District Democratic Party organization, she was drawn into the Democratic circle that included Franklin Delano Roosevelt.

By the late 1920s, Anna Rosenberg was reputedly the busiest woman in New York, so successful in her work as a labor consultant and public relations counsel that her income was over $60,000 a year. Not only were her services sought by the largest business firms in the country, city and state officials consulted her about their problems. As time passed, she took on more and more work for government bodies. She served in consultative and administrative posts in manpower and labor relations for three Democratic presidents, several New York State governors, and several New York City mayors. Roosevelt, then governor of New York, first called on her for consultation in 1928. Her first appointment to a federal post was in the National Recovery Administration in 1934; in 1935 she became regional director. In 1938, President Roosevelt sent her abroad to study industrial relations for him. In 1944 he sent her to Europe as his personal observer, and a year later she went again to help President Truman untangle the great problems of repatriation and demobilization of our troops there.

She served on many committees and boards during World War II. She was the director of the Office of Defense and regional director of Health and Welfare Services. She was a member of the New York City and New York State war councils and held the secretaryship of the president's Combined War Labor Board.

Meanwhile, she served as the only woman regional director of the War Manpower Commission. And her services to the United States were finally capped in 1950 when she was brought to Washington to serve in her new post during the Korean War. As assistant secretary of defense from 1950 to 1953, she worked with Secretary George C. Marshall on a draft for the Senate Armed Services Committee that became known as the Universal Military Service and Training Bill, which attempted to allocate manpower equally between defense, farm, and military. Its chief provision, accepted by Congress, was the induction of eighteen-year-olds—an age group, Anna Rosenberg argued, whose induction would dislocate the economy at the least cost to the government for dependents. In her new post, she became the adviser of generals and the boss of millions of soldiers.

Mrs. Rosenberg personified what used to be called the American ideal. A self-made woman, foreign born, who was driven from Hungary at the age of ten, she carved out for herself such a position that large corporations paid huge sums for her advice and city and state officials consulted her about their problems. When she was attacked by anti-Semitic forces and the baselessness of the attacks was exposed, the small, hardworking, dynamic Jewish woman of the Pentagon was vindicated and applauded as was her due. With a quiet and great devotion to her work, she brought order out of chaos. She succeeded where stiff-necked generals failed.

For her outstanding services, Anna Rosenberg was awarded the Medal of Freedom in 1945 and the United States Medal of Merit in 1947, the first woman in history to be so honored.

After 1953, when she left the defense establishment, Anna Rosenberg served on New York State and New York City consultative bodies, including the 1966 Temporary Schwulst Committee on City Finances, which suggested a city income tax; the nonpartisan Urban Action Center, beginning in 1967; and on many Democratic fund-raising efforts. In 1968, President Lyndon Johnson appointed her to serve on the Commission on Income Maintenance, which examined all welfare and income-support programs.

Through the years as a public relations consultant, she worked closely with agencies that raised funds for Palestine (later Israel) and for the Joint Distribution Committee and the New York Federation of Jewish Philanthropies.

Her second husband was Paul G. Hoffman, industrialist and United Nations development-program administrator.

Anna Rosenberg Hoffman died on May 9, 1986, at the age of eighty-one. Leading American figures and the public at large voiced their admiration of the woman whose contributions to her adopted country had been unique and who held the highest position ever filled by a woman in the American federal and military establishment up to that time.

THE FIRST AMERICAN ACTOR AWARDED A DOCTORATE DEGREE

1951

Eddie Cantor, the banjo-eyed vaudevillian whose dancing feet and double takes brought him stardom in movies, radio, and television, was awarded an honorary Doctor of Humane Letters degree by Temple University on June 14, 1951—the first actor in America to rate the degree.

His citation appropriately read:

A great American, endowed with personal ideals and generosity of spirit, whose innate talents as an entertainer have made him a national institution . . . His great use of his life is to spend it for something that outlasts life itself, for his humane activities in bringing pleasure to mankind do not end at the footlights nor before the cameras.

For his humanitarian work he was also cited by the Congress of the United States.

No one could have achieved fame by his own efforts with fewer advantages than this entertainer.

Eddie Cantor was born in a crowded tenement flat over a Russian tea room on Eldridge Street in New York's Lower East Side on January 31, 1892. His real name was Isidor Iskowitch, and his parents were impoverished young Russian-Jewish immigrants. He really never knew them since his mother died in childbirth when he was a year old and his father, an unemployed violinist, perished of pneumonia a year later.

The orphan was brought up by his grandmother Esther, a widow who supported herself and the baby by peddling. She lived to see her grandson become a star, and he always revered her.

Cantor grew up a tough, unambitious youngster in the dirty ghetto. A poor scholar, he quit school without finishing it. His sole talent seemed to be for giving comic impersonations of the day. Ashamed to impose on his grandmother, Eddie left home for weeks, leaving one job after another.

Early in 1907 he and a friend managed to work for one week as a song-and-dance team at the Clinton Music Hall in their neighborhood. The next year, accepting a dare from taunting friends, Eddie Cantor, as he now called himself for "stage" purposes, entered the weekly amateur contest at Miner's Theater on Broadway.

Even at the age of sixteen, his native-born talent asserted itself. He won first prize of $5. On the strength of that triumph, Cantor got a job as a blackface comedian with a touring burlesque show, but it soon stranded him in Shenendoah, Pennsylvania. His grandmother came to the rescue again.

Back in New York, Cantor found his mark as a singing waiter in Carey Walsh's saloon in Coney Island, where the piano player was a clever tunesmith named Jimmy Durante.

Attracted to the theater, Cantor joined the fabulous Gus Edwards "Kid Cabaret" in 1912, along with George Jessel and Walter Winchell, who was then a dancer. A good part of his musical-comedy act followed, as did an offer from the legendary Florenz Ziegfeld to appear as the star in *Midnight Follies*. It was during this early part of his career that he married Ida.

Soon came *Broadway Brevities* (1920), *Make It Snappy* (1922), and stardom in *Kid Boots* (1923), which ran for three years. Reaching the top, he made many movies, including such hits as *Whoopee* (1928), *The Kid From Spain* (1933), *Roman Scandals* (1934), *Strike Me Pink* (1936), and *Ali Baba Goes to Town* (1937). All these musical comedies were under the aegis of Samuel

Goldwyn, who surrounded Cantor with dozens of beautiful Goldwyn girls who filled in the background for his antics.

In 1931 Cantor entered radio work and devoted more and more time to it as the medium developed through the next two decades. He became one of the greatest stars of radio. Besides entertaining millions, he introduced such headliners as Deanna Durbin, Dinah Shore, George Burns and Gracie Allen, and Eddie Fisher.

After television attracted major sponsors, he began appearing on a monthly show. Radio had consumed most of his time in this period, although he made a few films. The last one was *If You Knew Susie* in 1948, named for a song he had made enormously popular.

He made other songs so familiar that they were associated with him as distinctively as his own name. When radio audiences heard the lyric "Potatoes are cheaper, tomatoes are cheaper, now's the time to fall in love" or "Ida, sweet as apple cider," they knew at once that Eddie Cantor was on the air.

Despite his rise to fame, he never forgot the underprivileged youth. It is said that he never refused a legitimate request for aid, either personal or educational. His "loans" to impecunious actors were uncountable. He played in as many as six benefit shows in one night and toured the country endlessly for the United States Service Organization in World War II.

In the early 1930s he financed a camp in New York for impoverished children. He raised hundreds of thousands of dollars for Jewish refugees from Hitler and for Palestine. When the State of Israel was faced with an unprecedented economic emergency situation, he led a great drive for Israel Bonds, giving unstintingly of his time and talent. He also aided Christian and nondenominational philanthropies.

For all the joy he afforded audiences and all the fine work he did for the underprivileged and oppressed, Eddie Cantor was equally admired for what he did in the struggle against the terrible killer, polio. Not only did he originate the famous "March of Dimes," he gave the nationwide campaign its name.

Begun by him in 1936, the March of Dimes became one of the most widespread and best-known campaigns against disease. (It is now known as the March of Dimes Birth Defects Foundation.)

It was for his work on behalf of the March of Dimes as much as for his eminence as an actor and philanthropist that Temple University in 1951 awarded Eddie Cantor the honorary degree of Doctor of Humane Letters.

Hollywood itself placed its stamp of approval on the famous and universally beloved human being when it made the motion picture known as *The Eddie Cantor Story*. Often hilarious, often touching, it tells the story of the unconquerable spirit with which Eddie Cantor fought his way out of the slums to the utmost peak in the entertainment world, with his name flashing among the brightest lights on Broadway and from there across the country and around the world.

Semiretired after suffering a heart attack in 1953, Cantor continued to be a show-business figure for a decade after giving up his public appearances. He published his autobiographies, *My Life Is In Your Hands* (1932), *Take My Life* (1956), *The Way I See It* (1959), and a book of reminiscences, *As I Remember Them* (1963).

He was a founder and president of the Screen Actors' Guild and the Jewish Theatrical Guild. In 1964 he was awarded a medal by President Lyndon Johnson for his service to the United States and humanity.

After more than fifty years in show business, Eddie Cantor died on October 10, 1964, at the age of seventy-two.

As actor, comedy star, philanthropist, and originator of a great humanitarian campaign, Eddie Cantor richly deserved the praise he received from his own people and the love of all Americans.

THE FIRST ATOMIC-POWERED SUBMARINE

1954

In January 1954 the world's first atomic-powered submarine, the *USS Nautilus*, succeeded in finding a path across the Arctic ice cap from the Atlantic to the Pacific. The *Nautilus* did not actually cross over, but rather under, the polar cap because of its ability to stay under water several times longer than submarines powered by conventional fuels. Three years later it startled the world by running submerged under the North Pole on a voyage from Pearl Harbor, Hawaii, to England.

The crucial discovery that atomic-powered motors were feasible gave impetus to the development of the atom for peaceful purposes and made it possible for submarines to remain away from their home bases for a year or more without refueling.

A fleet of nuclear-powered submarines and surface ships soon followed, as well as the world's first commercial nuclear power plant in Shippingport, Pennsylvania, which supplies power for the residents of Pittsburgh.

The supervision, planning, and construction of the *Nautilus* was directed by Admiral Hyman G. Rickover, a tough and dedicated naval captain from Chicago, who believed it was in the best interests of the country to develop vessels powered by the newest form of energy. He had to overcome great obstacles placed in his way by traditional naval planners and had to fight against almost the entire naval establishment to bring the

American Navy up to what he considered the minimum requirements for the sake of America's defense and freedom of the seas.

Hyman George Rickover was born in Poland to Abraham and Rachel Ungar Rickover on January 27, 1900. When he was six, his parents joined the wave of Jewish emigration to the United States and settled in Chicago. Hyman's father supported the family by working as a tailor. Young Rickover was determined to contribute to the family's meager income. In high school he worked after classes every day until 11:00 P.M. and on weekends as a Western Union messenger. He was never home before midnight but managed to do well in school nevertheless.

After graduating from John Marshall High School in 1918, he obtained an appointment to the United States Naval Academy at Annapolis. It meant a great deal to him, not so much because he loved the sea, but rather that he could receive a college education—something his family could not otherwise afford.

Rickover graduated in 1922 in the top quarter of his class and was commissioned an ensign in the United States Navy. After a tour of duty at sea, he returned to the Naval Academy five years later to pursue graduate work in electrical engineering. He continued his studies at Columbia University, where he received his M.S. degree in 1929. He then studied submarine science at the submarine base in New London, Connecticut. Several land assignments were followed by a return to sea duty.

He served aboard submarines from late 1929 to mid-1938. After duty on the battleship *New Mexico*, he had his only seagoing command in Asian waters as skipper of the minesweeper *Finch* from June 1937 to May 1939. When World War II started, he was placed in charge of the electrical section of the Bureau of Ships of the Navy Department in Washington, D.C., in the first of many wartime appointments.

His career was not spectacular at first, although he was credited with saving the lives of a number of enlisted men in the course of shipboard accidents. He was never afraid to say what he thought, even to the highest officers, earning for himself a reputation as a frank, outspoken Navy captain who could be counted on to get things done.

Rickover gradually rose through the Navy ranks in position and influence. By mid-1945, after serving briefly on the commanding staff of the U.S. Pacific fleet, he became industrial manager at Okinawa and was named commanding officer of the Naval Repair Base there. Later that year he became inspector general of the San Francisco-based Nineteenth Fleet and shortly thereafter received an assignment through the Atomic Energy Commission to work on the Manhattan Project in Oak Ridge, Tennessee, in which he participated in the development of the atomic bomb. Rickover visited other nuclear research centers and became convinced that ships could be powered by nuclear energy.

Almost alone in his belief, he worked out a plan and submitted it to the Navy. The plan was put aside by Congress, but Rickover appealed to Admiral Chester Nimetz, chief of Naval Operations. A former submariner himself, Admiral Nimetz approved the idea, and Captain Rickover recruited a staff that included civilians from universities and industry and set up a three-year course at the Massachusetts Institute of Technology devoted to atomic submarine technology. Rickover's success in pushing through what was justifiably considered to be risky, hugely expensive, and an unwieldy project reflected his insuperable will, which did not endear him to many of the older Navy career officers and government officials.

Rickover's plans for the nuclear submarine, to be named *Nautilus*, called for expenditures of more than $40 million. To save time, the nuclear propulsion reactors were built separately in Idaho, while the submarine construction took place in Groton, Connecticut. When the *Nautilus* was well underway, Rickover began designing a second nuclear submarine as well as a nuclear aircraft carrier and a related project. But these never got off the planning board as a controversy concerning his naval status created an uproar in Congress.

Rickover had been passed over twice for promotion to the rank of admiral. (The naval codes require retirement if promotion is denied twice.) But the newspapers, the Senate Armed Services Board, and others raised such a furor that another board was convened with tacit orders to promote Captain Rickover.

The Navy's official explanation for its refusal to promote him was that they felt he was too much of a specialist to meet the qualifications of a flag officer. Underneath, however, was the fact that he was "not Navy" by reason of his unconventional methods and outspoken opinions. After an investigation in the matter, he was finally promoted to the rank of Rear Admiral in 1953 and Vice Admiral in 1959. Eventually, as full admiral, Rickover achieved an eminence unmatched by any Jew in American military history.

As a permanent fixture in the Navy, Rickover became an outspoken critic of the institution and other aspects of American life, particularly its education system. Comparing American schools unfavorably with British schools, he wrote a blistering attack on American education and offered proposals for reform in *Education and Freedom* (1959).

He was an enemy of progressive schooling in civilian life, and once called for the abolition of service academies if steps were not taken to improve their teaching of engineering.

Rickover was frequently credited with having been the mentor of former President Jimmy Carter, who was a graduate of Annapolis with training in nuclear engineering and who had once served as a naval officer under Rickover.

In 1980, as president of the United States, Jimmy Carter presented Admiral Rickover with the Medal of Freedom. On that occasion, President Carter said: "With the exception of my father, no person has had such a profound impact on my life."

As he neared his eighty-second birthday, Admiral Rickover was eased into retirement by Secretary Lehman, who at thirty-nine was the youngest secretary of the Navy. When Rickover retired, he expressed regrets on the role he had played in nuclear proliferation and called for an international agreement to outlaw nuclear weapons and reactors because of the radiation dangers they pose.

After his retirement, Admiral Rickover set up the Rickover Foundation (now known as the Center for Excellence in Education), which is dedicated to improving American education.

The Navy named a nuclear-powered attack submarine for Admiral Rickover, a rare honor for a living person. The *Hyman G. Rickover* was commissioned in July 1984 by the admiral's wife, Eleonore.

Over the years Admiral Rickover's nuclear Navy recruited and trained more than ten thousand officers and sixty thousand enlisted men. Thousands of men and women have taken what they learned from him into every part of American government and industry.

Admiral Hyman G. Rickover died on July 8, 1986. He was eighty-six years old. He was buried with full military honors at Arlington National Cemetery.

During the course of his career, Admiral Rickover generated controversy on all sides. He attacked naval bureaucracy, ignored red tape, lacerated those he considered stupid, bullied subordinates, and assailied the country's educational system. And he achieved in the production of the first nuclear-powered submarine in the early 1950s, what former Secretary of the Navy Dan Kimball called "the most important piece of development work in the history of the Navy."

THE FIRST COLLEGE OF LIBERAL ARTS FOR WOMEN UNDER JEWISH AUSPICES

1954

Stern College for Women, the first degree-granting college of liberal arts and sciences for women under Jewish auspices in the United States, was founded in 1954 by Yeshiva University as a counterpart of Yeshiva College, the university's college of arts and sciences for men.

In September of that first year, a pioneering handful of faculty and administrators offered thirty-three students a choice of nine liberal arts and sciences majors, along with Jewish studies. During its growth from that original class of thirty-three to a student body of over 750, the college continues to offer a four-year course of study leading to a bachelor's degree in the arts, sciences, or religious education and affords students the opportunity to major in the natural sciences, humanities, social sciences, preprofessional studies or programs of the Sy Syms School of Business. Courses in Jewish studies are offered on both the elementary and advanced levels. For sufficiently qualified students, courses are given leading to a Hebrew Teacher's diploma and an Associate in Arts degree in Jewish Studies.

Jewish traditions are part of the college's way of life. Classes are not held on the Sabbath and Jewish holidays, nor are they held on legal holidays, and Jewish dietary laws are observed in its dining room.

Stern College is housed in its own building at Thirty-fifth Street and Lexington Avenue in midtown New York City and has as its campus the great avenues, parks, and landmarks for which New York City is famous.

The opening of Stern College at such a particular opportune time was intended to help remedy what was a critical situation in regard to the Hebrew-teacher shortage. Jewish educators looked to Stern College as a reservoir of talent from which to draw the personnel they so urgently needed.

Today, women from all over the world—the United States, Israel, Canada, Latin America, Europe, and the former Soviet Union—come to study at Yeshiva University's Stern College for Women. Each year seventy percent of Stern College graduating seniors go on to graduate schools. They not only strengthen Jewish life, they enrich all professions as well.

Since Stern College held its first graduation, it has graduated 3,681 women, many of whom fill a unique role in Jewish life as teachers, scientists, psychologists, social workers, doctors, and community leaders.

The establishment of Stern College was made possible through an initial gift of $500,000 made in 1954 by Max Stern, a New York businessman, philanthropist, and honorary chairman of Yeshiva University's board of trustees. A German-Jewish immigrant who arrived penniless in the United States in 1926, he made a fortune from the sale of birds and bird seed. The gift, made in memory of his parents, Emanuel and Caroline Stern, represented the largest single contribution to Yeshiva University up to that time.

When in 1950 Yeshiva University obtained a charter for a medical school, Max Stern was among a group of five who visited Albert Einstein in Princeton, New Jersey, and prevailed upon him to lend his name to the new school. Initial donations from Stern and his four colleagues launched a campaign to found the Albert Einstein College of Medicine in the Bronx, New York, on whose board he served. In June 1961 Max Stern started the university's $25 million Midtown Center development program with a surprise gift of $1 million.

In 1962 Max Stern was cited in *Who's Who in America* for his significant and substantial gifts to education in America, specifically Yeshiva University.

Max Stern was a brilliant and cogent fund-raiser who always set an example by his own giving. By 1976 he had contributed a total of over $10 million to Yeshiva University and major gifts to other institutions as well.

In 1981, in recognition of Stern's contributions to Jewish educational projects in the United States and Israel, Prime Minister Menachem Begin of Israel and Mayor Teddy Kollek of Jerusalem dedicated a park in his name in Jerusalem and gave him the key to the city. He was awarded the Jerusalem Medal in 1976.

In addition to his leadership at Yeshiva University, Max Stern served as president and honorary president for over thirty years of the Jewish Center, one of New York City's most prominent Orthodox synagogues. He was also one of the original founders of the New York City United Jewish Appeal—Federation of Jewish Philanthropies, a Master Builder of Shaare Zedek Hospital in Jerusalem, honorary chairman of Torah Umesorah, the National Hebrew Day School society, and president of the Manhattan Day School in New York.

One of the foremost Jewish communal leaders in the nation, Max Stern attributed his abiding interest in educational and charitable efforts to the disciplined training of his parents, Caroline and Emanuel Stern, in whose memory Stern College was named. Born in Fulda, Germany, near the Hartz Mountains, on October 27, 1898, he received his early Jewish and general education there. His father was president of the Jewish Congregation of Fulda for almost forty years. The congregation itself had existed for more than five hundred years. As a youngster, Stern was encouraged to devote himself to learning, to be concerned with the welfare of the less fortunate, and to become independent. At eighteen he opened his own linen factory, a venture that flourished until Germany's depression in the 1920s. It was then, in 1926, that he came to the United States and established a bird seed and accessories business that became known throughout the world as Hartz Mountain Products Corporation. The company pioneered in what was popularly thought to be "outlandish ideas"—the importation of singing canaries, the distribution of birds and pets to chain stores, the concept of national radio product advertising, and major research to combat bird diseases and to perfect bird food medications. He also founded Sternco Industries, which specialized in tropical fish and accessories.

In the 1930s Max Stern was responsible for the popularization in the United States of the singing canary. In the 1950s he was responsible for the breeding establishment and distribution of the system that brought millions of parakeets into the homes of Americans.

It was under his guidance that Hartz Mountain Products invented a medicated food so that birds of the psittacine family could be free of psittacosis disease (believed to be common among many newly imported parrots and caused by a large virus called rickettsia). This made it possible for this type of bird to be sold again in the United States.

In 1969 Cyril H. Rogers, author of a pet book entitled *Parrot Guide*, the most authoritative publication of its kind throughout the world, dedicated his book to Max Stern—"industrialist, philanthropist, pioneer in the art of birdkeeping and 'father' of the American bird cage industry."

At the age of seventy-three, Max Stern turned over most of his corporate duties to his son, Leonard Norman Stern, who became president of Hartz Mountain Pet Foods, Incorporated. When Leonard Stern, armed with an M.B.A. from New York University, took over, he added dog and cat supplies. Now the company has over one thousand pet supply products, and the number is constantly increasing.

It is the world's largest manufacturer of pet products. Leonard Stern also built a separate real estate fortune by developing the New Jersey Meadowlands (empty marshlands near New York City). After two decades of cleanup and land reclamation, the Meadowlands area of New Jersey is shedding its image as an environmental wasteland and emerging as one of the busiest centers of commercial development in the Northeast. The Meadowlands has also become a mammoth experiment in urban development.

By 1988 Leonard N. Stern occupied twenty-second place on *Forbes* magazine's list of America's four hundred richest people. In October of that year he gave his alma mater, New York University, a $30 million contribution. The university announced that henceforth its undergraduate and graduate schools of business would be simply and jointly known as the Leonard N. Stern School of Business.

Today among the new buildings at New York University is the Stern Building at 44 West Fourth Street in Manhattan.

Leonard Stern also owns the *Village Voice*, a New York City weekly newspaper.

THE FIRST TO CONQUER POLIO

1955

A number of American Jews have achieved eminence in the medical sciences, which have been traditional Jewish fields of interest since the Middle Ages. Several have made significant medical discoveries.

At the age of forty, Jonas Salk became world famous as the discoverer of the poliomyelitis (infantile paralysis) vaccine that bears his name. The

Salk Vaccine became mankind's first effective weapon to beat back the forces of this dreadful viral disease that always crippled or paralyzed and sometimes killed its victims.

Dr. Salk utilized the technique of developing a way of injecting the dead—and therefore harmless—polio virus into the bloodstream so that the body could build up immunities and fight off any living polio virus that might enter the body later on.

The Salk Vaccine changed medical history, preventing many thousands of cases of polio and saving thousands of lives. In the United States the vaccine soon ended the yearly threats of polio epidemics and the toll of paralysis and death.

It was an odd set of circumstances that led the quiet and modest scientist to one of the world's outstanding discoveries in the continuous struggle against the dreaded diseases of mankind.

Born in New York City on October 28, 1914, Jonas Edward Salk was the eldest of the three sons of Daniel B. and Dora Press Salk. His father was a manufacturer of ladies' blouses and scarves. The family lived in the Bronx, where Jonas went to public school. After graduating from Townsend Harris High School, which was reserved for exceptionally bright students, he was admitted to City College of New York at the age of fifteen. His intention was to study law, but as a freshman he suddenly decided to add science to his curriculum, purely to give himself a broader background. At once he saw where his real interests were. From then on his life was to be all science.

He entered New York University's School of Medicine in 1935. After his first year he won successive fellowships in chemistry, bacteriology, and experimental surgery. After earning his M.D. degree in 1939, he interned at Mount Sinai Hospital in New York City from 1940 to 1942, but now his full interest was in medical research.

He began his work on the influenza virus while still a medical student and resumed it once again in 1942 when the National Research Council awarded him a fellowship at the University of Michigan's School of Public Health. There he rejoined a former teacher, Dr. Thomas Francis Jr., an internationally known virologist, and together they developed the influenza vaccine now in use.

When the University of Pittsburgh's School of Medicine expanded its virus research program in 1947 after World War II, Dr. Salk joined its staff as professor of bacteriology and director of its Virus Research Laboratory. There his scientific interests moved gradually from influenza virus to the urgent effort to develop a polio vaccine at a time when polio seemed to be on the increase.

Dr. Salk's concentrated efforts against polio began when he was part of a team assigned to survey polio viruses throughout the United States to see how many varieties could be linked to the disease in humans. In the course of time and with a March of Dimes grant, Dr. Salk acquired the first prerequisite: a collection of representative strains of all three types of the polio virus, now known simply as polio viruses types I, II, and III. A second prerequisite was furnished by the discovery—by Dr. John Enders of the Harvard Medical School and Dr. Thomas Weller of the Children's Medical Center in Boston—of a simple method of growing the polio virus in cultures of various types of tissue in an artificial media—a test tube—for which they received the Nobel Prize in medicine in 1954.

In the course of work on immunoclassification of polio viruses to distinguish the different types of virus, Dr. Salk made observations pointing toward the development of noninfectious or killed polio virus that could induce immunity without causing infection. When Salk—working with persistent determination often twenty hours a day, every day of the week—finally discovered the vaccine he thought would be effective, he chose to use his wife and three young sons and himself as subjects for the first experimental injections. When that worked, further experiments continued on a broader scale. And then, in 1954, the National Foundation for Infantile Paralysis put the Salk Vaccine to the test in the greatest medical experiment ever undertaken. At a cost of $7,500,000, more than a million school children in nationwide field tests received three injections for the three types of viruses. Others got placebos (blank shots), while still others were merely observed.

Some of those who did not get the Salk Vaccine got polio; many were crippled and some died. Of those who got the vaccine, up to ninety percent were spared the effects of the disease. Now for the first time in medical history an effective means of preventing the polio scourge had been found. The Salk Vaccine was safe, highly effective, and potent.

The result was announced, and the vaccine was licensed for public use on April 12, 1955, to a grateful world. Salk's vaccine was recognized internationally as one of the great advances in immunology and as an important event in the beginning of the modern era of vaccine development.

In the meantime, Dr. Albert Sabin, an American-Jewish virologist, devoted his career to the development of protective vaccines against viruses that cause death and crippling diseases in children. In particular, he had been conducting experiments for thirty-five years on developing an oral live-virus vaccine against the three identified strains of poliomyelitis. His own war on polio ended in 1961, when the live, orally administered Sabin Vaccine that he developed reached the point of mass usage.

Since 1961 more than 260 cases of paralytic polio have occurred in this country among the recipients of Sabin's Vaccine. While the effectiveness of the oral vaccine is more than ninety-five percent in this country, it drops to about seventy-five percent in tropical countries.

The successful development of the oral vaccine led to a long scientific debate over the relative merits of Dr. Salk's version, which used the killed polio virus, and the later one developed by Dr. Sabin that used the live polio virus. Eventually, the Sabin Vaccine entirely supplanted the Salk Vaccine in the United States, and a sharp rivalry persisted between the two scientists throughout their lives.

The live-virus vaccine promised lifetime immunity, while the original Salk Vaccine did not. But Salk never lost faith in killed virus polio vaccine and continued to champion the cause all his life. On several occasions he pointed out that the live-virus vaccine did, on rare instances, produce the disease as well as immunity, while the killed virus vaccine, properly made, carried no such risk.

After the success of 1955, the Commonwealth of Pennsylvania established a Chair in Preventive Medicine for Dr. Salk at the University of Pittsburgh. Two years later, Dr. Salk's title was changed to Commonwealth Professor of Experimental Medicine.

No cases of polio were reported in 1969 in the United States for the first time, and the disease is on the verge of being eradicated around the world.

Dr. Salk conceived of the idea of an institute to bring together scientists and scholars from different disciplines who share common interest in science and the human implication of their work. He founded such an institute with the financial support committed by the March of Dimes (now the March of Dimes Birth Defects Foundation). The Salk Institute for Biological Studies began operation in 1963, and Salk directed it thereafter. It is housed in an architecturally grand group of buildings, designed by Louis Kahn, on a piece of land donated by the City of San Diego in La Jolla, California, overlooking the Pacific Ocean.

The group of fellows invited to work there included several winners of the Nobel Prize, an award that eluded Dr. Salk, although many other honors were conferred upon him in his lifetime. These included a United States Presidential Citation (1955), the Congressional Medal for Distinguished Civilian Achievement (1955), the Lasker Award (1956), the Robert Koch Medal (1963), the Mellon Institute Award (1969), and the Presidential Medal of Freedom (1977).

He was named a Chevalier de la Legion d'Honneur by the French Government (1955) and was awarded honorary degrees from universities in the United States, Israel, Great Britain, Italy, and the Philippines.

At the Institute that bore his name, Dr. Salk continued biomedical research on a wide range of subjects, including the immunological aspects of multiple sclerosis and cancer.

In 1986 Dr. Salk initiated a strategy for studying the prospects for the immunological control of H.I.V. infection and AIDS. With the collaboration of several research groups internationally, he coordinated studies to develop a method of immunization using a killed virus preparation in investigating the prospects for the control of H.I.V. infection before the disease develops and to prevent infection and/or disease in those not yet infected. Scientists have been testing such an experimental immunization on hundreds of people.

Dr. Salk's scientific publications numbered more than one hundred. He has written several books that are extensive explorations of human development from scientific and philosophical points of view intended for general readers. *Man Unfolding* (1972) discusses the biological processes that led to the evolution of humankind and compares these processes to theories about the evolution of the universe. In *Survival of the Wisest* (coauthored with Jonathan Salk in 1973), Dr. Salk continued his speculations on whether the human species can coexist with nature and its evolutionary processes comparatively rather than destructively. His other books include *World Population and Human Values: A New Reality* (1983) and an essay entitled *An Evolutionary Philosophy for Our Time,* included in a volume on *Living Philosophies* (edited by Clifton Fadiman, 1990).

He came to believe that it was the force of evolution that guided him in the early 1950s to reject the common wisdom and develop a polio vaccine that used killed viruses instead of live ones.

In his later years, Dr. Salk broadened his horizons to include painting, poetry, and writing on themes as much philosophical as scientific.

On the fortieth anniversary of the licensing of the Salk Vaccine, on April 11, 1995, the March of Dimes announced that it was creating a $100,000 prize to be awarded annually in Dr. Salk's name to an investigator who makes major advances in developmental biology.

Dr. Jonas Salk died on June 23, 1995, of heart failure in La Jolla, California, at the age of eighty.

"Few have made one discovery that had benefitted humanity so greatly. Jonas Salk was a man, who, right to his last day, was actively in pursuit of another," said Dr. Francis Crick, the Nobel laureate, president of the Salk Institute.

THE FIRST MEDICAL SCHOOL UNDER JEWISH AUSPICES

1955

The Albert Einstein College of Medicine, a constituent college of Yeshiva University, is the first medical school established under Jewish auspices in the entire history of the Diaspora. Formally opened on September 22, 1955, delegates from thirty states and Canada were among the more than seventy-five hundred persons attending the dedication exercises. Governor of New York, Averell Harriman, Senator Irving M. Ives, Mayor Robert F. Wagner, Dr. Hans Albert Einstein (son of Albert Einstein), and many other prominent leaders in government, medicine, science, and education took part in the ceremonies.

Nathaniel L. Goldstein, chairman of the Board of Overseers of the college and former attorney general of New York State, who presided over the dedication exercises, saw in the opening of the college "a fitting climax to the celebration of three hundred years of Jewish participation in American life." In his congratulatory message, President Dwight Eisenhower said: "The dedication of this new medical college is of vital significance to the health and welfare of the nation."

For many years the idea of creating a Jewish-sponsored medical school in America was a subject of much discussion. After considerable deliberations, notwithstanding arguments that such a school would lead to segregation and isolation of Jewish students, it was found that there unquestionably existed a need for additional medical schools, confirmed by the president's commission on the health needs of the nation.

Finally on December 15, 1950, Yeshiva University, the first American university under Jewish auspices, under the leadership of Dr. Samuel Belkin, its president, was granted a charter by the New York Board of Regents, permitting it to open medical and dental schools and grant the degrees of M.D. and D.D.S. When these plans became known, the City of New York offered to establish a professional teaching relationship with it. The city's Bronx Municipal Hospital Center, then under construction at a cost of $40 million in the Westchester Heights section of northeast Bronx, became affiliated with it. A drive for funds was initiated, and a building program was agreed upon. Michael M. Nisselson, noted civic and communal leader, was appointed director of development of the college, and the building was rushed to completion on schedule. On October 14, 1953, Dr. Marcus Kogel was chosen dean. Formerly commissioner of hospitals of New York City, Dr. Kogel thenceforth devoted all his energies to the development of the project and took the lead in establishing the college. Dr. Abraham White, a biochemist internationally recognized for his role in the isolation of ACTH, was named associate dean.

At the dedication ceremonies held on October 23, 1955, the new school, the first medical school established in New York City in fifty-five years and the first in the state in twenty-six years, pledged itself "to carry on in the spirit of warm humanity and scientific integrity exemplified by Albert Einstein, justifying high hopes for the college as a valuable instrument for advancing medical science and the national welfare."

The medical college opened its doors with a faculty consisting of nationally and internationally recognized medical specialists. With a curriculum emphasizing the relationships existing among the subjects comprising the study of medicine, the program of the college was based on the fact that medicine is a social as well as a natural science.

The new medical college was the core of a $100 million "Medical City," which included the $40 million Bronx Municipal Hospital Center and the $45 million Bronx Psychiatric Center, to be built by the state (now the Bronx Psychiatric Center, a six-hundred-bed facility of the New York State Department of Mental Health).

The first unit of the Municipal Hospital Center, the 511-bed Nathan B. Van Etten Hospital, named for a former president of the American Medical Association and first president of the Bronx County Medical Society, opened in 1954. Its second unit, the 898-bed Abraham Jacobi Hospital, named for the "father of pediatrics in America," was in operation in 1955. These hospitals adjoin the college and serve as clinical teaching centers, with the college exercising full professional responsibility for the care of patients.

Today five additional buildings stand on the original sixteen acres on the campus proper: the Florsheimer, Ulmann, and Mazur buildings; the Belfer Educational Center for Health Sciences; and the Chanin Institute for Cancer Research. The combined facilities constitute one of the largest and most comprehensive centers of medical education, care, and research in the country.

Since 1963 Montefiore Hospital became an affiliated hospital of the Albert Einstein College of Medicine. In addition to its 765-bed Henry and Lucy Moses Division on its West campus and the 431-bed Jack D. Weiler Hospital on the East campus, Montefiore includes long-term care facilities, family health centers, and home health services where medical students go for clinical experience. With over forty-three thousand admissions annually, Montefiore serves as both the major health care provider for 1.2 million Bronx residents and as a tertiary care referral center for patients from elsewhere.

In 1988 the Long Island Jewish Medical Center was designated the Long Island campus and a major affiliate of the Albert Einstein College of Medicine. In 1993 the Beth Israel Medical Center in lower Manhattan became its Manhattan campus.

In 1994 Rachel Sussman, president of Renette Foundations Corporation, gave $1 million to establish the Leo and Rachel Sussman Computer-Based Education Fund, which supports computer programs that enhance students' learning at the Albert Einstein College of Medicine.

Although the Albert Einstein College of Medicine is under Jewish auspices and the traditions of the Jewish religion are adhered to, the college is open to all academically qualified students without regard to race, creed, or gender. It is now historically significant as the institution that catalyzed the dissolution of discrimatory practices in the admission of students and faculty appointments among medical schools in the United States.

From an original class of fifty-six students in 1955, the student body now numbers over twelve hundred, including postgraduate students attending the Sue Golding Graduate Division of Medical Sciences and the Belfer Institute for Advanced Biomedical Studies. More than forty-eight hundred alumni currently serve the nation as physicians, medical educators, and biomedical scientists.

Nine members of Einstein's faculty, including Einstein's dean, Dr. Dominick P. Purpura, an internationally recognized neuroscientist, have been elected to the National Academy of Sciences.

A full-time faculty of over one thousand teachers delivers health care and conducts studies in every major medical specialty and area of biomedical research. Traditional barriers between departments and among specialists at work in separate physical facilities have been overcome through the formation of a variety of centers and institutes that are staffed by the educators and investigators from many medical fields.

This interdisciplinary approach is widely utilized at the Albert Einstein College of Medicine of Yeshiva University and has resulted in important advances in clinical care; scientific understanding of cancer; mental retardation; liver, heart, and kidney disease; diabetes; Alzheimer's disease; and AIDS. The centers are also integrated with the college's training programs, providing opportunity for students to train in an environment that reflects the dramatically changing nature of medicine as it advances toward the twenty-first century.

It serves as an enduring memorial to Albert Einstein, who during his lifetime was deeply interested in the project and lent it his encouragement and support.

THE FIRST JEW IN BASEBALL'S HALL OF FAME

1956

Among Jews who have won fame in the world of sports, no one was accorded more national respect and admiration for his ability than Henry "Hammerin Hank" Greenberg, one of baseball's greatest first basemen and one of the most famous Jewish baseball heroes in history.

Henry Benjamin Greenberg was born on January 1, 1911, in the Greenwich Village section of New York City, the son of Orthodox Jewish parents from Bucharest, Romania. He was reared there and, from the age of seven, in the Bronx.

As a student in James Monroe High School, the boy spent the summers working in his father's textile firm but snatched a few minutes of baseball at sundown and went to see Babe Ruth play as often as he could. Although naturally awkward, Hank's big frame carried a lot of power. (He was a six-foot-four-inch 215 pounder.) He helped his high school win championships in baseball, basketball, and soccer. He played baseball the year round and in the school gym during the winter. By the age of sixteen he had found his adult batting style. "I hit now exactly as I did then," Greenberg wrote in 1939.

Before entering college, Hank joined a semiprofessional Brooklyn baseball team on which one of his friends was a pitcher. A scout from the world champion New York Yankees had discovered Greenberg in high school. Later he was sought by three other league teams. Although he yearned most to play for his home team, the New York Yankees, the scout from the club failed to appear to keep an appointment, so he accepted a contract with the Detroit Tigers. He was then barely nineteen.

With that team Hank Greenberg became one of the greatest baseball stars of all time. In 1935, his first full season as a Detroit regular, he helped the Tigers to a pennant, their first in twenty-five years, and won their Most Valuable Player Award. He also received the American League's Most Valuable Player Award, thus becoming the first person ever to receive it at two different positions.

In the 1937 season he won the runs batted crown with 183, only one less than Lou Gherig's All-League record. In 1938 he hit fifty-eight home runs, second only to Babe Ruth's record of sixty in one season. Hank was the only man to bat the ball into the center field bleachers of Cominsky Park in Chicago, where the center field wall is 340 feet from home plate. In the thirteen years he starred in the major leagues, he hit 331 home runs. He was paid more than $60,000 a year to play baseball.

At the peak of his career in 1941, World War II intervened, and Hank Greenberg became one of the first big leaguers to lay aside his baseball uniform and fight for his country. He served as a lieutenant and then as a captain in the Army Air Force. He took part in the first land-based bombing of Japan and was discharged with a Presidential Unit Citation and four battle stars.

In 1945, after a four-year interval, he returned to baseball, rejoined the Detroit Tigers, and led his team once again to a pennant, by hitting a ninth-inning grand slam. Two years later, he returned to first base and won his third American League home run title.

Greenberg was traded to the Pittsburgh Pirates in 1947 and ended his playing career after one season in the National League. He compiled a lifetime batting average of .313, hit 331 home runs, and batted in 1,276 runs in 1,394 games.

He was responsible for a number of changes in baseball law.

Success never spoiled him nor made him forget his religious heritage. When the "bomber from the Bronx," as Hank was often called, refused to play on Rosh Hashanah, the Detroit Free Press praised him and published a special Happy New Year's greeting in Hebrew to him.

Edgar Guest had written a poem after Hank spent Yom Kippur praying and fasting in the synagogue:

"Said Murphy to Mulrooney, We shall lose the game today!
We shall miss him in the infield, and shall miss him at the bat,
But he's true to his religion—and I honor him for that!"

In 1956, ten years after he played his last game, the greatest honor that can befall a professional baseball player came to Hank Greenberg. He was elected to baseball's Hall of Fame, the first Jewish player to be given this honor. He called it his "ultimate satisfaction, something I never dreamed about."

A great exponent of America's favorite sport, Hank Greenberg was a credit to the country that gave him the opportunity to develop in the work of his choice and in the national pastime's most colorful era.

On September 4, 1987, the Detroit Tigers baseball team lost three to two in the Seattle Mariners' King Dome. The loss, however, was inconsequential compared to the loss the Detroit franchise and baseball fans everywhere suffered that day when it was announced that Henry Benjamin Greenberg had passed away at his Beverly Hills home at the age of seventy-five.

Commenting on his passing, the *Sporting News* writer thought and wrote: "God must have been down a couple runs in the ninth and needed a long one."

THE FIRST AMERICAN-BORN CONDUCTOR OF THE NEW YORK PHILHARMONIC

1958

On November 14, 1943, a virtually unknown young man of twenty-five was suddenly called upon to conduct the New York Philharmonic Orchestra—without rehearsing—substituting on just a few hour's notice for Bruno Walter, its conductor, who had become ill. So extraordinary was his talent and so electrifying his personality that his unscheduled appearance was front-page news the next day. Music critics and concert-goers alike hailed Leonard Bernstein's "brilliant musicianship," "the authenticity of his interpretations," as well as "the excellent and exciting qualities of his performance."

The young man went on to repeat his triumph many times. He appeared as guest conductor with the world's major symphony orchestras. Wherever he conducted, here or abroad, he received ovation after ovation for his "absolute fidelity to a composer's score," "flawlessness of detail," and "genuine luminosity of tone."

In 1953, Leonard Bernstein became the first American conductor at the La Scala Opera House in Milan where he directed Maria Callas in Cherubini's *Medea*.

The citizens of Israel packed the streets as for a conquering hero, when Bernstein first came to conduct there in 1948 while the War of Independence was being fought.

It was that way, too, when he went to Israel on July 9, 1967, immediately after the Six Day War, to conduct the Israel Philharmonic in a victory concert on Mount Scopus in Old Jerusalem, which had just been liberated.

For almost forty-seven years, the name of Leonard Bernstein was the mark of soul-stirring music to the people of four continents.

Nevertheless, Leonard Bernstein's fame did not rest on his achievements as a conductor alone. He excelled in several different roles—as conductor; composer of symphonic music, musicals, ballets, and operas; and as a pianist and academician. And he was master of television and an eloquent explainer of his art. Stravinsky called him "a department store of music."

The first of Bernstein's compositions to win wide fame was his *Jeremiah Symphony*, a blending of biblical themes with melancholy yet inspiring music for soprano. It won the award of the Music Critics Circle of New York as the "Most Outstanding Work By an American Composer Introduced During the 1943–1944 Season." In the same year came the first performance of his popular music, *Fancy Free*, a ballet that attained an enormous popularity. In October 1946 the Ballet Theater introduced his *Facsimilie*, which like his *Fancy Free* was choreographed by Jerome Robbins.

In December 1944 he made his foray into the rigors of the Broadway theater with the youthful gaiety and vivacity of *On the Town*. His second musical was a hit of even greater proportions, the 1953 *Wonderful Town*. In the fall of 1956 his *Candide*, a comic operetta written in collaboration with Lillian Hellman, was introduced on Broadway. *West Side Story*, which opened in New York in September 1957 and in London a little over a year later, was a "smash hit" in both cities. The British production won the 1960 London Critic's Award for the best musical of the year. The movie production of *West Side Story* was hailed as the "Best Picture of 1961" and received the Academy Award. Bernstein also composed the incidental music for the 1950 production of Barrie's *Peter Pan*, for the 1957 Broadway production of

Christopher Fry's *The Lark*, and the score for the Oscar-winning film *On the Waterfront*.

Throughout the years of writing musical comedies, Bernstein continued composing serious compositions, and among these works are his Second Symphony, *The Age of Anxiety*, which was first performed by Koussevitsky with Bernstein as piano soloist in 1949. The Boston Symphony and the Koussevitsky Foundation together commissioned his Third Symphony, subtitled *Kaddish* (the traditional Jewish prayer in memory of the dead). It was composed in 1963 and dedicated to the memory of John F. Kennedy.

Other major compositions by Leonard Bernstein include *Serenade for Violin, Strings, and Percussion* (1954); *Five Anniversaries for Piano Solo* (1964); *Mass: a Theater Piece for Singers, Players, and Dancers,* commissioned for the opening of the John F. Kennedy Center for the Performing Arts in Washington, D.C., and first produced there in 1971; *Chichester Psalms* for chorus, boy sopranos, and orchestra (1974); *The Dybbuk* (1974), which set to music S. Ansky's Yiddish drama; *Songfest,* a cycle of songs for singers and orchestra (1977); *Divertimento for Orchestra* (1980); *Arias and Barcarolles* for piano duet and two singers; and *Concerto for Orchestra* (subtitled *Jubilee Games*), the latter two works completed and first performed in 1989.

Bernstein's one act opera, *Trouble in Tahiti*, from 1951, was followed in 1983 by *A Quiet Place*, a sequel meant to be performed with it.

This unusual man who grew up to be a vital force in the musical life of our country was born in Lawrence, Massachusetts, on August 25, 1918. He was the son of Samuel, a beauty supply and hair goods businessman, and Jennie Resnick Bernstein and grew up in Boston.

Leonard showed no particular interest in music until his tenth year when a divorced aunt sent her old upright piano to the Bernsteins for storage. Leonard found it irresistible. "I touched it, it made pretty sounds. Right away I screamed, 'Ma, give me lessons,' " he later wrote. A month of lessons convinced him that he was going to be a musician, a decision his father opposed up until the time of his son's first professional success.

Bernstein attended Boston Latin School, where he received a well-rounded education. He graduated from Harvard University in 1939, where he majored in music. As a student he demonstrated his uncanny ability to memorize entire scores. While yet a student he met such notables as Dimitri Mitropolous and Aaron Copland, who suggested that he study conducting. To this end Bernstein spent two years of graduate study at the Curtis Institute of Music in Philadelphia, where he studied under Fritz Reiner, then conductor of the Pittsburgh Symphony Orchestra.

In the summer of 1940, Bernstein became a student of the Boston Symphony's reigning conductor, Serge Koussevitsky, at the Tanglewood

Music Center in Lenox, Massachusetts, where in 1942 he was named his conducting assistant.

This position gave him entree to many other opportunities. In the 1942–1943 musical season, he conducted concerts in New York. In 1943 he was appointed as the assistant conductor of the New York Philharmonic under Arthur Rodzinski, then its musical director.

In 1945 Bernstein served as conductor of the New York Symphony. During his three-year directorship in this post, Bernstein began to develop his flamboyant brand of podium showmanship. He attracted young, enthusiastic audiences by emphasizing modern music neglected by older, more conservative orchestras.

From 1951 through 1955 Bernstein was head of the Orchestra and Conducting Department at Tanglewood, and from 1951 to 1956 he was professor of music at Brandeis University.

At frequent intervals he appeared on the New York Philharmonic podium as guest conductor. With Dimitri Mitropoulos, he was one of the two principal conductors of the Philharmonic in 1957–1958 before he became permanent conductor in 1958.

The first American-born and trained musical director of the New York Philharmonic, he brought new prestige, popularity, and informality to America's oldest symphony orchestra. He organized its seasons around themes such as "Keys to the Twentieth Century," "The Middle Eastern Tradition," "Spring Festival of Theater Music," and "The Gallic Approach."

During the 1950s and early 1960s, Bernstein's international reputation flourished. He was the first to take the New York Philharmonic Orchestra to South America, Israel, Japan, New Zealand, the USSR, Turkey, and several European countries.

In Vienna he led the Vienna Philharmonic Orchestra in Beethoven's nine symphonies, which was telecast to large audiences by the Public Broadcasting Corporation. He conducted in London and at the International Music Festival in Prague, ultimately playing hundreds of concerts in seventy cities throughout thirty-five countries.

For an international tour that commemorated the United States Bicentennial in 1976, he programmed only American music and played to sold-out houses wherever he went.

Bernstein's conducting repertory encompassed all the major musical literature, old and new, as well as integral performances and recordings of the symphonies of Beethoven, Brahms, Schumann, and Mahler. Today's renaissance of interest in Mahler's music can be directly attributed to Bernstein's pioneering performances and recordings of all nine symphonies with the New York Philharmonic in Mahler's centennial year, 1960.

Leonard Bernstein made his television debut in 1954 on the "Omnibus" television program, a forerunner of his later CBS "Young People's

Concerts" with the New York Philharmonic, which extended over four-teen seasons, beginning in 1958, an eleven-time Emmy Award winner. His infectious ability to communicate ideas about music and composers brought a new understanding of serious music to millions of viewers and listeners.

Bernstein's eminence as a writer is based on his books *The Joy of Music* (1959), *The Infinite Variety of Music* (1966), and *Findings* (1982), and their translations into a score of foreign languages. Six lectures given at Harvard University in 1972–1973 when he was Charles Eliot Norton Professor of Poetry were later collected in a book entitled *The Unanswered Question*.

Leonard Bernstein retired in 1969 as conductor of the New York Philharmonic to devote himself to composing, although he continued conducting for a number of weeks each season. That same year he was named "Laureate Conductor" of the New York Philharmonic, a title created especially for him. By then he had conducted more concerts than anyone else in its history. His 1,244th concert was given in 1990.

The Israeli Philharmonic Orchestra had also tendered him with a lifetime title of "Laureate Conductor" in 1988.

His link to Israel was deep and permanent. In 1982 he composed *Hallil*, a nocturne for solo flute, string orchestra, and percussion, which received its premiere in New York City and afterward was performed by Jean-Pierre Rampal and the Israel Philharmonic. The piece was composed in memory of nineteen-year-old flutist-soldier Yadin Tannenbaum, who was killed in the Yom Kippur War in Israel. Bernstein dedicated *Hallil* (Hebrew for "flute") to Yadin and his fallen brothers.

Bernstein's fervent absorption in music did not shade his awareness of world problems. As a Jew, he felt deeply the problems of "a whole people in a world of no security," which moved him to write his *Jeremiah Symphony*. While he did not feel obligated to project a specific type of Jewish music, he maintained that when a musician expresses himself sincerely, he creates out of his own integrity without self-consciousness.

Bernstein recorded more than one hundred albums.

He was the recipient of dozens of honorary degrees and awards from colleges and universities, including his alma mater, Harvard, from which he received the Man of the Year Award in 1966. He won Grammys, Tonys, and Emmys. He was given ceremonial keys to the cities of Oslo, Vienna, and Beersheba, among others, and high honors from many nations, including Italy, Israel, Denmark, Germany, England, and France, where he was successively made Chevalier, Officer and Commander of the French Legion of Honor. In his own country he received the Kennedy Center honors in 1980.

The National Fellowship Award in 1985 applauded his lifelong support of humanitarian causes, and he received the Gold Medal from the

American Academy of Arts and Letters, to which he was elected in 1981, the MacDowell Colony's Gold Medal, medals from the Beethoven Society and the Mahler Gesellschaft, and New York City's highest honor in the arts, the Handel Medallion.

Festivals of Bernstein's music are continuously produced throughout the world, most recently at the Beethoven/Bernstein Festival in Bonn, Germany, and in London, produced jointly by the Barbican Centre and the London Symphony, of which he was honorary president from 1987.

In June 1990 Bernstein was among the first recipients of the Paemium Imperiale, an international prize created in 1989 by Japan Art Association and awarded for lifetime achievement in the arts. He used the $100,000 prize to found the Bernstein Education Through the Arts Fund.

When Leonard Bernstein died in New York City on October 14, 1990, his name was known all over the world. He had blazed across the firmament as possibly the most renowned musical figure of the late twentieth century.

THE FIRST PRIVATE APARTMENT HOUSE BUILDER TO FOUND A CITY IN THE UNITED STATES

1961

Samuel Jayson LeFrak, Chairman of the LeFrak Organization, one of the world's largest building and development companies, is the nation's largest apartment house builder and the first to found a city bearing his name. The LeFrak Organization built more than two hundred thousand apartments and homes and millions of square feet of retail, commercial, and industrial space.

With eighteen thousand employees and a reported $3 billion in revenues, the LeFrak Organization was ranked thirty-seventh in *Forbes'* 1994 list of the four hundred largest privately held companies in the United States.

It has been estimated that one of every sixteen New Yorkers lives in a LeFrak-built apartment. The builder of moderately priced apartments, he is regarded as a hero of the middle class.

Samuel LeFrak, a business leader and an expert on urban affairs, is also an engineer, architect, sportsman, and patron of the arts. In recent years, LeFrak has expanded his commercial interests into the fields of finance, communications, agriculture, music publishing, record production, oil and gas exploration, and entertainment.

He has often been called upon by the United States Government, international agencies, and other nations to participate in creating housing and economic development programs. He spoke on the future of middle-class housing in America before the eighty-third United States Congress. Completing a world trip in 1963 under the auspices of the United States State Department, LeFrak recommended important changes in housing programs and financial planning subsequently adapted by many nations. He has lectured at American and foreign universities and before professional and trade associations throughout the United States.

Samuel Jayson LeFrak was born in New York City on February 12, 1918, to Harry and Sarah Schwartz LeFrak. His father, a cut-glass manufacturer, had been born in Palestine and emigrated to the United States from Paris, France, in 1898. Building had long been the family's traditional occupation, and with the knowledge of construction that Harry LeFrak had acquired from his father and grandfather, he founded a business of his own in 1905. The family lived in Brooklyn, where Samuel attended Erasmus Hall High School, graduating in 1936.

Intending to major in business, LeFrak enrolled at the University of Maryland. He discovered, however, that he wished to follow his father into the building business. He transferred to the study of economics and engineering and graduated in 1940 with a B.S. degree.

During his free time as an undergraduate, LeFrak worked at various occupations in Washington, D.C., as well as with his father during summers and vacations. With earnings, savings, and graduation gifts of about $5,000, LeFrak invested in the family construction business. In 1948 he was elected president of the LeFrak Organization, which by then was building apartment houses throughout New York City, some of which it also managed. In 1951 LeFrak persuaded his father to begin building outside the city and attempt major developments. They took out loans and started building simultaneously on several large sites. Within six years LeFrak had constructed thousands of new apartments in the tri-state area. By 1960 he had constructed major developments costing $48,500,000.

In 1955 when the Mitchell-Lama Law, which subsidized middle-income housing, was passed by the New York State Legislature, the LeFrak Organization became the first private construction firm to be associated with the plan. Through cooperation with city housing authorities, LeFrak put up thousands of additional apartments. A major consequence was the development of the $8 million cooperative development, the King's Bay Houses in the Sheepshead Bay section of Brooklyn, one of the pioneer urban renewal housing developments in the country privately built with city financing in 1957.

LeFrak was one of the first to merge luxury apartments with office space when he built the Parc Vendome in 1959 in Queens, which in this instance included the construction of the Municipal Court of the City of New York within the building.

LeFrak is most famous for his cities – huge, self-contained complexes with virtually every facility. He opened his first, LeFrak City, in Queens, New York, in 1961. The land had once been owned by William Waldorf Astor, who obtained it from King George II. Known as the "City within a City," LeFrak City is a forty-acre, $150 million housing development made up of twenty eighteen-story buildings bordering on the Long Island Expressway in Forest Hills-Elmhurst. Housing twenty-five thousand, it is one of the largest privately financed apartment developments in the world. LeFrak City has won several awards for distinctive design and community planning. A self-contained development of five thousand apartments with its own office park, it provides residents and office workers year-round on-site facilities for shopping, education, recreation, entertainment, and transportation.

The organization has also developed such communities as the ninety-two-acre Battery Park City, the first major waterfront landfill community in New York in more than one hundred years.

Other notable projects that LeFrak has undertaken since the 1960s include the West Side Manor, a high-rise building containing 246 apartments, and the James Tower with 261 apartments. Both were constructed as part of Manhattan's West Side Urbal Renewal Project.

LeFrak's success is due to his obsessive control of costs. He minimizes costs by buying early and warehousing his building materials until needed and producing bricks in his own plants. He also keeps large amounts of cash on reserve, enabling him to borrow at lower rates of interest.

Today LeFrak is building a six-hundred-acre $10 billion waterfront site called Newport in New Jersey, across from downtown Manhattan along the Hudson River. Newport will be a four-hundred-acre mixed-use community consisting of retail, residential, office, commercial, leisure, and entertainment facilities.

Since construction began early in 1986, $2 billion has been invested and more than eleven million square feet has been constructed in Newport. The first office building in Newport Office Park – the 455,000-square-foot, fourteen-story Recruit/Newport Financial Center – has been leased to Recruit USA, a computer-services corporation based in Tokyo. It represents the largest office lease undertaken by a Japanese corporation in the USA. Ground-level space has also been leased by a branch of the United Jersey Bank.

The second office building is Newport Tower, a one-million-square-foot structure leading directly to the Newport Centre Mall and the Pavonia-Newport PATH subway station. With its thirty-six stories, Newport Tower will be among the tallest buildings in New Jersey.

Comprised of almost five million square feet, Newport Office Park – in which Newport Tower and the Recruit/Newport Financial Center are located—will be one of the most extensive of its kind in the New York-New Jersey region.

Landlord to about half a million people in New York, LeFrak has long divided his time between business and civic affairs. He has served his state and city as commissioner of the Saratoga Springs Commission; as commissioner of Landmarks Preservation of New York; as commissioner of the Interstate Sanitation Commission of New York, New Jersey, and Connecticut; as a member of the Industrial Development Corporation; and on the executive committee of the Citizens Committee of New York City.

He has received honorary doctoral degrees from the University of Maryland, New York Law School, Colgate University, Pratt Institute, and the University of Rome.

A noted philanthropist, he has served on the boards of directors of dozens of hospitals, colleges, schools, and organizations. He is a trustee of the Jewish Hospital in Denver, a founder of the Albert Einstein College of Medicine of Yeshiva University, and a former chairman of the national board of Histadrut Ivrith of America, a national society that promotes the study of the Hebrew language. He is a recipient of the President's Award for Humanitarian Services from the University of Haifa, Israel, and has been awarded the Gold Medal Man of the Year Award by the Israel Bonds organization. Through the Jewish National Fund, he has received the John F. Kennedy Peace Award.

Among LeFrak's countless awards are also honors and recognition from a spectrum of international societies, philanthropies, and educational institutions, such as being knighted a Knight Commander by the king of Norway and receiving a Cross of the Royal Norwegian Order of Merit, knighted a Knight Commander by the king of Sweden and receiving the Royal Order of the North Star, knighted a Knight Commander by Pope John XXIII and receiving the Knights of Malta Cross of Merit and Honor, knighted a Knight Commander by the president of Finland and receiving the Order of the Lion of Finland and the Medal of Parliament.

One of his most recent recognitions as a builder and planner came from the People's Republic of China, which invited LeFrak to present his views on mass housing and modern construction technology to that nation's leaders to help them solve their shelter crisis.

Samuel LeFrak is an avid art collector. He has often talked of building a major museum wing or creating his own museum in Newport. In December 1993 Samuel and his wife, Ethel, announced a major unrestricted gift of $10 million to the Solomon R. Guggenheim Museum, home to one of America's finest collections of modern and contemporary art. The LeFrak's names were added to the rotunda of the Frank Lloyd Wright building to honor the donors of the largest gift the museum had theretofore received.

Today, Samuel LeFrak, chairman of the board of the LeFrak Organization, and his son, Richard LeFrak, president of the firm, are leading the LeFrak Organization into the future while preparing the way for the next generation of LeFraks, Richard's sons Harrison and James LeFrak—currently Princeton undergraduates—to assume the mantle of leadership.

THE FIRST SONGWRITER TO COMPOSE FIFTEEN HUNDRED POPULAR SONGS

1966

Many of the songs we sing, the Broadway shows we see, and the tunes we whistle have something in common. They were composed, introduced, and publicized by American Jews.

For the better part of this century, America has heard and sung the songs of Irving Berlin. The most successful Tin Pan Alley "graduate," he achieved legendary status among twentieth-century American popular composers. His ever-popular "God Bless America" has become accepted as America's second national anthem. His "Easter Parade" and "White Christmas" have become fixtures of the holidays they celebrate. His paeans to blue skies, ragtime, romantic waltzes, America, the Army, show business, and music are etched on the American consciousness.

With a life that spanned more than one hundred years and a catalog that boasted some fifteen hundred ballads, dance numbers, novelty tunes, and love songs, plus twenty Broadway musicals and revues and seventeen feature films, Irving Berlin epitomized Jerome Kern's famous maxim, "Irving Berlin has no place in American music . . . he *is* American music. Emotionally, he has absorbed the vibrations emanating from the people, the manners, and the life of his time and in turn gave these expressions back to the world—simplified, clarified and glorified."

Irving Berlin was born Israel Beilin on May 11, 1888. One of eight children of Moses and Leah Lipkin Beilin, his exact place of birth is unknown, although his family had been living in Tolochin, Byelorussia, where his father was a cantor in the village synagogue. When, in 1893, the family was forced to flee their home after a pogrom during the reign of Czar Alexander III, he was brought to the United States at the age of five. They settled in a crowded tenement on Cherry Street in the heart of New York City's Lower East Side among other Yiddish-speaking immigrants.

Irving Berlin grew up well versed in the lifestyle and milieu of the Lower East Side. Profoundly interested in singing even as a child, he was a member of a synagogue choir. His musical ear, as well as his ability to recall any melody he heard, was clearly an inheritance from his father the cantor, but whereas his father had enjoyed cantorial music, young Irving developed a taste for the sentimental ballads of the 1890s.

The family's financial problems were compounded by the death of Moses Beilin in 1901. To help support his mother and brothers and sisters, young Irving sold newspapers on the streets and earned pennies leading a blind singer on his rounds through the streets of the Bowery, in those days the Broadway of the Lower East Side.

At fourteen, having completed only two years of formal schooling, he ran away from home and began to earn a living as a singing waiter in saloons and bars.

From 1905 to 1907 Berlin worked as a singing waiter at the Pelham Café at 12 Pell Street in the heart of New York City's Chinatown, where he sang, waited on tables, and learned how to pick out tunes on a battered upright piano. In his off hours, he laboriously picked out the tunes of new songs on the keyboard, though unable to read or write music. In fact, he had no idea how to transcribe his tunes to compose musical scores. Throughout his career his technique remained primative, and when he composed at the piano, he did it only in one key—F sharp. For this reason he later had a special piano built in such a way that with the turn of a lever it could play in any key he wanted while he continued to play only the black keys.

It was at the Pelham Café that Berlin wrote the lyrics for his first published song, "Marie From Sunny Italy," which was released by the Joseph Stern Company on May 8, 1907, with music by Nick Nicholson, the saloon's pianist. It brought him the measly pittance of thirty-seven cents in earnings. The printer inadvertently changed his name from Israel Beilin to Israel Berlin. Taking the change one step further, the budding composer adopted Irving as his first name.

His second tune, "Dorando," brought him twenty-five dollars the following year and a staff position with the Ted Snyder Music Publishing Company. For the next three years most of Berlin's output was in collaboration with Snyder or one of his stable of composers. Berlin was soon made a junior partner in the firm.

In 1911 came the song—the words and music both by Berlin—that swept the nation and the world, a syncopated creation that set a new style in song: "Alexander's Ragtime Band." It had a strong influence on contemporary composers. Jazz concerts and jazz symphonic works were unknown before its appearance, but when serious musicians were caught up in the sweep of its irresistible melody, they began to sense a new idiom in American music. The tune sold a million copies of sheet music within three months of its publication. Decades later, it became the theme song of a successful motion picture.

As the sales of this song were multiplying, Berlin came out with two additional songs in the ragtime idiom—"The Ragtime Violin" and "Everybody's Doin' It Now"—which helped make the turkey trot a dance craze. While still in his early twenties, the "ragtime king" was earning $2,000 a week.

Drafted into the United States Army in World War I as an infantry private, Berlin served at Camp Upton, Long Island, an embarkation point for troops leaving for Europe. He was commissioned to write the songs for *Yip, Yip, Yaphank*, "A Musical Mess Cooked Up By the Boys of Camp Upton." After a limited engagement at the camp, the show opened on July 26, 1918, at the Century Theater on Broadway. From it came "Oh, How I Hate to Get Up in the Morning," a hit that was inspired by Berlin's fondness for sleeping until noon. *Yip, Yip, Yaphank* earned $150,000 for the building of a service center at Camp Upton.

After his discharge from the Army with the rank of sergeant, Berlin formed his own music publishing house in 1919—the Irving Berlin Music Company—to market his own songs. The decision would make him a millionaire many times over. Berlin then began composing music for a long line of Broadway shows including the *Ziegfeld Follies*, an annual revue noted for its lavish sets, rich costumes, and great names in show business.

Around the same time, Berlin became a theater owner. The Music Box Theater, which he established in partnership with veteran showmen Sam Harris and Joseph Schenk, opened with a specially written Berlin musical, *The Music Box Revue*. The revue continued for three years, producing several of Berlin's most successful hit songs, among them "Say It With Music." Now for the first time a theater was given a theme song.

Berlin was married for only one year to Dorothy Goetz, who died from typhoid fever contracted while on their honeymoon in Cuba in 1913. He married the social debutante Ellin McKay in 1926. She was the daughter of a wealthy non-Jewish industrialist, Clarence McKay, president of Postal Telegraph, who opposed the wedding.

It was in the 1920s that Berlin wrote some of his most memorable ballads, some inspired by events in his own life such as "All Alone," "What'll I Do?" "Always," "Remember," "The Song Is Ended," and "Blue Skies."

After a fallow period during the early years of the Depression, Berlin again became productive in 1932 and composed "How Deep Is the Ocean?" and "Say It Isn't So," which became enormous hits for RCA and the Berlin Music Company.

Devoid of the frivolity of his earlier musical scores, his next two musicals were sobered by social awareness of the early 1930s. *Face the Music* dealt with political corruption, and *As Thousands Cheer*, which opened on September 30, 1933, introduced "Heat Wave," a dirge about a lynching, along with the classic "Easter Parade."

In 1935 after sound was introduced into motion pictures, Berlin was recruited by the motion picture industry and wrote the score for his first film musical, *Top Hat*, in which Fred Astaire and Ginger Rogers introduced "Isn't This a Lovely Day" and "Cheek to Cheek." It was succeeded by *Follow the Fleet* (1936), *On the Avenue* (1937), and *Carefree* (1938). That same year a film compendium of Berlin songs was assembled for the movie *Alexander's Ragtime Band*, starring Alice Faye and Tyrone Power.

In 1940 Berlin wrote the most popular movie of his career, *Holiday Inn*. The film was a fantastic box-office smash that starred Bing Crosby and introduced one of the most popular songs ever written. In Bing Crosby's version alone, "White Christmas" sold over twenty-five million records. All told, the song has been recorded in more than three hundred versions, and new ones come out each holiday season.

Other films for which Berlin composed original songs include *Blue Skies* (1946), *Easter Parade* (1948), *There's No Business Like Show Business* (1954), and *White Christmas* (1954).

Annie Get Your Gun (1950) and *Call Me Madame* (1953) were film versions of his stage musicals.

Berlin's "God Bless America" was originally written in 1918 as the finale of the second act of *Yip, Yip, Yaphank*. Deciding that the song was not needed since the soldiers in the cast had already expressed their love for their country without having to sing about it, Berlin put it aside. More than twenty years later, the popular singer Kate Smith asked him to give her a song for a patriotic broadcast she was doing. Berlin recalled the melody he had written for *Yip, Yip, Yaphank*, slightly altered the lyrics, and made Smith promise that any profits from the song be donated to America's scouting movements. She agreed and introduced the song on her Armistice Day program in 1939. It immediately swept the country—so much so that the song was used at both political conventions in 1940.

World War II brought another all-serviceman musical, *This Is the Army*, to raise money for the USO. Berlin wrote the entire show at Camp Upton, where he was stationed during World War I. He supervised the staging and appeared in it singing, "Oh, How I Hate to Get Up In the Morning," taken from his World War I show. The show opened on Broadway on July 4, 1942, and played in most major cities of the United States. It went on tour throughout England, Italy, and various bases in the South Pacific. Berlin stayed with the show during its three and a half years of travel and appeared in it when it was made into a motion picture by Warner Brothers.

The show earned about $10 million for the Army Relief Fund. Berlin did not receive any money for his efforts but was awarded a Medal of Merit by General George Marshall. Among the hit songs in this musical were "Any Bonds Today," "This is the Army, Mr. Jones," and "I Left My Heart at the Stage Door Canteen." His patriotic motivations to boost production in defense plants led Berlin to compose "Arms for the Love of America." He also composed "Angels of Mercy" for the American Red Cross.

Berlin's last prewar show had been *Louisiana Purchase*, a satire on political bossism that opened on May 28, 1940, at the Imperial Theater. With the end of World War II he returned to Broadway with *Annie Get Your Gun*, based on the exploits of the sharpshooting Annie Oakley. The songs in *Annie* included such all-time favorites as "They Say It's Wonderful," "Doin' What Comes Naturally," "The Girl That I Marry," and, most of all, the song that became the theme song of the entertainment industry, "There's No Business Like Show Business."

There were other musicals after *Annie Get Your Gun*, including *Miss Liberty* in 1949, a story about a woman who posed for the Statue of Liberty, highlighted by such numbers as "Let's Take an Old-Fashioned Walk" and "Give Me Your Tired, Your Poor." A year later he had another hit, *Call Me Madame*, based on the life of Perle Mesta, the socialite and party giver who was appointed U.S. Ambassador to Luxembourg. Berlin's last musical, written in 1962, was entitled *Mr. President*. The show told the story of a president and his family after they leave the White House.

For five decades, Irving Berlin remained the acknowledged master of popular music, and in 1966 songs were still coming from his ever-lively imagination. When *Annie Get Your Gun* was revived in 1966, Berlin added another hit song entitled "Old-Fashioned Wedding."

Irving Berlin supported Jewish charities and organizations and donated large sums of money to worthwhile causes. Over the years he was honored by the National Conference of Christians and Jews and by the YMHA as "an outstanding American of the Jewish faith." He made large contributions to the United Jewish Appeal of New York and was a generous supporter of the State of Israel.

An unabashed patriot, his love and generosity to his country was legendary through several of his foundations, including the God Bless America Fund and This Is the Army, Inc. He donated millions of dollars to the Army Emergency Fund, the Boy and Girl Scouts of America, and the Campfire Girls. His actions were acknowledged by such accolades as the Army Medal from President Truman in 1945, a Congressional Gold Medal in 1955 from President Eisenhower for composing "God Bless America" and other patriotic songs, and the Freedom Medal from President Ford in 1977.

Irving Berlin's one hundredth birthday on May 11, 1988, was celebrated worldwide, culminating in an all-star tribute at Carnegie Hall benefitting the hall and the American Society of Composers, Authors, and Publishers, of which he was a cofounder.

On September 22, 1989, at the age of 101, Irving Berlin died in his sleep in his town house in New York City. Many of the songs he wrote will live on as long as America loves to sing a song.

THE FIRST AMERICAN JEW TO RECEIVE THE NOBEL PEACE PRIZE

1973

Jews have been lovers of peace from the days of Solomon and Jeremiah. Some have been absolute pacifists like Alfred Fried and Tobias M. S. Asser, two European Jews who won the Nobel Peace Prize in 1911. Others have fought for peace alone; through their governments; or through legal, peace, or humanitarian organizations.

The political scientist and presidential counselor Henry Alfred Kissinger, who served as secretary of state under Presidents Richard Nixon and Gerald Ford, was the first American Jew to receive the Nobel Peace Prize, which was awarded to him in 1973. In July 1983 he was appointed by President Ronald Reagan to chair the National Bipartisan Commission on Central America, until it ceased operation in January 1985. From 1984 to 1990 he served as a member of the president's Foreign Intelligence Advisory Board. Foreign and domestic leaders sought him for guidance and advice or blamed him for American policy failures.

Born Heinz Alfred Kissinger on May 27, 1923, in the Bavarian town of Fürth, Germany, he was the elder son of Paula Stern and Louis Kissinger, a teacher in a girl's secondary school. He grew up in a cultured and devoutly Orthodox Jewish home in Germany.

Less than three months before the mobs of Kristallnacht destroyed their synagogue in 1938, the Kissingers fled Nazi Germany for London and then America. They settled in the Washington Heights section of New York City. Heinz—now "Henry"—attended George Washington High School in the evening, where he was a straight A student, and worked in a shaving brush factory during the day. While attending City College of New York in 1943, he was drafted into the United States Army for service in World War II. He was assigned as a German interpreter and interrogator for the 970th Counterintelligence Corps. After Germany surrendered to the Allies in May 1945, Kissinger was appointed district administrator and set up functional governments in areas of Germany captured by American troops. For his service in this capacity, the young Army captain was awarded a Bronze Star.

After the war, Kissinger entered Harvard University under a New York State scholarship. There he specialized in political science and earned his M.A. degree in 1952 and his Ph.D. in 1954. He used his doctoral dissertation as a basis for his first book, which was published in 1957 as *A World Restored: Castereagh, Metternich, and the Restoration of Peace, 1812– 1822.* In it he viewed modern history as a struggle between the forces of revolution and the conservative statesmen of the established order.

Remaining at Harvard, Kissinger served from 1954 to 1969 as a member of the faculty for both the Department of Government and the Center of International Affairs. At Harvard, Kissinger quickly established himself as an authority on foreign policy and strategic defense. One of his colleagues, the American historian Arthur Schlesinger, Jr., recommended him as director of a study sponsored by the Council on Foreign Relations. The result of this eighteen-month study was a book Kissinger wrote, *Nuclear Weapons and Foreign Policy*, in which he examined the alternatives to the strategy of massive nuclear retaliation that had been formulated by Secretary of State John Foster Dulles. This book proved to be a best-seller and brought him to the attention of Nelson Rockefeller, who in 1956 appointed him director of the Rockefeller Brothers Fund. From 1959 to 1969 Kissinger headed Harvard University's Defense Studies Program.

During the administration of President John F. Kennedy, he became a part-time consultant to several policy-making agencies and in 1965 was a consultant to Henry Cabot Lodge, Jr., who was posted in Vietnam.

When Richard Nixon was elected president in 1968, Kissinger was brought into the administration by him. He assumed the position of assistant to the president for national security affairs, with the responsibility of advising the president on foreign relations and military policy as head of the powerful National Security Council.

As chief foreign policy advisor to President Nixon, Kissinger initiated the Strategic Arms Limitation Talks (SALT) in 1969. Two years later he played a prominent role in negotiations that led to the initiation of the detente policy with Russia and to the Soviet Union's promising access to West Berlin in exchange for recognition of East Germany. During the summer of 1971 Henry Kissinger secretly met with Premier Chou-En-Lai in Peking to pave the way for Nixon's trip to the People's Republic of China in February 1972, which reestablished a relationship with China.

Espousing a policy based on an international balance of power, Kissinger played a major role in advising the president on the United States policy in Vietnam, Laos, and Cambodia. He worked tirelessly in pursuit of the right strategy for ending the war in Vietnam, the longest in American history.

Richard Nixon, in his second term as president, named Henry Kissinger secretary of state on September 22, 1973, the highest position ever attained by a Jew in any American administration. Kissinger had helped Nixon formulate the so-called Vietnamization policy, whereby United States troops were progressively disengaged and replaced by South Vietnamese. On January 27, 1973, Kissinger reached a peace agreement with the chief North Vietnamese negotiator, Le Duc Thou. It was agreed that the United States would withdraw its troops while continuing to send aid to South Vietnam. In turn, North Vietnam would release

American prisoners of war. The two men were awarded the 1973 Nobel Peace Prize for their efforts to end the fighting.

Kissinger gave his share of the $122,000 prize money to establish a scholarship fund for the children of American servicemen killed or missing in action in Vietnam.

In the fall of 1973 when the Yom Kippur War broke out between Israel and the Arab states of Egypt and Syria, Kissinger made numerous visits to seven Middle Eastern capitals in an effort to end the fighting. This "shuttle diplomacy," as it came to be known, led to a cease-fire agreement between Egypt and Israel, resumption of full-scale diplomatic relations between Egypt and the United States, the reopening of the Suez Canal, and, in May 1974, the signing of the agreement between Israel and Syria, thereby launching a peace effort in the Middle East.

In 1974 when President Richard Nixon resigned from office in the wake of the Watergate scandals, Kissinger remained secretary of state under President Gerald Ford until 1977. Then, leaving government service, he taught at Georgetown University's School of Foreign Service. In addition to writing books; publishing numerous articles on United States foreign policy, international affairs, and diplomatic history; and lecturing, he formed Kissinger Associates, a private consulting firm, and is widely sought out to purvey foreign policy expertise to private corporations.

After seventeen years on the diplomatic sidelines, in April 1994 Kissinger, along with Lord Carrington, the former British Foreign Secretary, agreed to help mediate the fierce dispute in South Africa between the African National Congress and the Zulus who wanted an autonomous homeland. He flew to South Africa in what some experts called a long-shot effort to end the strife that threatened to undermine that country's first all-race elections from April 26–28.

In addition to the books mentioned above, Henry Kissinger was also the author of *The Necessity of Choice* (1961) on the prospects of United States foreign policy, *The Troubled Partnership: A Reappraisal of the Atlantic Alliance* (1965), *The White House Years* (1979), *Years of Upheaval* (1982), *Observations: Selected Speeches and Essays 1982–1984* (1985), and *Diplomacy* (1994), a history of western diplomacy from Richelieu down through Metternich and Bismark to modern times.

Henry Kissinger's memoirs—particularly *White House Years* and *Years of Upheaval*, written from the vantage point of the Nixon White House—were eagerly anticipated by all those interested in understanding the inner workings of American foreign policy. His volumes are seminal books written by a gifted historian and political scientist transformed into a statesman who admirably succeeded in digesting, analyzing, and presenting an enormous amount of major developments in American foreign policy in a perspicuous, coherent, and engrossing fashion.

A moving passage in Kissinger's *White House Years,* so reminiscent of Mary Antin's paeans to America as a haven for persecuted Jews, reveals Kissinger's deep feelings of gratitude and identification with his adopted country, which made possible his meteoric rise to the pinnacle of policy making in Washington. He writes: "America acquired a wonderous quality for me. When I was a boy, it was a dream, an incredible place where tolerance was natural. . . . I always remembered the thrill when I first walked the streets of New York City. Seeing a group of boys, I began to cross to the other side to avoid being beaten up. And then I remembered where I was."

In addition to receiving the Nobel Peace Prize in 1973, Henry Kissinger was awarded the Presidential Medal of Freedom in 1976 by President Gerald Ford and the Medal of Liberty in 1986.

Kissinger's column, syndicated by the *Los Angeles Times Syndicate,* appears in leading United States newspapers and in over forty foreign countries.

On June 20, 1995, Henry Kissinger was honored for "his contribution toward Anglo-American relations."

Henry Kissinger did not have to bend when he was knighted by Queen Elizabeth in Buckingham Palace. The Queen made Mr. Kissinger an Honorary Knight Commander of the Most Distinguished Order of St. Michael and St. George, one of the top honors Britain can bestow on a foreigner.

Because he is an American, he did not get the title "Sir," but he is allowed to add K.C. after his name.

THE FIRST AMERICAN JEWISH WOMAN TO RECEIVE THE NOBEL PRIZE IN MEDICINE

1977

On October 13, 1977, the Caroline Institute in Stockholm, Sweden, called Dr. Rosalyn Yalow to inform her that she had been awarded the Nobel Prize in medicine (jointly with Dr. Roger Guillemin and Dr. Andrew Schally, who worked independently in different parts of the United States) "for the development of radioimmunoassays of peptide hormones." In the seventy-seven years since the founding of the Nobel Prizes, 106 laureates had been named in physicology or medicine. Dr. Yalow was the first American Jewish woman and the second woman ever in the history of the prize to join this select group.

The Nobel Prize was awarded to Dr. Yalow for having perfected a testing procedure that combines "immunology, isotope research, mathematics, and physics." The test is known as RIA, for radioimmunoasy, a technique used in more than five thousand clinical and research laboratories throughout the world to measure small amounts of peptide hormones and other substances in blood and tissues. It is so sensitive that it can detect the billionth part of a gram. As one member of the Nobel Prize Committee explained it, the RIA is like finding a lump of sugar in a lake sixty-two miles long, sixty-two miles wide, and thirty feet deep.

Rosalyn Yalow was born Rosalyn Sussman on July 19, 1921, in the Bronx, New York. She was the daughter of Simon, the owner of a small paper and twine business, and Clara Zipper Sussman. She obtained her early education in the Bronx public elementary schools and then attended Walton High School, where her chemistry teacher urged her to study science. She was determined to become a physicist as an undergraduate at Hunter College (now part of the City University of New York) at a time when recent developments in nuclear physics aroused great interest. However, she had been advised that it was virtually impossible for a woman to receive a graduate assistantship in physics.

As a senior she accepted a position as secretary to a scientist at Columbia University so that she could take tuition-free courses after graduation. She graduated with a Bachelor of Arts degree from Hunter College in January 1941 magna cum laude and Phi Beta Kappa and as that institution's first graduate with a major in physics. A month later, she received word that she had been accepted as a graduate teaching assistant in physics at the University of Illinois in Urbana.

The only woman among four hundred men on the faculty of the College of Engineering, she became in 1945 the second woman in the history of the University of Illinois to earn a doctorate in physics. Since her research was in nuclear physics, she became skilled in making and using apparatus for the measurement of radioactive substances.

On her first day in graduate school, Rosalyn Sussman met Aaron Yalow, the son of a leading rabbi in Syracuse, New York, who was also beginning graduate studies in physics. In 1943 he became her husband. Two years later, after obtaining their Ph.D. degrees, the Yalows returned to New York, where for one year Roslayn Yalow worked as an electrical engineer for the Federal Telecommunications Lab—a research laboratory for ITT. When the research group left New York in 1946, she returned to her alma mater, Hunter College, to teach physics to veterans in a pre-engineering program.

After World War II, the Veterans Administration initiated a research program to explore the use of radioactive substances in the diagnosis and treatment of disease. One of the hospitals chosen for the nuclear medicine project was the Veterans Administration Hospital in the Bronx, which hired Dr. Yalow as a consultant in nuclear physics in 1947. In that capacity she established and equipped one of the first radioisotope laboratories in the United States (radioisotopes are radioactive atoms).

Three years later she was appointed physicist and assistant chief of the hospital's Radioactive Service. That year Yalow also met Dr. Solomon A. Berson, a young internist who joined the Radioisotope Unit and with whom she began what would be a twenty-two-year complementary collaboration that lasted until his death in 1972. Together they began the pioneering work of radioimmunoassay that culminated in the Nobel Prize. Unfortunately, Dr. Berson did not live to share the Nobel Prize with her, as he would have had he survived.

Initially the two researchers explored the use of radioactive iodine in the diagnosis and treatment of thyroid disease. Later, they measured blood volume by tagging red blood cells with radioisotopes of phosphorus and potassium or plasma proteins with radioiodine. They subsequently used radioactive iodine to tag insulin and other hormones and proteins to study how the body used such substances. While conducting those studies, Dr. Yalow and Dr. Berson developed their revolutionary method of radioimmunoassay, a laboratory procedure that employs radioisotopes and immunologic methods to measure with a high degree of precision substances in blood and other body fluids. In the past, those substances had often been impossible to measure because they were present in such minute quantities that biologic assay systems could not readily detect them.

Since that time, RIA has permitted scientists to utilize this methodology to measure the concentrations of hundreds of pharmacologic and biological substances in the blood and other fluids in the human body, in animals, and in plants.

Doctors carrying out diagnoses of their patients are now able to detect what may sound like trivial changes in their patients' hormones that in turn can produce radical effects on their health. The new method of testing and evaluation continues to lead to new discoveries and understanding of the nature of the human body.

RIA has been used by thousands of blood banks to prevent the use of blood contaminated with the hepatitis virus. The technique may be employed to detect if a person has recently taken drugs such as heroin, methadone, or LSD. It has been used for the early detection of cancer and to measure the levels of neurotransmitters (substances that allow nerve impulses to be transmitted across the gap between nerve cells) or hormones in tissue or plasma.

During the many years that the testing procedures were being developed, Dr. Yalow was available as a guinea pig, participating as a volunteer in many laboratory studies.

Dr. Yalow has been associated with the Bronx Veterans Administration Medical Center since 1947, serving as acting chief of the Radioisotope

Service from 1968 to 1970 and until 1980 as chief of the Nuclear Medicine Service. In 1972, she was named Senior Investigator by the Veterans Administration, only one of six scientists so designated by the VA's 140-hospital complex throughout the United States.

Dr. Yalow joined the Mount Sinai Medical School of City University of New York faculty when the medical school was founded in 1968 and was named Distinguished Service Professor in 1974. She was the fifth faculty member, the first woman and the first nonphysician to be so honored by that institution.

Between 1979 and 1986, Dr. Yalow was Distinguished Professor-at-Large of the Albert Einstein College of Medicine of Yeshiva University. She was concurrently chairman of the Department of Clinical Sciences at Montefiore Hospital and Medical Center in the Bronx from 1980 until 1986. Since 1986 she has been Solomon A. Berson Distinguished Professor-at-Large at the Mount Sinai School of Medicine.

In 1976 she was the first woman and the first nuclear physicist to receive the prestigious Albert Lasker Basic Medical Research Award. Among Yalow's many other awards and honors are the American Academy of Achievement Gold Plate Award for Salute to Excellence (1977) and the A. Cressy Morrison Prize in Natural Sciences of the New York Academy of Sciences (1975). She is a Fellow of the New York Academy of Sciences and a member of the American Academy of Arts and Sciences, the New York Academy of Medicine, the Radiation Research Society, the American Association of Physicists in Medicine, the Endocrine Society, and the National Academy of Sciences.

Dr. Yalow has delivered distinguished lectures before numerous societies and at medical centers throughout the world. She has been awarded fifty-one honorary doctorate degrees and has received over fifty additional awards from medical, scientific, and other societies. In 1980 she was presented with an honorary Doctor of Science degree by the University of Hartford in Connecticut. At the commencement address she reflected on some of her early experiences as an aspiring scientist and her observations since then, saying: "If we are to have faith that mankind will survive and thrive on the face of the earth, we are dependent on the revolutions brought by science. These revolutions will set us free from hunger and permit us to set our sights on the stars."

THE FIRST JEWISH ASTRONAUT

1984

On January 28, 1986, seven brave men and women began a space shuttle mission aboard the *Challenger* from the Kennedy Space Center in Florida.

Only one minute and 12.2 seconds after lift-off a major malfunction caused the explosion of the spacecraft, taking the lives of all seven astronauts— seven people whose dreams of space sprang from roots as diverse as the country itself.

The crew included three trained pilots—Francis Scobee, the space-craft commander; the mission pilot, Mike J. Smith, a commander in the U.S. Navy; and Air Force Lieutenant Colonel Ellison Onizuka, a former aerospace engineer. Aboard, too, were Dr. Ronald E. McNair, a laser expert; Gregory Jarvis, an engineer; and Christa McAuliffe, a New Hampshire schoolteacher who was to be the first civilian in space. And there was Judith Resnik, the first Jewish astronaut and the second American woman to fly in space back in 1984. (Dr. Sally K. Rand, who flew a mission in 1983, was the first American woman to fly in space.)

On her first trip into space, Resnik was a mission specialist on the maiden voyage of the shuttle *Discovery*. After *Discovery* was in orbit, she radioed back to NASA that "the earth looks great." Part of her job on that mission was pointing a camera on the craft's robotic long arm to inspect initial efforts to shake a chunk of ice off the craft's side. The crew managed to make the robotic arm knock off the piece of ice. Resnik had logged 144 hours and 57 seconds in space.

A classical pianist who had earned her doctorate in electrical engineering from the University of Maryland, Judith was born on April 5, 1949, in Akron, Ohio. As a student, math and science were her favorite subjects. One of her teachers in high school declared that she was the best math student he had ever had. Carnegie-Mellon University in Pittsburgh, known for its excellent science program, was where she earned a bachelor of science degree in electrical engineering in 1970, and she obtained a doctorate in electrical engineering from the University of Maryland in College Park in 1977.

After her graduation, Resnik held a number of jobs before entering the space program. Her first work was with the RCA Corporation in Morristown, New Jersey, where she worked on circuitry for specialized radar control systems. While working for RCA, Resnik authored a paper on design procedures for special-purpose integrated circuitry.

Resnik was a biomedical engineer and staff fellow in the laboratory of neurophysiology at the National Institutes of Health in Bethesda, Maryland, until 1978. Prior to her selection by NASA in 1978, she worked for the Xerox Corporation in El Segundo, California. When in 1977 she was completing her studies for her doctorate at the University of Maryland, she saw a notice on the bulletin board of her office, announcing the National Aeronautics and Space Administration's plan to recruit new astronauts. NASA received six thousand applications from women. Judith did not feel that she had a chance, but decided to apply. She went on a strict diet and exercise program and became very knowledgeable about flying, even studying to receive a pilot's license. Finally after much waiting, in January 1978, Judith, almost twenty-nine years old, was accepted by NASA as one of the new astronaut candidates along with four other women.

She completed her one-year training evaluation period in August 1979. NASA then assigned her to work on a number of projects in support of the *Orbiter* development, including experimental software, the Remote Manipulator System, and training techniques.

Interviewed before her first space flight in 1984, Resnik said she had strong commitments to her religion. Her grandparents had fled Kiev, Russia, in the 1920s and emigrated to Palestine. As a boy, her father, Dr. Marvin Resnik, an optometrist, studied at the Hebron Yeshiva in Palestine and was among the children who survived the pogrom there in 1929. That same year his family fled to the United States and settled in Cleveland, where her grandfather, Jacob Resnik, worked as a *shochet*.

Judith Resnik received a Jewish education, spoke Hebrew and celebrated her Bat Mitzvah (confirmation) at the Beth El Synagogue in Akron, and continued attending Hebrew School until her graduation from Akron's Firestone Hebrew High School.

She was determined to do everything she possibly could. She was a classical pianist and a gourmet cook. When questioned about her intensity at the piano, she replied: "I never play anything softly."

On the morning of January 28, 1986, Resnik was awaiting the launch of her second space mission, after months of intensive training. The *Challenger* shuttle had been delayed over and over again. Once there was a dust storm in Western Africa where they might have had to make an emergency landing. Another delay was caused because it was raining heavily and space shuttles do not take off in the rain. Judith was on the upper deck of the *Challenger*, strapped to a couch, flat on her back, on the third try, but it became too windy for them to take off, and after five and a half hours in this position, the astronauts climbed out of the spacecraft.

NASA finally decided to launch the spacecraft at 11:38 A.M. on the morning of January 28, 1986, although there were icicles on the launch pad and cold temperatures they knew might cause problems. At 11:39 A.M., just one minute and 12.2 seconds after lift-off, the *Challenger* space program had come to an end. The spacecraft exploded and all those inside were killed, including Judith Resnik.

All seven members of *Challenger*'s crew were mourned as American heroes. Their deaths in what was the first in-flight disaster in fifty-six United States space missions was a national tragedy, mourned by all Americans.

A Jewish funeral was held for Judith Resnik in Akron. She was just thirty-six years old when the tragedy occurred. She had once said, "It does not enter our minds that we are doing something dangerous." This must be the way they have to think or there would be no space programs.

The *Dr. Judith Resnik Challenger Memorial* was established in 1989 in Haifa, Israel, by the American Friends of the Bnai Zion Medical Center in honor of Judith Resnik and her fellow *Challenger* crew members.

The memorial consists of a rehabilitation gymnasium furnished with physiotherapeutic equipment and advanced instrumentation. The facility is an integral part of the Orthopedic and Prosthetic Departments of the Medical Center. It serves many thousands of disabled war veterans, stroke victims, handicapped children, and others similarly disabled in Northern Israel who face the challenge of rehabilitation daily in order to live a full and productive life.

THE FIRST SPIRITUAL MENTOR TO ORDAIN TWO THOUSAND RABBIS

1985

Among Orthodox Jews, Rabbi Joseph Dov Soloveitchik, the twentieth century's preeminent Talmudic scholar, renowned philosopher, and theologian, was simply known as "the Rav," an affectionate Hebrew name for teacher. He held no elective office and occupied no pulpit, yet the breadth of his learning and the depth of his piety was such that on matters of *Halakhah* (Jewish law) his authority was unchallenged. Orthodox rabbis around the world called him with queries about how to apply Jewish law to modern problems.

For nearly half a century, from 1941 to 1985, Rabbi Dr. Soloveitchik was professor of Talmud and Jewish philosophy at the Rabbi Isaac Elchanan Theological Seminary of Yeshiva University in Upper Manhattan, where he trained, inspired, and ordained some two thousand rabbis, leading the Yeshiva to claim that he had conferred the title more often than any other American spiritual mentor or seminary teacher.

His students and followers in all branches of Judaism have shaped the character of modern Orthodox Judaism; his teachings have stood as paradigms of philosophic insight and religious sensitivity. In a milieu in which religious faith is challenged to the utmost by the modern intellectual temperament and the practitioners of rabbinic Judaism are distrustful of the tools of the Western intellectual tradition, Rabbi Soloveitchik championed the validity of applying the most sophisticated and rigorous philosophic and analytic methods of understanding the corpus of Jewish law, construed both as a metaphysical system and a practical way of life.

Equally at home in the works of Shakespeare, Kant, and the laws of nature, as well as the deep-welled springs of Jewish tradition and learning,

Rabbi Soloveitchik wove together concepts of Jewish and Western scholarship, forging innovative and creative approaches to man's place in relationship to God and to the scheme of the universe.

He demonstrated that modern culture and intellectual thought are not incompatable with total observance of *Halakhah*. He was one of those instrumental in helping Orthodox Judaism secure a foothold in America. In his lectures and writings he chartered out a philosophy of Judaism rooted firmly in *Halakhah*, yet fully aware of the soul's conflicts as an existentialist (philosopher or psychologist).

Born in Pruzhan, Poland, on February 27, 1903, Joseph Dov Soloveitchik was the descendant of a prominent East European rabbinic dynasty. His maternal grandfather, Rabbi Chaim Soloveitchik, rabbi of Brisk-Litovsk, Poland, was responsible for revolutionizing Talmudic scholarship. Joseph spent his childhood in Khoslavitch, a White Russian town, where his father, Rav Moshe, served as rabbi. Under his father's tutelage, he mastered his grandfather's method of Talmudic study. In remarkable contrast to the education of all Orthodox rabbis of that era, his mother provided him with an extensive secular education, introducing her son to the writings of Ibsen, Pushkin, and Bialik.

In 1931 he earned his doctorate in philosophy from the University of Berlin. His dissertation dealt with the epistemology and metaphysics of the neo-Kantian Jewish philosopher Hermann Cohen.

That same year he married Tonya Lewitt, the recipient of a Ph.D. degree in education from the University of Jena. In 1932, together with his wife and newborn child, Dr. Soloveitchik emigrated to the United States to accept the position of rabbi of the Orthodox Jewish community of Boston, the city that remained his home. There in 1938 he founded the Maimonides School, the first Hebrew Day School in New England and at that time one of only two such schools outside of New York City. He nurtured it from infancy to the great institution it has become. In 1995, the Maimonides School was still under the guidance of the Soloveitchik family.

In 1941, Rabbi Soloveitchik was appointed Professor of Talmud at Yeshiva University's Rabbi Isaac Elchanan Theological Seminary, succeeding his father who had held the post since being recruited by Dr. Bernard Revel in 1929. He became the spiritual mentor of a majority of today's American Orthodox pulpit rabbis, thus influencing hundreds of thousands of Jews in America and throughout the world.

Although his home was in Boston, Rabbi Soloveitchik conducted Talmud classes at the Rabbi Isaac Elchanan Theological Seminary (RIETS) until 1985, when he became ill, shuttling each week to New York by plane, train, or car.

As a teacher, he kept his students in awe of his knowledge and in fear of his rebuke. When he first came to Yeshiva University, students began to skip their regular college classes to attend his lectures. Soloveitchik taught his students that the key role of a rabbi is "to redress the grievances of those who are abandoned and alone, to protect the dignity of the poor, to save the oppressed from the hands of the oppressor."

In 1952, Rabbi Soloveitchik began to conduct *shiurim* (talmudic discourses) regularly at Congregation Moriah in Manhattan. What began as small, weekly gatherings for laymen in the synagogue became a meeting place for thousands from all parts of New York. The weekly lectures continued for some thirty years.

Rabbi Soloveitchik's annual *shiurim*, often lasting from four to five hours that he delivered at Yeshiva University on the occasion of his father's *Yahrzeit* (anniversary of death), attracted thousands of listeners and was regarded as the major annual academic event for United States Orthodox Jewry.

Rabbi Soloveitchik's study is said to have been knee-deep in manuscripts of his commentaries of holy works and everyday problems and tapes of his *shiurim*. Even so, continuing his family's reluctance to appear in print due to the demands of perfectionism, his published writings are few and far between.

Rav Soloveitchik described himself as "a stranger in modern society that is technical-minded, self-centered, and self-loving."

"My doctrines are not technical. My law cannot be laboratory tested. What can I say to a functional, utilitarian society?" he asked in *The Lonely Man of Faith*, first published as an essay in the journal *Tradition* in 1965 and reprinted as a book by Doubleday in 1992.

He outlined his basic theological position in "Ish Halakhah" (Halakhic Man), a lengthy essay that appeared in the Hebrew journal *Talpiot* in 1944. The essay was published in English in 1993 by the Jewish Publication Society of America. The rabbi argued in the essay that man becomes master of himself when he lives in accordance with Jewish law. Then he is no longer a creature of habit; his life becomes sanctified, and God and man are drawn into a community of existence that he termed "a convenental community." This community, he maintained, brings God and man together into an intimate relationship. "To see the world through the eyes of *Halakhah*," he wrote, "is as valid and as noble as to see it through the eyes of an artist or scientist. It is only through the observance of *Halakhah* that man attains his goal of nearness to God."

In 1974 Yeshiva University published *Shiurei HaRav: A Conspectus of the Public Lectures of Rabbi Joseph Dov Soloveitchik*, which was republished in 1994. Three additional essays that were published separately revealed his compelling interest in people as divided beings, active and passive. Contradictory and paradoxical as people are, he argued, torn as they are by stress and conflict, lured and repelled by divinity, he nonetheless concluded that every human being was capable of childlike innocence and faith no matter how cynical he or she had become.

In addition to his position at Yeshiva University, Rabbi Soloveitchik was chairman of the *Halakhah* Commission of the Rabbinical Council of America. In this capacity he took strong positions on many issues in American life. He was also president of Mizrachi, the Religious Zionists of America.

Following the death of the Ashkenazic Chief Rabbi of Israel, Isaac Herzog, in 1959, Rabbi Soloveitchik declined an invitation to succeed him, not trusting the mixture of religion and politics that it entailed. In an interview with the Boston *Jewish Advocate* in 1964 he explained: "I was afraid to be an officer of the State. A rabbinate linked up with the State cannot be completely free."

Rabbi Soloveitchik pioneered advanced Jewish studies for women, believing that only the study of the sources of *Halakhah* could ensure its observance. He studied Talmud with his daughters, and such a policy was carried out at the Maimonides School. When Yeshiva University's Stern College for Women began offering Talmud courses over two decades ago, he silenced the controversy that arose by delivering the inaugural lecture.

Although much of Rabbi Soloveitchik's work involved reconciling traditional Judaism with the modern world, he opposed aspects of the dialogue initiated by the Catholic church with Jewish leaders as part of the church's ecumenical movement in the 1960s. He said there could be no dialogue concerning the uniqueness of each religious community since each is an entity that cannot be merged or equated with a community that is committed to a different faith. He maintained that such conversations should be restricted to issues of social policy, like the needs of the poor and race relations.

Through his ordination of some two thousand rabbis, the force of his personality, his inexhaustible knowledge of Torah and Talmud, his incisive logic and analysis, his lectures and writings, Rabbi Soloveitchik became the recognized leader of Orthodox Jewry all across the spectrum.

He died in his home in Brookline, Massachusetts, on April 8, 1993, at the age of ninety and was mourned around the world.

"What a link he was to so many strands of the convenental people, to everything from the particular genius of his grandfather, originator of the 'Brisker Method' of Talmudic analysis, to the world of East European Jewry that is destroyed, to the 'anonymous Jew' of the centuries with whom Soloveitchik had so much sympathy, to the world of the Patriarchs and Matriarchs, with whom Soloveitchik seemed to be on such intimate terms . . . and now he leaves a void because he bridged two worlds, and the bridge is not to be reconstructed because the worlds are gone," wrote Rabbi Hillel Goldberg, editor of the Denver *Intermountain Jewish News*.

THE FIRST CHRONICLER OF THE HOLOCAUST TO RECEIVE THE NOBEL PEACE PRIZE

1986

Sixty years ago the world stood mute during the most unspeakable event in history: the cruel and systematic murder of six million innocent men, women, and children. While the German Nazi Holocaust consumed its victims, while Jews were herded into ghettos and concentration camps and brutally starved, gassed, and burned, the nations of the world were silent. For nearly two decades surprisingly little was written or said publicly about the Holocuast.

Elie Wiesel, writer, philosopher, novelist, and playwright, is known throughout the world for his extraordinary efforts to rescue the Holocaust from historical and literary oblivion.

Through his novels, collections of essays, stories, and plays, Elie Wiesel has given us not only an eyewitness account of what happened but also an analysis of the evil powers that lay behind these events. His main concern is the question of what measures can be taken to prevent a recurrence of these events.

It was for his devotion and dedication to exemplification of these themes that Elie Wiesel was awarded the 1986 Nobel Peace Prize. He was the first chronicler of the Holocaust to receive the award.

"Wiesel is a messenger to mankind," said Egil Aarvik, chairman of the Norwegian Nobel Committee in announcing the award. "His message is one of peace, atonement, and human dignity. His belief that the forces fighting evil in the world can be victorious is a hard-won belief. . . ." Aarvik also noted that "Wiesel's commitment, which originated in the suffering of the Jewish people, has been widened to embrace all oppressed peoples and races." On accepting the award, Wiesel recalled "the kingdom of night" he encountered—and survived—in the death camps. "I have tried to keep memory alive," he said. "I have tried to fight those who would forget. Because if we forget, we are guilty, we are accomplices." In conclusion, he declared, "Our lives no longer belong to us alone; they belong to all those who need us desperately."

Elie Wiesel was born on September 30, 1928, in Sighet, a small town in the Carpathian Mountains of Transylvania, in Romania. He was the only son of Shlomo and Sarah Feig Wiesel, having two older sisters and a younger one. His father, a middle-class shopkeeper, instilled the values of Western humanism in the boy. It was at his mother's insistence that Elie obtained a sound grounding in the Torah, Talmud, and the mystical teachings and doctrines of kabala and Hasidism. In 1944, at the age of fifteen, he was deported by the Nazis to the Auschwitz concentration camp with his family and the rest of Sighet's fifteen thousand Jews. His mother and younger sister perished in the gas chambers of that camp. His two older sisters, from whom he was separated, survived the camp. Wiesel and his father were later transported to Buchenwald. There he watched his father die from starvation and dysentery, a scene grippingly related in his first memoir, *Night*, an autobiographical account of a youngster thrust into the death camps with his family.

Liberated toward the end of the war by American troops, he and some four hundred other Jewish orphans were sent to France and became wards of a French Jewish children's agency. There he mastered French, which remained his favorite literary language, and met Francois Mauriac, a Nobel laureate in literature and eminent Catholic philosopher who encouraged him to write about the Holocaust and who later wrote a moving introduction to *Night*, in which Wiesel describes in striking detail the living death he saw at Auschwitz and Buchenwald.

Between 1948 and 1951 Wiesel studied philosophy at the Sorbonne, hoping it would help him deal with the monstrous evil he had experienced. To earn a living, he became a teacher of Hebrew and the Bible and worked simultaneously as a foreign correspondent for the Tel Aviv newspaper, *Yediot Achronot*.

Eleven years after he entered Buchenwald, he arrived in New York City, where he joined the staff of the *Jewish Daily Forward*, a Yiddish-language newspaper, as a writer of feature articles. He also wrote for *L'Arche*, the official publication of organized French Jewry. In 1963 he became an American citizen.

In the meantime, Elie Wiesel had published a number of books, of which *Night* was the first. *Night* was born on the day he met Mauriac. "He was talking about Christ," Wiesel recalled in an interview with Samuel G. Freedman that appeared in the *New York Times* on October 23, 1983. "I simply told him, 'Ten years ago I knew hundreds of Jewish children who suffered more than Christ did and no one talked about it.' And he wept. Mauriac said to me, 'You know, you should talk about it.' And that moved me more than anything."

Writing in longhand, Wiesel produced an eight-hundred-page memoir in Yiddish entitled *Un Di Velt Hut Geshvigan* (*And the World Kept Silent*). After publication of a condensed version of the book in 1956 in Buenos Aires, Wiesel shortened it even more and translated it into French in 1958 as *La Nuit*. When it appeared in 1960 in English as *Night* in the United States, the effect was shattering.

As a result of the book's publication, not only did the Holocaust become a proper subject for public discussion by Jews and Christians, it transformed Wiesel into a major American and world Jewish figure, "a conscience of world Jewry" and "a modern Job" who would not permit the Holocaust to be forgotten.

To date, Elie Wiesel is the author of thirty-eight volumes, including novels, collections of essays, stories, dialogues, and plays. The Holocaust lies at the core of all his writing. His works depict the personal and historical events that have structured his universe, life in the Jewish *shtetl* (small town) of Eastern Europe, the encounter with death in the concentration camps, survival, and the aftermath of catastrophe. His characters, their faith, language, and problems, are exclusively Jewish. The perennial problems of reconciling the concept of a benevolent God with the prevalence of evil in the world is a basic theme in his work, which superimposes modern existentialism on traditional Judaism. In one way or another, each one of his books addresses itself to the question with which Camus and other existentialist philosophers have struggled: How can one be, how can one affirm life, after having experienced unrelieved and absolute evil?

Among Wiesel's best-known works are *Dawn*, a novel (1961); *The Accident*, a novel (1962); *The Town Beyond the Wall*, a novel (1966); *The Gates of the Forest*, a novel (1966); *Legends of Our Times*, essays and stories (1968); *A Beggar in Jerusalem*, a novel (1970); *One Generation After*, essays and stories (1970); *The Oath*, a novel (1973); and *Twilight*, a novel (1988). He has also written two plays, *Zalman, or the Madness of God* (1974) and *The Trial of God* (1979).

He has written an eyewitness account of the plight of Soviet Jewry, based on a trip he made to Russia, entitled, *The Jews of Silence* (1966).

In other works he has drawn on the wisdom of the past to illuminate and empower the present. This work includes *Souls on Fire: Portraits and Legends of the Hasidic Masters* (1972); *Messengers of God: Portraits and Legends of Biblical Heroes* (1976); and *Four Hasidic Masters: More Portraits and Legends* (1978).

Wiesel is one of the totally committed Jews making a significant impression on rootless American-Jewish scholars and intellectuals of the "New Left," whose assumptions he effectively challenges in lectures and debates.

Wiesel has supported the cause of Soviet Jews, Nicaragua's Miskito Indians, Argentina's "disappeared," Cambodian refugees, the Kurds, South African Aparteid victims, famine victims in Africa, and the victims of the continuous war in Bosnia.

Three months after receiving the Nobel Peace Prize, Wiesel established the Elie Wiesel Foundation for Humanity. Its mission is to advance the cause of human rights and peace throughout the world by creating a new forum for the discussion of urgent ethical issues.

The first major project undertaken by the foundation was the international conference of Nobel laureates convened jointly by him and

French President Francois Mitterand. Seventy-five Nobel laureates from five continents met in January 1988 in Paris to explore issues and questions related to the conference theme, "Facing the Twenty-first Century: Threats and Promises." This was followed by seminars in Boston on "The Anatomy of Hate," cosponsored by the University of Haifa, Israel.

Another major conference was convened by the foundation and the Norwegian Nobel Committee in August 1990 in Oslo. Next came a conference sponsored by the journal *Ogonyok* in December 1991 in Moscow. Some of those attending were Helmut Schmidt, Bronislav Geremk, and Jack Matlock. A special session was held in the Kremlin offices of Mikhail Gorbachev. It was Gorbachev's last official function as president of the USSR.

In addition to receiving the Nobel Peace Prize, Elie Wiesel has been the recipient of numerous literary and humanitarian awards. Wiesel's efforts as chronicler of his experiences as Holocaust survivor and defender of peace and human rights have earned him the Presidential Medal of Freedom (1992); the United States Congressional Gold Medal (1984); the Medal of Liberty Award (1977); and the rank of Grand Officer (Commander) in the French Legion of Honor (1990).

His books have won numerous awards, including the Prix Medicis for *A Beggar in Jerusalem* (1968); the Prix Livre-Inter for *The Testament* (1980); and the Grand Prize for Literature from the City of Paris for *The Fifth Son* (1983).

His most recent books published in the United States are *Sages and Dreamers* (1991) and *The Forgotten* (1992). In December 1995 Alfred A. Knopf, Publishers, will follow with Elie Wiesel's memoirs *All Rivers Run to the Sea*.

Elie Wiesel was Distinguished Professor of Judaic Studies at the City College of the City University of New York from 1972 to 1976 and Henry Luce Visiting Scholar for the Humanities and Social Thought at Yale University from 1982 to 1983. Since 1976 he has been the Andrew W. Mellon Professor of the Humanities at Boston University.

From 1980 to 1986 Wiesel was chairman of the United States Holocaust Memorial Council, an independent federal agency set up by Congress in 1980 to raise funds to create a Holocaust memorial on the Mall in Washington, D.C.

On April 22, 1993, Elie Wiesel lit the eternal flame at the dedication ceremonies of the United States Holocaust Museum and presented the dedication speech declaring, "Not only are we responsible for the memories of the dead, we are also responsible for what we are doing with those memories. . . . For the dead and the living we must bear witness."

On September 30, 1993, the exhibit *Journey of a Witness* opened at Boston University's Mugar Library on the occasion of Elie Wiesel's sixty-fifth birthday. On public display through August 1994, it showed hundreds of items—photographs, speeches, books, notes, correspondence, awards, and manuscripts—from 1928 to the present, filling twenty-two cases in the Grubosky-Rosenfeld Exhibition Hall. The theme that emerged from this collection was the voice of one man who has dedicated his life to rescuing history by preserving memory and demanding justice in the face of adversity.

As the exhibit at Boston University's Mugar Library demonstrated, the message of universal caring is paramount in Wiesel's mind. His actions, which flow from a seemingly inexhaustible wellspring of energy, continue to confront the troubling issues of our day.

On November 20, 1994, Steven Spielberg—director and producer of *Schindler's List*, the Holocaust film that won seven Academy Awards—received the State of Israel Bonds Elie Wiesel Holocaust Remembrance Award for his efforts to preserve the memory of the Holocaust.

Survivors of the Holocaust, a foundation Spielberg started in the previous ten-month period, has already conducted more than thirteen hundred interviews. Its goal is to speak with one-fourth of the three hundred thousand Holocaust survivors worldwide in the next two years.

Bibliography

Adams, James Truslow. *Album of American History.* 3 vols. New York: Atlantic Monthly Press, 1944–1946.

——. *The Founding of New England.* Boston: Atlantic Monthly Press, 1927.

Adler, Cyrus. "Adolphus S. Solomons and the Red Cross." *Publications of the American Jewish Historical Society* XXXIII (1934): 211–30.

——. *Jacob Schiff: His Life and Letters.* 2 vols. New York: Doubleday, Doran & Company, 1928.

Agresti, Olivia Rossetti. *David Lubin: A Study in Practical Idealism.* Los Angeles: University of California Press, 1941.

Alpert, Zalman. "Lubavitcher Rebbe: Menachem Mendel Schneerson," in *Jewish-American History and Culture: An Encyclopedia* (New York: Garland, 1992) 373–375.

Angel, Marc. *La America: The Sephardic Experience in America.* Philadelphia: Jewish Publication Society of America, 1982.

Angoff, Charles. *Emma Lazarus: Poet, Jewish Activist, Pioneer Zionist.* New York: Jewish Historical Society of New York, 1970.

Baron, Salo Wittmayer. *The Jewish Community: Its History and Structure to the American Revolution.* 3 vols. Philadelphia: Jewish Publication Society of America, 1942.

——. *Steeled by Adversity: Essays and Addresses on Jewish Life.* Philadelphia: Jewish Publication Society of America, 1971.

Barish, Louis., ed. *Rabbis in Uniform: A Century of Service for God and Country, 1862–1962.* New York: Jonathan David, 1962.

Barrett, Mary Ellin. *Irving Berlin: A Daughter's Memoir.* New York: Simon and Schuster, 1994.

Barrett, Walter. *The Old Merchants of New York City.* New York: Carlson, 1863.

Beard, Annie E. *Our Foreign Born Citizens,* 9th ed. New York: Crowell, 1968.

Bergreen, Laurence. *As Thousands Cheer: The Life of Irving Berlin.* New York: Viking, 1990.

Bernstein, Joanne, and Blue, Rose, with Alan Jay Gerber. *Judith Resnik: Challenger Astronaut.* New York: Lodestar Books, 1990.

Besdin, Abraham R. *Reflections of the Rav: Lessons in Jewish Thought: Adapted from the Lectures of Rabbi Joseph D. Soloveitchik.* Hoboken, NJ: Ktav, 1981.

Bigelow, Baruch M. "Aaron Lopez, Merchant of Newport." *The New England Quarterly* Vol. IV, No. 4. (1931).

Birmingham, Stephen. *The Grandees: America's Sephardic Elite.* New York: Harper & Row, 1971.

———. *Our Crowd: The Great Jewish Families of New York.* New York: Harper & Row, 1967.

———. *The Rest of Us: The Rise of America's East European Jews.* Boston: Little, Brown and Company, 1984.

Blau, Joseph L. and Baron, Salo W., eds. *The Jews in the United States 1790–1840: A Documentary History.* 3 vols. New York: University Press, 1963.

Bloom, Herbert I. "A Study of Brazilian Jewish History, 1653–1654, Based Chiefly on the Findings of the Late Samuel Oppenheim." *Publications of the American Jewish Historical Society* XXXIII (1934): 43–125.

Borgenicht, Louis. *The Happiest Man. The Life of Louis Borgenicht as told to Harold Friedman.* New York: Putnam's Sons, 1942.

Brown, Robert McAfee. *Elie Wiesel: Messenger to All Humanity.* Notre Dame, IN: University of Notre Dame Press, 1983.

Burton, Humphrey. *Leonard Bernstein.* New York: Doubleday, 1994.

Butler, Pierce. *Life of Judah P. Benjamin.* Philadelphia: G. W. Jacobs and Company, 1907.

Carvalho, Solomon Nunes. *Incidents of Travel and Adventure in the Far West.* New York: Derby and Jackson, 1857.

Chyet, Stanley. *Lopez of Newport: A Colonial Merchant Prince.* Detroit: Wayne State University Press, 1970.

Cohen, Naomi W. *American Jews and the Zionist Idea.* New York: Ktav Publishing House, 1975.

———. *Dual Heritage: The Public Career of Oscar S. Straus.* Philadelphia: Jewish Publication Society of America, 1972.

———. *Encounter With Emancipation: The German Jews in the United States, 1830–1914.* Philadelphia: Jewish Publication Society of America, 1984.

———. *Not Free to Desist: The American Jewish Committee, 1906–1966.* Philadelphia: Jewish Publication Society of America, 1972.

Columbus, Christopher. *The Diary of Christopher Columbus's First Voyage to America, 1492–1493,* abstracted by Fray Bartolome de las Casas. Trans. Oliver Dunn and James E. Kelley Jr. Norman, OK: University of Oklahoma Press, 1989.

Daly, Charles P. *The Settlement of the Jews in North America.* New York: Philip Cowen, 1893.

Dawidowicz, Lucy. *On Equal Terms: Jews in America, 1881–1981.* New York: Holt, Rinehart and Winston, 1982.

Dexter, Franklin B., ed. *Literary Diary of Ezra Stiles.* New York: Charles Scribner's Sons, 1901.

Dinnerstein, Leonard. *Anti-Semitism in America.* New York: Oxford University Press, 1994.

Dix, Marc H. *An American Business Adventure: The Story of Henry A. Dix.* New York: Harper & Brothers, 1928.

Dyer, Albion. "Points in the First Chapter of New York Jewish History." *Publications of the American Jewish Historical Society,* III (1894): 41–60.

Elzas, Barnett A. *The Jews of South Carolina From the Earliest Time to the Present Day.* Charleston: The Daggett Printing Co., 1903. Reprint, Spartanburg, SC: Reprint Company, 1972.

Evans, Eli. *Judah P. Benjamin: The Jewish Confederate.* New York: The Free Press, 1988.

——. *The Provincials: A Personal History of the Jews in the South.* New York: Atheneum, 1973.

Ewen, David. *The Story of George Gershwin.* New York: Henry Holt & Company, 1944.

Ezekiel, Moses Jacob. *Memoirs from the Baths of Diocletian.* eds. Joseph Gutmann and Stanley Chyet. Detroit: Wayne State University Press, 1975.

Feingold, Henry L., ed. *The Jewish People in America.* 5 vols. Baltimore: Johns Hopkins University Press, 1992.

——. *A Midrash on American Jewish History.* Albany, NY: State University of New York Press, 1982.

——. *The Politics of Rescue: The Roosevelt Administration and the Holocaust, 1938–1945.* New Brunswick, NJ: Rutgers University Press, 1970.

——. *Zion in America: The Jewish Experience from Colonial Times to the Present.* New York: Twayne Publishers, 1974.

Fermi, Laura. *Illustrious Immigrants: The Intellectual Migration from Europe, 1930–1941.* Chicago: University of Chicago Press, 1968.

Fernow, Berthold., ed. *The Records of New Amsterdam from 1653 to 1674.* 7 vols. New York: Knickerbocker Press, 1902–1907.

Fine, Ellen S. *Legacy of Night: The Literary Universe of Elie Wiesel.* Albany, NY: State University of New York Press, 1982.

Fineman, Irving. *Woman of Valor: The Life of Henrietta Szold, 1860–1945.* New York: Simon and Schuster, 1961.

Finkelstein, Louis. *The Jews: Their History, Culture, and Religion.* 2 vols. New York: Harper & Brothers, 1960.

Fischel, Jack, and Pinsker, Sanford, eds. *Jewish-American History and Culture: An Encyclopedia.* New York: Garland, 1992.

Fish, Sidney M. *Aaron Levy: Founder of Aaronsburg.* New York: American Jewish Historical Society, 1951.

——. *Barnard and Michael Gratz: Their Lives and Times.* Lanham, MD: University Press of America, 1994.

Frank, Philipp. *Einstein: His Life and Times*. Trans. George Rosen. New York: Alfred Knopf, 1947.

Frazer, Nancy. *Jewish Museums in North America: A Guide to Collections*. New York: John Wiley, 1992.

Fredman, J. George, and Falk, Louis A. *Jews in American Wars*. New York: Jewish War Veterans of the United States, 1942.

Freund, Miriam K. *Jewish Merchants in Colonial America, Their Achievements and Their Contributions to the Development of America*. New York: Behrman's Jewish Book House, 1939.

Friedman, Lee M. *Early American Jews*. Cambridge, MA: Harvard University Press, 1934.

——. *Jewish Pioneers and Patriots*. Philadelphia: Jewish Publication Society of America, 1945.

——. *Pilgrims in a New Land*. Philadelphia: Jewish Publication Society of America, 1948.

Gal, Allon. *Brandeis of Boston*. Cambridge, MA: Harvard University Press, 1980.

Gartner, Lloyd P. "Salo Wittmayer Baron (1895–1989)." *American Jewish Yearbook*, Vol. 91 (1991): 544–554.

Goldberg, Isaac. *Major Noah: American Jewish Pioneer*. Philadelphia: Jewish Publication Society of America, 1936.

Goldman, Shalom. *Hebrew and the Bible in America: The First Two Centuries*. Hanover, NH: University Press of New England, 1994.

Goldstein, Philip R. *Centers in My Life: A Personal Profile of the Jewish Center Movement*. New York: Bloch Publishing Company, 1964.

Gompers, Samuel. *Seventy Years of Life and Labor: An Autobiography*. 2 vols. New York: E. P. Dutton and Company, 1925.

Goodman, Abram Vossen. *American Overture: Jewish Rights in Colonial Times*. Philadelphia: Jewish Publication Society of America, 1947.

Goren, Arthur A. *The American Jews and the Quest for Community*. Cambridge, MA: Harvard University Press, 1982.

Grinstein, Hyman B. *The Rise of the Jewish Community of New York: 1654–1860*. Philadelphia: Jewish Publication Society of America, 1945.

Grose, Peter. *Israel in the Mind of America*. New York: Alfred A. Knopf, 1984.

Grusd, Edward E. *B'nai B'rith.: The Story of a Covenant*. New York: Appleton, 1966.

Gutstein, Morris A. *The Jews of Newport: Two and a Half Centuries of Judaism, 1658–1908*. New York: Bloch Publishing Company, 1936.

Hadassah Chronology: Eight Decades of Service to the Jewish People. New York: Hadassah, 1986.

Handlin, Oscar. *Adventure in Freedom: Three Hundred Years of Jewish Life in America*. New York: McGraw-Hill Book Company, 1954.

Harap, Louis. *The Image of the Jew in American Literature: From Early Republic to Mass Immigration.* Philadelphia: Jewish Publication Society of America, 1974.

Harris, Leon. *Merchant Princes: An Intimate History of Jewish Families Who Built Great Department Stores.* New York: Harper & Row, 1979.

Helmreich, William B. *The World of the Yeshiva: An Intimate Portrait of Orthodox Jews.* New York: The Free Press, 1982.

Hertzberg, Arthur. *The Jews in America: Four Centuries of an Uneasy Encounter.* New York: Simon and Schuster, 1989.

Hirsh, Joseph, and Doherty, Beka. *The First Hundred Years of the Mount Sinai Hospital of New York.* New York: Random House, 1952.

Hoffman, Miriam. "Yiddish Theater." In *Encyclopedia Americana.* Vol. 29 pp. 678–679. Danbury, CT: Grolier, 1991.

Howe, Irving. *World of Our Fathers.* New York: Harcourt Brace Jovanovich, 1977.

Huhner, Leon. "Asser Levy: A Noted Jewish Burgher of New Amsterdam." *Publications of the American Jewish Historical Society,* VIII (1905): 9–23.

——. "Francis Salvador: A Prominent Patriot of the American Revolutionary War." *Publications of the American Jewish Historical Society,* IX (1901): 187–95.

——. *The Life of Judah Touro, 1775–1854.* Philadelphia: Jewish Publication Society of America, 1946.

Isaacson, Walter. *Kissinger: A Biography.* New York: Simon and Schuster, 1992.

Jablonski, Edward. *Gershwin: A Biography.* Garden City, NY: Doubleday, 1987.

Jacob, H. E. *The World of Emma Lazarus.* New York: Schocken Books, 1949.

Janowsky, Oscar I., ed. *The American Jew: A Reappraisal.* Philadelphia: Jewish Publication Society of America, 1972.

Janvier, Thomas A. *In Old New York.* New York: Harper Brothers, 1894.

Jewish Encyclopedia. 12 vols. New York: Funk & Wagnalls, 1901–1906. Reprint, Ktav, 1966.

Johnson, Melvin M. *The Beginnings of Freemasonry in America.* New York: George A. Doran & Company, 1924.

Johnston, Mary. *Pioneer in the Old South.* New Haven: Yale University Press, 1918.

Joselit, Jenna Weisman. *New York's Jewish Jews: The Orthodox Community in the Interwar Years.* Bloomington, IN: Indiana University Press, 1990.

Kagan, Solomon. *Jewish Contributions to Medicine in America, 1654–1934.* Boston: Boston Medical Publishing Company, 1934.

Kanter, Kenneth A. *The Jews on Tin Pan Alley: The Jewish Contribution to American Popular Music, 1830–1940.* New York: Ktav Publishing House; Cincinnati: American Jewish Archives, 1982.

Karp, Abraham. *Beginnings: Early American Judaica.* Philadelphia: Jewish Publication Society of America, 1976.

——. *Haven and Home: A History of the Jews in America.* New York: Schocken Books, 1985.

Kaplan, Mordecai M. *Judaism as a Civilization. Toward a Reconstruction of American Jewish Life.* New York: Thomas Yoseloff, 1957.

Kayserling, Meyer. *Christopher Columbus and the Participation of the Jews in the Spanish and Portuguese Discoveries.* New York: Longman's, Green and Company, 1894. Reprint, New York: Hermon Press, 1968.

——. "Isaac Aboab, the First Jewish Author in America," *Publications of the American Jewish Historical Society,* V (1897): 125-36.

Kissinger, Henry. *The White House Years.* Boston: Little, Brown and Company, 1979.

——. *Years of Upheaval.* Boston: Little, Brown and Company, 1982.

Klapperman, Gilbert. *The Story of Yeshiva University.* New York: Macmillan Company, 1969.

Kohler, Max J. "Civil Status of the Jews in Colonial New York," *Publications of the American Jewish Historical Society,* VI (1897): 81-106.

——. "Judah Touro, Merchant and Philanthropist," *Publications of the American Jewish Historical Society,* XIII (1905): 93-111.

——. "Phases of Jewish Life in New York Before 1800," *Publications of the American Jewish Historical Society,* III (1894): 73-86.

Korn, Bertram. *American Jewry and the Civil War.* Philadelphia: Jewish Publication Society of America, 1951.

——. *Eventful Years and Experiences: Studies in Nineteenth Century American Jewish History.* Cincinnati: American Jewish Archives, 1954.

Kranzler, George. *Williamsburg, U.S.A.: The Face of Faith; An American Hasidic Community.* Baltimore: Hebrew College Press, 1972.

Landman, Isaac, ed. *Universal Jewish Encyclopedia.* 10 vols. New York: Universal Jewish Encyclopedia Company, 1939-43. Reprint, New York: Ktav Publishing House, 1969.

Lebeson, Anita Libman. *Jewish Pioneers in America, 1492-1848.* New York: Behrman's Jewish Book House, 1931.

——. *Pilgrim People.* New York: Harper & Brothers, 1950.

Levin, Alexandra Lee. *The Szolds of Lombard Street: A Baltimore Jewish Family, 1859-1909.* Philadelphia: Jewish Publication Society of America, 1960.

Levin, Marlin. *Balm in Gilead: The Story of Hadassah.* New York: Schocken Books, 1973.

Levine, Peter. *Ellis Island to Ebbets Field: Sports and the American Jewish Experience.* New York: Oxford University Press, 1992.

Levitan, Tina. *The Laureates: Jewish Winners of the Nobel Prize.* New York: Twayne Publishers, 1960.

——. *Islands of Compassion: A History of the Jewish Hospitals of New York.* New York: Twayne Publishers, 1964.

——. *Jews in American Life: From 1492 to the Space Age.* New York: Hebrew Publishing Company, 1969.

Lewis, Theodore. "History of Touro Synagogue." *Bulletin of the Newport Historical Society* Vol. 48, Part 3 (Summer 1975): 281–320.

Lifson, David. *The Yiddish Theater in America.* New York: Thomas Yoseloff, 1965.

Liptzin, Sol. *The Jew in American Literature.* New York: Bloch Publishing Company, 1966.

London, Hannah R. *Portraits of Jews by Gilbert Stuart and Other Early American Artists.* Rutland, VT: Charles E. Tuttle, 1969.

Lyman, Darryl. *Great Jews in Music.* Middle Village, NY: Jonathan David Publishers, 1986.

Lyons, Eugene. *David Sarnoff: A Biography.* New York: Harper & Row, 1964.

Madariaga, Salvador de. *Christopher Columbus.* New York: Macmillan Company, 1940.

Madison, Charles A. *Eminent American Jews: 1776 to the Present.* New York: Frederick Ungar Publishing Company, 1970.

Maginnis, John J. "My Service With Colonel David Marcus," *Publication of the American Jewish Historical Society,* LXIX (March 1980): 301–324.

Marcus, Jacob Rader. *The American Jewish Woman: A Documentary History.* New York: Ktav Publishing House; Cincinnati: American Jewish Archives, 1981.

——. *The Colonial American Jew, 1492–1776.* 3 vols. Detroit: Wayne State University Press, 1970.

——. *Memoirs of American Jews, 1775–1865.* 3 vols. Philadelphia: Jewish Publication Society of America, 1955–1956.

——. *Concise Dictionary of American Jewish Biography.* 2 vols. Brooklyn, New York: Carlson Publishing, 1994.

——. *United States Jewry, 1776–1985.* 4 vols. Detroit: Wayne State University Press, 1989–1993.

Markens, Isaac. *The Hebrews in America.* New York: The Author, 1888. Reprint, New York: Arno Press, 1975.

Masserman, Paul, and Baker, Max. *The Jews Come to America.* New York: Bloch Publishing Company, 1932.

McCall, Samuel Walker. *Patriotism of the American Jew.* New York: Plymouth Press, 1924.

Millman, Herbert. "The Jewish Community Center." In *American Jewish Yearbook,* vol. 66, New York: American Jewish Committee; Philadelphia: Jewish Publication Society of America, 1966.

Merriam, Eve. *Emma Lazarus: Woman With a Torch.* New York: Citadel, 1956.

Moise, Penina. *Poems of Penina Moise.* Charleston, SC: Charleston Section, Council of Jewish Women, Nicholas G. Duffy, 1911.

Moore, Deborah Dash. *At Home in America: Second Generation New York Jews.* New York: Columbia University Press, 1981.

Morais, Henry S. *Eminent Israelites of the Nineteenth Century.* Philadelphia: E. Stern and Company, 1880.

Noveck, Simon. *Great Jewish Thinkers of the Twentieth Century.* Washington, D.C.: B'nai B'rith Books, 1985.

O'Callaghan, E. B., ed. *Documents Relative to the Colonial History of the State of New York. Procured by John Romeyn Broadhead.* 15 vols. New York: AMS Press, 1969.

Oppenheim, Samuel. "The Early History of the Jews in New York, 1654–1664," *Publications of the American Jewish Historical Society,* XVIII (1901): 1–91.

——. "More About Jacob Barsimson, the First Jewish Settler in New York," *Publications of the American Jewish Historical Society,* XXIX (1925): 39–52.

Pais, Abraham. *Subtle Is the Lord: The Science and the Life of Albert Einstein.* New York: Clarendon Press, 1982.

Peters, Madison Clinton. *Justice to the Jew: the Story of What He Has Done for the World.* New York: McClure Company, 1908. Reprint, New York: Bloch Publishing Company, 1921.

Philipson, David, ed. *The Letters of Rebecca Gratz.* Philadelphia: Jewish Publication Society of America, 1929.

Plaut, W. Gunther. *The Growth of Reform Judaism in American and European Sources until 1948.* New York: World Union for Progressive Judaism; Union of American Hebrew Congregations, 1965.

Polner, Murray. *Jewish Profiles. Great Jewish Personalities and Institutions of the Twentieth Century.* Northvale, NJ: Jason Aronson Inc, 1993.

Pool, David de Sola. "Hebrew Learning Among the Puritans of New England Prior to 1700," *Publications of the American Jewish Historical Society,* XX (1911): 31–83.

——, and Pool, Tamar de Sola. *An Old Faith in the New World: Portrait of Congregation Shearith Israel, 1654–1954.* New York: Columbia University Press, 1955.

——. *Portraits Etched in Stone: Early Jewish Settlers, 1682–1831.* New York: Columbia University Press, 1952.

Postal, Bernard, and Koppman, Lionel. *Jewish Landmarks of New York: A Travel Guide and History.* New York: Fleet Press Corporation, 1978.

——. *A Jewish Tourist's Guide to the United States.* Philadelphia: Jewish Publication Society of America, 1954.

Rakeffet-Rothkoff, Aaron. *Bernard Revel: Builder of American Jewish Orthodoxy.* Philadelphia: Jewish Publication Society of America, 1972.

Raphael, Marc Lee. *Jews and Judaism in the United States: A Documentary History.* New York: Behrman House, 1984.

Reznikoff, Charles, and Engleman, Uriah Z. *The Jews of Charleston: A History of an American Jewish Community.* Philadelphia: Jewish Publication Society of America, 1950.

Ribalow, Harold, ed. *Autobiographies of American Jews.* Philadelphia: Jewish Publication Society of America, 1973.

——. *The Jew in American Sports.* New York: Bloch Publishing Company, 1959.

Rischin, Moses. *The Promised City: New York's Jews, 1870–1914.* New York: Harper & Row, 1972.

Rosenbaum, Jeanette. *Myer Myers, Goldsmith, 1723–1795.* Philadelphia: Jewish Publication Society of America, 1954.

Rosenfeld, Alvin, and Greenberg, Irving, eds. *Confronting the Holocaust: The Impact of Elie Wiesel.* Bloomington, IN: Indiana University Press, 1978.

Roth, Cecil. *A History of the Marranos.* Philadelphia: Jewish Publication Society of America, 1941.

——, ed. *Encyclopedia Judaica.* 17 vols. Jerusalem: Kefer Publishing House, 1972.

——. *The Jewish Contribution to Civilization.* New York: Harper, 1940.

Runes, Dagobert, ed. *The Hebrew Impact on Western Civilization.* New York: Philosophical Library, 1951.

Sachar, Howard M. *Farewell Espana: The World of the Sephardim Remembered.* New York: Alfred A. Knopf, 1994.

——. *A History of Israel: From the Rise of Zionism to Our Time.* New York: Alfred A. Knopf, 1976.

——. *A History of the Jews in America.* New York: Alfred A. Knopf, 1992.

Sanders, Ronald. *Shores of Refuge: A Hundred Years of Jewish Emigration.* New York: Henry Holt, 1988.

——. *The Downtown Jews: Portraits of an Immigrant Generation.* New York: Harper & Row, 1969.

Sarna, Jonathan. *Jacksonian Jew: The Two Worlds of Mordecai Noah.* New York: Holmes and Meier, 1981.

Schappes, Morris U. *A Documentary History of the Jews in the United States, 1654–1875.* New York: Citadel Press, 1950. Reprint, 3rd ed. New York: Schocken Books, 1971.

Schoener, Allon. *The American Jewish Album, 1654 to the Present.* New York: Rizzoli International Publications, 1983.

——. *Portal to America: The Lower East Side, 1870–1925.* New York: Holt, Rinehart and Winston, 1967.

Schulzinger, Robert D. *Henry Kissinger: Doctor of Diplomacy.* New York: Columbia University Press, 1991.

Stiles, Ezra. *The Literary Diary of Ezra Stiles.* Ed. Franklin B. Dexter. New York: Charles Scribner's Sons, 1991.

Silberman, Charles E. *A Certain People: America's Jews and Their Lives Today.* New York: Summit Books, 1985.

Simonhoff, Harry. *Jewish Notables in America, 1776–1865.* New York: Greenberg Publisher, 1956.

——. *Saga of American Jewry, 1865–1914.* New York: Arco Publishing Company, 1959.

Sklare, Marshall. *Conservative Judaism: An American Religious Movement.* New York: Schocken Books, 1972.

Slater, Robert. *Great Jews in Sports.* Middle Village, NY: Jonathan David Publishers, 1983.

Soloveitchik, Joseph B. *Halakhic Man.* Trans. Lawrence Kaplan. Philadelphia: Jewish Publication Society, 1983.

Stern, Malcolm. *First American Jewish Families: 600 Geneologies, 1654–1977.* Cincinnati: American Jewish Archives, 1978.

——, ed. "The Sheftall Diaries: Vital Records of Savannah Jewry (1733–1808)," In *American Jewish Historical Quarterly* LIV (March 1965): 243–277.

Straus, Oscar S. *Origin of the Republican Form of Government in the United States.* New York: Putnam's Sons, 1901.

——. *Under Four Administrations From Cleveland to Taft.* Boston: Houghton Mifflin Company, 1922.

Strum, Philippa. *Louis D. Brandeis: Justice for the People.* Cambridge, MA: Harvard University Press, 1984.

Suhl, Uri. *Eloquent Crusader: Ernestine Rose.* New York: Julian Messner, 1970.

Todd, A.L. *Justice on Trial: The Case of Louis D. Brandeis.* New York: McGraw-Hill, 1964.

Traux, Rhoda. *The Doctors Jacobi.* Boston: Little, Brown and Company, 1952.

Urofsky, Melvin. *American Zionism from Herzl to the Holocaust.* Garden City, NY: Doubleday, 1975.

Vorspan, Albert. *Giants of Justice.* New York: Union of American Hebrew Congregations, 1960.

Wald, Lillian. *The House on Henry Street.* New York: Henry Holt, 1915. Reprint, New York: Dover, 1971.

——. *Windows on Henry Street.* Boston: Little, Brown and Company, 1934.

Weinryb, Bernard D. "Noah's Ararat Jewish State in Its Historical Setting," In *Publications of the American Jewish Historical Society,* XLIII (March 1954): 170–191.

Wertheimer, Jack. *A People Divided.* New York: Basic Books, 1993.

Wiernik, Peter. *History of the Jews In America From the Period of the Discovery of the New World to the Present Time.* New York: The Jewish History Publishing Company, 1931. Reprint, 3rd ed. New York: Hermon Press, 1972.

Williams, Beryl. *Lillian Wald: Angel of Henry Street.* New York: Julian Messner, 1948.

Wile, Frederick. *Emile Berliner: Maker of the Microphone.* Indianapolis: Bobbs-Merrill Company, 1926.

Wise, Isaac Mayer. *Reminiscences.* Trans. David Philipson. Cincinnati: L. Wise and Company, 1901. Reprint, New York: Central Synagogue, 1945.

Wise, Stephen S. *Challenging Years: The Autobiography of Stephen Wise.* New York: Putnam's Sons, 1949.

Wischnitzer, Mark. *To Dwell in Safety: Jewish Migration Since 1800.* Philadelphia: Jewish Publication Society of America, 1948.

Wiznitzer, Arnold. "The Exodus from Brazil and the Arrival in New Amsterdam of the Jewish Pilgrim Fathers, 1654." In *Publications of the American Jewish Historical Society,* XLIV (December 1954): 80–97.

Wolf, Edwin, 2nd, and Whiteman, Maxwell. *The History of the Jews of Philadelphia From Colonial Times to the Age of Jackson.* Philadelphia: Jewish Publication Society of America, 1957.

Wolf, Simon. *The American Jew as Patriot, Soldier and Citizen.* Philadelphia: The Levytype Company, 1895. Reprint, Boston: Gregg Press, 1972.

Wolfson, Harry A. "Judah Monis." In *Dictionary of American Biography,* VII. pp. 86–87. New York: Charles Scribner's Sons, 1934.

Zacuto, Abraham Ben Samuel. *Almanach Perpetuum Celestium Motuum (Radix 1473).* Trans. Joseph Vizinho. Geneva: Société Sadag, 1917.

Zielonka, Martin. "The Fighting Jew." In *Publications of the American Jewish Historical Society,* XXXI (1928): 211–17.

Zwierlein, Frederick. *Religion in New Netherland.* Rochester, NY: John P. Smith Printing Company, 1910.

Index

ABOUT THE AUTHOR

Tina Levitan is one of the few American authors with books published in both Hebrew and English. Born in Boston, she received her early education there, attending the Boston Hebrew College Prozdor (High School) and later was graduating from Hunter College and the Herzliah Hebrew Teachers Seminary in New York. A trail-blazer in a field where few women are encountered, she is the author of *The Laureates: Jewish Winners of the Nobel Prize* (1960), *Islands of Compassion; A History of the Jewish Hospitals of New York* (1964), the two volume *Baolam Hechadash*, written entirely in Hebrew (1968), *Jews in American Life; From 1492 to the Space Age* (1970), and *Viewpoints on Science and Judaism* (1978). She lectures frequently and has had over 450 articles and reviews on American Jewish history and Jewish life published in scholarly and popular Jewish journals. Ms. Levitan lives in New York City.